David L. Francis
Exploiting Agility for Advantage

David L. Francis

Exploiting Agility for Advantage

A Step-by-Step Process for Acquiring Requisite
Organisational Agility

DE GRUYTER

ISBN 978-3-11-063645-1
e-ISBN (PDF) 978-3-11-063726-7
e-ISBN (EPUB) 978-3-11-063745-8

Library of Congress Control Number: 2020939127

Bibliographic information published by the Deutsche Nationalbibliothek
The Deutsche Nationalbibliothek lists this publication in the Deutsche Nationalbibliografie;
detailed bibliographic data are available on the Internet at http://dnb.dnb.de.

© 2020 Walter de Gruyter GmbH, Berlin/Boston
Cover image: cowii/iStock/Getty Images Plus
Typesetting: Integra Software Services Pvt. Ltd.
Printing and binding: CPI books GmbH, Leck

www.degruyter.com

Preface

I was six years old when I noticed that my father did not go to work like my friends' parents. Rather, he was always involved in one enterprise or another. Dad had left school at the age of 12 and, for the rest of his life, he undertook many ventures, from making earmuffs for wartime soldiers to running a small loan company for people buying second-hand cars. These endeavours provided our family with security in insecure times. The term agility was not used then, but Dad was a master practitioner. He was not always successful but never defeated. My father's life experience taught me much about the promise and perils of being agile.

Organisational agility has fascinated me throughout much of my working life. It began when I took a job in Harrods department store in London. I had been hired to develop executive training in a shop that was the largest in Europe but was firmly stuck in the past. As I walked around the store it felt as if I had been transported back to the 1930s. In particular, the men's clothing department looked as if it was a set for an early black and white movie, with dingy lighting, pre-war fixtures, a ban on women being sales assistants and uninspiring merchandise. There were two great exceptions. Those departments that sold elegant fashion for women were exciting, bold and always modish. The fishmonger was so inventive that few visitors missed the famous quirky daily displays. These differences were fascinating. How could one department be vibrant, and another be completely unenterprising?

Fortunately, Harrods' top managers had identified the problem. An inspiring management team led a change programme during the seven years that I worked in the store. Harrods was transformed. It attracted the most fashionable young people. The store became successfully agile in a way that honoured its traditions, yet made it a trendsetter—its 'personality' had changed fundamentally (Harrod, 2017).

Participating in this transformation taught me that there are close links between individual and organisational agility. Harrods' directors were exceptional people. They would not accept the status quo, realising that the world had changed but Harrods had not. Those senior managers saw an opportunity and they became change leaders. They took inspiration from the style of the Beatles, searched the world for progressive ideas about retailing and spent endless hours seeking ways to recreate Harrods so it retained its distinctive personality but would become a magnet for well-healed and fashion-conscious young people. This was far from being an easy task. A deeply embedded conservative but proud culture had to be realigned. Huge investments were made, including replacing the dark mahogany cabinets and dingy lighting in the new men's department, that now had stylish fixtures and bright young women and men as sales staff. It took a special kind of leadership to respond boldly to external change, embrace opportunities, create a quite different organisational personality for Harrods and provide the focused energy to bring about a far-from-easy transformation. Harrods' leaders did not simply respond to change.

https://doi.org/10.1515/9783110637267-202

Rather they *used* change to create and find opportunities. From this experience I learnt that agile enterprises must have agile-friendly leaders.

About the same time, I became transfixed by the sociology of NASA's Apollo program. Here was a vast venture that began not with a plan, but with an ambition. I visited TRW Systems, in Redondo Beach, to meet the engineers involved in designing the Abort Guidance System for the Lunar Lander Module. They talked about the Apollo program in ways that reminded me of accounts of Christopher Columbus's enthusiasm as he set sail from Spain in 1492 on a voyage of discovery. It felt almost as if NASA had its own life force. The managers and engineers who were working on the Apollo program in TRW Systems were empowered by an ethos of boldness and they were aligned by a unified ambition.

The individuals who were successful in Harrods and TRW Systems seemed to have distinctive personality characteristics. They were proactive, effective, creative, adaptable and resilient. It was clear that grit, courage, resolve and strength of character can help a person to thrive, despite uncertainties and difficulties. Sociologists have a special term for this form of proactivity. They call it 'agency', which can be described as an ability of people to make a difference in the world around them.

Agility was entirely driven by human agency when I worked in Harrods. This is no longer true. Recently, I undertook a research assignment in a financial services company that buys and sells stocks and shares. Its decisions are taken in microseconds by computer algorithms, without any human intervention. In this company, like many others, machines are taking an ever-greater role in enabling agility, extending its reach and potency. Those who seek to lead a successful agile organisation today must integrate social and technical capabilities.

Agility is more than a strategy for survival or a formula for gaining comparative or competitive advantage. It provides a lifeboat for individuals, communities and enterprises in turbulent times. Without agility we become victims of change. So, it is difficult not to become concerned when we reflect on the life chances of today's young people. For many, the old certainties will be unavailable. They must find ways to thrive through waves of disruptive change and they will be buffeted by unpredictable global issues. Most will become close partners with intelligent machines and find that their hard-won knowledge has a disturbingly short half-life. I hope that many will acquire the mindsets and skillsets required to be agile in their own careers.

The core of organisational agility has always been exploiting opportunities for advantage. Increasingly, we question what 'advantage' really means, as we have found that gains for the initiator may result in losses for others, including our polluted planet. In previous generations commercial organisations were largely dedicated to exploiting opportunities to maximise shareholder value. Today the landscape of opportunities has changed, as environmental and social issues have, rightly, become targets for responsible agency.

That agility is more than an organisational development strategy was shown wonderfully during the dark days of the 2020 coronavirus epidemic. During long periods of isolation people developed multiple initiatives. Online support groups helped the elderly, orchestras played in digital concert halls and yoga teachers taught online. Countless opportunities were created to alleviate suffering in troubled times. Some agile minds created novel ideas, others adopted formats used elsewhere, but the agile activists had the grit, and found the resources needed, to transform opportunities into benefits.

Possessing agility is a strength that can be used for good or ill. When people of good faith use skills of managing agility to enhance the human condition then almost no problem will be too large, no opportunity too stretching. So, we see the Gates Foundation creating opportunities to save poor people from avoidable illnesses and UN agencies finding better ways to react to natural emergencies. Humanistic-driven agility is a great instrument for transforming hope into action.

Mastery of organisational agility will be needed widely as we search for ways to thrive in a new sociological and technocratic age that will transform societies in ways that cannot be predicted. It is managers who need to create the conditions in which prudent and responsible opportunism can thrive. This is why leaders and managers need to understand where, when and how to embed 'requisite agility' into their organisations.

Why 'requisite'? It is because not all organisations need to be equally agile and that agility can sometimes be dysfunctional. This became clear to me when, some years ago, I met Stuart, then chief executive of a UK company that had developed and patented exciting new technologies for medical analyses, winning a Queen's Award for Export Achievement. Stuart shared with me his experience of managing a business that, when we met, had been supremely agile and was then bankrupt. Our discussions were seminal. I came to realise that agility is neither easy to manage nor is it a sure-fire recipe for success. This book owes much to Stuart's willingness to share his painful managerial experiences, as it was this that initiated my interest in finding out what was needed for an organisation to be successfully agile.

Understanding agility can come from unexpected sources. For some years I have been privileged to act as a member of the advisory board for a Christian charity known as the Salvatorian Office for International Aid. I recall attending a meeting in Rome where a nun told the story about how four German missionaries reached remote Assam in 1890. They were the first to arrive and, within just a few years, churches and schools had been built. The missionaries could not have been in a more remote place; they did not speak the local language, had few resources and lived amongst suspicious villagers. Yet they found ways to achieve something truly remarkable. They were driven by an unshakeable inner conviction that created opportunities and overcame barriers. It would be difficult to find a more vivid description of an agile enterprise than this missionary outpost. From this we learn that agility has deep roots in beliefs, commitment and passion and is not confined to high-tech or commercial enterprises.

Many conversations shaped my thinking about organisational agility, and I can only mention a few friends and colleagues who have been particularly influential. My co-author on other books, Mike Woodcock, taught me many secrets about the art of opportunism during our many writing breaks. John Bessant, professor of innovation management, and an inspiring intellectual leader, showed me just how useful good theories really are. Professor Yves Doz, of INSEAD, led me on a journey to discover the essence of the craft of agile strategy making. Henry Mintzberg's brilliant practical intellect opened my mind to contingency thinking as we worked, unfortunately for just a few days, to apply his theoretical models in practice. I learnt much about the pivotal importance of personal mastery from Helen Price. Barry Goodfield demonstrated that reservoirs of human potential lie waiting to be released in all of us. Eric Winkler's own remarkable entrepreneurial journey convinced me that honourable values lie at the core of organisational health and the late Roger Harrison helped me to understand that human-centred Organisation Development could, and should, be deliberately undertaken. Father Milton Zonta enabled me to see that individuals who are deeply committed to a shared set of beliefs can overcome apparently insuperable obstacles, energised by their collective inner strength.

My academic colleagues in the Centre for Entrepreneurship, Change Management and Innovation Management (CENTRIM), in the Brighton Business School, located on the South Coast of the UK, have been continuously supportive. Led by our proactive director, Dr George Tsekouras, CENTRIM's three interdependent areas of intellectual specialisation have enriched the eclectic theoretical base that underpins this book. My colleague, Despina Kanellou, leader of our Team Academy initiative, has helped me to see how bold educational formats can help students to acquire personal agile competencies. Professor Toni Hilton, Head of the Brighton Business School, contributed more than she knows to my understanding of the need for responsible agility. The University of Brighton's vice chancellor, Debra Humphris, is striving to make our university future-ready and participating in this initiative has taught me much about the realities of installing agility into a large organisation.

My long connection with the UK's Henley Business School provided irreplaceable opportunities to test the validity of the concepts presented in this book with senior managers. Without their input this book could not have been written. Clair Hewitt, head of learning design, powerfully explained the importance of managers mastering organisational agility and this conversation helped me decide to write this book.

Many individuals, companies and institutions have tested earlier versions of the concepts and tools presented in the book and their comments changed my thinking. I have gained many valuable insights from Katiusca Alvarez, Carlos Seaton, Jasper Gilder, Henry Wu, James Holloway, Dominic Swords, Leonardo Joel Muñoz, Peter

Augsdorfer, Simon Parisca, Søren Houmølle and Ray Charlton. Dave Adrian contributed greatly to my understanding of the relationship between values and agility. Professor Howard Rush helped me to understand the dynamic relationship between agility and innovation. Don Young's insight into work groups, and his wonderfully bold creativity, has left a lasting intellectual legacy. I want to recall my gratitude to the late Dr Juer, who taught me that the debilitating untidiness of the world is normal, but we can work to rise above it. Two of my sociology teachers, Norbert Elias and Tony Giddens, gave me insightful perspectives that have increased in value over the years.

Sam Treacy was brilliant as my editorial guide, especially on the arcane mysteries of grammar. The great team of change agents in Richmond Consultants Ltd., have, as always, been the best kind of critical friends.

Dr Miladys Parejo has been a constant source of creativity, challenge and support. She created a prize-winning arts-based social enterprise in which I took an administrative role for more than a decade. This experience has taught me more about agile organisations than reading dozens of books. Miladys's enterprise is enriched by the creative and willing cooperation of many artists and helpers, but it was she that provided the driving force. I have realised that organisational agility is more than a bundle of dynamic capabilities or a set of aligned processes. It is a loved creation, with its own life force, that needs unreasonable dedication.

Lastly, I owe a great debt to Steve Hardman, Maximilian Gessl and the entire production team at De Gruyter publishers. They have been a joy to work with! It makes a big difference.

As always, the responsibility for errors and inadequacies is mine alone.

David L. Francis
Hove, UK

Contents

Part III: **Resources**

Key Abbreviations Used

ACA   Agility Change Agent
ADT   Agility Development Team
CEO   Chief Executive Officer
EAfA   Exploiting Agility for Advantage
LoB   Line of Business
OD   Organisation Development
TMT   Top Management Team

https://doi.org/10.1515/9783110637267-204

Part I: **Requisite Agility**

1 Exploiting Agility for Advantage

You will not be alone if you are interested in organisational agility. A McKinsey global (McKinsey & Company, 2017) survey discovered that agility is a top-three priority for about 75% of senior managers. A study by PA Consulting (paconsulting.com, 2019) found that about 70% of business leaders believe cycles of invention and innovation are accelerating at an almost overwhelming rate, requiring an agile organisation to survive. Many not-for-profit organisations see agility as a key 21st century organisational requirement. For example, NATO (Soykan & Alberts, 2015) is focused on using emergent technologies to improve military agility and UNICEF (Amatullo, 2015), the global charity, is working to create an agile workforce and workplaces.

Many organisations, large or small, commercial or not-for-profit, have recognised the truth of Charles Darwin's observation that all organisms struggle for existence and it is those organisms that adapt successfully that survive and thrive (Darwin, 1909). These rules of nature also apply to organisations. We will describe the ability to adapt proactively to opportunities and threats as 'agility'.

The McKinsey survey, mentioned above, contained a disturbing observation. It found that the construct of organisational agility is elusive for many. It seems that managers recognise that their organisation needs to be capable of exploiting agility for advantage but are unsure how to turn this insight into action.

About this Book. . .

The purpose of this book is to make the management of agility less elusive. It provides a step-by-step process to help managers assess whether their organisation is sufficiently and appropriately agile. If not, ways will be suggested as to how fit-for-purpose or requisite agility can be acquired.

This book does not seek to sell agility as the answer to all the 21st century's managerial problems. It takes a position that the enthusiastic pursuit of organisational agility is neither always necessary nor will it always be constructive. Rather, adopting agility as a wanted dimension of organisational effectiveness should be a strategic choice and has extensive implications for management practice and for organisational development. For this reason, this book was titled *Exploiting Agility for Advantage*. The real management challenge is not to adopt agility principles universally but to develop agility requisitely, meaning selectively, in ways that can strengthen an organisation for both short- and long-term advantage.

Senior managers will find that *Exploiting Agility for Advantage* (hereafter *EAfA*) provides a methodology to enable an organisation to put the principles of agility into practice. But this is not a book for top executives. Those who manage organisational sub-units can use the step-by-step process described in this book without the need

https://doi.org/10.1515/9783110637267-001

for their parent organisation to have formally adopted the EAfA Process for increasing their organisation's capacity to exploit agility for advantage.

The term 'organisational sub-units' is not commonly used in management practice and requires explanation. We will describe all the components of an organisation as sub-units. This includes divisions, departments, lines of business (LoBs), workgroups, project teams, linkages with suppliers, liaison devices and autonomous systems. These may be permanent, temporary or ad hoc organisational arrangements and can combine technical resources and ecosystems. There are two reasons why all these different organisational formats have been categorised as sub-units. Firstly, it greatly simplifies the explanation of the EAfA Process. Secondly, our knowledge of how agility can be effectively implemented in different types of sub-unit is, at the time of writing, too thin to be authoritative.

EAfA's secondary audience is those who influence organisational development or management practice, including management consultants, teachers and students of management, Organisation Development interventionists and executive coaches. They have a special role, as they are often objective, outward-looking and constructive critical friends who act as guides, mentors and expert advisors to managers. The EAfA Process may also be helpful to social analysts and policy advisers, as it provides insight into the developmental requirements of institutions in the 21st century.

The last intended audience for this book is academic researchers and students of management. Since the 1990s organisational agility has become an important area of interest for academic groups, with more than half a million articles and books mentioning the construct. EAfA is dedicated to the task of becoming successfully agile, which is an under-explored topic in academic literature. Those interested in agility from an academic perspective may find that four conceptual developments that have not previously been published are useful additions to academic knowledge in this important area of organisational development. These are (i) the EAfA Leadership Framework, (ii) the EAfA Agile Capabilities Reference Model, (iii) the 6Ps Model and (iv) the EAfA Agility Typology Model.

EAfA takes the view that selectively adopting organisational agility as a policy is a strategic commitment, like any other. There will be costs, both financial and non-financial and, hopefully, flows of benefits that we will describe as 'agility deliverables'. If agility is deployed effectively then it becomes an organisational asset that can be exploited in multiple ways, potentially providing many different deliverables.

The scope of the required strategic commitment may be modest or transformational. Much organisational agility is targeted at 'doing better'. I recall visiting a cookie factory in the United States and meeting Marilyn, the maintenance manager. She was passionate about destroying the host of insects that thrived under giant baking ovens. Marilyn spent her coffee breaks reading magazines, like the *Food Safety Weekly*, searching for new ideas to win battles against the roaches. She conducted experiments, led problem-solving teams, monitored the effectiveness of trials and so on. Marilyn had an agile mindset, and used agile practices, to do better. Other organisations will use agile principles and practices to drive strategic change, sometimes redefining the essence of an organisation. We will describe this as 'do different' agility.

It is a key managerial task to define the functions that organisational agility needs to play in an organisation and ensure that fit-for-purpose or requisite agile capabilities are acquired and used. Before we proceed further it is important to define the word 'function', as it will be used in two quite different ways in this book. One meaning of the word is a specialist unit of an organisation (e.g., the finance function). The other definition is less widely used as it comes from sociology but is a core construct in EAfA. We will define a 'function' as the contribution that a component of an organisation makes to increase the probability that the whole is fit-for-purpose (e.g., the function of rewarding people for being open about their errors is to enable collective learning about what not to do in the future).

The Structure of the Book

EAfA provides managers, and their advisers, with a seven-step structured learning journey to enable them to understand the functions and potential dysfunctions of organisational agility and decide how they can exploit agility for advantage. This will be described as the EAfA Process.

EAfA is organised in three parts. Part I has four chapters. The first introduces the rationale for the book, the second provides an overview of the construct of agility, the third chapter explores the nature of opportunities and the fourth describes the attributes of those who successfully lead agile organisations.

Part II is structured as a work programme with seven steps. These provide managers and facilitators with the constructs and tools needed to enable them to decide where and how agility can be exploited for advantage in their organisation. There are five possible pathways through this work programme and Part II can be read as a standard book, rather than as work programme, if readers find this more helpful.

Part III is for those who wish to study aspects of organisational agility in greater depth. It provides a theoretical underpinning to key topics, supported by selected references, additional comments and suggestions for further reading.

EAfA draws extensively from social-science research, as it was my wish to use research to improve practice, thereby providing an evidence-based perspective. However, the book is written for managers, practitioners, trainers and teachers, so it needs to be accessible and practically useful. Hopefully, readers will enjoy the informality of the approach and excuse the lack of an exploration of alternative viewpoints. Those interested in the conceptual framework of EAfA can use Part III to deepen their understanding of the academic underpinnings of the work.

The EAfA Process is relevant for all sizes and types of organisations. Agile strategy formulation, and related organisational development initiatives, are needed across a wide range of organisations, for example, in military units, government departments, educational institutions, hospitals, social enterprises and charities. Even religious orders have found the EAfA Process useful and there has been interest from the managers of a prison! In fact, some of the most significant thought leaders, including some of those who developed what became known as the Agile Paradigm, have been not-for-profit organisations.

The EAfA Process is, itself, an agile product. It is a work-in-progress and managers can improve it by incorporating findings from new research and enrich the methodology as they learn from their own experience. As the developer of EAfA, as well as the author, I welcome insights, comments and criticisms to improve later editions—my contact details are in the final chapter.

How EAfA was Developed

EAfA has developed over the past 25 years. It began when I joined an academic research team investigating the management challenges faced by companies striving to become agile. We found that progress was only made when decision-makers deeply understood the construct of agility and had found ways to integrate its principles and practices into their practice of management. Since then I have facilitated agility-orientated organisational development initiatives in commercial and not-for-profit organisations in the United States, South America, Asia, Africa, China and Europe to discover whether the EAfA Process is relevant in different cultures. I have learnt that organisational agility is not a product to be adopted off-the-shelf. It requires managers to embrace relevant mindsets and decide how to use the potential benefits of organisational agility within a wider set of managerial priorities.

People in agile organisations undertake personal development journeys. This is because agile organisations are adaptive, which means that individuals have stretching roles. Formal job descriptions decrease in importance and the person becomes more important. Undertaking the EAfA learning journey provides more than insight into a managerial methodology. It helps all involved to grow as people and acquire productive efficacy or agency.

From my research and prototyping of the EAfA Process seven truths have emerged, which are:
- Not all organisations need to be equally agile.
- Being agile is not the only thing that organisations need to do.
- Leading an agile organisation needs a distinctive set of competencies.
- Adopting the wrong type of agility can be dysfunctional.
- The sub-units of an organisation need distinctive pathways for operationalising agility as 'one size does not fit all'.
- Becoming requisitely agile is a long journey, with progress being made over time.
- Agility can be lost as well as gained.

These truths are the reason why it is necessary to strive to become requisitely agile, meaning 'not too much, not too little, of the right type and delivering wanted agility deliverables'. The construct of requisite agility is not original to EAfA, as it is used in military strategic planning, but EAfA has developed it in a unique way.

Why EAfA is needed: Our VUCA World

A key reason why gaining, sustaining and upgrading requisite agility has become a managerial and organisational development priority for many enterprises is that deep and extensive contextual changes are changing landscapes of opportunities and threats, often dramatically.

Few people can doubt that multiple, disruptive, forces are fundamentally reshaping sectors, industries, markets and national economies. The impact of such change forces is so extensive that many organisations are either affected now or will be soon. This era of business turbulence has been described as being characterised by VUCA (volatility, uncertainty, complexity and ambiguity).

Three categories of superordinate change drivers create a VUCA environment.

First is the transformational impact of new or emerging science-based technologies, such as self-healing systems, nanotubes, bioengineering and the quantum coherence phenomena. These have the potential to be value-creating for those that can capture advantage from exploiting them, and value-destroying for those committed to earlier, inferior technologies.

The breadth and depth of social, environmental and economic change that flows from science-based technologies has been described as Industry 4.0, meaning that we have entered a new era. For example, cyber-physical systems enable computers to cooperate with each other, and with humans, in real time providing previously unimaginable automation and control possibilities. Amongst many changes, Industry 4.0 requires that organisations need to be requisitely agile and it changes the ways that agility can be achieved. Technological boundaries are redefined as digital, physical and biological specialisations become integrated. We can expect to see entirely new industries emerging that can dramatically improve integration and productivity, but these changes will be accompanied by a host of social problems as traditional ways of working become redundant.

Second, the structure of competition is changing. For example, a few global enterprises have captured markets that are far larger than previously thought possible and venturesome small enterprises are gaining access to platforms that allow them access to markets previously too costly to reach. This degree of turbulence in the structure of competition has profound consequences.

Lastly, the environmental, sociological and political consequences of humanity's dominance as species are becoming dysfunctional, meaning that the pursuit of profit alone has become too narrow a definition of value added. Enterprises are being compelled to reconsider their role in a changing world. There are changing definitions of what gaining advantage means.

Today's managers are not the first to operate in a VUCA world. Times of social upheaval, war and uncertainty have occurred throughout history. However, 21st century managers are the first to confront the range of volatile and uncertain characteristics outlined above. Only requisitely agile organisations have the capabilities that are required to thrive in a VUCA dominated world.

The Changing World of Dog Food

The nature of VUCA change drivers can be illustrated by an example. Thirty years ago, dog food was broadly divided into dry and wet categories. In supermarkets there would be bags of dry dog food, made by international companies like Mars and Nestlé, and a variety of types of wet canned dog food, often made by the same companies. Dog owners would experiment with different foods to see which their dog enjoyed and many would buy the same product year after year.

Today, the same range of products is available in supermarkets, but it is just as easy to obtain supplies of food that have been prepared specifically for an individual dog. A owner simply needs to fill out an online form with key facts about their dog, such as name, age, breed, weight, health and activity level. Based on nutritional studies the food for this particular dog will be prepared to meet its specific requirements and supplies will be sent regularly to the owner, direct from the factory.

These developments in pet food have been profoundly disruptive. The complexity of providing customised food for dogs is achievable only by using advanced data processing and direct marketing. This enables many categories of operating costs to be reduced and has other benefits as well.

Dog owners receive a product that may be better for their animal and they feel they have taken every possible step to give their pet the best care. The food producer has direct contact with dog owners and knows what they prefer, thereby achieving what has been called 'customer intimacy'. Companies that mass-produce standard dog food are at a disadvantage as their assets and competences no longer place them at the cutting edge of competition and they must use costly distribution channels.

Of course, dog food is just one example of an era of competition changed using a newly available capability to deliver complex micro-customisation. Many industries are being disrupted in similar ways and more are predicted to change profoundly. It is organisations with deep strategic and operational requisite agility that will survive and thrive.

Successful Agility

Adapting to a VUCA and disrupting world is not as daunting as some might imagine. Throughout history, countless organisations have created or found and exploited opportunities, mitigated threats and profited thereby. Some industries, like news gathering, humanitarian aid and fashion retailing, are inherently dynamic and organisations that have thrived in these environments are invariably venturesome and adaptive. Much can be learnt from studying such successful examples. They have undertaken multiple acts of selective, decisive, prudent, timely, advantageous and well-executed opportunism. When we review these cases, an interesting conclusion emerges—there is no single formula for being successfully agile.

Notice that we use the term 'successfully' agile. Some have claimed that agility is a foolproof pathway to gain competitive or comparative advantage in today's world, but this is not true. It is possible (i) to have too much or too little agility; (ii) to adopt a dysfunctional type of agility; (iii) to be agile in the wrong places; (iv) to prioritise short-term agility, without developing sufficient resilience to cope with future challenges and (v) to fail to acquire the foundational capabilities required to underpin organisational agility. A managerial aim should be to avoid such potential errors by constructing and maintaining a requisitely agile organisation.

Dysfunctional Agility

One sleepless night in Colorado Springs I realised just how dysfunctional agility could be. I had been asked to undertake an organisational development assignment with a company called Inmos (McLean & Rowland, 1985), which was a UK semi-conductor company with factories in South Wales and the United States. The founders of Inmos had seen an opportunity for a then non-existing product that can be described as 'a working computer on a silicon chip' which used parallel processing technologies. The UK government financed the start-up but later Inmos was sold to my client, an international company. Why was I unable to sleep that night? I had been told that Inmos was losing more than half a million dollars a day and I found that their unique innovation, called a transputer, was more like an experimental prototype than a mass production product. Eventually, Inmos closed and I have been told that its accumulated losses approached a billion dollars.

Certainly, Inmos was opportunistic. Their owners had made a large bet and I know those involved were talented, dedicated and adaptive. So, why was their agility dysfunctional? Inmos' Silicon Valley competitors were more experienced, and they advanced much faster. More importantly, from my own involvement with the company, I know that no one had identified a big market opportunity for the transputer that could be grasped and defended by Inmos. The company has been boldly opportunistic but not prudently opportunistic.

If there are any doubts that adopting the wrong type of organisational agility can be dysfunctional then the history of Nokia's mobile phone business provides salutary lessons. It was Nokia that dominated the mobile phone market for much of the first decade of the 21st century, but this did not last. By 2012 Nokia's business share of the market had shrunk to 33% as momentum had moved to Apple and android smartphone manufacturers. In September 2013 Nokia sold its mobile phone business to Microsoft.

The decline and fall of Nokia's mobile phone business has attracted the interest of academic scholars. How was it possible for an organisation with excellent technical resources, a healthy cash flow and sector dominance to be outpaced by new entrants? For several years a team of researchers interviewed former Nokia executives to understand how such a catastrophic collapse could occur and their findings were published in an article entitled 'The Curse of Agility' (Lamberg, Lubinaitė, Ojala, & Tikkanen, 2019).

The article explained that, in the early 2000s, Nokia had wholeheartedly embraced a version of agile organisational concepts as its dominant philosophy for management. Nokia became a place where sub-units had considerable autonomy, competing technologies were explored, diversity was relished, strategies were changed frequently, reorganisation was almost permanent, and the CEO dedicated much time to satisfying external stakeholders.

I visited Nokia in 2008 and found that managers were well-schooled in the merits of what had become known as the Agile Paradigm. One informed me that 'being on the edge of chaos' was essential for world-leading innovation. Some Nokia managers were so immersed in agile management that several were giving keynote lectures in business schools on the agile enterprise. I was told their philosophy of management would enable Nokia to dominate the global market for mobile handsets for generations to come. Other Nokia managers had a different story to tell. They spoke about the 'then new iPhone' with respect and fear. One manager said: "We had all of the technology, but we were so fragmented that did not use it and now we are three years behind!"

So, what went wrong? In an executive Apple conference in 2003 CEO Steve Jobs declared the future of mobile communication and information exchange would be with mobile phones (Isaacson, 2011). From then on Apple's R&D was tasked to focus relentlessly on creating a smartphone concept that would become an irreplaceable digital life partner in years to come. In 2005 Google acquired Android Inc. and they began a similar developmental journey. The first iPhone was sold on June 29, 2007 and a Google android phone was launched in 2008.

Apple and Google had driven their visions relentlessly, with ample resources available. Many teams played well-defined roles to make this happen. Their challenge was not only technological as a smartphone would provide consumers with resources that had previously been impossible to imagine. In order to invent the concept of a smartphone Apple and Google were organised more like an orchestra than a jazz band. Huge effort was invested in driving state-of-the-art technical developments and funding basic research into scientific and technical innovation. The result was Apple's IOS ecosystem and Google's android platform.

Apple and Google's visionary, structured, unified and technologically driven development programmes contrasted dramatically with Nokia's complex and under-integrated matrix structures, their frequent changes of organisation, divergent development agendas in dispersed development groups, convoluted decision-making structures and leadership by general managers, some of whom openly admitted they were not technologically savvy. During my visit to Nokia I was told by the director of a research group that: "our top management has been seduced by the agile management philosophy: they deal with policy and leave concepts to emerge. This does happen but there are too many ideas and not enough commitment, and it is all too slow". Another senior executive told me that: "it's falling apart here. No-one knows what the right thing is to do. We have the greatest people but an unorganised organisation".

Reflecting on this case it is apparent that the form of agility that Nokia had adopted was unable to stand up to a challenge from Apple and Google. However, a top-down and orchestrated approach had enabled Apple to be supremely agile and create an opportunity to integrate telephone and web-based computing. We can suggest that the article entitled 'The Curse of Agility' could have been given the title 'The Curse of the Wrong Type of Agility'!

Managing Agility

Wherever there are gatherings of leaders and managers it is likely that agility will be discussed. This focuses attention but has a dark side. Organisational agility is in danger of becoming a bubble of short-lived enthusiasm. We need to move beyond seeing agility as a strategic magic wand, as this cheapens the construct. We should see agility as a potentially mission-critical organisational asset but one that has associated risks and needs to be fit-for-purpose.

Organisational agility requires that change becomes institutionalised. Rather than being an episode, change becomes a way of life. This requires assertive and creative adaptation, often to new or unpredicted challenges. Turbulence in the external environments must be matched by an equal organisational flexibility.

Some good news is that striving to become agile is more often beneficial than destructive! This occurs when requisite agility (i) supports an organisation's strategy for gaining and sustaining comparative or competitive advantage; (ii) is aligned with other organisational priorities; (iii) is responsibly executed and (iv) develops organisational robustness or hardiness, which we will define as a capability to survive and thrive despite difficulties.

In the next chapter the construct of agility will be explored in greater detail.

2 What is Organisational Agility?

In 2018 a pop-up café opened in Tokyo for just eight days. Its customers were served by robots that were about a metre tall (Berezina, Ciftci, & Cobanoglu, 2019). Elsewhere in the world there were other cafés staffed by robot waiters but the DAWN ver.β café was different. It was the first to have the robots controlled by paralysed people from their beds or wheelchairs at home. Ten disabled people, some only able to communicate using eye movements, took turns to control four robots that picked up plates, talked to customers, served drinks and offered snacks. The robots transmitted live video and audio over the internet so their disabled operators could direct them using specially adapted computers.

This venture could only be undertaken after the required technologies were available. Developments in robotics and disability-friendly control systems had advanced to a stage where, with further technical development, the café could operate in ways that everyone involved, especially the disabled operators, would find fulfilling. An opportunity was present, but it was not fully formed. It took Kentaro 'Ory' Yoshifuji, who was the CEO of Ory Lab, a Japanese robotics company, to invest his time, and Ory Lab's resources, in doing everything needed to acquire resources, coordinate an extensive development programme, win support and open this unique café.

Ori led the DAWN ver.β café initiative, undertaking much of the technical work and becoming a persuasive advocate of this great experiment. As a boy, he could not attend school for several years due to poor health. Later in his life, Ori developed technologies to help disabled people, including OriHime, a robot specifically designed to reduce the loneliness of disabled people. An OriHime robot attended a concert for a six-year-old girl who had been born with a muscle disease. From her bed, she could control the robot's movements and enjoy her favourite band. Her pleasure inspired Ori to do more.

The DAWN ver.β café is an example of an agile enterprise. An opportunity was identified by someone with the passion to become deeply involved and had the technical capabilities to know what could be achieved. Many other people also made distinctive contributions. For example, psychologists worked with technical experts to develop simulations that tested whether disabled people could control robots, as it was essential they not be overwhelmed with the complexities of their tasks.

Many streams of the work programme were integrated by an ambition statement that defined aims and explained why these were important. A temporary organisation was constructed to develop, resource, manage, fund, promote, launch and learn from the initiative. The DAWN ver.β café demonstrated that requisite agility is a quintessentially human endeavour in which passion, commitment, grit and human energy are as important as organisation, objectives, coordination, technology and controls.

https://doi.org/10.1515/9783110637267-002

Pinnacle Point

The energy, commitment, skill and resources that created the DAWN ver.β café provides an example of a capability that may be almost as old as humanity itself. About 72,000 years ago, near a place called Pinnacle Point in South Africa, humans began to make stone tools that recent research has shown required an advanced knowledge of the effects of heat on molecular structures (Brown et al., 2009). Imagine a scenario where a toolmaker who is a master of knapping (sculpting) stones, picks up a stone that was blackened from last night's fire. He begins to knap it to make a sharp stone blade. The stone splits easily and the blade is keener than any he usually knaps. Then he does something special. He realises there is a possibility that other stone tools would be improved if the stone was as easy to work as the one he had pulled from the fireplace. He has identified a possible opportunity for improvement.

At this stage there were many unknowns. No one could be sure why the heated stone provided superior raw material for knapping. Perhaps it had belonged to a God or a snake had slept on it. The toolmaker needed to experiment, perhaps by collecting different types of stone, marking them and putting them into a fire for varying lengths of time. After a while, evidence-based knowledge would be acquired so that knappers could predict which stones would benefit from being heated for a specific length of time. Achieving this depth of understanding required focused exploratory effort.

Assume that our toolmaker found evidence that stones dug from a specific geological stratum, heated to a temperature of 350 degrees centigrade, would reliably provide superior raw material. He now had a different challenge, which was to convince the other toolmakers in the knapping team that it would be worth the effort to find ways to build kilns and change their ways of working. Our agile toolmaker had to become a politician.

Thereafter, kilns were designed and built, new tools developed, processes changed, quality control introduced and so on. Unexpected problems must have occurred, and new knowledge would be gained through trial and error. In this phase, the energy of agility needed to be redirected towards developing an efficient factory system. Later, another set of activities would be needed for the initiative to be deemed a success. This was to convince hunters in nearby villages to use the superior tools. Our agile toolmaker had to become a marketeer.

As far as it is known, Pinnacle Point is the first example of humans undertaking this level of technological innovation. A wide variety of products were produced, including stone axes, scrapers, knives and arrow heads. I have handled stone tools from the Neolithic period and can confirm they were sharp enough to give a man a reasonably close shave. The early industrialists of Pinnacle Point undertook multiple forms of prudent opportunism including exploiting innovation in materials science, the development of mass production techniques and the formation of distribution networks.

These two examples enable us to see that agility is not an unreachable or unusual attribute. We learnt from the DAWN ver.β café story that organisational agility is a quintessentially human endeavour. We can assume that the stone knappers of Pinnacle Point were remarkably similar, as they developed previously unknown ways to heat silcrete rocks before knapping them.

The EAfA Definition of Organisational Agility

There are four interlinked streams of activities that characterise agile organisations. EAfA defines requisite organisational agility as an aligned set of attributes that enables an organisation to (i) adapt proactively and intelligently to situational changes; (ii) create or find, select, and responsibly exploit, sufficient numbers of promising opportunities to gain comparative or competitive advantage; (iii) robustly avoid or mitigate threats and (iv) acquire the full range of assets, resources and competences needed to thrive in a different future.

Let's unpick this definition.

Requisite organisational agility requires *an aligned set of attributes*. These can include human, technical, resource-based, systemic, network-based or managerial assets, depending on the type of agility needed. The word 'aligned' is key, as agile organisations can suffer from excessive fragmentation, as was experienced by Nokia described above. These attributes are bundles of capabilities, functioning rather like neuro-networks, to provide grand, systemic or meta-level deliverables.

Adapting proactively and intelligently to situational changes means using human and non-human assets to sense environments deeply, extensively and quickly; capturing insights about changes; interpreting their significance and responding effectively. Until recently, this capacity for proactively gathering and absorbing often weak signals has been a human endeavour but machine intelligence is playing an ever-greater role.

Creating or finding, selecting and responsibly exploiting sufficient numbers of promising opportunities to gain comparative or competitive advantage requires that an organisation or sub-unit is capable of being routinely prudently opportunistic. The word 'promising' is important, as no organisation could, or should, strive to exploit every opportunity. Requisitely agile organisations select opportunities that have a high probability of contributing responsibly to gaining comparative or competitive advantage. Note the word 'responsibly'. EAfA has adopted a stance that being agile has an ethical dimension as agility provides collective agency, which is the wellspring of action, and action always has a moral dimension.

Robustly avoiding or mitigating threats is a constant preoccupation of requisitely agile organisations. Threats are many and varied, with some being complex or unpredictable. Agile-friendly managers follow the advice of Andy Grove, a founder of Intel, who insightfully titled his book *Only the Paranoid Survive* (Grove, 1998). Grove knew that threats may not be recognised and can dramatically erode, or destroy, an organisation's distinctive advantages and transform its assets into liabilities. Requisitely agile organisations are aggressively defensive. They relentlessly look for possible threats and rigorously explore their likely consequences. The German general, Field Marshal Rommel (Rommel, 2006), once observed that to become a hero one must first survive. This stance is typical of those who lead and manage agile organisations. Processes for gaining early warning of impending threats, and developing proactive threat mitigation strategies, are key components of requisite agile capability. This has insightfully been described as 'robustness' as it enables an organisation to withstand shocks and thereby grow stronger.

Acquiring the range of assets, resources and competences needed to thrive in a different future is the last meta-level deliverable required from possessing requisite organisational agility. Those who manage requisitely agile organisations track and study trends, develop scenarios and predict the characteristics of future-ready organisations. This increases the probability that new or different ways will be found to retain competitive or comparative advantage and avoid becoming trapped in strategic cul-de-sacs. Managers may invest in innovation or acquisition to increase the probability of their organisation remaining viable, despite being impacted by new or different change drivers. Thriving in a different future may require the destruction of exiting activities. Requisite agility depends on possessing bundles of capabilities that can assist an organisation to thrive in best- and worse-case scenarios. Possessing a capacity to take intelligent decisive action in unforeseeable future circumstances is always required. The aim is to be wise in positioning strategically and tactically.

We can summarise by stating that the EAfA definition of a requisitely agile organisation is one that is appropriately (i) situationally adaptive, (ii) prudently opportunistic, (iii) threat mitigating and (iv) future readying.

Agility Deliverables

Organisations strive to become agile because their leaders and managers want to exploit agility for advantage. Only when the value of the deliverables outweighs the costs, or other downsides, can agility be said to be a successful strategy.

So, what is a deliverable? The answer is slightly complicated because requisite agility is not a standard to be reached but an ambition to be realised. Organisational sociologists refer to this as being contingent, meaning that it depends on the context and the decisions made by leaders (Mintzberg, 1998). There are systemic imperatives. Every organisation needs to have policies to enable it to be appropriately situationally adaptive, prudently opportunistic, threat mitigating and future readying. These meta-level agility deliverables are non-negotiable, as every requisitely agile enterprise is entitled to benefit from possessing them. This is a necessary, but not sufficient definition of the possible deliverables from agility, as they are contingent upon organisation-specific landscapes of opportunities, rival's capabilities, the nature and intensity of change drivers, the role of machine intelligence and choices made by owners and managers. The EAfA Process enables managers at every level of an organisation to decide where and how they can best exploit agility for advantage.

As industries and organisations differ, the meta-level agility deliverables need to be elaborated before they can become useful. For example, a pharmaceutical company with a mission to lead new drug development may define one of its required agility deliverables to be that it adopts scientific advances more rapidly than its rivals. However, a global children's charity may define a required agility deliverable as an ability to influence many governments to introduce child safeguarding legalisation.

Organisation-specific agility needs to support the corporate mission and strategic intent directly. For example, at the time of writing, Amazon's (Smith, 2018) mission statement is "we strive to offer our customers the lowest possible prices, the best available selection, and the utmost convenience". In the fast-moving online retailing sector this mission can only be realised if multiple opportunities are created, or found, to keep prices low, increase the variety of reliable selection options and find new ways to provide an ever more convenient service to customers. Amazon seeks to gain from its commitment to organisational agility streams of timely initiatives that will enable the business to remain ahead of rivals in its chosen mission-critical success areas, as mentioned above.

Agile deliverables only become real when they are delivered. There are cases where organisations have claimed to be agile, but they lack the depth of execution capability to transform intentions into realities. Put simply, an agile organisation will have a 'can-do' ethos and 'will-do' capability. Without this, requisite agility cannot be achieved.

Quantities of Agility

Not all organisations need the same quantity of agility. A simple example clarifies this point. Companies in fast-developing industries, like Google or Microsoft, need a much greater quantity of systemic agility than Whyte and Mackay, a maker of traditional Scotch whisky with production processes similar to those first used by Friar in 1495. Determining the optimal quantity of agility needed is a function of three factors: two external and one internal.

The two key external factors are (i) current rivals' agility and (ii) the impact of present and future change drivers. Managers should benchmark their own organisation's agility against best-in-class rivals to determine whether others are gaining superior agility deliverables. This specialised form of benchmarking helps to define whether greater agility-orientated investment (financial and non-financial) will be needed to strengthen competitive or comparative advantage. Predicting future change drivers, as we will see in Part II of this book, provides additional insights as it is possible that change drivers will change the logic of the situation and radical or do-different agility will be needed to remain viable.

The internal factor is an organisation's Agility Ambition. This is a form of strategic intent that specifies how agility fits into, and enriches, an organisation's identity or its collective personality. An Agility Ambition is always an act of leadership that needs to be explicit. Typically, there will be a written (explicit) ambition statement but, more important, will be the way that senior leaders behave, as this communicates what is really valued. The importance of Agility Ambitions is discussed in Part II of this book.

Fitness and Agility

There are similarities between organisational agility and core athletic capability, as possessed by people such as Olympic swimmers, ballet dancers and triathlon champions. All successful athletes have distinctive physical qualities, strong motivation, focused discipline, specialised equipment, balanced nutrition, skilful coaches, extensive practice and so on. Once possessed, some will use their core athletic capability for running marathons, others for practicing yoga and yet others for dancing all night. A person without core athletic capability cannot undertake any of these activities proficiently. Athletic capability, like requisite organisational agility, provides the readiness required to undertake defined categories of action successfully.

Sitting on top of core athletic capability is sport-specific fitness. Different sports require specific strengths. For example, rock climbers spend hours strengthening their fingers so they can hold onto a tiny crevice. In order to develop this specific strength climbers train by supporting their entire body weight with just two fingers from each hand hanging from fingerboards for 10 to 20 seconds at a time. Other sports, for example, boxing and gymnastics, require different types of sport-specific fitness. The notion of core capability being overlaid by issue-specific fitness provides an important metaphor for conceptualising requisite organisational agility.

The fitness analogy suggests that requisite agility cannot be gained by taking a decision alone, as enduring commitment, specific routines and hard work will also be required. We can conclude that organisational agility is more than an intent; it must be earned. There is another important similarity, as athletic capability will vanish if it is not nurtured. Likewise, organisational agility will be lost if it is not routinely nourished, practised and constantly recreated.

EAfA defines organisational agility as a two-level construct. We will describe the foundational level, analogous to core athletic capability, as 'systemic agility', as it enables an organisation, as a whole, to be situationally adaptive, prudently opportunistic, threat mitigating and future readying. Systemic agility needs to be overlaid by 'local agility', analogous to sport-specific fitness, as this provides requisite agility for sub-units.

Level One: Systemic Agility

Systemic agility refers to an entire organisation, including its ecosystem. For the purpose of this book an organisation will be defined as 'an entity aligned by the same mission, vision and values'. This Unit of Analysis is important as organisations develop 'their own way of being', which influences all sub-units. An example illustrates the pervasive influence of an organisation's culture. As mentioned above, I once worked in Harrods and, when I joined, the store was a relic of a bygone age. I recall suggesting to my manager that the tie section in the men's department should hire female sales attendants to help customers select ties they would enjoy. I was told, "this is not who Harrods is. Females have no place in selling clothing to men". This 'way of being' or ethos was a force that valued tradition rather than agility. An organisation's culture, systems, structures and choices about who will exercise power, greatly affects who has the potential to exercise agency and where this will be directed.

Systemic agility enables activities to be undertaken that otherwise would be impossible. When systemic agility is high it assists sub-units to develop requisite local agility. The common characteristics of a systemically agile organisation are described, in detail, in Part II of this book. The requirements are extensive. Twenty components are described, each of which, if present, enables systemic agility or, if weak, becomes an agility blockage. The components are interdependent and organised into five domains. The first domain focuses on strategic-level and top management team (TMT) issues, the second on organisational routines and processes, the third on the wider ecosystem, the fourth on resources and capabilities and the last on sources of momentum.

Systemic agility needs to be a property of an entire organisation as it provides a supportive ecosystem for the development of requisite local agility. Consider this analogy. Imagine a neglected garden where pests abound, the soil is unproductive, plants run wild, weeds flourish and invasive species have taken root. In such a garden, it is almost impossible that there could be an area that can grow prize-winning roses as horticultural skills are absent, the soil is depleted and inadequate resources are available. A supportive ecosystem is needed for a prize-winning rose garden. The same is true of localised organisational agility—it needs requisite systemic agility in order to thrive.

Requisite systemic agility requires that appropriate types of agility have been adopted and implemented effectively in each sub-unit that can benefit. This is a key feature of the EAfA Process. The model that we will use to explain this describes eight types of agility, namely *top down* (agility by centralisation), *routines-based* (agility by pre-planning), *project-based* (agility from temporary organisations), *socio-technical* (agility by optimising human and non-human capabilities), *skunk-works* (agility from cutting-edge specialists), *intrapreneurial* (agility from internal entrepreneurship), *granular* (agility from devolved teams) and *networked* (agility from inter-organisational collaboration). These types of agility are explained, in detail, in Part II of this book.

Agile organisations need strong social and operational cohesion as they frequently reorganise, and it is essential that barriers to organisational flexibility are low. Netflix provides an example that illustrates this point (Jenner, 2018). In order to strive to maintain its position as the leading provider of streamed digital entertainment in the second decade of the 21st century, Netflix undertook multiple agile initiatives, including pioneering technical developments, commissioning award-winning new content production, maintaining a strong social media presence, developing native apps for computing platforms, limiting illegitimate copying and so on. All these activities interacted to form a 'gestalt', meaning that the whole was more than the sum of the parts and, as a result, an extremely high level of organisational cohesiveness was achieved. Maintaining organisation-level cohesion, sometimes referred to as boundarylessness, is an essential task for those who wish to exploit agility for advantage.

Agile organisations aim to be comparatively superior to rivals, and potential rivals, in relation to the four meta-level agility deliverables described earlier. This requires systemic agility and it is necessary for TMTs to define the meta-level deliverables as entitlements, interpret them in ways that make sense to their own organisation and find ways to assess their current comparative strengths and weaknesses in each area (perhaps by using the EAfA Process in Part II of this book).

Systemically agile organisations have an interesting characteristic—the organisation is more important than the tasks currently being undertaken. Stable organisations are held together (made cohesive) by everyone knowing what is required of them, and they know they can rely on others to perform their assigned specialised tasks. Systemically agile organisations cannot depend on role clarity to provide cohesiveness as some roles will be inherently flexible. Agile organisations need to develop what we will refer to as a distinctive organisational personality or identity, that is held in place by shared beliefs, common values and a commitment to the 'kind of organisation that we want to become'.

A requisitely agile organisation is a cared-for, and energised, sociological entity that makes intelligent choices about what to do in order to gain the required meta-level agility deliverables. This is not a task to be done only once. Managers need to find ways to renew requisite agility permanently, recognising that the journey will be long, arduous, confronting and never completed.

Level Two: Local Agility

Not all parts of an organisation need to be equally agile and not all sub-units need to be agile in the same ways. The following example illustrates this point.

Consider a busy sports centre where the operations department will have a team looking after the swimming pool. This team will have strict routines for checking whether the water quality is safe, standard procedures are used for dealing with noisy children or amorous couples and standard operating procedures for dealing with emergencies are in place. Those working in the team will only be marginally affected by a requirement to be agile as, for them, discipline is more important. The marketing department at the sports centre will have a quite different work experience. They will study customers and potential customers and learn from similar facilities elsewhere to find or invent new and different ways to exploit the sports centre's facilities. Those working on the marketing team must be venturesome and creative. They have a much greater need for agility than does the pool team, as multiple flows of initiatives are required.

A localised approach to the development agile capability adds complexity but improves the probability that agility will provide requisite agility for sub-units. Localised agility capability can be targeted at one or more of six domains: (i) product (outputs), (ii) process (sequences of activities), (iii) positioning (communicating outside), (iv) paradigm (business model), (v) provisioning (obtaining resources) and (vi) platform (facilitating utilisation). This framework, known as the 6Ps Model, will be described in more detail in the next chapter.

Agility and Innovation

Agility and innovation have a close, but complex relationship, rather like that sometimes seen between brother and sister. An organisation with requisite agile capability exploits opportunities responsibly and effectively. An organisation with high innovation capability undertakes the work needed to develop and exploit opportunities that are new to the unit of adoption. Is there a difference between agility and innovation? The answer is yes, as the nature of work, the driving force and the associated risk profiles, are different for each. The kind of differentiation is clarified by two examples.

The XYZ company is *agility* orientated and their mission is to profit from property development. XYZ's directors had spent months studying good practice in this industry and thereafter followed tried-and-tested methods for locating, buying, improving and renting or selling properties. XYZ's core work requires finding properties with potential, purchasing them at lowest cost, configuring ways to improve them, ensuring that improvements are made economically and making a sale, or finding tenants, that yield a good profit margin. If the directors of XYZ lack ideas, they study what more experienced property development companies have done and adopt their relevant ideas. Their dominant driving force is the flexible imitation of existing best practice.

The ABC company is *innovation* orientated and their mission is to develop a new generation of equipment that will improve the productivity of mushroom farms. ABC's work is targeted at discovering, developing, testing and (eventually) marketing a differentiated and superior mushroom growing system. Their work modality is dominated by scientific investigation; their building is full of experimental equipment and several million dollars have been invested in studies, investigations, laboratory services, field tests etc. Their dominant driving force is creating valuable outputs that are new and capable of being patented. They focus relentlessly on making valuable discoveries.

Agility and innovation have different clock-speeds. Innovation requires finding and exploiting new ideas and is frequently time-consuming, uncertain, expensive and difficult. This is true in many industries, including that of being an author! Writing this book took many months of research and development but, once published, it can be copied in seconds. Those investing resources in innovation will be successful only if they can capture value from what they create. Notice the 'if' word. Failure is common.

Agility has a rapid heartbeat. It is rapid, lean and acquisitive, perhaps taking advantage of others' weaknesses. It is possible to be agile without a commitment to innovation, as is demonstrated by strategies used by manufacturers of generic drugs or by the XYZ property company mentioned above. But agile organisations can lack ownership of unique assets so their competitive advantage can be imitated more easily. Momentum is essential.

Why is the relationship between agility and innovation complex? Many organisations must, like the ancient Roman god Janus, must face two ways and be both agile and innovative, as was demonstrated in the sports centre example explained earlier. Work groups rightly, adopt mindsets, skills and activities to support their specialised work requirements. As the modality of work is different between agile and innovative work-groups, silos or closed groups can develop and this will undermine systemic coherence. Boundaries can become high walls. Requisitely agile organisations must find ways to overcome such potential barriers.

Not just being Nimble

It is important that we recognise the breadth of the construct of requisite agility. In management magazines agility is sometimes described as nimbleness, flexibility and being fast-to-react. But this is only part of the story. It is necessary to be prudent as well as quick. Some decisions will have big consequences. Managers in requisitely agile organisations know that big bets need to be based on the best possible analysis. The founder of Amazon, Jeff Bezos, once described himself as the chief slowdown officer as he knew that sometimes it is more important to be right than fast (Denning, 2018). Deep agile capability is intelligent, selective and incisive. It is this that we seek to achieve.

Context is a Capability

Agility flourishes more in some contexts than others. If someone wants to be a jewellery designer, they may go to Florence where a 600-year-old tradition continues to this day. A company undertaking advanced pharmaceutical research could locate in Research Triangle Park, North Carolina, as the resources that are needed to support state-of-the-art science are readily available, including three highly-ranked research universities. An electronic products manufacturer will feel at home in Shenzhen where, for example, there is the pioneering Open Innovation Lab that develops digital intelligent hardware and a complete ecosystem of packers, shippers, suppliers and other resource providers. When such clusters form, specialised capabilities develop naturally and able people gravitate to the locality.

Today, in Silicon Valley, it feels as if that agility is in the air, as organisational agility is a deeply understood imperative. There have been historic periods when entire societies embraced agility as a prized way of being. The Vikings embedded agile principles deep into their social fabric and conquered much of the known world. Ancient China was a leader in creative opportunism, for example, inventing the pulp papermaking process in the 2nd century BCE. Since the 19th century Germany has excelled in the manufacturing of printing presses, following the establishment of Koenig and Bauer near Würzburg in 1818. Societal cultures can provide a context for agility to thrive, and it makes sense to exploit their potential.

Organisms not Machines

Agile organisations are best viewed as organisms, not machines. They are capable of being venturesome, intelligent and self-healing. Agile organisations have such delicate dynamism that it is useful to think of them as possessing a life force of their own. It is a key managerial challenge to nourish this energy system, so that the organisation becomes capable of surviving and thriving in times of change.

This life force is impossible to measure yet can be felt in every agile organisation. Visitors sense a hard-to-define vibrant energy, and an empowering ethos, as soon as they enter the building. This is sustained by the aligned constructive agency or efficacy of individuals, especially those in leadership positions who energise proactive, cohesive, intelligent and ongoing momentum.

Agility is deeply rooted, like the DNA in a living creature. The people that work in an agile enterprise have a can-do and will-do mindset and this will be embedded in new recruits. They possess a desire to win and are open to ideas, possibilities and the experiences of others. Agility is not optional, as it becomes a cultural imperative—it is 'the way that we do things here'.

A ubiquitous sense of can-do optimism in agile organisations has some similarities with the placebo effect in medicine. A placebo is an inert treatment that has no known effects, so it should not provide medical benefits. But something strange can happen. Researchers in Harvard Medical School (Howe, Goyer, & Crum, 2017) have found that placebos have physical and psychological effects as participants in placebo groups show changes in heart rate, blood pressure, anxiety levels, pain perception, fatigue and brain activity. Our psychological state may not be a passive response to circumstances but, if an optimistic mindset can be adopted, then it will act as a creative force.

The same is true for agile organisational organisms. Agile organisations do more than scan for promising ideas. They have packs of skilled hunters who are resilient and persistent, communicate fully with fellow hunters, have heightened senses, possess powerful problem-solving skills, are often led by a skilled guide and will use aggression or guile to gain advantage.

Agility requires grasping selective opportunities and making the most of them, despite setbacks, uncertainties and risks. Although some forms of opportunism can be automated, much depends on the optimism of key people. Personalities are important. There is a role for those who are sceptical, as their wariness can improve decision-making. But pessimists cannot dominate, as agility must be nourished by collective boldness and shared optimism. Agile organisations need to be emotionally healthy, as Bing Crosby's World War II song expressed: "You've got to accentuate the positive: Eliminate the negative: Latch on to the affirmative: Don't mess with Mister In-Between" (Arlen, Mercer, Crosby, & Andrews Sisters, 1944).

Agile Organisations have Distinctive Personalities

Although not proven by research, it seems that agile organisations are more highly differentiated than non-agile enterprises. Every agile organisation seems to possess a distinctive personality and ethos, meaning that it operates in ways that feel 'special' when compared with other organisations in the same industry.

Why should this be? An accounting company that offers routine auditing services will have standardised routines, many of which will have been automated. Its rivals are not likely to be significantly different and customers can switch easily. Rival companies seem largely similar. In contrast, a management consulting company that specialises in bringing new thinking to top managers, must be agile to survive. Many managers have observed that strategic consultancies are markedly different from each other. They search for different kinds of recruits, their training is highly specialised, conceptual frameworks are differentiated and so on. Each has its own distinctive personality and ethos. This form of organisational differentiation occurs as agile organisations are aligned by a shared ambition, rather than by shared routines. Sociologists describe this as a distinctive form of social cohesion (Durkheim & Halls, 1984).

Agility: A Dynamic Construct

Agility is, itself, a dynamic construct. As new resources become available, such as machine intelligence, enterprise management systems, digital communications or artificial intelligence, they can extend the capacity of an organisation to be agile. In the third decade of the 21st century it has become evident that almost every organisation is technology dependent. Agility has become a socio-technical dependent driving force. Nevertheless, the essence of agility, which is timely prudent opportunism, is enduring, as we will explore in the next chapter.

3 Prudent Opportunism

Requisitely agile organisations exploit promising opportunities. And they do so strategically, efficiently, rapidly and frequently. Of the four meta-level deliverables that can be gained from requisite agility, prudent opportunism is the core. The other meta-level deliverables relate directly to opportunism. A key reason why it is necessary for a requisitely agile organisation to be highly situationally responsive is to gain a deep understanding of the forces that may redefine landscapes of opportunities. Proactive threat mitigation requires that opportunities be identified to avoid future hazards. Becoming future-ready depends on increasing the probability that an organisation can thrive in future, often quite different, landscapes of opportunities.

Opportunities often exist in relation to others, in ways that we will describe as landscapes. For example, the transition from motor vehicles running on fossil fuels to electric-powered vehicles created a new landscape of opportunities, including needs for charging stations, battery technologies, diagnostic equipment and sensor technologies. Landscapes that were once promising often become unattractive, as new categories of opportunity become available.

Promising opportunities are pivotal as they may, if grasped effectively, result in advantage. If we consider an organisation to be akin to an organism, then opportunities are its major food source. Requisitely agile organisations will have mastered the art, science and craft of managing prudent opportunism, at both strategic and local levels. This requires that many dimensions of leadership, management, organisation and resourcing have been configured to facilitate, not hinder, this mission-critical capability.

The EAfA Definition of Opportunity

EAfA defines an opportunity as a potential wellspring of advantage. Prudent opportunism is defined as the craft of detecting or creating, evaluating and selectively grasping promising opportunities. This requires four interlinked sets of activities we will describe as (i) seeking, (ii) choosing, (iii) adopting and (iv) executing.

Only activities related to seeking and choosing are examined in this chapter, as adopting and executing are included in the topics dealt with in Part II of this book.

The Two Levels of Opportunity

EAfA identifies two levels of opportunism: strategic and local. At the strategic level issues that need to be addressed will include answering questions like 'where will we compete?' 'What is our ambition?' 'How should we organise?' 'What are our priorities?'

https://doi.org/10.1515/9783110637267-003

'What is our philosophy of winning?' And 'what will be our legacy to people, planet and profit?' In order to answer these questions, adapting an approach suggested in an earlier book (D. Francis, 1994) I recommended that this requires 12 inter-dependent work programmes, namely: exploring industry scenarios, assessing market dynamics, evaluating profit potential, analysing competitors, hearing outside perceptions, clarifying values, finding opportunities, exploring opportunities, adopting a competitive strategy, defining required capabilities, implementing strategy and remaining agile.

The local level relates to sub-units. Here opportunities to develop agile capabilities can be radical but will be shaped and contained by (i) the wider organisation's strategy, (ii) the requirements of other sub-units and (iii) resource restrictions. At the local level the types of issues to be addressed will include exploring questions like 'where do we need to improve?' 'What is hindering us from doing better?' 'Who else is doing what we do more efficiently and effectively?' And, 'which of the 6Ps is most promising for us?'

Aligning both strategic and local levels, so that each has a comprehensive understanding of the other, is essential in providing the high degree of coherence required in an agile organisation.

What are Opportunities?

The nature of opportunities becomes clearer as we reflect on an example. There is a smartphone app called *Be My Eyes*, which enables sight-impaired people to connect with a sighted volunteer if they 'need to borrow a pair of eyes' (Avila, Wolf, Brock, & Henze, 2016). It might be that a blind person is standing at a bus stop and cannot read the timetable, or a visually impaired mother is preparing her child for school and cannot tell whether a pair of socks are matching. A visual and sound connection is made between a visually impaired person and a volunteer who can see through the lens of the smartphone. Almost always, questions will be answered immediately.

The originator of *Be My Eyes* was Hans Jørgen Wiberg who had a severe visual impairment himself. Hans's experience of progressive sight loss, and his strong desire to help others, meant that he searched for possible ways to help people like himself. He realised that the increasingly versatile capabilities of smartphones could provide a platform to connect sighted and non-sighted people. Technological advances had opened a window of opportunity for effective and free audio-visual communication.

Hans was a consultant to the Danish Association for the Blind and this connection helped a latent opportunity to be transformed into an initiative. Resources were invested in building a virtual platform and many volunteers helped to test and improve the system. It gathered momentum. To date, *Be My Eyes* has approximately

2.3 million volunteers offering help in 185 languages. One user observed that technology is great, but it is the beautiful people behind it that make it special.

The *Be My Eyes* story enables us to identify many of the key features of an opportunity. First, opportunities are not simply found, rather they are hunted by people who are open to new possibilities and have a personal investment in finding ways forward. Secondly, landscapes of new possibilities can arise from technical, demographic, political and other forms of change. These give birth to latent opportunities that can become triggers for innovation initiatives. Thirdly, fragments of embryonic opportunities often need to be creatively combined to construct a mature opportunity. Lastly, opportunities will fail to be exploited for advantage and lie unused unless resources are found, managed initiatives are undertaken and driven to completion.

Opportunities are many and varied. Some exist today whilst others can be predicted to become available in the future. Others will not be pre-prepared opportunities as they can be created by 'new combinations' of resources, ambitions and action initiatives. Some opportunities can be adopted without difficulty whilst others will require selecting and deploying different types of modalities for managing agility (more about types of agility in Part II of this book). Opportunities will vary in their deliverables, some providing little utility but can be useful 'small wins', others may be transformational and yet others can be dysfunctional in various ways. Nevertheless, a deep and wide flow of opportunities provides nourishment to agile enterprises.

Alertness

An example clarifies the importance of entrepreneurial alertness to find opportunities. Until recently, many people in the UK smoked cigarettes that were purchased from small shops. Some would buy a box of matches at the same time. One day an entrepreneur happened to be in a tobacconist's shop and heard several people ask for a 'box 'o matches, please'. An opportunity crystallised in his mind and he registered a new brand name, which was for 'Boxer Matches'. For many years afterwards, when people asked for a 'box 'o matches please', they were given his Boxer brand! It took extreme alertness to realise that asking for a 'box 'o matches' sounded similar to boxer matches. With that insight, a fortune was made.

Hunting Opportunities

Opportunities can be created, found, constructed or borrowed but it is too much to hope that serendipity will provide an adequate flow of opportunities, as they need to be hunted. The word is appropriate as good hunters have specialised skills, access to appropriate resources which they expend on dedicated and focused effort.

Hunting is a craft that, above all, requires extreme, sustained alertness. I recall an experienced hunter telling me that he would spend up to six hours motionless and tied halfway up a tree waiting to see if a wild boar might come within range. Good hunters are tenacious. They know where there are promising hunting grounds, how to behave and they have customised tools and techniques.

Good Hunting Grounds

Hunting opportunities successfully requires that hunters are empowered and what they bring back is valued and used. If hunting is counter-cultural in an organisation then it will be neglected. Five productive hunting grounds for finding opportunities are:

Customers, both internal and external, provide an infinite quantity of insight into needs, wants and ways to improve. Bringing their experience into an organisation enables weaknesses to be identified, opportunities to be defined and strengths to be built upon. Increasingly, big data analyses and artificial intelligence is providing new insights into customers' needs and wants. Being close to lead users is a powerful tool, as it provides an opportunity to co-create the next generation of innovative ideas with those who are practical experts in a specific area. For example, if a company wants to develop a new mountain bike then it will be productive to work intensively with riders that win tough international races. They know what would help them do even better.

Potential customers are an often-neglected source of information, partly because they are more difficult to access. There are cases when companies have missed out on next generation product development because they failed to hear the views of people who could be their customers but went elsewhere. When found, potential customers are uniquely valuable as their decision-making processes provide insight into the range of factors that underlie their purchasing decisions.

Stakeholders, including shareholders, advisers, employees, suppliers and distributors, provide added insight into opportunities. This can be especially valuable, as they have a close relationship with the organisation but also have a degree of distance. For example, a supplier may know that a few customers are benefiting from a specific technology and will share this knowledge with their other customers, thereby alerting their laggard customers to opportunities that have already proven their value.

Mavericks think differently and are prepared to speak their mind. Particularly valuable are people who understand the factors that may influence the organisation in the future. Their great contribution is to think in unfamiliar ways. It is paid, and unpaid, consultants who can make a significant contribution, as they are not only industry specialists but have intervention skills, meaning that they are likely to be especially influential.

Rivals are a boundless source of insight into opportunities, especially those who are leaders as they have practical knowledge of the realities of being comparatively or competitively successful. An effective way to find new or different opportunities is to study others who do similar things, but in different ways.

Blockages to Opportunism

The concept of unblocking is derived from Gestalt psychology (Farrands, 2012) and figurational sociology (Elias & Jephcott, 2000). A key insight from Gestalt psychology is that it is important to zoom out and see elements as being part of a bigger picture that figurational sociology views as being constantly in flux, so understanding the process is as important as understanding the situation. These theoretical approaches take a wide perspective and examine how parts interrelate to form a whole. The framework has useful practical implications, as we find that inadequate or dysfunctional parts of a system will inhibit it from operating effectively, so become blockages.

A blockage is a factor that inhibits the output of a system, which can be a whole organisation, a sub-unit or an individual. Blockages need to be defined as such, understood and weakened or, preferably, removed. A simple example clarifies the construct. A café offers an online home delivery service for its famous cakes, but its website is often unavailable, so the lack of connectivity is a blockage. The cakes are tasty, the prices are low, the delivery team is friendly and so on. But the fact that customers are frequently unable to order is enough to undermine the efficacy of the total socio-technical system.

Focusing on blockage removal (Woodcock & Francis, 1990) is central to the EAfA Process, as the prompt removal of significant blockages is a managerial imperative in requisitely agile organisations. The blockage approach does not come from a soft school of Organisation Development methodologies and needs to be counter-balanced with strength-based approaches.

Many organisations have blockages that inhibit or prevent prudently opportunism. I have often heard that "our organisation is full of people who can say 'no'". This is understandable. Managers are frequently measured on whether they achieve efficiency, deliver conformance, reduce risks and avoid waste. Progressing such activities requires targeted do-better agility. Other forms of agility, especially those that are do-different, will be neglected. For example, recently, I investigated the effects of a newly installed, integrated information management system, powered by artificial intelligence, in an international company on organisational agility. The system required that processes and information conformed to detailed specifications but the algorithms favoured a narrow form of opportunism and eliminated others. In effect, the discipline of the system strangled do-different opportunism and had become an agility blockage.

Opportunity Maturity

Some opportunities are immature (conceptual, latent, embryonic, fragmented or unproven), while others are mature (tested, costed and have been demonstrably shown to be valuable to the unit of adoption). The readiness of an opportunity to be exploited varies considerably. We refer to this as 'opportunity maturity' and it can be considered as a sliding scale. The fact that opportunities will vary in maturity complicates decision-making and means that judgement calls about readiness are frequently required.

Relatively immature opportunities have an unknown potential for exploitation. In such cases managerial bets will have a high chance of failure but the costs of raising the maturity level of the opportunity can be low. There are different types of immature opportunities, including *conceptual* opportunities, that do not exist but can be imagined; *latent* opportunities could probably be realised but work needs to be done for this to be proven; *embryonic* opportunities do exist but need to be developed further; *fragmented* opportunities will need to be combined with others if they are to become viable and *unproven* opportunities, which exist but are untested or their costs and benefits are unknown.

Mature opportunities allow for managerial bets to be taken with a lower probability of failure but a higher risk of competitive intensity, as others are likely to have grasped the same opportunity. Mature opportunities can be exploited with little adaptation, perhaps on an experimental basis. Again, there are types. *Tested* opportunities can be adopted with confidence; *costed* opportunities have been proven to add value faster than cost and opportunities that are *demonstrably perceived as being valuable* will have been preferred by customers to rival's offers. A simple example of a mature opportunity helps us to visualise the construct. A grocery store has developed a new line of business supplying customers with a weekly delivery of fresh foods in their homes. The owner of a similar shop in a different town, without such a service, learns of its success and decides to offer an identical service. She discovered a mature opportunity with proven value.

Rigorously assessing the current level of the maturity of opportunities clarifies what needs to be done for them to become ready to be proposals. This is important as many opportunities will be 'good for someone but not good for us'.

Strategic Opportunity Seeking

No one is sure of the exact date, but about 1766, in the early years of the Industrial Revolution, a group of scientists, engineers and industrialists began to meet monthly for an afternoon's discussion and a fine dinner close to the developing industrial city of Birmingham in the UK (Schofield, 1966). They met when the moon was full, to be safe as their carriages took them home after dinner. For this reason, the group became known as the Lunar Society. Their first leader was a physician, Erasmus Darwin, who developed pioneering ideas on evolution. Other members included Matthew Boulton, who had designed a state-of-the-art factory that would be capable of uniquely precise engineering, the brilliant engineer James Watt, who invented compact steam engines that enabled railways to be constructed, Joseph Priestley, who discovered oxygen and the social reformer and entrepreneur Josiah Wedgwood, whose pottery became world famous.

During their lengthy discussions many ideas were shared, issues debated, and social and economic problems discussed. The members of the of the Lunar Society were socially committed men (as far as is known there were no regular female members). They spent much of the time together considering the social and moral impact of rapid technological change that had been brought about by the industrial revolution. There were rules as to how discussions should be conducted. Every member was expected to contribute and to be open to the views of others. These scientists, engineers and industrialists used the meetings of the Lunar Society to, metaphorically, stand back from their normal worlds and develop an informed broad perspective. Viewpoints from different specialisations were synthesised and became integrated into visions of what could be. In effect, the Lunar Society became a policy think-tank or a salon that provided a forum where leading thinkers would become aware of the different ways in which issues could be framed, air their own views and be tested by equally accomplished others.

The Lunar Society facilitated strategic opportunity seeking as it set policy decisions into a broad social, moral, technological and economic context. It helped those present to become industrial statesmen rather than entrepreneurs. Today, annual meetings at Davos have a similar function. The members of the Lunar Society had recognised that their power had consequences.

This form of networking facilitated strategic level prudent and responsible opportunism. It opened minds and fed imaginations. It had a moral quality, required for those whose decisions were shaping a revolution that was changing society fundamentally. From notes left by members it is clear that the capabilities of each member of the Lunar Society to take wise and progressive decisions was enhanced.

Local Seeking

Seeking opportunities for sub-units in an organisation requires four sets of searching activities, specifically: looking inwards, upwards, outwards and forwards.

Looking inwards collects observations, ideas and guidance from those who work in the organisation. Perhaps surprisingly, these inputs are rarely collected systematically. However, they provide a low cost and valuable resource for those who are seeking opportunities to do-better and to do-different. A survey can be used to gather ideas from everyone in an organisational sub-unit or is in some way connected to it. The insights gained will enrich understanding of possible opportunity landscapes and new hunting grounds.

Looking upwards is facilitated by a similar data gathering exercise but is targeted at gaining inputs from senior management, both in person and from studies of corporate strategy and policy documents. The aim is for the sub-unit to benefit from the wider perspective of senior people. Two key questions are: 'What does the organisation need from us that it is not getting at the moment?' and 'how might this change in the future?'

Looking outwards requires searching to find examples of leading best practice, as these provide tried-and-tested insights into where opportunities can be found and what can be done to exploit them. It will often be wise to look for exemplars that are in different industries to the Unit of Analysis. For example, a company installing charging points for electric vehicles may find that conventional telephone companies have valuable ideas about how to lay cables in public places.

Looking forwards requires a future search to consider opportunities that are currently not available but may occur, driven by political, social, technological or other changes. This will be important as developments, often technological, greatly change landscapes of opportunity.

It is often necessary to align strategic and local opportunism, as was shown by Netflix. When low-cost technologies became available for fast digital data distribution, it enabled films to be streamed globally, in high resolution, thereby partly replacing the need for cinemas. Netflix exploited this opportunity by providing an on-line film library. They knew that the companies that would win in this new market segment were those that could capture a very large market share. Within Netflix, many sub-units contributed to achieve the required dominance. For example, one sub-group led a project to upgrade the user interface with mini-preview videos and a separate sub-group undertook the less structured task of commissioning original new content. This required more than a cluster of projects, as there were extensive interdependencies and frequent adaptations to initial plans. It is true to say that Netflix evolved through the work of dynamic orchestrated local agility.

Targeted Opportunism

Requisite agility provides organisations with a capability to do things that would otherwise be impossible. Once an organisation has acquired a degree of agile capability it becomes important to ask the question: 'where should we exploit our agile capability for the greatest benefit?'

In order to answer this question, we can use the 6Ps Model, which is an updated version of a framework (D.L. Francis & Bessant, 2005) that I developed with John Bessant some years ago. This model provides a structured approach to examining the six dimensions of the opportunity space for agile initiatives. The agility target areas are *product, process, position, paradigm, provisioning* and *platform*. The 6Ps are not tight categories, as they have fuzzy boundaries, but they are sufficiently differentiated to act as a pragmatic framework.

Product Agility (P1) targets what is produced. Specifically, the outputs of an organisation or a sub-unit that are, or could be, provided for external and/or internal customers and/or other stakeholders. Products are tangible goods or forms of service that will be upgraded as opportunities occur. For sub-units, internal customers can be more important than external customers. For example, a production engineering team may evaluate developments in nanomaterials and deliver a presentation to senior managers. By producing this analytical product, the team will have provided an input to an internal customer. Many products produced for external customers are inherently complex, as choices need to be made about issues such as branding policies, market development trajectories, industry logics, resource availability, technological developments and other factors. Targeting innovation capability on developing new and/or improved products can involve multiple actors engaged in complex and inter-linked processes with a single end in view, which is creating superior value at an acceptable cost for the customer.

Process Agility (P2) targets how work is done. Processes are sequences of activities that enable tasks to be accomplished and integrated. Agility in processes aims to make them faster, more responsive, cheaper, more reliable, accurately measurable and/or better integrated. Much of the lean thinking agenda is designed to facilitate process agility. Processes are extensive, interdependent and routinised. For example, even in a simple organisation like a dentist's reception area there will be multiple processes, such as registering patients, keeping records, stock management, making appointments, arranging rotas, logging staff time, arranging maintenance work, cleaning the waiting room, reminding patients of forthcoming visits and so on. Requisite process agility is acquired by systematic analysis and comparative benchmarking. Process agility will extent outside of the boundaries of an organisation into its value stream or ecosystem. Multiple small improvements can accumulate into large gains.

Positional Agility (P3) targets how meanings and interfaces are managed. Specifically, how an enterprise communicates with its customers (internal and external), potential customers, entities in its ecosystem and other stakeholders or influential bodies. It includes two-way communication, both transmitting and receiving. An example demonstrates one dimension of positional agility. Lucozade is a soft drink that is now manufactured by the Japanese company, Suntory. William Owen, a chemist, had developed the formula for this product in 1927 to provides calories and energy for people who were ill. A bottle of Lucozade occupied a prominent place on the bedside table of many ailing people for decades. Some years ago, a major advertising campaign repositioned Lucozade as a wellness drink, rather than as sickness aid. It was not significantly changed in formula, but Lucozade is now widely drunk in gyms and sports clubs. The meaning of the product changed fundamentally. Positional agility has wide relevance as it includes many aspects of an organisation's interplay with the environment.

Paradigm Agility (P4) targets principles of organising and systems of thought. The paradigm that an organisation adopts is often referred to as its business model, but paradigm also includes the shared constructs that people within an organisation use to make sense of the world. Paradigms can, often with difficulty, be changed, as was shown, for example, in aviation where it used to be commonplace for a flight crew to hide mistakes but, as it was recognised that errors facilitate learning, the paradigm has been changed so that pilots now feel that they can admit errors openly. Organisational paradigms are a social fact that develops as people within an organisation come to share values, possess a common history and, to use a sociological phrase and, adopt embedded norms ('the ways that we do things here'). Paradigm agility can be described as 'changing the rules of the game' and is relevant at all levels of an organisation.

Provisioning Agility (P5) targets where and how resources are obtained. These can include financial, knowledge, technological, locational, contractual, reputational or legal assets. As we learnt from the *Be My Eyes* case, many forms of agility cannot progress to execution unless adequate tangible and intangible resources are made available. Determining what provisions will be needed to transform an agile intention into an agile reality can be daunting, especially if do-different agility is being undertaken. Sometimes an approach known as frugal innovation facilitates provisioning, as its ethic is 'doing more with less' so risks are reduced. Provisioning requires an facilitating ecosystem. This can include users, supporters, actual and potential customers, kindred organisations, funding sources, online special interest groups, networking sites, advisors and resource providers.

Platform Agility (P6) targets how outputs are integrated to be useful or accessible. Platforms are made possible by standardisation and the use of communication networks. An example would be if all the hotels in a city provide information in a standardised form in real time to a website platform, then users can see where there are vacancies and what types of facilities are available. Such a platform adds value as it reduces complexity for travellers and increases the utilisation of hotels in the city. Many platforms are technologically enabled but the construct can be used more widely as platforms can facilitate many forms of intermediation. The cost of creating platforms can be low and they permit an ease of collaboration that was previously unachievable. Digital platforms are enabled by the extraordinary power of internet searches and the increasing universality of access to digital resources.

The 6Ps Model enables managers to target searching systematically by looking at P1, P2 and so on. Consider targeting 'P1' (Product) for example. Earlier we considered changes in the dog food industry where it is now possible to get food supplies that have been prepared specifically for an individual dog. Here a combination of largely technical developments had created hitherto unavailable opportunities for product innovation. These included web-based marketing, an ability to interface cheaply with individual customers, developments in canine nutrition resulting in knowledge of optimal feeding of different breeds of dog and integrated automated production specifically designed for mass customisation.

Inner-Directed Opportunities

Not all opportunities will be identified by external seeking. Important opportunities are inner-directed. For example, radical artistic movements, like impressionism in painting or modernism in literature, evolved as groups of artists meet informally, challenged each other, shared their experiments and collectively developed a different way of seeing the world. The same process can be seen with new business models, like digital platforms, some of which were conceptualised in late night conversations in vegan cafés in San Diego or in a surfer's bar at Ocean Beach. Inner-directed opportunism will be examined in greater detail in the section on salons in the next chapter.

Need-Driven Opportunities

Opportunities can be sought where a need has been identified, even though a way forward is not immediately available. In 2014 there was an outbreak of the Ebola disease in West Africa, but no effective vaccines were available. Pharmaceutical companies' resources were quickly targeted towards Ebola and, because of the extent of the health emergency, accelerated research was undertaken. This involved extensive cooperation between normally rival companies and new public-private partnerships, including technical support from China and Russia. It is common for a new pharmaceutical product to take ten years to develop. In this case, prototype vaccines were being trialled less than a year after the outbreak. A few years later, in 2020, the Covid 19 virus pandemic prompted a wonderfully agile international response with multiple laboratories doing work in days that normally took months to complete.

Fragmented Opportunities

Fragmented opportunities require new combinations, incur greater risk, need more developmental effort but may provide a first-mover advantage, with the range of benefits this brings. Imagine the owner of the grocery store learns that a local farmer is producing juices from rare varieties of fruit trees from an ancient orchard and that a local ice cream manufacturer has begun making fruit sorbets from concentrate. The owner of the grocery store brings the farmer and ice cream maker together and they decide to create a new range of sorbets called Yesteryear Flavours, to be sold online. An opportunity with intermediate maturity had been created by a synthesis of existing resources that required limited adaptation.

Emerging Opportunities

Opportunities may be deeply hidden and can change over time. In the 1990s it became commonplace for internet users to share music without paying royalties to artists or record companies. This was illegal but regulation was weak, so illegal music sharing sites, often based in countries with few restrictions, captured a huge share of the market. Traditional music companies saw this as a mortal threat and sought to defend their copyrights through aggressive legal cases. One company, Apple, saw the emergence of a new landscape of music distribution as an opportunity. Their reach was global and Apple realised they had an opportunity to create an entirely new market segment—monetised online music sales. Apple lacked the organisational capability to develop an attractive product rapidly and purchased a small company called SoundJam that had developed a working version of an MP3 music player. SoundJam's software developers moved to Apple and were bound by a two-year secrecy clause. They developed iTunes, described as the 'World's Best and Easiest to Use Jukebox Software', which was launched in 2001. For other companies the launch of iTunes radically changed the landscape of opportunities. It opened a door for companies like Spotify who provided free streams of music interspersed with advertisements with the option of paying a fee for advertisement-free streaming. Later, other entrants entered the market with alternative offers, for example, Amazon included a similar service with their Prime subscription.

Innovation-Based Opportunities

Exploiting opportunities for advantage can require innovation, which, if successful, we define as transforming an idea into an asset by gaining advantage from ideas that are new to the unit of adoption, where the benefits gained are greater than the costs, financial and otherwise, incurred. In order to explain this point, we will return to the example of the changing world of dog food. In that industry a strategic opportunity became available to combine three constructs: disintermediation, mass customisation and manageable complexity. Disintermediation removed the need for chains of costly intermediaries, like wholesalers and retailers. Mass customisation provided a means to retain the economic benefits provided by mass production while meeting the needs of specific categories of customers (micro-markets), sometimes even a market size of one. Manageable complexity meant that it was possible to deal with millions of customers individually, without adding excessive cost. The availability and integration of these business concepts changed the landscape of opportunities. Simply recognising this new reality was important for all dog food makers as it was a threat to traditional suppliers.

For some companies, not necessarily existing players, there was a big-bet opportunity. This was to disrupt the dog food industry by innovating in paradigm and supplying customised food for individual dogs. Those who could capture this new market segment would need ample resources, a strategic ambition, a willingness to make a large speculative commitment and the capability to undertake multiple aligned developmental initiatives, some of which would require innovation. Areas where innovation was required included research into veterinary science related to animal nutrition (now needed as insight was needed into the special requirements of different breeds of dog etc.) and finding ways to relate positively with dog owners using web-based tools.

Notice that not all of the required developments required owned innovation initiatives. Some required capabilities could be purchased, hired, copied or the work could be outsourced. Although owned ('we do the work ourselves') innovation is a primary route for transforming an idea into an asset, it is not the only one. It might be, for example, that acquisition would provide a faster and less risk-laden way forward.

If innovation is chosen as the selected exploitation pathway then it can deliver four major benefits. Namely the innovator (i) can be a first-mover, which often provides substantial advantages; (ii) owns the innovation and, if ownership can be protected, this can create high barriers for rivals; (iii) having developed a new product or service means the innovators understand it in depth, this becoming a springboard for further developments and (iv) being innovative mobilises organisational energy, which reinforces an organisational personality that nourishes agility. Successful innovation provides momentum and opens previously unavailable opportunity spaces, which are a core characteristic of organisational agility, as the DAWN ver.β café example demonstrated.

Innovation requires a specialised form of agility, as the pathway from finding an opportunity to acquiring an asset requires distinctive clusters of activities that have different functions and are rarely sequential. In my research into 106 innovative organisations (Humphreys, McAdam, & Leckey, 2005) I found that one cluster of activities is needed to find, create or integrate opportunities; a second and different cluster of activities is needed to explore potential advantages and disadvantages of possible ideas; a third, different cluster undertakes activities to decide whether to commit resources to a specific option; a fourth, is needed to undertake the work of producing a wanted product or service and a fifth cluster of activities is dedicated to gaining maximum advantage from the innovation process.

Each of these clusters of activities can be described as a modality, as it is a particular way of doing or experiencing something. The five modalities are M1 Searching, M2 Exploring, M3 Committing, M4 Realising and M5 Exploiting. Since each must be a good example of type it is important that innovation managers know what modality is needed to make progress, how they need to act to manage it and when to transition to another modality. Modalities are rarely undertaken in sequence, as they are characterised by unexpected leaps forward, unsuccessful trials and difficult trade-off decisions.

The (M1) *Searching Modality* provides new (to the Unit of Analysis) ideas, opportunities, lines-of-enquiry, sources of inspiration, ways of proceeding and alternative perceptual schemas. It requires a temporary sub-culture that challenges existing viewpoints and requires those involved to be open-minded, inquisitive and outward-looking. The Searching Modality may find or create hundreds of ideas and possibilities. It requires micro-level agility to promote behaviours that are enquiring, energised and non-judgemental.

The (M2) *Exploring Modality* assesses the strengths and weaknesses of possible options. It requires a temporary sub-culture that investigates ideas before they are evaluated. Some may contain nuggets of gold while others will be impractical, irrelevant or unlikely to create value. Solid, disciplined detective work is needed to understand which initiatives have merit and whether they fit with their organisation's strategic intent and Agility Ambition. The output will be a shortlist of viable and potentially value-adding options. Options must be developed into coherent, comprehensive and evidence-based proposals since it will be impossible to adopt every suggestion. It requires micro-level agility to promote rigorous analysis, a balance between creative optimism and judicious pessimism and insightful evaluation of possibilities, thereby providing the evidence needed for effective decision-making.

The (M3) *Committing Modality* determines which of the available innovation options should be adopted and building the required degree of commitment needed to see that the initiative will be supported. It requires a temporary sub-culture of prudent opportunism. The key questions are 'should we do this?' and 'can we do this?' Answering these questions requires moving beyond assessing whether a proposal is a 'good idea'. It requires deciding whether it is a good idea for us. Only so much can be done at once. If an innovation initiative is adopted as a managerial priority, then those whose support will be needed must 'sign-up' to become proactive enablers. The Committing Modality provides the organisational momentum to move forward with focus, energy and resources. It requires micro-level agility to promote insightful, bold and considered decision-making supported by the aligned mobilisation of supportive managerial effort and the provision of enabling resources.

The (M4) *Realising Modality* transforms a commitment into an actuality. It requires a project management sub-culture. Usually an effective temporary team will be built. Team members will need to work within the disciplines of agile project management and be adaptive to cope with inevitable difficulties. Inevitably there will be set-backs, changes in direction and opportunities to improve. The membership of the task-team may change over time, but its main requirement remains the same—to make a service, product or other artefact that creates greater value than the costs incurred. It requires micro-level agility for flexible project work that is focused, coordinated, results-orientated, time-efficient and effective.

The (M5) *Exploiting Modality* increases the benefits that have resulted from undertaking an innovation journey. It often happens that those who develop something new fail to appropriate all possible advantage from their innovation initiatives. For this reason, there is a need for an Exploiting Modality that focuses attention on gaining benefits from innovating. It requires a sub-culture that emphasises gaining maximum advantage. Marketing, internally and externally, is a primary discipline that facilitates optimisation. It requires micro-level agility to promote entrepreneurship and continuous improvement.

Re-Found Opportunities

It is sometimes assumed that organisational agility relates to finding newly available opportunities that have been made available by cutting-edge technologies. This is incorrect, as an organisation can become requisitely agile by re-finding lost opportunities. For example, one of Europe's most agile companies is one of its most traditional. It is the supermarket chain Aldi that owns about 10,000 stores, including some in Australia and the United States. Two brothers developed Aldi and succeeded in upscaling the traditional principles of street markets. Aldi focuses on low fixed costs, avoiding high-priced brands, astute purchasing, having a narrow but well-chosen product range, emphasising exceptional value for money and offering time-limited bargains. Aldi's founders had identified and captured an available opportunity space as other supermarket chains had failed to meet a deep-rooted desire of shoppers to find genuine bargains day-after-day. Maintaining this business model requires significant requisite agility in many but not all sub-units, as some parts of Aldi are dedicated to providing consistency and conformance. Aldi shows that is possible to bond time-honoured retailing principles with current best practice management in areas such as supply chain and HR management, demonstrating that opportunities can sometimes be found by looking backwards.

Windows of Opportunity Open and Close

Just as windows of opportunity for agile initiatives open, others close. In 1833 an entrepreneur in Boston had 180 tons of ice cut from a local pond and sent to India to be sold. At the end of the voyage there was still 100 tons to sell. Forty years later, firms in the Boston, Massachusetts area were cutting almost 700,000 tons of ice annually and 90,000 men were engaged in the ice cutting industry. It was not to last. In 1851 a medical doctor, Dr John Gorrie, was granted a patent for a machine to make ice. Mechanical icemaking technology developed and in 1868 New Orleans had the first large commercial ice making plant, closely followed by many others.

By the 1920s the natural ice cutting industry was dead. We can conclude that many landscapes of opportunities, like radioactive substances, have a half-life.

Opportunity Famines

An opportunity famine 'changes the game'. When this happens, organisational agility becomes an urgent strategic issue as do-different agility may be required. Consider what occurred when the coronavirus epidemic swept across the world in 2020 and, within weeks, shut down schools, factories, sporting events and many businesses. One of the companies that was hit was the McLaren motor racing manufacturer, as Formula One race meetings were cancelled. However, almost immediately, McLaren repositioned itself as an advanced manufacturer used its facilities to make medical equipment, showing great strategic agility. They were quick to take three initiatives. First, to acknowledge that their existing business model was temporally unsustainable. Secondly, to look proactively for different ways to use existing capabilities, lastly, to establish project teams to drive initiatives forward.

Organisations operating in changing landscapes of opportunities need to excel in what Joseph Schumpeter (Kurz, 2012) described as creative destruction, meaning that they are not burdened by out-of-date rigidities. Great agile organisations, like the Red Cross, Google or Harvard University, have these characteristics.

Selecting Promising Opportunities

Opportunism must be prudent. There are cases where opportunism has been so destructive that it has resulted in bankruptcy (Malmsten, Portanger, & Drazin, 2001). As a consequence, requisitely agile organisations invest considerable resources to become competent in speculative decision-making as, on balance, the bets taken need to add value, not destroy it. They need to find and exploit promising opportunities.

No organisation can, or should, exploit every potential or available opportunity, so being requisitely agile requires saying 'not for us' often. The aim is to select all the opportunities that have a probability of contributing responsibly to gaining comparative or competitive advantage and becoming future-ready.

Note the word 'responsibly'. Actions need to be morally justifiable, as organisations are key components of societies and their impact can either heighten the quality of civilisation or diminish it.

There is no foolproof method for differentiating between promising and unpromising opportunities, but risks are diminished when managers use evidence-based decision-making to understand likely costs, risks, strategic fit and potential benefits. Increasingly help is available from using machine intelligence to run scenarios. Using explicit decision selection criteria facilitates prudent opportunism, as these assist managers to select opportunities that are intended to further their organisation's Agility Ambition (more about Agility Ambitions later).

Choosing which decision selection criteria to use is increasingly challenging, as the range of criteria that must be considered has expanded considerably. It used to be that financial advantage was the sole criterion used in most cases. Today, it is widely recognised that all those who are influenced by an organisation, including the natural environment and human communities, are stakeholders. Opportunities need to be evaluated as to whether they are likely to add value to various stakeholders and trade-off decisions are inevitable. This multidimensional decision-making perspective can be institutionalised. For example, the Articles of Association of the Danish pharmaceutical company, Novo Nordisk, require triple bottom line (TBL) accounting methods be used to balance financial, social and environmental considerations (Morsing & Oswald, 2009).

The range of available opportunities may be large and diverse, increasing the managerial challenge of selecting only those who are likely to be beneficial for an organisation at a particular time. The complexity of the managerial task is increased as opportunities are often interconnected, so exploitation will need to be aligned and sequenced, as exploiting each opportunity requires resources that are invariably limited. The aim is to select sets of promising opportunities for which the required organisational resources can be found to exploit them.

Help comes from the Good Judgment Project (Schoemaker, 2016), which was undertaken after it had been shown that even top experts in the US National Intelligence Council were capable of making costly and wrong judgement decisions. The research project found that some generalists, described as super-forecasters, can predict more accurately than specialists, training can improve the prediction efficacy, and well-functioning teams can outperform individuals. Super-forecasters are fast in acquiring and processing information and can detect patterns reliably. They intentionally work to make accurate predictions, ask many questions, reflect deeply when they are incorrect and frequently try to improve their methods. They tend to be open-minded and will flex their opinions according to new evidence.

Agile organisations must work to become better at selecting promising opportunities. Where possible they gain access to super-forecasters and, as training and team working have been shown to improve the reliability of predictions, they use findings from organisational psychology to improve the probability that only promising and prudent opportunities are chosen.

It can be Done

Despite the complexity of choosing, it remains true that the capability to exploit selected opportunities is mission-critical for delivering agility. Even small enterprises can progress multiple initiatives at the same time. For example, a takeout restaurant in the UK called Finnegans Fish Bar won a national prize for innovation some years ago. When I visited this business, it had only six employees but was successfully developing more than 40 separate opportunities at one time. Mostly, these were concerned with improvements to existing processes. We can conclude that there is much to be gained by extensive micro-opportunism, providing that the opportunities selected fit the needs of an organisation's business model and support its Agility Ambition.

Achieving these ends requires that managers at all levels understand the construct of agility, know what it takes to become requisitely agile, undertake agility initiatives, remove blockages, and utilise agility-enabling technologies such as artificial intelligence, self-healing systems or other digital resources where this is cost-effective and agility enhancing. Aligning managerial action to achieve these ends is a leadership function, a point that we will explore in the next chapter.

4 Leading Agile Enterprises

EAfA sees the role of a leader in an agile organisation as facilitating the emergence of a deep consensus as to their organisation's chosen Agility Ambition, designing an organisation with the capabilities to deliver it and persuading others to adopt the Agility Ambition as an enduring personal mission. This requires teaching (not selling to) members of the organisation 'what is important and not important to us', 'what we need to do to win', 'how we are special' and 'what we must do collectively to create value faster than cost'.

Agile-friendly leaders are highly influential in creating (and re-creating) an organisation's distinctive personality, or identity. Their primary task is to mobilise aligned and functional (not dysfunctional) action. They do this by developing three managerial philosophies, that can be described as theories (although leaders are unlikely to use this terminology). These are a Theory of Winning, a Theory of Change and a Theory of Action.

The Theory of Winning specifies how aims, ambitions, capabilities and measures become integrated into an organisation-wide driving force. The Theory of Change specifies how flows of initiatives are configured to achieve defined ends and the Theory of Action clarifies where responsibility lies for proactive and timely invention and adaptation, and how required resources are to be made available, thereby building change capability into sub-units.

As leadership is a collective function in all but the smallest enterprises, it is imperative that those with leadership roles, sometimes called the upper echelon of the organisation, develop a shared understanding of how these theories will be used to shape decision-making and transformed into action programmes. Although the three theories conceptualisation is modern there have been countless examples throughout history where leaders have shown great prowess in performing these functions. Almost always, there is an emphasis on prompt action. Time is seen as the scarce resource and proactivity as the quintessential attribute. It is reputed that, about 400 BC, the Greek scholar, Demosthenes, observed that speech is empty unless accompanied by action (Trevett, 2011). About the same time the Chinese general, Sun Tzu, advised his army commanders that they should be as rapid as the wind (Tzu, 1981). Shakespeare, captured the vital importance of intervening decisively into flows of events (Shakespeare, 2018) in his play, *Julius Cesar*, when Brutus said:

> There is a tide in the affairs of men.
> Which, taken at the flood, leads on to fortune;
> Omitted, all the voyage of their life
> Is bound in shallows and in miseries.
> On such a full sea are we now afloat,
> And we must take the current when it serves,
> Or lose our ventures.

https://doi.org/10.1515/9783110637267-004

A business that has succeeded in building agility deep into its organisation's personality is Jardine, Matheson & Co. (175 Years of Looking to the Future, 2007). The company was founded in 1832 in Canton, China, by William Jardine and James Matheson. Early records show that the founders had many discussions about what was necessary to develop a great trading company (developing their Theory of Winning). Substantial funds were invested in infrastructure and great care taken to hire entrepreneurially talented managers to be able to take advantage of short-term opportunities (their Theory of Change). Jardine and Matheson configured their company so that it would be requisitely agile (their Theory of Action). This enabled them to change their business strategy as the Far East became the energising hub of world trade. Jardine, Matheson & Co.'s current business model remains true to the principles of the founders. By 2020 Jardine had almost half a million employees and profitable businesses across the world. The company had benefited greatly from previous generations of leaders and managers, who were masters of agility. Their theory of change remains mobilised by a policy of hiring talented and inner-directed people who are willing and able to work within a strong corporate culture characterised by a demanding work ethic, an independent spirit, financial prudence, an emphasis on developing business foresight and an unrelenting determination to succeed.

Agile-Friendly Leadership

Many 21st century leaders are becoming masters of requisite agility. They have had little choice, as disruptive external forces meant that business as usual had ceased to be a viable strategy for many. Interestingly, spending time recently with members of TMTs showed me that many have enjoyed this challenge. Being an agile-friendly leader makes great demands on a person as how she or he acts is consequential. This requires well developed personal attributes, like boldness, visionary thinking and proactivity. Many leaders grow as people when they are required to be agile-friendly.

Agile-friendly leaders act as visionary entrepreneurs and organisational architects. They create an organisation that has the capacity for frequent, aligned and prudent opportunism only where this is needed (not everywhere needs to be agile). The leader will, without suffering debilitating stress, deal constructively with the many forces that drive frequent and sometimes disruptive change, while reinforcing or revising the extant theories of winning, change and action.

Two questions are important when we seek to identify what it takes to lead an agile-friendly organisation effectively: Is agile leadership distinctive? If the answer is 'yes', what are characteristics of agile-friendly leaders? In order to answer these questions, we will draw from a two-year study of organisational agility undertaken by the CENTRIM research group in the University of Brighton, UK (Meredith & Francis, 1998). The original research data from the research team has been re-examined for this book and has been integrated with later longitudinal investigations undertaken by the author, to construct an 11-factor model that describes what agile-friendly leaders do. We will describe this as the EAfA Leadership Framework and use it to explore the role of leadership in agile organisations.

Is Agile Leadership Distinctive?

It has become fashionable to argue that agile organisations require little or no central leadership, as those at the edge of an organisation can take better decisions locally. EAfA takes an opposite view. A successfully agile organisation needs strong, hands-on leadership that varies in style from facilitative to directive according to the quantity of agility needed, where it needs to be located and which types of agility are required to deliver the enterprise's Agility Ambition.

Leaders must be decisive, but this will not be sufficient. Wise decisions will need to be made as to which opportunities to grasp and how to drive them forward. This requires aligned, capable and attuned, hands-on, leadership. That hands-on leadership has a decisive effect on an organisations' systemic agility, is illustrated reviewing Steve Job's contribution to Apple Computer, Inc. Consider what Jobs said during a talk that he gave to Apple employees (Jobs, 1997):

> Apple (has) suffered for several years from lousy engineering management . . . there were people going off in eighteen different directions doing arguably interesting things, each one of them. Good engineers. Lousy management. What happened was, when you look at the farm that was created, these different animals going in different directions. It doesn't add up. The total is less than the sum of the parts. So, we had to decide what are the fundamental directions that we are going in . . . The result of that focus, of saying no, will be great products.

This is not the voice of a CEO who has abandoned hands-on leadership. Neither is it the voice of a boss supporting unconditional empowerment or embracing anarchic decision-making. Job's criticisms were blunt. His diagnosis opinionated. And the message was clear: 'this is who we are!' and 'this is how we must be'. By statements and actions Jobs shaped Apple's Agility Ambition and he, more than any other leader in Apple, constructed its distinctive corporate personality.

Steve Jobs practiced 'Top Down Agility', which is a type described in Part II of this book. Other leaders have chosen different stratagems for managing agility and gained advantage, or suffered disadvantage, thereby.

Agile-Friendly Leadership

A core leadership role is to configure the organisation so that it becomes requisitely agile and remains so. This is a complex and ongoing task. As agility is a capability for retaining relevance over time, it requires that an organisation acquires, and sustains, a confident, vibrant, adaptive, proactive, experimental and flexible organisational personality. This cannot be achieved without those in leadership positions acting as directors, designers, champions and role models. What they do, how they do things, and what they do not do, really matters.

Leaders need to do more than adopt agility as a dimension of their organisation's personality. They need to understand the paradigm in depth and master the craft of weaving requisite agility into wider managerial practice. The EAfA Process, described in Part II is designed to provide a useful format for moving this developmental agenda forward.

Achieving requisite agility is important as inappropriate agility management can be dysfunctional, as was demonstrated by Nokia's loss of leadership in the mobile phone industry. If this occurs then agility becomes a force of disintegration, it promotes ill-considered decision-making, results in missing potentially productive opportunities or adds cost without increasing value. Agile-friendly leadership is needed to avoid such risks and find ways to exploit the potential of agility for gaining advantage.

Agility has different functions in different situations, even in the same organisation. Consider a police force, for example. It will have specialist units to deal with issues as diverse as the protection of children, cyber-crime and the scientific analysis of forensic evidence. Each unit may need to possess agile capability but the agility deliverables that each unit is entitled to expect will differ markedly. This means that leaders need to ensure that sub-units clarify their locally relevant agility deliverables within the context of the overall organisation's Agility Ambition.

In addition, agility requirements shift over time. In a theatre, for example, the lighting department can have periods when the requirement for agility is low but changes in directors' requirements or in technologies will introduce phases characterised by a high requirement for agility. This can result in major reconfigurations of people, equipment and resources. Such agility was needed about twenty years ago. At that time, in many theatres, lighting was controlled in real-time by an operator seated at the back of the auditorium. When affordable computer control desks became available then lighting states could be programmed as memories into a control desk. Mastering the potential of this new and capable technology required substantial agility as many roles changed, new opportunities for creativity became available and previous routines abandoned.

Fighting Fires

Some years ago, research was published (Boyatzis, Thiel, Rochford, & Black, 2017) on the brave people who lead teams that fight wildfires in the United States. This is relevant to our study as there can be few leadership tasks that require a greater degree of agility than this form of firefighting.

Incident Commanders is the title given to leaders of wildfire firefighting teams. Their responsibilities are immense, as they must deal with extremely dangerous events in landscapes that are unfamiliar in rapidly changing conditions. An Incident Commander will lead a team that coordinates the work of hundreds, or thousands, of firefighters who control many resources, such as specialised aircraft or emergency services.

Technical knowledge of specialised firefighting techniques is essential for all incident commanders but those who have been shown to be outstandingly effective share additional characteristics. Namely, they possess (i) high emotional self-control; (ii) the ability to adapt to different challenges; (iii) a positive outlook; (iv) high empathy and (v) a capacity to inspire others. Successful incident commanders cope with stressful situations without losing their poise; they find ever more effective ways to get things done; never give-up; understand others' emotions and provide everyone involved with a positive sense of purpose.

The Incident Commanders research study demonstrated that those who lead agile organisations need high levels of emotional maturity and must be interpersonally skilled. These human qualities lie at the heart of what we will describe as 'Agile-Friendly Leadership'.

Strategic Agency

Agile-friendly leaders bring meaning to work. They take decisions that specify their organisation's intended contribution to the wider world, whether they do so deliberately or not. We will describe this as 'strategic agency'.

Sometimes I use the movie Sister Act to help managers explore the nature of strategic agency. The film tells the story of Deloris, a nightclub singer who witnessed a murder but is in danger of being attacked, probably killed, by the murderers. The police need Deloris to be protected so she can serve as a witness. She is secretly enrolled as a nun in a failing convent and the Reverend Mother forces her to join the struggling convent choir, which she transforms into a high energy gospel group. Eventually the choir sings to a packed audience and receives a standing ovation from everyone present, including the Pope. The energy Deloris brings to the convent transforms the range of social initiatives being undertaken by the nuns and the neighbourhood is cleaned up. She energises the nuns and transforms the convent's future. Watching the movie demonstrates how one person can exercise agency.

Prudent strategic agency needs a width of understanding of issues, opportunities, threats and priorities. These inform the development or reformulation of a Theory of Winning, especially enabling it to incorporate an ethical dimension incorporating stances towards fairness, transparency, socially responsibility and global futures.

Leaders who adopt agility as a strand of their organisation's strategy are, in effect, saying: 'we do not know how the future will unfold but we will be ready to do what it takes to be viable whatever happens'. This stance is different from that taken by an organisation that sets a long-term goal and works relentlessly to achieve it. An agile organisation's strength is rooted in its capacity to react intelligently to situations that cannot be fully predicted. Benefiting from changing circumstances requires superior situational responsiveness; an ability to be prudently opportunistic, robust threat avoidance and taking active steps to be future-ready. Each of these bundles of activities requires leaders to decide: 'what is important, and not important to us now?' 'What do we need to do to win in the foreseeable future?' 'How can we be special in the changing context?' 'What must we do collectively to create value faster than cost?' And 'How do we act responsibly for all of our stakeholders?'

The path will not be easy. In most types of agile organisations the benefits of standardisation decrease and the requirement for ad hoc initiatives increases. Hands-on and capable agile-friendly leadership will be needed to align and attune decision-making and to develop deep execution capability (the ability to get things done). Agile-friendly leadership needs to construct organisations that are permanently effective in dealing with multiple complex, important, often novel, initiatives.

The EAfA Leadership Framework

EAfA requires that leaders take action to:
1. Build an agile-friendly TMT
2. Define the organisation's Agility Ambition
3. Select facilitative types of agility
4. Embed effective integrating mechanisms
5. Adopt an agility-oriented organisational personality
6. Relentlessly unblock blockages
7. Promote optimistic discourse
8. Take fast go, no-go decisions
9. Sponsor a salon culture
10. Acquire individuals with grit
11. Exploit multiple technologies

These leadership characteristics are examined briefly below. In Part II of this book we will explore how these characteristics can become incorporated into a wider definition of requisite organisational agility.

Leadership Characteristic One: Build an Agile-Friendly TMT

Business angels are professional investors in start-up companies and they have a reputation for being uniquely skilled in identifying enterprises that can grow profitably and cope with whatever fortune throws at them. Understandably, business angels are choosy and will only support about one start-up in 40 that apply for funds. What do business angels look for? They say that the most important factor is the quality of the team at the top (Mason, Botelho, & Zygmunt, 2017). A TMT needs to be adaptable, willing and effective, otherwise the start-up will be one of the 39 that are rejected.

Personal qualities and team coherence are vitally important factors, especially proactivity, opportunism, achievement-orientation, openness and trustworthiness. Key questions they ask include: 'Is the lead entrepreneur capable, motivated and honest?' 'Are team members committed to making a success of their enterprise?' 'Do they work together constructively as a team?' 'Do they have the competencies needed, both specialised and managerial?' 'Is there a deep consensus about ends and means?' 'Are they a learning organisation?' 'Do they have an informed view of what it will take to gain a competitive or comparative advantage?' 'Can they accurately describe the challenges that they will face?' TMTs need to be able to answer 'yes' to all these questions if they are to be an effective brain and heart of their requisitely agile organisation.

Personal qualities matter at the top of organisations. Many choices need to be made and it will be impossible to gain sufficient information for entirely evidence-based decision-making. Operating in this reality requires that every top team member possesses the apparently opposite personality characteristics of assertiveness and humility. A TMT must gain and sustain a deep consensus about ends and means. Often the issues that top teams must resolve are complex, with strong plausible arguments supporting different viewpoints and time will be short. All the members of a TMT need to contribute thoughtfully, assertively and knowledgeable and have sufficient loyalty to implement decisions fully, whether or not they agree with the decision made.

The work of TMTs often seems chaotic to observers. There may be a short meeting to decide whether to invest in a new machine, then a few minutes later an investor's questions will need to be answered, shortly followed by a presentation from a marketing company on a new branding initiative. Structured meetings of top team members will be just one element of a fluid, dynamic and frequently informal nexus of processes where senior people come together, in various combinations, to share insights, discuss issues, prepare proposals, meet customers, have learning sessions, give presentations and, sometimes, disappear from their organisation for days to run deep-dive sessions into difficult strategic issues.

Agile-friendly top managers will: (i) decide upon the membership of the TMT and upper echelon, including specifying the roles of support teams and defining how inter-relationships will work; (ii) embed an agile-friendly top team culture; (iii) install processes for facilitating prudent opportunism; (iv) clarify decision-making processes in terms of quality, velocity and implementation effectiveness; (v) proactively construct leadership messages to signal the commitment of leaders to requisite agility and (vi) configure the architecture of the organisation so that it facilitates requisite systemic and local agility.

Leadership Characteristic Two: Define the Organisation's Agility Ambition

We learnt from the study of successful incident commanders of wildfire teams that leaders in agile organisations need a capacity to inspire others. This requires that everyone connected with the work of an agile organisation knows what the organisation is seeking to become. EAfA describes this hard-to-define characteristic as an Agility Ambition. An example helps to explain the role of an Agility Ambition in agility-orientated organisational development.

Médecins Sans Frontières (Doctors Without Borders) has a mission to provide medical care for those most in need (Sheather et al., 2016). The organisation has a distinctive set of values and operating principles. They set high standards for the ethical and professional behaviour of everyone involved in providing their medical care, so that their work will continue to be valued universally. As Médecins Sans Frontières works in areas of conflict they insist on maintaining neutrality, as this reduces risks and increases the probability that they can work with anyone who needs medical help. Medical standards are high, despite the difficulties of providing care in places with few resources. Médecins Sans Frontières undertakes original research to improve its capacity to be of service to humanity.

This set of operating principles defines the essence of Médecins Sans Frontières. It shapes the personality of their organisation and underpins their ability to be requisitely agile; able to respond efficiently, effectively and quickly. Their Agility Ambition is an elaborated description of 'what opportunities we will grasp and how we will make the best of them'.

An Agility Ambition acts as a container for initiatives, as it specifies the kinds of things that 'we want to do and need to do'. Notice that these activities are not fully defined. The ambition is not a plan, rather it provides clarity as to the desired direction of travel. An Agility Ambition becomes an integrating and aligning force when it is understood and adopted by all of those who are directly connected with the work of the organisation, including employees, volunteers, funders, suppliers or other stakeholders.

An Agility Ambition is more than a managerial communication as it becomes deeply embedded in the values of those whose actions can move the ambition forward. I recall meeting Médecins Sans Frontières' workers in Asia and they all had a deep commitment to their mission that had become part of their being. Sociologists describe the process of embedding values and beliefs as 'socialisation', as it explains how people come to share ways of thinking and acting.

Insufficient research has been done to be definitive, but it seems that the sociology and psychology of agile enterprises must be shaped by their organisation's Agility Ambition. Everyone needs to know what 'we intend to become'. This develops a shared ambition that will be used by each team member to guide their actions, thereby becoming an integrated collective driving force.

In Part II of this book you will find a method that can be used to prepare a productive Agility Ambition.

Leadership Characteristic Three: Select Facilitative Types of Agility

There has been little examination of typologies of agility but the fact that agility can be achieved by very different organising modalities is mission-critical to leading and managing requisitely agile organisations. When we examined the fortunes of Nokia, Apple and Google in the mobile phone industry during the first decade of the 20th century it became clear that Nokia had adopted an 'intrapreneural' modality for managing agility whereas Apple and Google had adopted a 'orchestrated, top-down' modality. In this case, it was the top-down type of agility that proved successful but cases can be found where the top-down type of agility has proved to be dysfunctional, deminstrating that 'one size does not fit all'.

Even in mature organisations a variety of types of agility can be needed. This point becomes clear if we consider the following example. In a Bank a centralised top-down type of agility will be needed to devise the architecture of Corporate Information Technology, as IT systems must work seamlessly across boundaries. In the same Bank a granular type of type of agility, using quasi-independent small work groups, may be functional as it liberates the creative energy of entrepreneurial teams to devise new banking products for micro-market segments. These types of agility require quite different organising modalities, but each can contribute to the achievement of an Agility Ambition.

Using devolved types of agility (such as the granular modality mentioned above) inevitably increases differentiation. This facilitates entrepreneurship but undermines organisational coherence, which may be dysfunctional. A brilliant solution, developed by Hans-Jürgen Warnecke is to conceptualise the organisation as a fractal entity (Warnecke, 1993). This construct requires some explanation! In Norway there are many fjords, each of which has a unique shape. But all are fjords, as they have shapes that share mathematically common characteristics. Fjords are fractals as they have self-similar design principles.

In a fractal organisation those in leadership roles need to decide what self-similar characteristics must apply to every sub-unit of the organisation. Earlier we looked briefly at the Médecins Sans Frontières. For them, core values, like the need to safeguard children or not take sides in a conflict situation, are organisation-wide imperatives that are self-similar and non-negotiable requirements. However, the tasks undertaken by different teams of doctors will vary greatly. There will be big differences between organising a vaccine campaign against measles in Tanzania and providing surgical services in a war zone. Médecins Sans Frontières workers need to conform to the organisation's required self-similar principles but will need to adopt differential organisational modalities for their tasks. They have a fractal organisation, with self-organising and self-optimising units configuring their own operations according to the local reality they face, within self-similar organisation-wide requirements specified by the mission, vision and values of the organisation.

Agile-friendly leaders ensure that the parts of their organisation that need to be agile adopt a type of agility that is optimal. They investigate where the organisation needs to become effectively requisitely agile, in both the short- and long-term. Original research conducted by the author has identified eight types of agility, each having a different leadership and managerial modality. This typology is described in Part II of this book. Key leadership tasks related to type choice include (i) deciding why agility is required, (ii) selecting the most relevant agility type available, (iii) understanding its required modality in depth, (iv) constructing a fit-for-purpose organisation to support the selected agility type and (v) removing any agility blockages.

Leadership Characteristic Four: Embed Effective Integrating Mechanisms

In all organisations, in order to gain deep competence, individuals, groups and autonomous entities must specialise, enabling them to develop the range of specific capabilities required for their area of expertise. Some see this form of specialisation as creating silos, which is dysfunctional for organisational agility.

This viewpoint is largely, but not totally, incorrect. Deep specialisation helps organisations to be requisitely agile, as competent performance is only available from those with proven capabilities. Consider, for example, a film director who needs dialogue to be recorded on a windy mountain. The director will depend on the sound team to have the right equipment and specialised knowledge to deal with this tricky technical task quickly and effectively. Should this specialisation be unavailable, and a less competent technician attempts to record the sound, then multiple experiments are likely to be needed and the result may be inadequate. In effect the film unit has become less agile as required specialised capabilities were unavailable.

Although silos are necessary, they can become closed systems; almost acting as organisations-within-organisations. When this happens a lack of constructive integration becomes an agility blockage, sometimes causing sclerotic organisational rigidity. This risk can be countered by using specialised inter-team organisational development interventions, for example, by adopting the fractal organisation model outlined above or by promoting a culture whereby specialist groups come to see themselves as service providers proactively meeting the needs of internal, ecosystem or external customers. This orientation requires each sub-unit to answer the following question: 'how can we help our organisation to achieve its Agility Ambition?'

In high intensity agile organisations sub-units work together frequently, often forming new temporary organisations. This requires that technical systems can talk to each other, for which the term interoperability is used. It provides an ability for sub-units, disparate systems or processes to collaborate, exchange data, information and knowledge. Advances such as cyber-physical systems, artificial intelligence and machine learning provide previously unavailable integrating mechanisms that improve communication and reduce errors between sub-units, specialists, platforms, machines, sensors, users and systems.

Providing leadership in an agile organisation requires doing more than developing a culture that supports boundarylessness, as state-of-the-art interoperability is needed in parallel. Advanced interoperability makes it possible to develop ultra-effective integrating mechanisms so that parts of the organisation will work together seamlessly, efficiently and effectively in the interest of the whole.

People and systems must work closely together in agile organisations. Interoperability is more than a set of mechanisms for achieving systemic efficiency. It is a pathway towards becoming future-ready and a tool for collective learning. Knowledge needs to flow easily across boundaries so that current best practice is effectively diffused. This helps intrapreneurs to find people in other parts of the organisation, or in the wider ecosystem, that can help them to find or create opportunities, solve problems, win support and make a proactive contribution. Those in leadership positions need to be well informed about developments in the policies and practices of interoperability as this is a foundational requirement for a modern systemically agile enterprise.

Leadership Characteristic Five: Adopt an Agility-Oriented Organisational Personality

In 1990 the police department in New York Police Department (NYPD) registered 1.1 million crimes. Ten years later the crime rate had fallen by almost 50%. In order to understand how this remarkable improvement had been achieved I visited the

NYPD to interview senior police officers. Six extracts from my interviews stood out as being important:

> One of the most innovative processes we've developed is Comstat, an acronym for Computerised Statistics. It's a problem-solving model. Each week, all of the precinct commanders gather together in our War Room; a hi-tech facility modelled on the war room at the Pentagon. Basically, we talk about crime for three hours.

> Once a month every precinct commander in the City has to come downtown and face the music. Each commander has to give an account of himself or herself—not just for the last month but for their whole tenure.

> We have developed eight crime-reduction, or quality of life, strategies. These are policy documents based on an analysis of past-practice and describe the dimensions and scope of the crime problem.

> This is the first administration that the top executives not only have a very high regard for the experience, the expertise, and the perception of street cops, but they reach out to them. Street cops contribute as much to these strategies as the management did.

> With a lot of input from the private sector. The Commissioner, Mr Bratton, has been a student of management for many years and, he has sought to educate himself outside and develop relationships and to pick the brains of some of American's top and most innovative business brains.

> The successful precinct commanders have been promoted, those who are less successful have not been promoted, and those that are really less successful have been moved to less important positions.

These extracts from my interviews illustrate some of the key leadership initiatives taken by the then NYPD's police commissioner, William Bratton. Many police departments from around the world, including London's Scotland Yard, visited New York to learn how to achieve the same level of situational responsiveness, prudent opportunism, threat mitigation and future readiness. As will be discussed in Part II of this book, the NYPD case provides strong evidence that large organisations can become requisitely agile.

The adoption of agility as a key attribute of the NYPD organisational personality resulted in major changes. These included defining the fight against crime as a task that could be achieved, rather than a lost cause; using real-time data to plan fast-response initiatives; developing evidence-based policies; involving those at the cutting-edge of the organisation (the street cops) in policy development; using managerial expertise from outside policing; requiring managers to account for themselves and ensuring that only competent people held key jobs. It was policy decisions such as these that accumulated to transform the personality of the NYPD from being an institution "that had given up the role of defeating crime for the last 25 years" to asserting that "we are back to the philosophy the police exist to prevent crime".

We will use the term *organisational personality* to describe a distinctive form of identity, characterised by multiple vibrant and venturesome initiatives that can be described as a collective life force. A central characteristic is the coherence of shared values. These are inner messages that tell us what is important or unimportant, good and bad. Values tell us what to work for and what to neglect. What to cherish and what to despise. They are the beliefs that we fight for when the going gets tough. Values give meaning to our work; at the deepest level they make us part of humanity. They are subterranean as they manifest themselves only indirectly through behaviour.

Values are the foundation of decision-making and they profoundly affect management style, and the emotional climate that leaders and managers generate around them. Once shared, values become the energising force that underpins organisational personality. In mechanistic organisations values are less significant. For example, those with the task of evaluating train drivers will examine their knowledge, safety record and skills. They only consider values that are related to performance as significant, as this is the sole criterion of fitness-for-purpose. Conversely, in an agile organisation, like Médecins Sans Frontières, volunteers must decide what is the best thing to do in the circumstances of the moment and they draw from shared values to guide them.

Leadership Characteristic Six: Relentlessly Unblock Blockages

Many factors can hinder agility. Proactive and speedy action is needed to diminish or remove them. If this is not done, then hindering factors become blockages and they act in the same way as something awful stuck in a household's plumbing system. Factors that inhibit requisite agility cannot be tolerated. Blockages must become the targets for urgent remedial action so as to avoid the demoralising experience of people in an organisation feeling 'everyone knows the problems, but nothing gets enough done to remove them'.

The inspiring organisational scholar, Henry Mintzberg (Mintzberg, 2004), studied the history of the Steinbergs's supermarket chain in Canada. Some time ago the owner, Sam Steinberg, noticed that sales in one of eight stores was declining slowly. Steinberg categorised the problem as a crisis that needed drastic remedial action. He closed the ailing store one Friday night and a host of workers modernised it over the weekend. The store's name was changed, prices were cut by about 15% and it reopened on Monday morning. Steinberg had seen the gradual decline in this store as a symptom of a systemic blockage that can be defined as 'we have become trapped in an older, inefficient model of merchandising'. As a quintessentially agile leader, he addressed the problem head-on.

Organisational blockages are dysfunctional for three main reasons: (i) they absorb resources that should be spent on constructive activities; (ii) the fact that a blockage is not being removed has a negative psychological impact, as it is a silent signal that 'we are not a can-do organisation' and (iii) a blockage becomes a resisting force that counteracts the forces that are helping an organisation to become requisitely agile.

Relentless unblocking requires a degree of assertive intolerance that is sometimes unwelcome. This is because blockages frequently occur because of avoidable errors. Confronting the blockage means confronting the error, and this can be an uncomfortable experience for all concerned. Unblocking is an approach to organisational development that addresses weaknesses head-on but, interestingly, this can be experienced as being therapeutic as there is pride in being able to overcome setbacks, especially when used in conjunction with 'build on strengths' approaches.

It is often more rewarding to remove blockages than to add new helping or driving forces. In an earlier work Mike Woodcock and I identified typical organisational blockages (Woodcock & Francis, 1990), some of which are summarised below to illustrate the range of factors that can undermine organisational agility.

1. Unclear aims: a lack of clarity about direction, purpose and what 'success' means.
2. Unclear values: possessing values are inconsistent, undeliverable, vague or not practiced.
3. Inappropriate management philosophy: leadership and management style failing to facilitate wanted behaviours.
4. Lack of management development: managers lack key competencies, and this is tolerated.
5. Dysfunctional organisational structure: the ways that power is allocated hinders effective opportunism.
6. Inappropriate control: Processes and activities are insufficiently efficient or effective.
7. Inadequate people skills: people lack the capabilities to succeed.
8. Slow technology adoption: potentially useful technologies are not used effectively.
9. Poor teamwork: people fail to work together constructively.
10. Low motivation: there is a generalised lack of energy and commitment.

Blockages such as these undermine the systemic agility as they create psychological, sociological and operational waste. An agile organisation needs to become a learning entity that is focused on identifying, defining and resolving blockages as they occur and taking steps to reduce the probability that they will be repeated. This will not be a once-only task. New blockages will occur, and old ones reappear. All need to be vanquished.

Leadership Characteristic Seven: Promote Optimistic Discourse

We use the term 'discourse' to describe the character of how people communicate about the things that concern them. It is a rather abstract concept that requires some explanation. In Germany in the 18th century the world was changing and a new 'spirit of the times' was rapidly emerging. The word 'zeitgeist' was coined to describe the distinctive discourse of an era.

Why are the constructs of discourse and zeitgeist relevant to managers seeking to construct an agile enterprise? The reason is that, in agile organisations, discourse needs be overwhelmingly positive as realistic optimism is an essential mobilising force in a can-do organisation. This means that leaders need to proactively promote optimistic discourse across their organisation and into the wider ecosystem. This zeitgeist needs to be a key feature of an agile organisation's identity or personality.

When those who work in an organisation buy-in to optimistic discourse it becomes an agility-enhancing cultural phenomenon with deep emotional roots. People develop a 'can do' and 'will do' mindset, meaning that they have a shared desire to win and are open to ideas, possibilities and the experiences of others. Agility becomes a true organisational asset only if people embrace the construct wholeheartedly and act in ways consistent with this ethos and zeitgeist.

Discourse shapes how people develop shared views of the world, which becomes embedded in collective behaviour by a process described by sociologists as adopting a set of norms. Put simply, a norm is a way of acting that is socially required. For example, in a household with children it may be a norm that every child has to wash their hands before a meal and the parents adopt a norm that they will always supervise handwashing.

In agile organisations norms are actively managed, which is a key task for managers at every level. The web of norms needs to promote situational adaptiveness; prudent opportunism; threat mitigation and future readying. This requires expertise in establishing which norms are functional (emergence) and how they are maintained (enforcement). Maintaining agile-enhancing norms can only be effective if leaders and managers behave in the ways that they seek to encourage. This applies to all those who exercise leadership, including team and thought leaders.

Agile-friendly leaders shape discourse and norm-setting across their organisation, in order to provide social coherence. This is too important a topic to be self-regulating. Behavioural science research and neuroscience provides useful tools that leaders can use to increase their capacity to become effective opinion leaders and norm makers. Leaders that succeed in embedding norms are outgoing, accessible, engaging and authoritative. They respect others, take steps to help them, communicate with people as equals and take time to explain issues in depth. Authenticity is more important than slick presentations.

A way to understanding the importance of discourse in organisational development is to imagine it as the music under a scene in a film. Imagine co-workers having a coffee break and each makes negative observations about what is happening in the organisation. The music underlying this discourse would be heavy, dull, discordant and uninspiring. If the opposite were true and co-workers were sharing stories about successes, and helping each other to solve problems, then the music would be light, engaging, inspiring and harmonious, thereby facilitating organisational agility.

Promoting a zeitgeist with an optimistic discourse is an essential leadership success factor in an agile organisation as it legitimises and promotes grasping selective opportunities and making the most of them, despite setbacks, uncertainties and risks.

Leadership Characteristic Eight: Take Fast Go, No-Go Decisions

In agile organisations decision-making will be frequent, important and frequently speculative. Multiple decisions are inevitable if sufficient numbers of promising opportunities are to be found, selected and grasped, and threat avoidance stratagems implemented.

It is far from easy to make prudent decisions where speculation cannot be avoided. Decision-making based on historic analysis will not provide all the inputs that are necessary for future-orientated decision-making. Accordingly, managerial judgements are needed. These will be leadership acts, as the trajectory of flows of commitment decisions becomes the de facto strategy of an organisation. The phenomenon is not new, as leaders have always had to make decisions about things they do not fully understand, or when outcomes are speculative. However, the scale of the decision-making challenge increases in agile organisations as they must be fundamentally opportunistic and future-orientated, with a generalised requirement for rapid decision-making cycle times. Not all opportunities can be promising and some opportunities will be promising for others, but not for you. Judgements, that can rightly be described as bets, must be made.

Decision-making requires making the most of evidence. With big data capability it has become possible to make certain categories of decisions almost in real time. This can use cross-functional teams in newsroom-like control centres. Such data analysis processes greatly increase the clock speed of decision processes. But there will always be irreducible uncertainties. Bets will need to be made.

It is wise gamblers who make good bets. As any gambler will tell you, it is not possible to predict the winners of a horse race so the safest (but, maybe, not the most profitable) stratagem is to make an each-way bet, meaning betting on several horses in the same race. The same principle applies for leaders making decisions about risk-laden opportunities. If more than one proposal can be pursued at the same time, at least in the early stages when investigation is relatively cheap, then more will be known about the efficacy of each option. Making sound speculative commitment decisions is improved if alternative pathways are explored to reduce the risk that a wrong choice will be made.

Contrary to popular belief, a key challenge in agile organisations is not finding ideas but killing many of them. If all proposed ideas were to be adopted, then the quantity of resource required for implementation would far exceed that which could be made available. This is true even in the world's largest organisations. In addition, many ideas will be unworkable, inappropriate or uninspired. It will be necessary for many proposals, probably most, to be culled. How effectively the idea-killing process takes place is an important element in the management of agile organisations.

Those who take go or no-go decisions need to be skilled in this aspect of the craft of management. We use the word 'craft' intentionally, as decision-making is neither a science nor an art, although both domains of knowledge are relevant. Prowess in decision-making is learnt by doing and reflecting on consequences. Craft skills are vitally important as those in leadership positions can be blinkered, self-serving, ignorant, overwhelmed, short-sighted or foolishly bold.

Exceptional decision-making capability is unfortunately rare, which is why agile organisations invest heavily in the selection, development and retention of leaders and managers with proven decision-making craft skills. There is no alternative, as many decisive decisions must be made if the organisation is to exploit promising opportunities and, at the same time, avoid being overwhelmed or fragmented by the pursuit of excessive novelty.

Leadership Characteristic Nine: Sponsor a Salon Culture

This leadership characteristic is one that you may find surprising. Agile enterprises need to develop what can be called a salon culture, as this provides an environment for exploring concepts, perspectives, ideas, experiences and predictions of future states. The word 'salon' is used to describe gatherings in which individuals become deeply engaged in conversations that enrich their understanding of what is happening and what can be done to improve things.

It was about 300 years ago when a formal culture of salons began to flourish in Europe. Salons occurred regularly and were usually open to new contributors. They were spaces devoted to developing new and better ways of thinking. Salons embraced difference and ideas would be critically examined. Those involved developed reflective skills, as being a good listener was an important attribute of a salon attender. Everyone understood the values that underpinned the life of a good salon, so trivial conversation, self-promotion and unnecessary repetition were unacceptable. Ideas for creative projects could be presented so feedback could be received, which was unrestricted by a need to serve a particular purpose. Salons became major contributors to the 18th century period known as Enlightenment, which led to an explosion of creativity in the arts, literature, philosophy and science.

The role of discussion in clarifying opportunities is profound. There is evidence that in ancient China and Greece gatherings of informed people would be organised to discuss important issues before decisions were taken. The aim was not to acquire a consensus but to clarify everyone's thinking by opening minds to differing perspectives and having one's own viewpoint challenged. The Lunar Society, discussed in Chapter 3, is a good example of a salon.

It is the creative potential of salons that make them of interest to those who lead agile organisations. They provide a resource to develop and test assumptions, concepts, proposals and plans. Today we might describe such institutions as workshops, seminars, focus groups, brainstorming sessions or ideation events. With web-based technologies, salons can be virtual. In an agile enterprise there needs to be a place where future-orientated constructs can be developed, which is invariably time-consuming.

Salons are particularly important in agile organisations as they provide opportunities for people who might otherwise not talk deeply with each other to develop an informed view of a progressive future. They are especially valuable at times when decisions must be taken, but no one knows the right answer. Strong, robust and extensive debates serve to clarify thinking. Without sacrificing respect for others, it is necessary for people to question, dispute and question the logic of others' positions. Only through a 'trial of fire' can the integrity of a viewpoint be tested. The management of an agile organisation is improved by institutionalising a salon-style approach.

Leadership Characteristic Ten: Acquire Individuals with Grit

Leadership in agile organisations requires a depth of character. This somewhat unfashionable insight is central to understanding the attributes of the elite leadership group that is ever-present in successful agile enterprises.

James Kerr wrote a vivid explanation of how New Zealand's national rugby team, known as the All Blacks, succeed in becoming top performers year after year in his book *Legacy* (Kerr, 2013). The first section of Kerr's book is devoted to explaining the importance of character, which can be defined as individuals possessing clear and coherent values and doing whatever it takes to put these into action, no matter what difficulties occur. Increasingly, those who coach sports teams, like the All Blacks, require that each player develops deep self-knowledge, as this enables them to discover their own inner strength and find ways to use it for the benefit of the wider organisation.

Kerr's book demonstrated that there are enduring qualities in people who thrive in situations that are replete with uncertainty and difficulty. The most important is that they have 'grit' meaning, they possess purposeful personal resilience. Examples of people with grit abound in every era of history, including Mao Zedong during the Long March, Mother Teresa in the slums of India and Alfred Pritchard Sloan Jr., the great American industrialist. Grit is not necessarily positive as it is also found in people whose motives are questionable or destructive. Agile organisations need people with grit who are dedicated to exploiting agility for advantage.

An emphasis on the development of character used to be an important component of education in the 19th century but is less pronounced today, although the popularity of self-help books demonstrates that there is a widespread interest in personal development. Character is not built by study alone as it requires working on oneself, undertaking a personal exploration of values, recognising the vital importance of feedback and the development of an ability to be in the moment. Developing emotional intelligence and mindfulness are some of the ways that managers in agile organisations can learn to cope constructively with the inevitable stresses of their role.

In Chapter 2 we analysed research that examined the characteristics of men and women who lead teams fighting forest fires. Those incident commanders who are rated as the most successful demonstrate that they possess grit. They have a deep commitment to reflective learning, knowing that striving to be the best that one can be is an endless journey.

Many impediments to organisational agility are psychological. In the past standardised behaviour was often seen as constructive, as good habits provide inner guidelines that assured capable performance. In a VUCA world the habitualisation of thought and practice is undesirable, as people need to adopt new ways of perceiving, thinking and doing. This requires deep learning as the intention is not to acquire new knowledge and skills but to unlearn as well.

Acquiring individuals with grit for key roles in an organisation is more than a task for specialists in human resource management, as it is a strategic act. It is remarkable just how far world-class agile enterprises will go to seek, find, motivate and honour individuals with the combination of advanced technical prowess and personal grit. Not everyone possesses an inner commitment to pursue aspirational goals with unstoppable zeal and diligence. Interestingly, people with grit do not necessarily demonstrate superior talent; rather superior diligence, confidence to be proactive and sufficient humility to be a team player. Organisations that retain people with grit repay their commitment by valuing them greatly as individuals.

Leadership Characteristic Eleven: Exploit Multiple Technologies

It has been said that 'all organisations are tech-based now'. It is not entirely true but even unlikely occupations, like archaeologists, vehicle breakdown technicians and religious evangelists, have become digitally enabled.

The significance of commitment decisions regarding technologies grows in importance as the centrality of digitally enabled systems expands. There is no escape.

Leaders and managers must be sufficiently technologically literate to supervise key decision-making processes. This is a substantial task as technologies evolve rapidly, fuse together and can be so complex that even experts may not be able to absorb all of the recent developments in their specialist areas.

Achieving decision quality in technological areas requires that senior leaders, including Board members, understand how technology may change their industry, or make it obsolete. They need to develop a shared, evidence-based and future-orientated conceptualisation of likely changing technological landscapes as these create and destroy opportunities. An informed and collective view is essential to guide decision-making, investment and capability development.

Many requisitely agile organisations favour a fast-follower stance in relation to technologies. Being a technology innovator brings first-mover advantages but is often costly in terms of managerial effort and R&D expenditure. Conversely, being a late adopter is a low-cost strategy but means that new capabilities will be acquired after rivals have benefited, thereby reducing the availability of opportunities. The rapid rate of technological development means that difficult predictions, perhaps guesses, need to be made as whether and when to opt into a new technology or a major upgrade.

Commitments to core technologies can lock an organisation into a mode of operating that either helps or hinders different types of agility to be implemented. Organisations that are locked into legacy architectures or outdated infrastructures will have a slower clock speed, which becomes an agility blockage. This has practical and psychological consequences, as task performance will be less efficient, and people can feel that they are working in an environment that lacks a 'can-do' ethos.

In a requisitely agile organisation technological investments contribute positively to enabling an organisation's Agility Ambition to be realised. This means that they will have been specifically designed to facilitate situational adaptiveness, prudent opportunism, threat mitigation and future readying.

Bibliography for Part I

175 Years of Looking to the Future. (2007). Jardines. Hong Kong.

Amatullo, M. V. (2015). Innovation by Design at UNICEF: An Ethnographic Case Study. Case Western Reserve.

Arlen, H., Mercer, J., Crosby, B., & Andrews Sisters, T. (1944). You've got to accentuate the positive. Los Angeles: Capitol Records.

Avila, M., Wolf, K., Brock, A., & Henze, N. (2016). Remote assistance for blind users in daily life: A survey about Be My Eyes. ACM International Conference Proceeding Series, 29-June-20.

Berezina, K., Ciftci, O., & Cobanoglu, C. (2019). Robots, Artificial Intelligence, and Service Automation in Restaurants. (S. Ivanov & C. Webster, Eds.), Robots, Artificial Intelligence, and Service Automation in Travel, Tourism and Hospitality. Emerald Publishing Limited.

Boyatzis, R. E., Thiel, K., Rochford, K., & Black, A. (2017). Emotional and Social Intelligence Competencies of Incident Team Commanders Fighting Wildfires. Journal of Applied Behavioral Science, 53(4),498–516.

Brown, K. S., Marean, C. W., Herries, A. I. R., Jacobs, Z., Tribolo, C., Braun, D., . . . Bernatchez, J. (2009). Fire as an engineering tool of early modern humans. Science, 325(5942),859–862.

Darwin, F. (1909). The Foundations of the Origin of Species: Two Essays Written in 1842 and 1844. Cambridge: University Press.

Denning, S. (2018). The Seven Things A Highly Agile CEO Does: Jeff Bezos. Forbes. Retrieved from https://www.forbes.com/sites/stevedenning/2018/09/17/the-seven-things-a-highly-agile-ceo-does-jeff-bezos/

Durkheim, E., & Halls, W. D. (1984). The Division of Labour in Society. London: Macmillan.

Elias, N., & Jephcott, E. (2000). The civilising process: sociogenetic and psychogenetic investigations (Revised). London: WileyBlackwell.

Farrands, B. (2012). A Gestalt Approach to Strategic Team Change. OD Practitioner, 44(4),18–23.

Francis, D. (1994). Step-by-Step Competitive Strategy. (J. Cranwell-Ward, Ed.), Self Development for Managers. London: Routledge.

Francis, D. L., & Bessant, J. (2005). Targeting innovation and implications for capability development. Technovation, 25(3), 171–183.

Grove, A. S. (1998). Only the Paranoid Survive: How to Exploit the Crisis Points that Challenge Every Company and Career. New York: Doubleday.

Harrod, R. (2017). The Jewel of Knightsbridge: The Origins of the Harrods Empire. Stroud, UK: The History Press.

Howe, L. C., Goyer, J. P., & Crum, A. J. (2017). Harnessing the placebo effect: Exploring the influence of physician characteristics on placebo response. Health Psychology, 36(11),1074–1082.

Humphreys, P., McAdam, R., & Leckey, J. (2005). Longitudinal evaluation of innovation implementation in SMEs. European Journal of Innovation Management, 8(3),283–304.

Isaacson, W. (2011). Steve Jobs. London: Little, Brown.

Jenner, M. (2018). Netflix and the re-invention of television. Cham, Switzerland: Palgrave Macmillan.

Jobs, S. (1997). Strategy is About Saying NO. YouTube. Retrieved from https://www.youtube.com/watch?v=H8eP99neOVs

Kerr, J. (2013). Legacy, 15 Lessons in Leadership: What the All Blacks Can Teach Us About the Business of Life. London: Constable & Robinson.

Kurz, H. D. (2012). Schumpeter's new combinations: Revisiting his Theorie der wirtschaftlichen Entwicklung on the occasion of its centenary. Journal of Evolutionary Economics, 22(5), 871–899.

https://doi.org/10.1515/9783110637267-005

Lamberg, J. A., Lubinaitė, S., Ojala, J., & Tikkanen, H. (2019). The curse of agility: The Nokia Corporation and the loss of market dominance in mobile phones, 2003–2013. Business History, 1–47.

Malmsten, E., Portanger, E., & Drazin, C. (2001). boo hoo: a dot.com story from concept to catastrophe. London: Random House Business Books.

Mason, C., Botelho, T., & Zygmunt, J. (2017). Why business angels reject investment opportunities: Is it personal? International Small Business Journal: Researching Entrepreneurship, 35(5), 519–534.

McKinsey & Company. (2017). How to create an agile organization. McKinsey & Company.

McLean, M., & Rowland, T. (1985). The Inmos Saga: A Triumph of National Enterprise. London: Frances Pinter.

Meredith, S. E., & Francis, D. L. (1998). Journey Towards Manufacturing Agility: Exploring the essential sixteen elements of the Agile Wheel. In R. L. Chapman & R. Hue (Eds.), Proceedings of the first international conference: World Innovation and Strategy Conference (WISC98) incorporating the 4th International Symposium on Quality Function Deployment (pp. 1–12). Sydney, Australia.

Mintzberg, H. (1998). The Structuring of Organizations. In H. Mintzberg, J. B. Quinn, & S. Ghoshal (Eds.), The Strategic Process (European, pp. 332–353). Hemel Hempstead, UK.: Prentice Hall Europe.

Mintzberg, H. (2004). Managers Not MBAs: A Hard Look at the Soft Practice of Managing and Management Development. London: FT Prentice Hall.

Morsing, M., & Oswald, D. (2009). Sustainable leadership: Management control systems and organizational culture in Novo Nordisk A/S. Corporate Governance, 9(1),83–99.

paconsulting.com. (2019). The Evolution of the Agile Organisation: Old dogs. Ingenious new tricks. Retrieved from http://www2.paconsulting.com/rs/526-HZE

Rommel, E. (2006). Infantry Attacks. Barnsley, UK: Greenhill Books.

Schoemaker, P. J. H. (2016). Superforecasting: How to Upgrade Your Company's Judgement. Harvard Business Review, 94(5),72–78.

Schofield, R. E. (1966). The Lunar Society of Birmingham; A Bicentenary Appraisal. Notes and Records of the Royal Society of London, 21(2),144–161.

Shakespeare, W. (2018). Julius Cesar (eBook). Forgotten Books.

Sheather, J., Jobanputra, K., Schopper, D., Pringle, J., Venis, S., Wong, S., & Vincent-Smith, R. (2016). A Médecins Sans Frontières Ethics Framework for Humanitarian Innovation. PLoS Medicine, 13(9),1–10.

Smith, J. (2018). How Jeff Bezos Built an E-Commerce Empire: The Unwritten Story of Amazon.com.

Soykan, B., & Alberts, D. S. (2015). Moving C2 Agility from a theory to a NATO Practice. In 20th ICCRTS "C2, Cyber, and Trust.

Trevett, J. (2011). Demosthenes, speeches 1–17. Elsevier B.V.

Tzu, S. (1981). The Art of War. In J. Clavell (Ed.). London: Hodder and Stoughton.

Warnecke, H.-J. (1993). The Fractal Company: A Revolution in Corporate Culture. Berlin: Springer-Verlag.

Woodcock, M., & Francis, D. (1990). Unblocking Your Organization. Aldershot: Gower.

Part II: **The EAfA Process**

5 Introduction to Part II: Using the EAfA Process to Exploit Agility for Advantage

Being capable of exploiting agility for advantage provides a hard-to-copy strength that provides competitive or comparative advantage. If possessed in appropriate ways, and used effectively, requisite agility increases the probably that an organisation will thrive in changing times. It is, therefore, a driver of organisational effectiveness that managers cannot ignore.

The EAfA Process is a structured intervention for transforming an intention (to become requisitely agile) into an organisational capability. It provides a step-by-step structure to provide logic, rigour and confidence. Organisations vary in many ways, so the EAfA Process is indicative, not prescriptive. EAfA should be adapted and enriched by users, as a structured approach must never become a straitjacket.

The EAfA Process (i) focuses organisational development on a single issue (achieving systemic and local requisite agility); (ii) uses methods that ensure those who will be involved in execution will have been involved in planning; (iii) does not adopt a one-size-fits-all policy, as this oversimplifies the task of becoming requisitely agile and (iv) enables a TMT to be informed leaders of the process.

The purpose of the EAfA Process is to help managers determine (i) what agility deliverables the organisation (whole or sub-unit) seeks to gain, (ii) what is the gap between existing and wanted agile capability, (iii) where is agility-orientated organisational development needed and (iv) what type or types of agility can best deliver the wanted agility deliverables.

An organisation can be said to have achieved requisite agility when it is gaining specified agility deliverables, both systemically and locally. This requires that all sub-units that have been identified as needing to be agile-capable, whether permanent or temporary, will devise and drive towards delivering their local Agility Ambition that conforms with organisation-wide guiding principles and systemic requirements.

The EAfA Process described in this part of the book recommends the use of a workshop-based approach, although the work programme can be completed by an individual manager, or by an external advisor or consultant. The process is most effective when all the steps are completed in sequence. However, each step can be used separately and can be easily adapted for this purpose.

Units of Analysis

The EAfA Process can be used with 10 units of analysis, which are (i) the organisation's ecosystem; (ii) entire organisations; (iii) business units; (iv) Lines of Business or

https://doi.org/10.1515/9783110637267-006

LoBs; (v) departments; (vi) work groups; (vii) inter-group relationships; (viii) autonomous systems; (ix) projects and (x) key individuals.

Advanced users of the EAfA Process can devise separate agility development strategies for each of these possible units of analysis. In this book, a simpler categorisation is used to reduce complexity. Only two units of intervention will be examined, which are the organisation as a whole (the systemic level) and all other groupings, such as departments, major projects, ecosystems or work groups, that we describe as 'sub-units' (i.e., the local level).

Defining Sub-Units

It is important to define sub-units carefully. For example, a local Unit of Analysis could be 'The Genomics Division', 'the South Asia Expansion Project' or 'The Corporate PR Department'. A Unit of Analysis will have coherent agility deliverables. This becomes easier to understand when an example is considered. The EFG Joinery Company has three LoBs, each serving a different market segment: government institutions, private customers buying high quality domestic fittings and libraries buying prestigious handmade bookcases. Would a local agility strategy be needed for each of these LoBs? The answer is 'yes', as the landscape of opportunities will be different in each market segment of the company's business.

EAfA is not only relevant to core business activities. Sub-units, that see themselves as support functions, such as maintenance, catering, finance, R&D or human resource management, will benefit from undertaking the EAfA Process. Where an organisation has not adopted EAfA as an organisation-wide development framework, managers or individual contributors (such as experts or specialists) can use the EAfA Process with their own sub-units independently. Also, many individuals have a need to be personally agile and aspects of the EAfA Process can help to facilitate the development of agile-friendly leadership and management skills.

When should the EAfA Process be used?

Regarding timing, the simple answer is 'as soon as possible'. If the EAfA Process is to be used as a wide-scale organisational development programme then the TMT should start the process, for reasons that are explained below. It is best to address the need to develop requisite agility as a serious task and that may mean waiting until the members of a TMT have found the time to complete the process themselves, with the same degree of attention that they give to other mission-critical strategic issues.

Using the EAfA Process Selectively: The Five Paths

Not all TMTs will want to commit their organisations to adopt the EAfA Process comprehensively. For this reason, five paths can be taken through the steps of the EAfA Process. The first four have the colours of ski runs: *green* for a gentle slope, *blue* for beginners, *red* is the intermediate level path and a *black* run is for those who want to make a full commitment and possess the resources that this will require. The fifth path is for readers who do not want to use EAfA as a process but wish to learn from its novel tools and techniques.

The *Green Path* is a gentle orientation to the construct as it only provides a theoretical orientation to organisational agility. If you choose to take the Green Path, then a group of interested managers should read Step One and complete the workshop assignment as suggested. This should be followed by a discussion to assess the relevance of agility for your own organisation. This helps managers to decide whether acquiring requisite agility is an organisational development priority for their enterprise. *To follow the Green Path only complete Step One.*

The *Blue Path* is more rigorous. If you choose to take this path, then a group of managers should be given the task of assessing whether the organisation is systemically agile and reporting their findings to a senior management team. The Unit of Analysis for the Blue Path can be the organisation as a whole or a sub-unit. The required method is to compete Step Three ('diagnosing') and use the EAfA Agile Capabilities Reference Model to assess whether the selected Unit of Analysis has the required capabilities to be systemically agile. *To follow the Blue Path only Step Three should be completed.*

The *Red Path* is comprehensive but localised. If you choose to take this path then one or more sub-units (e.g., a division, department, team or LoB) should be selected and asked to complete all the seven steps of the EAfA Process as directed. This can be facilitated with the help of an agility change agent (ACA). The Red Path provides an opportunity to test the EAfA Process without making a full commitment. As the sub-unit groups undertake their journey through the steps their experience should be viewed as an experiment, with detailed records kept, to be reviewed later. *To follow the Red Path all seven steps should be completed by the identified sub-units.*

The *Black Path* is for organisations that have already decided that improved agility is an organisational development priority. If you choose to take this path, then the members of the TMT need to become deeply involved from the beginning. Detailed guidance on how TMTs should use the EAfA Process is given below. Subsequently, all the sub-units that could benefit from acquiring requisite agility should complete the EAfA Process within guidelines set by the TMT. *To follow the Black Path all seven steps should be completed by the TMT before the identified sub-units do the same.*

The *Individual Path* is for students of management, teachers of strategy and organisational development, executive coaches, management consultants, organisational sociologists and researchers. As much of the content in Part II of this book is original, research-based and has not been published elsewhere, the material may be of interest to academic and professional readers. Those who do not wish to apply the EAfA Process as an organisational development intervention can read the material conventionally, by ignoring the instructions provided for facilitating workshops.

Who Leads the EAfA Process?

Leadership must be taken by the TMT when the EAfA Process is an organisation-wide organisational development initiative. In larger organisations the human resource department will generally take responsibility for administration, coordination and the development of ACAs, so that professional support will be available for the leaders of sub-units.

For local or sub-unit EAfA Processes the leader will be the manager of a sub-unit. Where sub-units are networks of activities, for example, in supply chains, then a manager who is an experienced chairperson can take this role. The EAfA Process must be led and managed separately from the normal work of a sub-unit.

What is an Agility Development Team?

The usual way to undertake the EAfA Process is establish an Agility Development Team (ADT). One ADT will be needed for each sub-unit.

The ADT must have at least some members who have a deep understanding of the work of the sub-unit. Also, ADT members should be chosen to contribute creativity, analytical skills, lateral thinking, critique and realism. Membership of an ADT can include outsiders or attendees who are not managers. An ADT should bring together everyone who can make an informed or creative input that facilitates sub-unit specific, agility-orientated organisational development. It may be that additional people will join an ADT for some, but not all, of the steps. In small sub-units all the members of the group can become the ADT. In larger sub-units, a representative group will be selected. ADTs with about six to eight members are often the most successful.

What will the ADT do?

An ADT uses the EAfA Process to determine what needs to be done to establish requisite agility in a defined Unit of Analysis (more about units of analysis later). This includes assessing whether (i) organisational capabilities are currently adequate to maintain requisite agility, (ii) what deliverables are required from possessing agility, (iii) what will the Unit of Analysis look like when it is requisitely agile and (iv) what managerial and organisational architecture is needed.

An EAfA Process begins with a kick-off meeting. It is important that all members of an ADT recognise the strategic significance of the intervention and agree to give it the time needed to complete it. Members of an ADT need to know that seven workshops will be held, each requiring pre-work that must be completed diligently. Further guidance on structuring the kick-off meeting is provided later.

Each of the steps has a similar structure, with specific guidance being provided for ADT leaders. A cycle begins when, about a week before the workshop, ADT members, and any additional attendees, receive a briefing about the purpose of the upcoming step and the required preparatory tasks. Usually it is best to organise a virtual or face-to-face meeting during which the ADT leader will outline the objectives, explain the requirements of the pre-work, answer questions and ensure that necessary practical arrangements are made.

Pre-work should be undertaken individually, or in pairs, in order to increase the diversity of input available for workshop sessions. It is important that all members of an ADT, and others that join for a particular workshop, complete the preparation as directed, as the quality of workshop discussion depends on all participants being well-informed about the specific tasks that they will undertake.

All workshops will be at least two-hours long, with target times given for each step. An effective format is for the seven workshops to be completed over a period of 12–14 weeks but they can be compressed into three-day off-site meetings if led by an experienced EAfA trainer.

For those involved in the EAfA Process, the experience can be as important as the outcome. Those participating will learn how to formulate a capability-based strategy. Informed debate is essential. The process must be kept vibrant and alive. An ADT leader should strive to sustain a team psychological climate that facilitates input, creativity, realism, active listening, thoroughness and challenge.

It will be important to see the steps as being interdependent. Breaking a complex topic into seven bite-sized chunks facilitates progress but can mean that connections are overlooked and the interactive nature of the steps of the EAfA Process will be under-explored.

For copyright reasons, all of the members of an ADT should have a personal copy of this book, as it includes pre-reading for workshops and guidance as to how to conduct them. This can be the e-book version.

The Role of ACAs

An ACA is a guide and an EAfA facilitator. The process has been designed to be self-managing and many ADTs will not want the help of an ACA. However, it can be helpful to have the help of a specialised change agent where increasing agile capability is an urgent or important organisational development priority.

An ACA will need a broad understanding of agility-orientated organisational development, deep knowledge of the EAfA Process and skills in acting as a critical friend for the leader, and the team's members, in order to help them (i) improve how they operate as a team and (ii) exploit the EAfA Process for advantage. It is important to note that an ACA will not act as a supervisor as this would undermine his or her ability to act as an effective facilitator.

In the explanations of each of the seven steps in the EAfA Process the role of the ACA is not specified, as this needs to be negotiated with the ADT leader before each workshop. For example, an ACA can act as the workshop process leader, a facilitator or a technical adviser. It is important that a written job description is prepared as this clarifies the role, which is beneficial for everyone. The purpose is to develop a set of mutually agreed expectations. The role can be revised as the EAfA Process is implemented in order to meet changing needs. Frequently undertaken tasks below can be used to develop the job description (sometimes called a psychological contract). ACA's frequently:

I.   Systematically observe the ADT's team process and make interventions that enable members of an ADT to reflect on how best to improve their teamwork.
II.   Help the ADT leader to understand the impact of his/her leadership style.
III.   Support the ADT leader in ensuring that the EAfA Process is used effectively.
IV.   Act as a guide to the technical content of EAfA.
V.   Move the ADT into a mental space where they are open to consider radical changes to their contribution to the wider organisation.
VI.   Act like a coach to a sports team, providing encouragement and guidance to help members to undertake the assigned tasks.
VII.   Watch for signs of emotional discomfort or distress and to arrange for psychological support to be available in cases of need (as some ADT members may find exploring alternative futures stressful and anxiety inducing).
VIII.   Add Organisation Development tools and techniques that are not included in the EAfA Process where these can help an ADT to move forward.

Of importance will be helping ADT leaders to prepare for each step of the EAfA Process. Accordingly, before each workshop, an ACA can meet with the ADT leader to:
– Study the suggested procedure
– Adapt the EAfA process to suit the special needs of the team
– Clarify the role of the ADT leader
– Plan how pre-work can be completed effectively
– Define the role of the ACA

During meetings of the ADT the ACA can encourage team members to:
- Be open, forthcoming and honest
- Adopt a positive approach
- Voice any concerns to the whole team as soon as possible
- Ensure that they will not be interrupted during the meetings
- Implement agreed action plans

If requested, an ACA can lead the Team Review Session that takes place at the end of every workshop. The outputs from this review-to-improve session should be noted, so that they can be used to remind the team of the suggestions for improvement at the start of the subsequent workshop.

It is important that ACAs are aware that becoming agile can have negative emotional consequences for some individuals. It is not always easy to feel comfortable when working in an agile organisation as old certainties become unavailable and new certainties are uncertain.

Who can be an ACA?

An ACA will be someone from outside the ADT, although he or she may be a colleague from another part of the wider organisation. An ACA needs to be a competent facilitator who understands EAfA fully and deeply. This expertise can be gained by studying the elements in this book, reviewing the experience of teams using the EAfA Process and studying Organisation Development tools and techniques. ACAs can assess their depth of understanding of Organisation Development by reflecting on the contents of the next section.

What are the Theoretical Roots of the EAfA Process?

The EAfA Process is a specialised derivative of a discipline known as Organisation Development or OD, as it widely known (Cheung-Judge & Holbeche, 2015). OD emerged in the early years of the 20th century when a group of efficiency engineers, led by Frederick Winslow Taylor (Taylor, 1911) analysed work processes in the Bethlehem Steel Company in the United States. They facilitated a raft of improvements that would have been difficult, or impossible, for the incumbent managers to achieve on their own. Taylor's work demonstrated that external interventions could be transformative if they were based on careful organisational diagnosis, evidence-based intervention and using well developed theories of action, change and winning.

In the late 1920s several social science experiments took place in Western Electric's Hawthorn Plant (Roethlisberger & Dickson, 1939). These demonstrated that human factors, such as the distinctive culture of work groups and how people make sense of the world, make a decisive impact on organisational efficiency and effectiveness. It was this sociological perspective that evolved into OD, differentiating its values and intervention methodologies from purely analytical approaches. Conceptually, OD belongs to a social engineering tradition, as its primary purpose is to provide constructs and tools to construct healthy and productive organisations.

OD uses social science methodologies that are orientated towards development, not necessarily change. There is an important difference between 'organisational change' and 'organisational development'. Organisational change is achieved by moving from one state to another. Organisation Development is based on a belief that organisations become better if they adopt humanistic values, assist people to deepen their emotional and conceptual intelligence and embrace socio-technical models of organising. We will not go into depth in describing the theoretical underpinning of OD, as the topic is too extensive. However, those who are considering using the EAfA Process, especially if they will act as ACAs, will find it beneficial to gain a deep insight into the policies and practices of OD.

OD practitioners advocate that the adoption of people-centred values is fundamental. For this reason, modern OD can be seen as a child of the Human Potential Movement, as it holds firm to a belief that people are able to grow personally, thereby becoming more capable of improving their organisations with understanding, skill and integrity. Put simply, the guiding principle of OD is that organisational effectiveness depends fundamentally on the agency of mature, wise, authentic, informed and learning-orientated people who use power responsibly.

OD practitioners are driven by a belief that people will give their best in situations where they feel that they are partners in an enterprise and are trusted, fairly treated, respected and empowered. OD holds that there is intrinsic merit in releasing latent potential (especially human). Also, if OD values are adopted by leaders then this will facilitate organisational health, meaning that all stakeholders, including the wider world, will benefit.

OD has amassed a large number of tools for improving organisational health, efficiency and effectiveness. Of great importance is systematic diagnosis. This facilitates people owning a shared vision of what needs to be done, which greatly increases the probability that constructive organisational development will occur. OD provides methods to improve needs assessments, intervention processes, collective learning and action-planning. It aims to influence the energy systems of organisations so they become proactively self-improving and can undertake effective deficit-based (solving problems) and vision-based (reinvention) initiatives.

Although some forms of OD can be self-managed there are times when help will be needed from internal or external change agents, who act as catalysts, coaches, guides and facilitators. For example, when an EAfA Process is undertaken an ACA can help to ensure that the seven steps are used constructively and can be strengthened further with relevant parts of the wider OD toolkit. Achieving requisite agility often requires unfreezing an existing social system. This task can be difficult as norms, patterns of behaviour and routines are often deeply buried in the modus operandi of an organisation and have become invisible to the members of the client system. An ACA can bring such buried issues to the surface, so that they can be examined.

EAfA's foundations are OD-based but the methodology has been influenced by five additional areas of academic enquiry: namely, strategic planning (Mintzberg, Quinn, & Ghoshal, 1998), innovation management (Tidd & Bessant, 2014), entrepreneurship studies (Duckworth, 2016), socio-technical systems (Crick & Chew, 2017) and emergence theory (Johnson, 2001).

An OD mindset is particularly valuable for those helping enterprises to exploit agility for advantage as it views organisations as organisms, not machines. It is wise for ACAs and managers to learn from recent perspectives of OD, as they have recognised that developments such as machine intelligence, neuroscience and complex adaptive systems provide valuable insights into the functioning of healthy and agile organisations. The EAfA Process goes into depth only on those OD topics that are specific to acquiring requisite agility. As managers work through the EAfA steps, they will identify organisational development needs. EAfA does not go into detail into how these should be managed as these processes have been described fully elsewhere (Vogelsang et al., 2012).

A Difficult Process

It is important for ADTs and ACAs to recognise that becoming requisitely agile will not be the easiest of OD initiatives. This is because acquiring agility provides an organisational capability that needs to be targeted dynamically, so it depends on the circumstances of the moment, rather than requiring the achievement of an absolute standard. For example, if a factory adopts the Six Sigma approach to process improvement, then everyone involved will know that success means that products are 99.99% free of defects. However, if an organisation decides to become requisitely agile then the deliverables cannot be specified with precision. A requisitely agile organisation possesses generalised dynamic capabilities that can be used in multiple ways.

Getting Started with the EAfA Process

Before a decision is made to use the EAfA Process, it is important to understand it. Usually, this begins with several senior managers reviewing this book to answer the question 'might this be right for us?' It is important not to make a full commitment decision immediately, as the EAfA Process should be trialled as a prototype before an extensive roll-out (by taking the Red Path, described above). This enables those who will facilitate the use of the EAfA Process to learn how to adapt it to a particular client.

If a decision is taken to move into the prototyping phase, then two or three sub-units need to be selected to undertake a trial of the EAfA Process. The trials should use all seven steps, so that the complete process can be evaluated. The trial sub-units should be selected on the basis that (i) their manager is willing to undertake an experimental initiative, (ii) it is considered that increased agility could be relevant to this sub-unit, (iii) those participating are prepared to systematically monitor their progress and (iv) they are open to share their experience with others.

Sub-unit trials are essential ways to learn about the EAfA Process in action. Notes should be recorded in detail of the experience of participants during the prototyping phase. Considerable effort should be invested in finding ways to implement the process and improve it, before EAfA is rolled out extensively. If internal or external facilitators are to be used as ACAs then they should be deeply involved in trials, as this will provide invaluable learning opportunities to enable them to facilitate the EAfA Process more effectively.

The Role of the TMT

If a decision is taken to roll-out the EAfA Process widely, then the members of a TMT will need to provide practical and emotional leadership and act as role models. Members of sub-units must feel aligned, supported and encouraged, especially when 'the going gets tough'. The EAfA Process requires a period of far-sighted thinking, which few managers find easy. There can be a tendency to return to the comfort of the known, rather than enter the void of the possible. A primary task for members TMTs is to create momentum, buy-in and openness to frequent revision, as requisite agility is never permanent, it is always being constructed and reconstructed.

If the members of a TMT decide to adopt the EAfA Process as an organisational development intervention then, before the roll-out, they must undertake the EAfA Process as participants, not simply for information. This is necessary for five main reasons:

i. Participating provides a first-hand experience of the EAfA Process that will help the members of the TMT to make decisions as to how it should be rolled out. The process does not have to be adopted universally as it is only relevant for those sub-units that need to possess agile capabilities.

ii. Requisite agility can only be achieved if the members of the TMT act as proactive role models. Participating personally in the EAfA Process enables members of top teams to clarify how their own, and top team's behaviour needs to change.

iii. TMTs must define their organisation's Agility Ambition (more about this later).

iv. The TMT must specify what high-level systemic agile deliverables are required by the organisation's Agility Ambition.

v. The TMT needs to define mandatory or self-similar requirements that all sub-units be required to accept. This provides coherence, alignment and helps to integrate interdependent sub-units as they need to be fractals of the whole.

The last point needs further explanation. A TMT will require that all sub-units have self-similar (i.e., be fractals) characteristics. For example, in my university all departments must adhere to defined standards for student safeguarding. Self-similar requirements can be difficult to define, as too many becomes oppressive, too few promotes under-integration and inappropriate self-similar requirements will be dysfunctional. See Chapter 4 for more details of the fractal organisation construct. An organisation's self-similar requirements can be captured in an Agility Playbook (discussed later) that has a similar purpose to the playbooks prepared by sports coaches to guide team players on how they should take advantage of any situation that may occur. This Agility Playbook will need to be available to sub-units before they begin their own EAfA Process as it will frame their EAfA Process.

The TMT's EAfA Workshop

Experience has shown that a TMT's EAfA Process can be particularly effective when it is takes place as a three-day residential workshop in a dedicated learning environment, like a business school, where professional staff act as skilled facilitators. A few weeks before a TMT's EAfA Process workshop there should be a kick-off meeting led by the chief facilitator to explain the process and provide the pre-work (which is completing Step One). Once in the business school environment the members of the TMT will work through all the seven steps at speed. Topics for further development will be identified, each of which should have a TMT member acting as the progress champion. It will be necessary to identify who will act as the ACAs to facilitate the process, should it be rolled out widely. Tactics for a wider roll-out of the EAfA Process should be agreed and a champion identified to coordinate the entire initiative. The TMT's EAfA workshop should conclude with each member of the top team describing how she or he will act as a role model in the months to come.

The purpose of the TMT's EAfA Process workshop is to develop a deep consensus on ends and means. The words 'deep consensus' are powerful and important. A shallow buy-in will not be sufficient. It is essential that a TMT achieves a consensus on the required functions of agility in their organisation and codifies this into an Agility Ambition, otherwise the initiative will be less than successful. In its entirety, the EAfA Process is demanding but TMTs have found it valuable to explore the process carefully as they realise that exploiting agility for advantage is a mission-critical dimension of organisational development, and provides a foundation for gaining and sustaining an enduring competitive or comparative advantage.

Terms of Reference for Sub-Units

The sub-units that undertake an EAfA Process must work within the self-similar policy/practice requirements specified by the TMT. Sub-units should report on how they intend to develop localised agile capability so that any systemic gaps can be identified and organisational cohesion maintained. Some proposed initiatives cannot be finalised without the commitment of key stakeholders, so sub-units will need to find effective ways to present their proposals upwards (to the TMT), sideways (to other teams that will be influenced) and downwards (to those who must develop agile capabilities).

What Deliverables will be Gained?

A successful EAfA Process identifies what requisite agility is needed now (a one-year view); in the foreseeable future (a three-year view) and it develops a scenario of possible agility requirements in the middle-distant future (a seven-year view). The seven-year view will be speculative but is essential as new or different capabilities may be needed that are not yet in place. These time intervals may be varied according to the pace of industry-specific changes.

Becoming requisitely agile liberates human and, increasingly, machine potential. Often, those who participate in the EAfA Process find that it is motivating to be directly involved in shaping the future of their own part of the organisation. Almost always, requisite agility will require that sub-units become proactive and venturesome, which is a form of job enrichment that many will welcome, but some will fear.

The Seven Steps of EAfA

The EAfA Process has seven steps. Each has a different purpose and will require at least one workshop. The first two steps provide an orientation to the process and the other five enable a requisite agility organisational development plan to be developed. The seven steps are briefly described below. This overview of the entire process should be shared with everyone who will be involved in the EAfA Process during a kick-off meeting.

Step One – Orientating: starts the learning journey by summarising findings from 30 years of academic research and practitioner experience into organisational agility, thereby providing a shared conceptual platform for those using the EAfA Process.

Step Two – Predicting: uses foresight techniques to define future agility capability requirements.

Step Three – Diagnosing: enables ADT members to assess their current state of agility readiness by comparing their own organisation against a research-based model of the systemic characteristics of a requisitely agile organisation.

Step Four – Envisioning: asks ADT members to conduct a thought experiment and develop a rich-picture description, an Agility Ambition, of what will, or will not, be happening when their sub-unit is requisitely agile.

Step Five – Scoping: defines what requisite agility is needed urgently (the one-year view); in the foreseeable future (the three-year view) and in the middle-distant future (the seven-year view).

Step Six – Customising: enables types of agility to be selected that meet the needs of the organisation.

Step Seven – Delivering: enables ADT members to develop a change agenda, select a theory of change and define the goals of an agility-orientated organisational development programme.

6 Step One – Orientating: *What is known about achieving requisite agility?*

The focus of this step is *orientating*. This is achieved by the members of an ADT gaining a conceptual appreciation of organisational agility by studying relevant academic research and authoritative case studies.

Guidance for the ADT Leader

Agile organisations are a conceptually distinct category, as they have distinctive features that separate them from non-agile organisations. Before detailed work using the EAfA Process is undertaken, it is essential that ADT members develop an evidence-based understanding of the distinctive properties of requisitely agile organisations. This task requires studying relevant research and scholarly analyses and debating the topic with others.

When introducing this step, ADT leaders, and ACAs if available, should emphasise the importance of developing a shared evidence-based conceptual understanding of organisational agility to underpin the work of the team during the EAfA Process. It may be that there will be resistance, as managers can view academic perspectives as being flawed or unrealistic. However, experience has shown that if those undertaking the EAfA Process are unaware of the width and depth of the construct of organisational agility then their work will be flawed. For example, many managers may view Scrum (discussed later) and agility as being synonymous, which greatly underestimates the breadth of the construct.

Undertaking an orienting study has another benefit. It enables team members to distance themselves from their current roles and view their task holistically and objectively. Becoming requisitely agile may require 'do different' as well as 'do better' changes. Having a considered and comprehensive view of the area of investigation facilitates radical thinking.

Before undertaking the Step One pre-work assignment and workshop the ADT must meet, physically or virtually for a kick-off meeting that will take about one hour. This meeting is essential, as the members of the ADT need to have an opportunity to tune into their task and decide how to become a high-performing team. The kick-off meeting concludes with a briefing session on how to prepare for the Step One Workshop. Guidance for structuring this meeting is given below.

During the Step One Workshop nine different theoretical lenses will be discussed. The ADT leader should seek to develop a consensus regarding the characteristics of requisite agility and the ways that it can be acquired. It may be that the Step One Workshop will end without a consensus being reached. If this occurs then

https://doi.org/10.1515/9783110637267-007

ADT leaders can arrange additional meetings, taking the form of academic seminars, to continue to explore agility constructs.

Throughout Step One ADT leaders shape discussions to (i) enable the team to acquire a shared set of authoritative concepts about what organisational agility is, and is not; and (ii) define the conditions that produce either requisite or dysfunctional agility.

Structuring the Kick-Off Meeting

All of the members of the ADT should attend the kick-off meeting in person or virtually. The agenda for this meeting is (i) an introduction to the EAfA Process, (ii) agreeing on our Unit of Analysis and (iii) introducing the Step One Workshop Pre-Work.

After opening the kick-off meeting, the ADT leader should ensure that introductions are made, especially if senior managers are present or there will be an ACA working with the team. The agenda should be summarised and the leader will introduce the EAfA Process, drawing from the list below:

1. *What does EAfA mean?* The acronym is short for 'Exploiting Agility for Advantage'. EAfA is an organisational development methodology that advocates that some, but not all, organisations will benefit from becoming either more agile or agile in different ways. Managers need to decide how much agility their own organisation needs now, and in the future. It is a management task to decide how best to exploit agility for advantage and EAfA offers a pathway for making these decisions efficiently and effectively.
2. *What is an agile organisation?* It is one that gains advantage from being outward looking, finding and grasping promising opportunities, minimising threats and being well prepared for a different future.
3. *What is the EAfA Process?* It is a step-by-step work programme that helps units of an organisation to develop the agile capabilities required to be fit-for-purpose in a changing world.
4. *What is requisite agility?* As not all parts of an organisation need to be agile in the same ways, requisite agility means 'not too much, not too little, of the right type and delivering wanted agility deliverables'.
5. *Why do units and teams need to complete the EAfA Process separately?* Parts of the same organisation will have different needs for agility, so it is essential that managers in each unit or team clarify their own needs, within the context of the requirements of the wider organisation.
6. *What is the role of an ADT?* An ADT is a temporary organisation formed to find effective ways to enable an organisational unit to become requisitely agile.
7. *What is the role of an ACA?* Sometimes it can help to have an external coach or facilitator who is experienced in using the EAfA Process and can provide an outside perspective to improve analysis and planning. If an ACA is helping the

ADT, then he or she should define their role and share their experience of what needs to be done to have a successful organisational development experience when using the EAfA Process.

8. *How will our EAfA Process fit into the wider Organisational Development Plan?* Sometimes an entire organisation will be working to exploit agility for advantage. When this happens, the TMT will have defined why agility is important to the organisation (by specifying the corporate Agility Ambition) and this will frame how different parts of the organisation should undertake the EAfA Process. (Where possible, senior managers should attend the kick-off meeting to explain the importance of the EAfA initiative to the enterprise.)

9. *Can groups use the EAfA Process without it being an enterprise-wide initiative?* Yes, groups can undertake the EAfA Process without it being an organisation-wide priority, but it is advisable to keep senior managers informed.

10. *Is EAfA suitable for small – and medium-sized enterprises?* Yes, the EAfA tools can be used successfully with small organisations.

11. *Is EAfA suitable for not-for-profit enterprises?* Yes, social enterprises and other types of not-for-profit organisations, like hospitals or charities can use EAfA. In fact, they often benefit greatly.

12. *What are the seven steps of EAfA?* The EAfA Process has seven steps. The first step orientates the team to their task by providing evidence-based concepts about how to achieve requisite agility. The second looks ahead to define future needs. The third enables an ADT to assess the current agility strengths of their part of the organisation. The fourth step helps an ADT to visualise what the unit will be like when it is requisitely agile. The fifth develops a roadmap to set priorities for an agility development programme. The sixth enables an ADT to select which types of agility to adopt. The last step defines the goals of an agility-orientated organisational development programme.

13. *How does the EAfA Process work?* A workshop process is used. Each of the seven steps requires pre-work and a workshop. Guidance notes for preparing for, and facilitating, each of the seven workshops are included in the process guidelines for each step.

14. *How much work will be required?* The time required for pre-work and the workshop varies with the degree of complexity of different steps. Overall, about 8 days should be allocated for completing all seven steps.

15. *How can we get the most from the process?* ADTs are most successful when (i) everyone prepares carefully for the workshops; (ii) the ADT becomes a high performing team and (iii) there is a strong emphasis on being proactive, positive and practical.

Following the overview presentation, it will be important that members of the ADT discuss the EAfA Process, raise concerns and review the practical implications of undertaking the seven steps.

Agreeing our Unit of Analysis

After the discussion following introductory presentation the ADT leader will work with the team to agree on a definition of the Unit of Analysis, which will specify clearly 'the part of the organisation' that the ADT will examine during the EAfA Process. The purpose of this discussion is to clearly define what the Unit of Analysis 'is' and 'is not'. A useful way to define a Unit of Analysis is to ask the question: 'what part of the organisation are we, as an ADT, able to influence greatly?' Subsequently, it will be necessary for the leader to write, and circulate, a description of the ADT's terms of reference, including clearly defining the specific Unit of Analysis that will be the focus of the ADT's work.

Introducing the Pre-Work for the Step One Workshop

The ADT leader should introduce the step one pre-workshop tasks (given below) and explain that it is essential that everyone involved in an EAfA Process has a deep understanding of how the construct of requisite organisational agility has evolved. This provides concepts that will orientate the members of the ADT as they complete the EAfA Process. For the first step, selective findings from 30 years of studies have been summarised, providing multiple insights into the construct of organisational agility. Nine academic research and authoritative case studies are described, each of which has contributed something substantially new to our understanding of organisational agility.

The review of research and practitioners' accounts assists members of the ADT to explore why agility is important in their context, understand how agility can be enacted and define the organisational characteristics that either drive requisite agility forwards, or block it from progressing. It provides those concerned with developing requisite organisational agility with a deep and wide set of research-based insights that enables them to demystify the construct.

The Pre-Workshop Task for Step One

Purpose
To explore the construct of organisational agility in depth and come to a shared understanding of what requisite agility means in practice.

Goals

i.   To assist the members of an ADT to explore deeply the construct of requisite organisational agility.

ii. To provide the ADT with an orienting set of concepts for the remaining steps in the EAfA Process.

Process

Undertake the pre-work individually, as the Step One Workshop will be more effective if everyone has an opportunity to make a distinctive contribution.

Core Task

To mine the nine studies of organisational agility for insights that might be useful for your ADT's work.

Sub-Tasks

1. Highlight all the insights that may have relevance to the work of your ADT.

2. Review your highlighted sections and select three insights that could be especially important for the work of your ADT. Briefly describe each of your selected key insights and say why it could be important (15 words or less) on one large Post-it type sticky note or similar. Take your three notes to the Step One Workshop.

3. If you wish, you can add additional theoretical perspectives, such as recent books and articles, to enrich your analysis.

Time Required

About 4 hours for the pre-work and 2 hours and 15 minutes for the workshop.

The Pre-Work for Step One

As you read the nine studies you will gain insights from the work of academics, managers, consultants, researchers and organisational development interventionists who have contributed to the development of a reservoir of constructs, tools, diagnostics and case-studies about requisitely agile organisations. These studies illustrate phases of evolution and revolution in ways of thinking about organisational agility and will assist you to understand the managerial challenges of acquiring requisite organisational agility. Each study provided valuable new insights. Later, it will be helpful if you extend your understanding by keeping up to date with newly published practitioner and academic literature.

A word of caution is needed. Requisite agility is not yet a coherent body of work. Maybe it never will be! Currently, it is sufficiently mature to provide a foundation for policy making but you should be open to future conceptual developments.

Study One: The Iacocca Report

Organisational agility only became a widely discussed managerial topic in the early 1990s. It was then that a influential report was published that many managers viewed as a nightmarish wakeup call (Nagel & Dove, 1991). America's corporate chiefs had contributed to a study that concluded Western industry had fallen far behind its Asian rivals and was at risk of being rendered redundant. The study was undertaken in the Iacocca Institute at Lehigh University, Pennsylvania.

The motive to undertake the Iacocca study was a major strategy review completed by the US military, that included a list of possible future conflict scenarios. More than 20 were described. Military planners assessed whether US forces could prevail in each scenario but, time and time again, the same weakness was identified. It was that the US military could not depend on America's industrial complex to provide the necessary back-up. The military analysts found many weaknesses, including slow responsiveness, a lack of flexibility, weak capacity to reconfigure resources, ineffective project-based management and an inability to undertake short-cycle innovation. They concluded that these inadequacies in American industry undermined the strength of the entire US military.

In 1991 an initiative was taken. The powerful Secretary of Defense Manufacturing Technology provided funds to form an industry consortium to look for ways to remedy the host of profound weaknesses in American productivity. This was a good time to act. Many senior executives in US enterprises had recognised the enormity of the problem but they did not see a solution. For as long as anyone could remember, the United States had been a manufacturing superpower but, by the 1980s, foreign competitors, especially Japanese, were offering better products at lower prices in many sectors.

Top managers from leading US companies, including General Motors, Boeing and AT&T, were eager to become deeply involved in what became known as the Iacocca Institute Industry Consortium. A high-powered temporary organisation was created and there was great dedication to their mission. The industry consortium was well resourced with access to high-level academic guidance. A core team of executives was seconded from 13 major companies and about 100 senior executives provided additional specialist input. They worked close to the dying Bethlehem Steel Plant, once a symbol of US manufacturing excellence, and this heightened the urgency of their task. The study was completed within six months and a two-volume report entitled the 21st Century Manufacturing Enterprise Strategy was produced (we will refer to this as the Iacocca Report).

The report presented a comprehensive critique of generic industrial weaknesses in the Western world and introduced the Agile Paradigm as the remedy to reverse the systemic decline of Western industries. It was argued that increased agility would be essential if US industry was to be saved. The report concluded that Western methods of managing were markedly inferior, especially in manufacturing industries, meaning that minor improvements would not be sufficient. Fundamental change was required if competitive advantage was to be regained.

The Iacocca Report stated that Western organisations had replaced a vibrant, entrepreneurial, aggressive and self-confident stance, a characteristic of those who had initiated the industrial revolution, for a commitment to order, hierarchy, efficiency, economy and risk-avoidance. These latter qualities had served well when substantial economies of scale could be achieved in manufacturing and rivals had nothing better to offer. But now, the report asserted, these organising principles were an industrial cul-de-sac from which more of the same would not provide an escape route. Three interdependent sets of changes were essential: one marketing-orientated, the second organisationally orientated and the third industry network-orientated.

From a marketing perspective, the report stated that companies would only regain sustainable competitive advantage if they met the specific requirements of micro-market segments with high-quality products that could be extensively customised and would provide long-term benefits. For example, using this logic, a bicycle manufacturer that mass-produced a standard range would be outclassed by a company that could rapidly configure tailor-made bicycles manufactured for each specific customer's body shape and personal cycling interests.

Profound changes in organisational design would be needed for companies to deliver such micro-market segment-specific offers. Production systems would need to be highly flexible and responsive without adding greatly to the cost base of the company. This would require organisations characterised by effective inter-disciplinary project teams, extensive use of scientific knowledge, modular production processes, the ability to provide information directly to production machinery and the adoption of socially responsible values. Such changes would require fundamental revisions of policies and practices in enterprises that had previously designed their production systems to be efficient machine bureaucracies, where workers' tasks were predetermined, controlled, simplified and repetitive. Agility would require an intelligent organisation that was capable of rapidly, reliably and cost-effectively exploiting selective opportunities that could not always be foreseen.

The Iacocca Report made another provocative assertion. It recommended that head-to-head competition between companies could be destructive and needed to be replaced by inter-organisational networking, meaning than companies should often collaborate rather than compete. This construct conflicted with the dominant view that companies only thrived when they succeeded in outperforming their rivals. Rather, it was argued, there were areas in which it was beneficial to cooperate (the term 'coopetition' is often used to describe this stratagem). The report suggested that coopetition could, and should, be practiced widely to enable organisations to be frequently reconfigured to meet short-term requirements.

These interdependent attributes—intense market customisation, intelligent and adaptable organisational designs and beneficial inter-organisational networking—became the first modern definition of the Agile Paradigm (the final report contained a cartoon that showed future leaders entering a door with a sign above that read 'Abandon Old Paradigms All Ye Who Enter Here!').

Not all the findings of the Iacocca study have stood the test of time. The report was partly wrong when it claimed that mass manufacturing organisations were no longer fit-for-purpose. We use mass-produced items every time we travel to work, clean our teeth or shop in a supermarket. However, many manufacturing organisations have found that mass-customisation, a valuable hybrid, is a viable business model. Later, many organisations exploited aspects of the visionary business models suggested in the Iacocca study, especially online platforms that have been highly creative in cutting fixed costs, gaining advantages from scale, providing user-specific services and involving customers in new product development.

We no longer believe that the form of agility described in the Iacocca study is the only available prescription for achieving lasting competitive advantage, although it has yielded highly beneficial breakthroughs in industries as dissimilar as dog food and pharmaceuticals. Neither has it been proven that adopting a strategy of wholesale commoditisation, facilitated by extensive inter-firm cooperation, is a reliable route to achieving national competitive advantage, as a one-size-fits-all prescription tends to freeze industries rather than encourage dynamic adaptation.

Nevertheless, the legacy of the Iacocca Report has been profound. It made an enduring contribution to agility theory by focusing on the future, asking the question 'what will be a winning formula for organisations like ours in ten- and twenty-years' time?' This laid the foundation for seeing future readying as one of the high-level deliverables required from organisational agility.

In Conclusion

The Iacocca Report had a catalytic effect on manufacturing businesses. No longer could they adopt the mass production paradigm as their sole guiding framework. From the early 1990s those constructing manufacturing systems began building agile capabilities into their designs. This trend accelerated as robotic and smart systems became available in the early 21st century and continues to develop as robotic machines become more capable and less expensive. Many enterprises became more situationally aware as they recognised that they could only succeed if they were equal to international best practice. Of great importance was the recognition that global supply chains could be developed to provide agility at low cost (with the emergent China spear-heading the development of a mindset that production could become a plug-and-play resource that could be quickly reconfigured as requirements changed). Lastly, the Agile Paradigm, promoted by the influential Agility

Forum that emerged from the Iacocca study, became a talking point around the world. Agility became a hot managerial topic.

Study Two: The Power of Lean

Shortly after the Iacocca study was completed, a quite different analysis of the causes of decline in Western manufacturing industries was published (Womack & Jones, 1996). This emphasised the importance of deeply embedding continuous improvement and effective processes into production systems, described as lean manufacturing.

It was in the late 1980s that a team of academic researchers, based at the Massachusetts Institute of Technology (MIT) compared Toyota's methods for automobile manufacturing with those of its American and European rivals. Their analysis caused deep anxiety for many Western managers, not only those working in the automobile industry. It became apparent that Western manufacturing industry was lagging far behind Japanese producers in production management concepts, competitive strategies, process innovation, human resource management and managerial practice: in fact, almost everywhere!

MIT's researchers found that Japanese carmakers, especially Toyota, had developed techniques of scientific analysis to study every dimension of production processes in great detail. Their conceptual rigour enabled Toyota's production engineers to assess the relative efficiency and effectiveness of processes in much greater depth that had been previously possible. From this, and the intentional use of the experimental method, a practice of focused continuous improvement was developed that could be adopted by every worker. Toyota's managers, and their shop-floor workers, had learnt to be proactive, to make evidence-based decisions and become skilled in effective problem-solving.

It was Toyota's breadth, depth and systemic perspective that was impactful. Not only did their production operations flow efficiently, equally rigorous study had been applied to supply and distribution chains, resulting in countless efficiencies. The MIT study concluded that Toyota had achieved mastery of a broad set of industrial capabilities through inspired leadership, years of structured experiments, highly effective process innovation and the development of coherent conceptual frameworks.

As it happens, I was working in the Far East at that time and I received an invitation to visit Toyota whilst I was in Japan. I was told that, "you can see everything that we do in Toyota. We will not hide anything. We know that should anyone decide to try to copy our system by the time that they have reached our level, we will have moved on to another stage!"

Toyota's production system was people-centred but deeply disciplined. It emphasised the importance of developing positive behaviours by clearly defining the roles of leaders, conducting extensive team-building sessions, reinforcing a culture of confronting problems with forensic commitment and striving to eliminate every non-productive activity or cost. Toyota used social engineering methodologies much more extensively than many Western organisations.

It was an MIT researcher, John Krafcik, who described the Toyota production system as being 'lean'. This became the name used to define a nest of methodologies that has transformed many manufacturing and process companies, and not-for-profit organisations, in recent decades. Applying lean methods has enabled organisations to remove much of the waste inherent in the previously dominant Fordist manufacturing model, especially a need for expensive inventory. It was found that a lean manufacturing model is inherently flexible and responsive to customers' needs, so it provides agile capability.

Although overlapping, agile and lean had a different emphasis. Using the definition of agility suggested by the Iacocca study team, an agile organisation gains advantage from being more able to exploit promising opportunities that have been created by changing market requirements. A lean organisation optimises the utilisation of resources, not just those who it owns but in its wider ecosystem, especially in its supply chain. The driving force of lean is finding ways to get difficult things done efficiently and effectively.

In the 1990s lean methods had an advantage that the Iacocca study lacked. Lean had been proven to be remarkably effective, as it had been 'battle-tested'. Moreover, there was evidence that versions of lean manufacturing could be successfully adopted in the West. For example, in 1984, Nissan opened a plant north of the UK, adopting a variant of lean production, and it quickly developed a reputation as being one of the most productive car plants in Europe. Lean was not, as some had claimed, only a workable business model in Japan.

The Iacocca Report was visionary, not an already proven formula for success. This had advantages, as it offered a new market-driven paradigm but had the disadvantage that it was speculative. As managers absorbed these two influential studies, they found a synthesis could be created that many called 'leagility' (Naylor, Naim, & Berry, 1999). This dominated much of production management thinking for many years and, more recently, has absorbed robotics and artificial intelligence constructs.

Since the MIT study was published many kinds of organisations have sought to transform themselves into lean enterprises. From their experience there are four important insights that have enriched our understanding of organisational agility.

First, in order to become lean, an organisation requires inner-directed agility, meaning that agile capabilities are targeted on improving organisational processes. After all, Toyota's production engineers were supremely agile as they sought to perfect production systems: they studied developments around the world, found promising opportunities, devised ways of avoiding or mitigating threats and took steps to enable their organisation to become better prepared to thrive in the future.

Second, lean provides agility through efficiency. Lean methods are most productive where repetitive tasks are undertaken. Lean emerged in an industry that was relatively stable. In most years the market for automotive products is predictable within definable limits. In this quasi-stable environment superior production methods based on lean provided order-winning efficiency, effectiveness and customer responsiveness. Improvements made in one year would be valuable for years to come.

Third, lean is not sufficiently dynamic for managing non-routinised activities, as Toyota itself demonstrated when it established a skunk works type organisational unit to design and build the world's first commercial hybrid electric vehicle. The Prius story demonstrated a quintessential need for an organic form of organisation in uncertain contexts. The story is important as it demonstrates that different types of agility have different functions. In the early 1990s Toyota's Chairman, Eiji Toyoda, had argued that it would be necessary to redesign cars for the 21st century, as environmental considerations would render the current designs obsolete. A decision was taken to make a Toyota hybrid car and a project team established with the code name G21. The first team leader was Takeshi Uchiyamada and the approach he took provoked a revolution in Toyota's development methods, including the formation of a co-located Vehicle Development Centre with a core team of ten outstanding young engineers. A new management process facilitated joint problem-solving with a dedicated physical space (obeya, or 'big room') where team members met daily. Toyota replaced its standard command-and-control managerial policy with open-access that enabled the best minds in the company to provide input on key issues. The Prius vehicle was successfully launched a year ahead of plan, and placed Toyota as a leader in electrically powered vehicles.

Fourth, being agile needs resources that being lean can provide. Organisations that master lean often enjoy superior profit margins. This means that they acquire sufficient resources to create new opportunities, not simply reacting to them when they appear. Toyota could afford to invest in large-scale innovation initiatives and the development of new technologies that were required for the next generation of automobiles as it was making reliable vehicles with order-winning features and making a substantial profit margin on each one. In effect, the lean part of Toyota's business was funding externally focused agile initiatives that served to future-proof the company. Some forms of agility require taking bets that organisations without investment funds find difficult or impossible to undertake. Being lean can generate the resources to fund speculative agility.

In Conclusion

Agile and lean mindsets are equally necessary. In 2004 two insightful scholars, Charles O'Reilly III and Michael Tushman, published a paper on the critical need for managers to master this duality (O'Reilly III & Tushman, 2004). When this was achieved an organisation would be truly 'ambidextrous', meaning capable of both exploiting and exploring.

Today, lean thinking has spread widely. It continues to provide an effective philosophy and discipline for improvement, but it does not focus sufficiently on innovation. Lean exploits left brain thinking using rational analysis and innovation does the same for the right brain, using synthesis and intuition. In an agile enterprise, both are required.

Study Three: Enterprise-Wide Agility

The Iacocca and MIT studies focused on manufacturing agility, but there was increasing evidence that entire organisations could become agile. During the 1990s several long-established organisations undertook major transformation programmes to acquire systemic agility and their experience enabled agility to be redefined as organisation-wide capability. This changed our understanding. In the early 1990s many considered that agility was a new manufacturing-specific business excellence model. A decade later, agility was being viewed as an essential characteristic for an organisation that operated in a dynamic environment.

That entire organisations can be agile is an age-old construct. However, its importance had been lost in the decades that followed the end of World War II, as a widespread shortage of manufactured goods meant that efficient producers were those who were successful. In many industries, agility was low on the list of priorities for achieving competitive or comparative advantage.

There are countless historic examples of past agile enterprises. For example, the Carthaginian general, Hannibal Barca (Gabriel, 2011), crossed the Alps with 30,000 soldiers, 9,000 cavalry and a herd of elephants. Recent research has shown that journey was more remarkable than had previously been believed, as evidence has been found that Hannibal chose a particularly difficult route along narrow paths to make a bold attack at the heart of the Roman Empire. More recently, the same kind of agility was shown by teams of code breakers who invented new technologies to enable enemy messages to be deciphered during the Second World War in the UK's Bletchley Park (M. Smith, 1998). Studying such organisations provides revealing insights into the nature of agile organisations.

A key finding is that organisations can be deliberately organised to be requisitely agile. Bold leadership is necessary to drive agility but this not sufficient. Cutting-edge expertise is needed. For example, the Erie Canal is a pioneering 363-mile (584 km) waterway built from the Great Lakes to the Hudson River in the United States in the 1820s (Bernstein, 2010). Senior engineers knew that they lacked the expertise for this major civil engineering task and deliberately sought to increase their knowledge base, sending an engineer named Canvass White to England to study canals and locks, as, at that time, the UK was the world leader in canal construction. White returned with detailed instructions for building locks, cuttings and bridges. This knowledge proved to be invaluable, as it enabled opportunities to be grasped efficiently and effectively.

The builders of the Erie Canal knew that many difficulties would need to be overcome to construct this canal, so local agility would be needed. Their organisational solution was to appoint assistant engineers, each responsible for a separate section. The assistant engineers were carefully chosen to be both knowledgeable and proactive and they would do whatever was required to solve problems. They did! Many local innovations took place including the invention of new processes, including one that enabled six men to remove 40 tree stumps in a day rather than one or two stumps that had been possible previously. The building of the Erie Canal demonstrated that systemic agility requires collective learning and can be facilitated by delegating decision-making authority to willing and able local teams.

Perhaps the world's most complex and agile organisation is the US National Aeronautics and Space Administration (NASA). They have been proactive in developing agility and pioneered many advances in complex-system, technology-based, organisational capabilities. Fortunately for us, NASA employed sociologists to study the development of an organisation that had no option but to be agile on a grand scale (Crawley & Kloman, 1972). Studies demonstrated that fluid networks of complex and capable organisations, aligned by a coherent goal statement, and supported by adequate resources, could achieve tasks that stretched beyond current human knowledge. A core dimension of NASA's identity during its preparation for the first moon landing was possessing an Agility Ambition, that they defined as being driven by an 'adventuresome spirit'. This drove a willingness to do whatever it took to overcome challenges, including constructing an organisation that was inherently adaptive, sometimes described as an adhocracy, meaning that it focused on what is right for the moment but may change soon. In preparation for the first moon landing NASA reorganised itself 11 times in eight years.

In order to understand more about agility-orientated organisational development journeys, we will briefly examine four cases of organisations that tried to reinvent themselves as agile enterprises. I personally investigated two of these case studies, the NYPD and Meubles De Chambre Innovante, and IBM and Google have been studied from published materials. These cases were selected as each contributed distinctive insights into the challenge of achieving enterprise-level requisite agility.

The New York Police Department

In the early 1990s crime was spiralling out of control across New York. It was the job of the NYPD to control the situation, but many senior officers had adopted the view that endemic criminality could never be defeated and the best that could be done would be to mitigate the worst effects of crime. In 1994 William J. Bratton became the new chief of police in the NYPD. He refused to accept this defeatist stance, holding that the police in New York could not stop criminals from committing felonies but they could prevent criminals from profiting from their actions. Moreover, Bratton emphasised that all crimes, including not paying a fare on a bus, must be seen by the NYPD as intolerable. He set the NYPD the mission of dramatically reducing crime, disorder and fear (Bratton & Knobler, 1998).

Bratton re-engineered the NYPD so that it could exploit promising opportunities, avoid or mitigate threats and become better prepared to thrive in the future. He empowered the commanders of districts and constructed a state-of-the-art war room where moment-by-moment tactics were planned. Specialist units were formed to address the root causes of crime, and teams of advisers from business schools and top corporations provided the NYPD with insight into state-of-the-art technologies. Bratton won the support of the mayor to increase the NYPD's budget by providing proof of the effectiveness of his police reforms, thereby ensuring that the organisation had sustainable viability.

Between 1994 and 1996 the murder rate in New York fell by 39.7%. Bratton had demonstrated that not-for-profit organisations could adopt many of the characteristics of the Agile Paradigm. The breadth and depth of organisational transformation in the NYPD illustrated the critical importance of leadership and the need to drive relentlessly towards a clear, stretching and well-communicated ambition statement. The NYPD case demonstrates that agile organisations are energised by releasing latent human potential, but only where this can be aligned with the overall mission. An organisational personality is needed that is confident, intelligent, proactive, purposeful, flexible, outward-looking and demanding. Moreover, they need to be good places to work as able and talented people must feel respected and rewarded.

IBM

That developing requisite agility was a viable organisational development strategy was demonstrated when Lou Gerstner published his book *Who Says Elephants Can't Dance? Inside IBM's Historic Turnaround* (Gerstner Jr., 2002). Gerstner had become CEO of IBM in 1993 when this great company was technically almost bankrupt, and he taught it to become agile and regain profitability. Gerstner took many initiatives. In every part of IBM cumbersome bureaucratic structures were dismantled, innovation demanded, prices became competitive and, importantly, latent energies were channelled into proactively creating new opportunities (not only responding to opportunities that were already there).

Gerstner did something that many who had studied organisational agility thought was wrong. He centralised power and limited the discretion of divisional managers.

That agility could be promoted by the disempowerment of cadres of senior managers ran counter to a persuasive managerial ideology that held that good leaders must always serve those who they lead. Gerstner centralised IBM to drive the company through an arduous and, for some, unwelcome transition, as he knew that the host of multiple organisational rigidities that had accumulated over many years would never allow such a depth of change to come from the bottom up.

Gerstner integrated the company as he saw the future as going to market as 'One IBM', with a capability to meet the next generation of customers' Information Technology requirements from IBM's newly aligned and extensive resources. Smaller companies could not offer such a comprehensive service. It was a demanding strategy that could only be delivered if IBM was an innovation leader in many highly technical and integrated areas. Accordingly, it would not be sufficient for IBM to have alignment between divisions, research centres, LoBs teams, project managers and marketing/salespeople. These relationships had to be much closer. All of IBM's organisational units needed to be proactively cooperative in contributing to the construction of an integrated corporate capability. Reorganisation followed. Divisions were organised into groups and a Worldwide Management Council was formed to oversee the structure. New core values were driven into every part of IBM, including operating as an entrepreneurial organisation with a minimum of bureaucracy and maintaining a never-ending focus on productivity. Processes became globally consistent. Cross-divisional teams focused on discovering what the major corporations, who were IBM's key customers, needed from a world-class one-stop-shop technology company.

Gerstner's organisational development strategy demonstrated that decentralisation was not the only way to achieve requisite agility. Sometimes, agility could only be achieved by centralisation. Gerstner did not ask: 'how can IBM become agile?' but 'how can the right kind of agility help us to win?'

Google

The story of this remarkably agile company began in 1998 when Larry Page and Sergey Brin, who were PhD students at Stanford University, founded the Google Inc. (Schmidt, Rosenberg, & Eagle, 2015). Its first substantial asset was an efficient search engine that enabled users to increase the utility of the world wide web. Google was, from the beginning, a buccaneering engineering enterprise. After a few years a list of "Ten Things We Know to Be True" was written, that did much to define Google's distinctive organisational personality. Amongst this list were two points that defined Google's Agility Ambition. One was "our hope is to bring the power of Search to previously unexplored areas and to help people access and use even more of the everexpanding information in their lives" and "we're always looking for new places where we can make a difference. Ultimately, our constant dissatisfaction with the way that things are becomes the driving force behind everything that we do" ("Ten Things We Know to Be True," n.d.)

The list of "Ten Things We Know to Be True" demonstrated that Page and Brin had thought long and hard about what would be the distinctive personality of the company that they were creating. The distinctive essence of Google would be intentional, considered, coherent and scalable. Their Agility Ambition provided clarity about what the company would seek to contribute to the world and defines a stance towards working that we can describe as constructive discontent, meaning 'we are proud of what we have achieved but there is more to do'.

Analysing Google's sustained and phenomenal growth shows that agile-friendly leadership plays an especially important role in agile enterprises. In fact, all the agile organisations that I have investigated as a researcher over the past 25 years not only have core values that support requisite agility, but they also live these values.

There was nothing particularly unique about Google's early mission; other companies had also identified the importance of finding better ways for users to exploit the internet. Google dominated because there was another (implicit) core value, that we can define as 'Business Matters'. Had Google simply been an R&D intensive digital engineering research company it is unlikely that it would have achieved platform dominance.

Google took its organisational design from the bold, collegial, technically intensive and achievement-orientated sub-culture that pervades Silicon Valley. Their complex management model envelops employees' lives so that personal identities and professional work become interfused. People do not play a role in Google; they inhabit a role. This stretches our understanding of bureaucracy that, traditionally, required that a role holder adopts predetermined mindsets and behaviours. Such regimentation would be a damaging rigidity in Google. The company employs people who have high cognitive agility and a strong learning orientation. They avoid hiring prima donnas, as large tasks require multiple forms of cooperation and excessive individualism would be a blockage, as it is a dysfunctional barrier to effectiveness.

Google has a deep and well-resourced commitment to large-scale radical innovation. Google did not see responsiveness as being sufficient. In order to achieve platform dominance, acting a fast follower would not enough. Google needed to create opportunities as its superiority lay in the capacity to change-the-game massively.

Strategically, Google was unconventional. It had more in common with the trading adventurers of the East India Company in the 17th century than with the efficient machine-like enterprises of 20th century corporate America. Conventional business processes include selecting target market segments, understanding industry attractiveness, studying rivals' offers and determining order winning and order qualifying criteria. This was not Google's only priority. They created markets rather than responding to them and sought global dominance by positioning themselves as free providers of widely used services like global maps and specialist databases. Their aim was for Google to become an invaluable partner in the lives of most people in the world.

The case of Google, and of companies such as Spotify, Netflix and Amazon, has improved our understanding of organisational agility. Almost unconsciously, scholars (me included!) had assumed that agility was a capability that organisations needed to acquire to enable them to survive and thrive in an increasingly demanding, and competitively aggressive, environment. The new generation of internet giants showed that a different logic was possible. Organisations could be established with a mission to create new opportunity spaces and have the twin aims of gaining a leadership position and finding ways to monetise at least some of their deliverables. To be a global leader in generic technological areas is expensive. Google needed to become so wealthy that it could afford to 'undertake speculative moon-shots'.

Not all of Google's ventures were successful, at least initially. Google X (now called X Company) was Google's semi-secret research and development facility with an almost unlimited budget. They developed Google Glass, a pair of spectacles with a tiny web-enabled computer and built-in screen that could search, take pictures and translate languages through eye movements, voice and gesture control. Google Glass became available in 2014 but was withdrawn two years later. This marketing failure was a business success, as Google learnt from the experience. Frontier-orientated agile organisations will take wicked problems, try to solve them and invest world-class talent to create different futures. These activities require taking big bets and some will fail. A risk-free regime is antithetical to frontier-level agility.

Meubles De Chambre Innovante

A company that I will call Meubles De Chambre Innovante (MDCI) undertook a journey towards enterprise-wide agility in 2018. Details of this case history have been disguised for reasons that will become apparent. It is a retail business that specialises in bedroom furniture and was the market leader in France in its category, with 327 stores across the country. A new chief executive had been appointed in 2017. She had read the Iacocca Report and believed that MDCI would benefit from adopting a version of the Agile Paradigm. Some months later, after she had visited many MDCI stores across the country she explained to her executive colleagues that the company currently offered the same bedroom furniture in central Paris, in suburban country towns and in exclusive resorts like Nice and Cannes. She pointed out that these places have very different populations. It was her opinion that each distinctive geographical areas needed to be treated as a separate micro-market segment so that people in each location could acquire bedrooms that they really want and can afford.

This strategy required major changes. MDCI's HQ building housed centralised departments like purchasing, marketing and human resource management. These functions were decentralised to eight new regional district offices. All 327 store managers attended management training courses to prepare them to take responsibility for selecting their own merchandise and managing local marketing. Previously merchandise had been purchased centrally and allocated to stores, with marketing being a HQ responsibility.

As power was devolved to store managers, they, helped by the regional teams, selected product ranges that they believed would be best suited to local market conditions. Many store managers initially responded positively, feeling that they had been empowered. Stores became much more diverse. Many managers were initially adventurous, buying merchandise that they thought would differentiate their store from its standardised rivals.

However, it was not to last. Two years later the CEO was clearing her desk as she had been instructed to resign from the company. The regional offices had been closed and the discretion of store managers was greatly reduced. Centralisation was reintroduced. Why? MDCI's profitability had collapsed. Turnover was down, there were large quantities of unsold merchandise in stores and costs had increased dramatically. A new CEO was then appointed. She returned the business to the previous standardised business model, allowing only a limited variety of range customisation for different categories of stores, and slowly the company regained profitability.

It was not only the increased costs of regional offices and unwise purchasing decisions by local store managers that had rendered MDCI's agile strategy unsustainable. There were a host of other difficulties. For example, the company's brand image had become confused; the complexity of its operations increased; quality control weakened; many store managers complained that they were not trained as entrepreneurs and felt over-stressed; experienced managers left the company and new generations of products became available from rivals but were not selected by the company's store managers, so increasingly competitive advantage was lost.

MDCI's experience in failing to implement the Agile Paradigm is revealing, as it helps us to understand the preconditions for achieving requisite agility. There were three sets of insights that add to our understanding of specific managerial challenges.

First, the Agile Paradigm, as described in the Iacocca Report, is suited to some business models but not to others. Deciding to offer customised products to individual customers, or to micro-market segments, should be viewed as a possible competitive strategy, not as a fool-proof solution to providing customer value in every situation. It is the customer who defines what 'value' means, and customers vary greatly. This is true for both external and internal customers.

Second: decentralising decision-making has the merit that managers who are close to customers are, arguably, better able to determine the specific needs of local customers. If managers are given the power to determine local strategies, then this may enable micro-segment strategies to be deployed effectively. In the case of MDCI this assumption, made by the CEO, was incorrect. When MDCI had been centralised the corporate marketing department possessed the professional skills to define patterns of customer value preferences and they would compare regional differences. After marketing decisions were decentralised, managers without marketing skills took key decisions based on inadequate local knowledge and without understanding fully the cost implications. We learn from this experience that that decentralising decision-making can reduce requisite agility and be dysfunctional, especially if decisions are to be taken by people who are ill-prepared for the responsibility or when devolved decision-making undermines organisational coherence.

Third: MDCI were ill-prepared for the transition to become an agile enterprise. When compared to the NYPD, it is obvious that the quantity and quality of their preparation was weak. For example, when I visited the NYPD in the 1990s I was told that: "we've completely re-staffed the top echelon by bringing in super chiefs who see the need for change" and "we have built a Command and Control Centre, a hi-tech facility modelled on the war room at the Pentagon." These are just two of the many resources that the NYPD had acquired that can be described as providing dynamic capabilities. The MDCI case teaches us that without the acquisition of mission-critical bundles of key dynamic capabilities, an agility-orientated strategy can fail, perhaps performing less well than the previous organisational model. The construct of dynamic capabilities has enhanced our understanding of the managerial challenges of being agile and will be discussed in the next section.

In Conclusion

These case examples demonstrate that enterprises can be created to be agile or, if leadership is agile-friendly and intensive organisational development takes place, then already established enterprises can acquire requisite agility. But becoming agile is neither easy nor risk free. Of particular importance is deciding where power lies. For the NYPD it was the district commanders and top HQ managers, perhaps 90 in total, that provided direction, coordination, and determined cultural values. For a period of time at IBM, the CEO was the single force driving the company to become an agile enterprise. Google gained its agility through its leaders' values and the acquisition of a vast proactive talent pool of world-class technical specialists who become intrapreneurs and entrepreneurs. MDCI failed to become an agile enterprise as it selected a micro-market orientated customer intimacy strategy without testing whether the inevitable increases in cost would be more than repaid by increased profit margins and it failed to develop the required dynamic capabilities. The conclusion? There is no one-size-fits-all solution.

Study Four: Dynamic Capabilities

In 1994 an academic paper was published that students of agility could not ignore. The authors, David Teece and Gary Pisano, (Teece & Pisano, 1994) had investigated how high-tech companies succeeded and they found that they possessed dynamic capabilities that provided competitive advantage in changing environments. This proved to be a missing link in our understanding of the managerial challenges in implementing requisite agility. It was, Teece and Pisano asserted, the possession, deployment and integration of dynamic capabilities that enabled companies to be proactively responsive, undertake rapid and flexible innovation, and realign internal and external resources to deal constructively with change.

Since the first paper was published, Teece, with different co-authors, has extended the analysis of dynamic capabilities by describing three primary clusters; specifically (i) those concerned with sensing opportunities and threats; (ii) those that enable seizing advantage from exploiting opportunities and (iii) those focused on transforming possibilities into value. Dynamic capabilities, it is argued, are supplemented by 'ordinary' capabilities, as it is these that enable an organisation to conduct business-as-usual tasks efficiently.

Although is not always easy to decide what is (or is not) a dynamic capability or assess how essential it is, the construct of dynamic capabilities has important implications for managers. No generalised guidance can be given, as there are differences between industries and individual organisations have their own strategic ambitions. So managers will need to decide what dynamic capabilities their own organisation should acquire, develop or improve so as to become engines of requisite agility. In addition, ways are needed to assess whether the dynamic capabilities that are possessed are used effectively and are adding value faster than cost.

Viewing dynamic capabilities from the organisational development perspective that is used in this book provides three frameworks that assist managers to use the construct for advantage. We will describe these as the Double Layer Dynamic Capabilities Model, Functional Dynamic Capabilities and the Dynamic Capabilities Deficit. These frameworks are explained below.

The Double Layer Dynamic Capabilities Model

The Double Layer Dynamic Capabilities Model emerged from a study of the KAO company in Japan. Despite intense competition from world-class companies like Proctor & Gamble, the KAO company has thrived for decades as it is a quintessentially agile enterprise. KAO is a chemical company that was ranked ninth by Nikkei Business in the list of excellent companies in Japan and third in terms of corporate originality. Input for the development of the Double Layer Dynamic Capabilities Model includes a case study written by Sumantra Ghoshal and Charlotte Butler (Ghoshal & Butler, 1992) and a personal visit to KAO in Japan by the author.

KAO has been highly creative in defining the optimal relationships between different types of capability and showing how these need to interact to become dynamic capabilities. The types of capabilities can be divided into two layers: institutional and task specific.

The *institutional layer* relates to the organisation as a whole and can be described as systemic capability. KAO's corporate philosophy, organisational design and management practices are based on Buddhist principles and they promote equality, emphasise the need for individuals to take initiatives in the interest of the company and facilitate the proactive sharing of information and ideas. For example, in Kao's R&D function there is a core value that everyone will cooperate in a continuous effort to deepen learning about all matters that could strengthen the company. Top management and researchers meet in monthly R&D meetings and open space gatherings are organised weekly, so that people from any part of KAO can become involved in research and development initiatives. There is a drive to transform individual wisdom into collective insight, so that a common perspective will be developed as multiple inputs are synthesised into a mature viewpoint. A person-centred culture underpins KAO's organisational structures, strategies, processes, initiatives and ambitions. It is indivisible nexus of values, cultural memes and social processes that provides the first layer of dynamic capabilities of this remarkable company.

The *task-specific layer* relates to technological and knowledge assets that are specific to the different industries and markets within which KAO competes. In order to feed a flow of innovations KAO needs to frequently upgrade its knowledge and technological assets. KAO's R&D department constructed a map showing how basic sciences, core-technologies, product-specific techniques, and managerial and social sciences underpinned product categories like cosmetics, skin care and household cleaning. Knowledge assets were aligned by contributing to KAO's core values (you can find an up-to-date version of this map on KAO's website). The map ("Kao: R&D Philosophy," 2020) enables managers and technical specialists to identify where required knowledge and technology assets were strong, weak or absent. From later investigations it has been found that knowledge and technology assets vary greatly between industries and each company, or not-for-profit organisation, can require a different configuration.

Functional Dynamic Capabilities

Conceptualising Dynamic Capabilities as functions uses a sociological perspective known as structural functionalism. Put simply, structural functionalism provides a way to assess how the components of a social system contribute to the maintenance of the whole. Sociologists ask: 'what is the function (i.e., the contribution) of this structural feature to the robustness of the entire social system?' This perspective is no longer considered to be adequate for examining societies but structural functionalism continues to be uniquely valuable in organisational sociology (Potts, Vella, Dale, & Sipe, 2016). An example helps to explain the structural functional perspective. One of NASA's values is integrity, which requires honesty, a commitment to ethical behaviour and candour, meaning that people can say what they believe without fear of being punished. A sociologist using the structural functional per-spective will ask the question: 'how does the adoption of the value of Integrity ben-efit NASA? Or, to put it another way, what are the functions of the integrity value for NASA?' The answer is that one of the functions that the integrity value provides is that errors are less likely to occur as anyone who suspects that something is wrong, no matter how junior he or she is in the organisation, will voice their con-cerns without fearing diapproval. This reduces the chances that known errors will not be addressed and functions to facilitate NASA in maintaining its status as a high reliability organisation.

One way to identify what functional dynamic capabilities are needed is to an-swer the question 'what do we need to be good at doing to be better than everyone else in doing these specific things?' If this question can be answered comprehen-sively then required functional dynamic capabilities can be identified. Another rele-vant question is: 'what would we need to do to reduce our ability to be better than everyone else in doing X?' When this question is answered then dysfunctional capa-bilities will be identified.

Dynamic Capability Deficit

Identifying a Dynamic Capability Deficit provides a managerial tool for identifying were needed dynamic capabilities are absent. There are three steps. The first asks 'do we have a comprehensive list of all of the dynamic capabilities that are required to do a great job?' The second step examines degree of readiness of our organisational capabilities to meet requirements. Our suggested criteria are (i) willingness (W), (ii) ability (A) and (iii) intention (I). These criteria can be assessed as being either 'low' or 'high'. The last step answers the question 'who is responsible for overcoming our Dynamic Capability Deficit?'

In Conclusion

The construct of dynamic capabilities rapidly became a topic of great academic interest. There have been numerous research investigations so, over time, we have become clearer about what dynamic capabilities are, and what they are not. For example, important insights were provided by Kathleen Eisenhardt and Jeffrey Martin in their paper published in 2000 (Eisenhardt & Martin, 2000) that included that:

- Bundles of dynamic capabilities include product development, forming alli-ances and other inter-organisational arrangements, timely reconfiguration of resources, co-evolving, patching (reorganising business units), strategic deci-sion-making and shedding assets that are no longer useful.

- Similar organisations need to have comparable dynamic capabilities, so it is possible to identify entry-level dynamic competencies that, if absent, result in the organisation being unable to achieve competitive or comparative parity.
- Patterns of required dynamic capabilities will vary according to the speed of industry and market changes. In relatively stable environments dynamic capabilities can be codified and routinised. In rapidly changing environments dynamic capabilities must be organic, as described in the Lean Startup approach (Blank, 2013).
- Temporary patterns of dynamic capabilities may be needed, for example, to take advantage of short-term opportunities.
- Dynamic capabilities can be developed from being non-existent through to best-in-class, although we do not have a way of assessing the maturity of dynamic capabilities objectively.

Study Five: CENTRIM's Agility Research Programme

The Centre for Research in Change Management, Entrepreneurship and Innovation Management, or CENTRIM, is part of the Brighton Business School and located on the south coast of the UK. CENTRIM was one of the first research groups in Europe to be established with a dedicated mission to study the management of innovation. Recently, CENTRIM has broadened its research scope, embracing entrepreneurship and change management. The interdependencies between these three areas of academic research provide a valuable intellectual framework for understanding the managerial challenges of organisations seeking to acquire requisite organisational agility.

In 1997 CENTRIM received funding from the UK's Engineering and Physical Sciences Research Council to undertake a two-year research programme that would investigate how managers could transform their organisation so that it would become a requisitely agile enterprise. We will refer to this research assignment as the Agile Management Research Programme (AMRP). An Agility Research Team (ART) was formed, led by Professor John Bessant, and I was the research team leader. The ART used action research methods to study how companies progressed on their individual journeys to adopt aspects of the Agile Paradigm. As far as we know, the ART's longitudinal investigation into the managerial challenges of adopting agility as a strategy is unique (Meredith & Francis, 2000).

Twelve medium-sized commercial companies became active members of the AMRP. They were diverse in markets and technologies, including one specialising in shop fitting, a manufacturer of lighting fixtures, a producer of automated medical equipment and a specialist Hi-Fi manufacturing company. Each case study company agreed to strive to adopt agile management policies and practices over an 18-month period. ART's researchers acted as facilitators, using a social science methodology known as Engaged Scholarship. The progress of each company was carefully studied to provide insights into the managerial challenges of becoming agile.

Shortly after the research programme started, an extended video film was taken of production processes in each case study company. The film included interviews with managers and shop-floor workers talking about the processes used in the company. Subsequently, ART's researchers introduced concepts about agile operations, undertook diagnostic surveys, observed management meetings, analysed workflows and led review workshops. They provided coaching to the senior managers in each company to assist them to adopt relevant aspects of the Agile Paradigm. Fifteen months later a second video film was made of the same processes that had been recorded previously. This enabled researchers to identify changes so that a longitudinal comparative analysis could be undertaken.

The ART found that managers invariably had very full agendas. For them, the key question was not: 'how can we become an agile enterprise?' But, 'how can we use this new managerial thinking to help us to improve?' After managers had been extensively briefed on the (then current) principles and practices of the Agile Paradigm, they viewed agility as a resource-bank of possible developmental initiatives, rather than a coherent discipline to be followed. This meant that each case study company undertook a different organisational development journey.

Agility was perceived by managers, rightly or wrongly, as aspirational and capable of being selectively adopted. Initially, the ART considered that this perspective underestimated the benefits of the Agile Paradigm but we came to realise that the managers were correct, as the context in which agility needed to be adopted was different for each enterprise. This insight led to the development of the requisite agility perspective that has been advocated throughout this book. Managers considered that it was vital for them to determine where agility was 'necessary or needed for a particular purpose' rather than 'it is a good thing to be agile'. Their perspective decoupled agility from being defined as a transformational industrial agenda into something that: 'we will implement because it will enable us to do the things that we want to do'.

The requirement for agility was not uniform within different sub-units of our case study companies, neither was it uniform over time or between the companies. This insight enabled the ART to understand the importance of enterprise-specific strategic choices in deciding 'where do we need agility?', 'what types of agility do we need?', 'how urgent and important is it?' and 'how can we gain the required level and type of agility in the most economical and effective ways?'

When the research investigation was complete, the ART identified seven findings that, at the time, advanced knowledge of the management of agility. The most successful case study companies adopted these principles:

Be Proactively Outward-Looking: Multiple external factors need to be tracked widely and deeply including competitors' strategies, technological developments, customers' needs and changes in the economic and market situation. Significant factors can occur anywhere; hence the need for wide scanning at all levels of the organisation, not only at the managerial level.

Take Advantage of Strengths: It is less costly, and less risky, to build on existing strengths than to enter unknown opportunity spaces. For example, one of the case study companies manufactured simulation display equipment for military use. They decided to supply similar products for the gaming and entertainment sectors. The technology was similar, but the customers were quite different, so new capabilities were required in marketing and sales but not in other parts of the value chain, thereby reducing risks and investment requirements.

Construct the Organisation for Flexibility: Managerial policies need to favour the acquisition of assets and systems that are inherently flexible and, if possible, have low exit costs. This applies to buildings, services, production layouts, technologies, IT, equipment, supply chains, human resources and control systems.

Don't Lose Quality in the Quest for Speed: Short-life cycles, demand for greater product variety and the narrowing of windows of market opportunity, means that fast new product or service development (or acquisition) is an important aspect of agility. But this should not be pursued at the expense of other key aspects of running a successful enterprise, like safety, evidence-gathering, adherence to ethical standards, financial stability and quality standards. Those case study companies that had sacrificed quality for speed found that their company's reputation suffered greatly.

Be Efficient to Provide Time to Be Agile: Being lean, reliable and capable reduces managers' workloads and provides time for the prudent exploitation of opportunities. Rapid problem-solving is an important driver of agility. If an organisation is slow in identifying and solving problems then its creative energies become absorbed by rectification and achieving minor improvements, rather than in seizing opportunities. Fast response to problems needs to become a way of life.

Multi-Skilled, Flexible People are Essential: Agile organisations are less dependent on systems, more dependent on the intelligence and opportunism of people. The capability, involvement, commitment and empowerment of people is mission-critical to agile operations. The full utilisation of people's skills, knowledge, judgement, experience and intelligence to their capacity is a powerful dynamic capability.

Be an Early Adopter of Technologies: Many technologies can facilitate agility. Agile enterprises need to embrace these early, even on an experimental scale, as this enhances collective learning and increases momentum for rethinking how to achieve requisite agility.

In Conclusion

CENTRIM's investigation was too limited in size and scope to provide definitive findings but follow-up studies have not fundamentally challenged the three main conclusions:

- Leading an agile enterprise is especially demanding for managers who sometimes will need to act as entrepreneurs and intrapreneurs. Some individuals relish this role, but others do not possess the motivation, willingness or ability to be sufficiently proactive (this finding will be discussed in the next section of this step). Agile enterprises must have people in the upper echelon who have strong entrepreneurial skills.

– Competence in managing current operations is a precondition for achieving requisite agility, as it reduces the burden on managers and, hopefully, provides flows of revenues that fund speculative initiatives. As ongoing problems in day-to-day operations become less demanding then managerial capacity is released, which enables agility-orientated initiatives to be undertaken.

– Becoming agile is a developmental journey that requires senior managers to work together to find ways to adapt agile management constructs for their own circumstances. Unlike other managerial methodologies, there is not a predetermined template defining what needs to be done. Rather agility is constantly defined and redefined over time.

Study Six: The Role of Agilepreneurs

CENTRIM's investigation, described in the previous section, found that those who act as leaders in agile organisations operate in somewhat different ways than those in non-agile organisations but the research team had not been able to collect sufficient data to analyse the nature of these differences.

Subsequently Dr Mike Woodcock and I built on the work of CENTRIM's AMRP by investigating the distinctive characteristics of agile leaders and managers, later publishing our findings in a book entitled *Developing Agile Organisations: Theory and Interventions* (Francis & Woodcock, 1999). Our data came from three sources. Biographical research provided insight into how leaders' mindsets facilitated agile-friendly behaviour. Data on agility facilitating processes came from observational studies of managers undertaking initiatives in organisations as diverse as Sun Microsystems, the London School of Hygiene and Tropical Medicine, Novo Nordisk (Denmark), Hong Kong's Mass Transit Railway and the International Fund for Agricultural Development in Vietnam. Lastly, the authors kept diaries of agile initiatives that they undertook personally. The framework presented below is not based on a statistically valid sample of informants, so should be viewed as hypothetical. It has, however, provided useful orienting concepts of the characteristics of a role that I will describe as agilepreneurship.

Agilepreneurs are the people in organisations that 'get things done, despite obstacles'. They are drive initiatives, often on a small scale but sometimes making a huge impact. They have developed their personal agency, so they are opinion leaders, activists, energisers and mobilisers of action. Their motto is 'can do, will do'.

Agilepreneurs have succeeded in synthesising strengths drawn from five different roles. Namely, those of the entrepreneur, intrapreneur, organisation builder, innovation manager and change maker. Agilepreneurs are not agility evangelists, as they know that other dimensions of management, like financial discipline, risk management, ethical governance and quality management, can be equally important. Rather agilepreneurs invest their energies on finding ways to exploit agility for advantage.

An agilepreneur uses her or his personal agency, business-sense and grit to (i) find and exploit promising opportunities (entrepreneurship); (ii) champion promising new initiatives (intrapreneurship); (iii) construct (often temporary) organisations to get new things done (organisation building); (iv) drive processes that gain advantage from ideas that are new to the unit of adoption (innovation management) and (v) shape people's mindsets and behaviours, so that organisational agility is widely perceived as being legitimate, desirable, achievable and becomes 'the way that we do things around here' (change maker).

The five dimensions of agilepreneurship are interdependent and blend into each other. During our observational studies several incidents were observed where an agilepreneur (i) detected an under-exploited opportunity that was external to his/her area of responsibility; (ii) formed an ad hoc group to focus collective energy on exploring the merits and demerits of the potential opportunity; (iii) worked with those who had power and influence in the organisation to make decision to proceed; (iv) incorporated new ideas into an action-plan and (v) embedded can-do, initiative-supporting cultural norms in relevant people and in the teams that drive progress.

Aligned agilepreneurship is a mission-critical asset in agile organisations for two main reasons. First, agilepreneurs add to an organisation's agile capability as they increase the quantity of agile initiatives that can be undertaken. Secondly, undertaking agile initiatives efficiently and effectively is often time-consuming, frustrating, inconvenient and characterised by setbacks. Focused dedication is required. The more talented agilepreneurs that are available, the more that can be achieved, but only if their energies are focused on contributing to the fulfilment of the organisation's Agility Ambition. Divergent agilepreneurship is often a dysfunctional force.

Agilepreneurship is a core capability of top executives in agile organisations, usually CEOs but sometimes other influential members of TMTs, as the cases of Google, IBM, Jardine Matheson and the NYPD have demonstrated. However, not all top managers need to have agilepreneurship mindsets and skills as checks and balances are needed to provide an environment within which the voice of prudence will be heard.

Agilepreneurs are future focused, dedicated to influencing decision-making and will be blockage removers. They know that agility requires flows of decisions that can never be entirely evidence-based. Judgements will be required, sometimes in real-time. Decisions that commit resources cannot be avoided, although it will often be possible to reduce exposure to risk. Over time the pattern of commitment decisions shapes the strategy and structure of the organisation.

Agilepreneurs take active steps to influence the organisation's psychological state, as people's emotions will either help or hinder the practice of agility. For example, a fear of failure can become a component of an organisation's personality and it will function as a hidden malevolent force that diminishes the capability to exploit agility for advantage. Agilepreneurs will take steps to reduce the factors that make people reluctant to change, such as countering pessimism that acts like a sheet anchor on a sailing boat, as it starves agility of the optimistic energy that it needs.

Unless machine intelligence can perform the role of an agilepreneur, as can happen in banking or military units, larger agile organisations have no option but to recruit, support and empower agilepreneurs for those parts of their organisation that require more radical types of agility. Agilepreneurship is not needed universally as other leadership and managerial capabilities, like ensuring conformance to standards, are needed in certain contexts. Agilepreneurship can be a team function as one team member may be strong in entrepreneurship but weaker as a change maker while a different team member has complementary attributes, meaning that the team as a whole becomes an agilepreneurial agent.

In the book *Developing Agile Organisations: Theory and Interventions* a seven-factor model of the competencies of agilepreneurs was provided. In the outline below, the original model has been revised.

Competency One: Active Searching (AS)

Agilepreneurs adopt a stance that can be summarised as: 'I am always looking for ways to move forward'. They are driven by a belief that opportunities are waiting to be discovered or can be developed. Opportunities may be latent, undeveloped or fragmented, so creative work will be needed before they can be evaluated. Frequently combinations of ideas must be integrated. Someone with a high AS competence sets time aside to search and is open to weak signals that indicate possible new avenues for enquiry. He or she will be curious, analytical and open minded in examining possibilities and avoid making early decisions to reject ideas.

Competency Two: Results Orientated (RO)

Agilepreneurs adopt a stance that can be summarised as: 'I want to be the person that puts us in a superior position'. They are achievement-oriented and competitive, taking energy from the act of winning. He or she wants to see results from their endeavours, for their own satisfaction and for the betterment of their organisation. They concentrate on gaining and protecting assets, advantages, improved positions and benefits. Their orientation is to optimise or exploit situations for advantage. Successful ROs are bold, cautious and prudent. But, once a decision is made, they will invest their energy and skill to overcome setbacks, maintain momentum and strive to achieve success.

Competency Three: Maintaining Self-Confidence (MSC)

Agilepreneurs adopt a stance that can be summarised as: 'I am the right person to get this done'. They are confident in their own efficacy, as they feel capable of getting things done, despite problems or difficulties. They are willing to lead but this will not be from a drive for control, as they possess sufficient self-confidence to take a follower role when it is logical so to do. Issues and conflicts will be confronted openly. They frequently seek input and support from others. There is an orientation towards being active. People with high MSC feel that they are strong but are constructively self-critical. They view themselves favourably, have high positive self-esteem and present themselves effectively.

Competency Four: Managing Organisational Processes (MOP)

Agilepreneurs adopt a stance that can be summarised as: 'I find and use resources to get things done'. They are skilled in managing processes and use effective and efficient ways to organise for different types of task. They bring people together, use technologies, set goals and build high performing task groups. In agile organisations this often requires the construction of temporary teams that are creative, skilled in situational analysis and capable of managing different forms of initiatives. People with high MOP are systematic, politically astute, skilled in organisational design and resilient.

Competency Five: Capturing Future Advantage (CFA)

Agilepreneurs adopt a stance that can be summarised as: 'I will enable us to be stronger in the future'. They have informed foresight and will have predictive capability, meaning that they take a long-term view and envision the potential benefits of adopting and developing selected opportunities. They know that risks will need to be evaluated and possible negative consequences reduced to the greatest extent possible. They recognise that the benefits of exploiting opportunities are rarely enjoyed immediately. Frequently, it takes time for advantages to be gained. Where the promise is strong, then long-term commitments will be made. People with high CFA are outward-looking, intellectually curious, seek diverse viewpoints, read widely and have considered world views.

Competency Six: Business Case Construction (BCC)

Agilepreneurs adopt a stance that can be summarised as: 'I increase the probability that good strategic decisions will be made'. They know that those who make strategic decisions, that require commitment and resources, will need to consider a comprehensive proposal, normally described as a business case. A strong business case is based on solid data and has explicit assumptions. The possible advantages of an investment are explained, with realistic forecasts about what success might provide. The business case will explore organisational and marketing implications, downsides, opportunity costs and ethical issues. Risk factors will be identified and assessed systematically. People with high BCC are data-based, methodical, cautiously optimistic, rational and pragmatic.

Competency Seven: Gaining Technology Advantage (GTA)

Agilepreneurs adopt a stance that can be summarised as: 'I use technologies to improve requisite agility'. They identify and acquire technological resources to supply information, clarity and analytical precision to decision-making processes. Machine intelligence is used to enhance requisite agility by enabling complexity to be managed. In the past, most of the functions of agilepreneurs were undertaken by people. Increasingly, technologies are playing a decisive role. Small enterprises use lower-cost technologies like web-search, blockchain, generic data analytics or scenario testing. Human service organisations, like public health schemes, gain from real-time modelling. Such technologies improve evidence-based decision-making and may be given independent decision-taking rights. As agile organisations thrive on information, agilepreneurship has become a socio-technical capability. People with high GTA are technically competent, systems-orientated and adopt design thinking frameworks.

In Conclusion

The skills of an agilepreneur are distinctive. He or she must be assertive, proactive and opportunistic. Rather than protect the status quo, an agilepreneur seeks improvement. In a sense, agilepreneurs need to have paradoxical qualities as they are both responsible role holders and entrepreneurs. Except in small enterprises those at the top of organisations cannot take the myriad of decisions needed, so initiative is required from all levels. In agile organisations managers are outgoing involved in 'the politics of creating our future' and ongoing learning has become a core-process. The development agenda is substantial, but it does provide the manager with new dignity in their increasingly central role.

Study Seven: Military Agility

Throughout history some military organisations became lead users of requisite agility, although they did not use this name. Other military organisations have been ossified, rigid, slow to change and outdated. Students of military history find that those with superior agility more often win wars (Tzu, 1981).

Military personnel must enter situations that are inherently complex, demanding, uncertain and dangerous. Often enemies will be resourceful, creative, bold and adopt new or unexpected tactics, each intended to weaken or destroy the opposition. Since the 1920s it has been widely recognised that armies, navies and air forces must be intentionally configured to possess agile capabilities for three main reasons. First, they are required to perform many varied tasks, like peace keeping, resolving conflicts large or small, disaster relief or ceremonial duties. Secondly, possessing agility has provided decisive advantages during combat, as opportunities occur without warning and need to be grasped quickly, wisely and boldly. Lastly, military technology is frequently cutting-edge, so units need to maximise the benefits from technological developments and find ways to counter threats from technological advances made by potential enemies.

Modern military forces see systemic agility as a core capability. A failure to be agile can be catastrophic. Situations that need military input can arise in minutes or hours. There can never be enough time to begin preparation once an alarm bell has sounded, so much must be planned in advance. Few other types of organisations have a greater need for requisite agility. It is not surprising that commanders and military instructors have invested substantial resources to learn how to embed agility successfully into organisations. This has intensified in recent decades as the nature of threats has changed dramatically and new technologies have emerged, such as cyber-warfare, that can be used to gain military advantage in previously unknown ways.

In military units, it has been found acquiring agility in turbulent times requires extensive organisational development. This is because agile military organisations require integrity, reliability and predictable performance. Military agility is not an alternative to disciplined management but a consequence of it.

The agility of military units is based on an extraordinary emphasis on learning, personal development and training. It has been recognised for many centuries (certainly since Roman times) that specific abilities, skills and knowledge need to be deeply embedded in each individual soldier. The breadth and depth of competencies developed in individuals provides a sound behavioural foundation for systemic organisation-wide agility.

Early in the 21st century, a major advance in the understanding of organisational agility came from a previously unexamined source. Military strategists, especially from NATO, published analyses of how the armed forces could acquire the capabilities required to deal effectively with new forms of threat. The military perspective on organisational agility has proved to be particularly informative as they invested substantial resources in developing concepts and undertook scientific experiments to determine which forms of agility were most effective in different scenarios, especially in evaluating the agility benefits of network-based organisations.

It is unusual for industry and not-for-profit organisations to draw examples from the armed services but, in this area, they are leaders. So, how do military organisations achieve and sustain a high degree of agility? Seven characteristics are significant:

- Information about situations is systematised, robust, fast and straightforward to use.
- All manner of potential problems will be simulated during training so that military personnel become experts in judgemental decision-making and finding optimal solutions.
- Those in command can form high-performing teams quickly and teams cooperate effectively together.
- When new situations occur practiced routines enable strategies, tactics and plans to be revised quickly.
- All work for a common cause, as units have a strong organisational personality.
- There is a can-do culture, meaning that opportunities will be identified and seized.
- Military training has gone beneath the level of skills to develop the character of each solder, meaning that people can rely on each other.

Three contributions from studies of military agility will be examined. The first is macro in scope, and concerns governance and organisation. The second is micro and enables us to examine how men and women are prepared to become agile military leaders. The third is managerial, as it provides a way of assessing whether an organisation has sufficient requisite agility, using an approach that is known as the METL.

Macro-Level Agility

Power to the Edge: Command, Control in the Information Age is the title of a very influential book (Alberts & Hayes, 2003). It was intended for military leaders but has far wider implications. This book, and subsequent studies, have increased our understanding of agility in three key areas: devolved decision-making, organisational design and interoperability.

Power to the Edge argued that digitally enabled forms of networking have fundamentally extended what we will call the agile envelope, meaning that military units can be more situationally responsive, prudently opportunistic and risk defensive than was ever possible before. This is because newly available technologies for communication, sharing and collective sensemaking do not simply facilitate existing constructs of military agility, they open new doors of possibility by enabling organisations to be more intelligent. This, of course, increases the importance of adopting agility as a core organising principle.

Military Decision-Making

Military decision-making used to be mainly centralised. Consider a platoon of 25 soldiers in active conflict. Historically, it would be the senior officers and staff members in Central Command that had the best available information about battlefield conditions. They took decisions that were passed to platoons as orders. This control method had two major benefits. Those making decisions had a battlefield-wide perspective, so could align resources behind a coherent strategy. Secondly, fast implementation of bold strategies was possible. However, there was a key disadvantage. Often decisions had to be made using fragmented information by people who did not fully understand local conditions, as information possessed by frontline soldiers could not be made available to decision-makers.

Information Age technologies enable platoon commanders and individual soldiers to contribute battlefield information in real-time. They can have equal access to situation reports. This enables a platoon, at the edge of the organisation, to be empowered to take autonomous evidence-based decisions, without reference to higher authority. This capability, if used prudently, increases military agility as decisions will be taken by people who know the reality of the local situation. It also helps those in Central Command, as they are less likely to be overloaded or required to take decisions from an inadequate understanding of the reality of the situation. *Power to the Edge* envisaged a military future where there is no distinction between line and support units. Information will be updated by those who know what is happening and soldiers can pull from an information cloud the data that they need to use devolved authority wisely, rather than following orders sent through formal communication channels. The term 'self-synchronisation' has been coined to describe this process. It was argued that self-synchronisation would enable Edge Organisations to benefit from the wisdom of the crowd and from peer-to-peer sharing, thereby democratising what military strategists describe as 'operational art'.

Military Organisational Design

Military planners know the importance of organisation. They analyse historic battles to understand what it took to win and discover why a force with superior resources can lose. The lessons learnt have shaped the design of military organisations through the ages.

The disintegration of the Soviet Union ended a relatively stable period for Western Armed Forces. It was replaced with a new 'workspace' that had VUCCA (volatile, uncertain, complex, chaotic and ambiguous) characteristics. This fundamental shift required that planners had to revise the principles of military organisation so that forces could deal with a wider range of threats, some of which could not be foreseen. It became clear that a military organisational design cannot be frozen, as organising needs to be an ongoing process in a VUCCA workspace. A variety of new organisational models were developed and their strengths and weaknesses evaluated in different scenarios. This knowledge enables commanders to select optimal organising principles that are contingent on the circumstances of the moment and the resources that are available. The question confronted constantly is: 'what is the best way to organise for current requirements?' This question needs to be answered at all levels, if an organisation is to acquire dynamic reorganising capability.

For senior officers the notion that organising needed to be proactively contingent provoked a dilemma. Command and control (C2) have long been core organising principles, as their absence has been shown to court disaster. If parts of a military organisation need to reorganise according to the immediate logic of the situation then, the question was asked 'how can C2 be maintained?

A multinational NATO team, with the code name SAS-085, did something that had not been undertaken previously. They conducted simulation experiments with live military personnel to acquire scientific data on which organisation design is effective in different workspaces (Alberts et al., 2014). Five NATO member nations (United States, Portugal, Canada, United Kingdom and Italy) participated in the Agility Campaign of Experimentation. The findings from these experiments are important and will be examined in some detail.

The Agility Campaign of Experimentation used realistic simulations of operations, such as transitions from major conflict to stability operations, peace-keeping operations and cyber warfare. Each scenario had different levels of complexity and unique mission objectives. As scenarios developed there were significant changes in complexity and other parameters. Four organisational models were tested. The least networked was stand alone, where each unit made its own decisions within the overall mission objectives; the de-conflicted model gave considerable autonomy but prevented conflicts between units; the coordinated model organised interacting activities and the coherent model fully enabled networking cooperation.

The experiments found that the level of complexity of the situation was the overarching determinate of which model of organisation would be most effective but, as time passed, and another phase of the scenario started, a different organisation model would often be more successful. There were two other important insights. The first was that network-based organisations required a hard-to-acquire deep level of interpersonal trust between agents. The second was that self-synchronisation was only effective when all involved understood, and adopted, an overall mission intent statement and they have the willingness and ability to fulfil the tasks required to achieve the specified mission.

The experiments demonstrated that organisational formats did not only need to be configured for the specific tasks being undertaken but optimal organisation would require that organisational designs needed to change dynamically as tasks were undertaken. This was a challenge to conventional thinking, as there had been a widespread practice of designing an organigram and seeing this as 'job done'. Agile organisations need much greater structural elasticity.

Interoperability

Interoperability means possessing the specialised capabilities that enable network-based organisations to work effectively. It is required at several levels in military organisations. For example, NATO counties, as different as the United States, Norway and Turkey, need to be capable of working together immediately in the confusion of conflict. Within each NATO country the air, land and sea services must be able to coordinate so they can launch effective joint operations.

Military organisations need extremely high levels of interoperability to achieve time-critical tasks, often in challenging situations. Networked entities need to be interoperable in information sharing and in what they describe as 'the cognitive domain' so that missions, priorities and ways of working are deeply aligned between partners. Systemic coherence or interoperability requires shared routines, common protocols, compatible technologies, aligned intellectual models and the so-called soft capabilities like openness, shared values and willingness to help each other.

Interoperability is an easy construct to explain but much managerial effort is needed to achieve it, especially when different forms of network-based organisation are required. Much depends on systems being seamlessly compatible. Therefore huge, complex and expensive war games are played. They act like rehearsals for a stage play, giving opportunities to test integration and enable the people concerned to get to know each other. With extensive simulations the capability for interoperability grows over time and provides an essential systemic alignment and coordination.

Military units have found that effectiveness in turbulent times requires more attention to structure, not less. Their experience and experiments demonstrate that agile organisations require integrity, reliability and a predictable quality of performance, otherwise they fail. Agility is not an easy-to-acquire organisational asset.

Socialisation, Character and Capability Development

Each year about 15,000 young people apply to be cadets in the US Military Academy at West Point. Fewer than 10% will be selected for a four-year programme that prepares them to become officers in the US military. There are four developmental themes at West Point, known as pillars, that are character, academic, military and physical. Of these, 'character development' and 'academic development' may seem, at first sight, to be something of a luxury.

Character development is mandatory, constant, tested and prescriptive. It requires that cadets internalise a set of values that include integrity, empathy, loyalty, respect, humility, duty, resilience and grit (persistence). Sociologists call this process 'socialisation' and West Point is explicit about its fundamental importance. They do not hide the requirement. Even dining etiquette is taught and required to be practiced. Graduates of West Point will have experienced a socialisation process that standardises what they value. The intent is to supply the armed services with leaders of character.

Academic development is intensive for all cadets as they must study for a Bachelor of Science degree. Only those with academic prowess will have been selected. The intention is for every cadet to develop a high-level capability for critical thinking and creative problem-solving. The curriculum includes liberal arts, engineering and experiential learning to facilitate the internalisation of a professional military identity.

West Point is not alone in its insistence that those who take decisions in the military will be 'leaders of character', with developed intellectual skills and accomplished proactivity. In the National Defence University of Malaysia those who wish to become officers must obtain black belts in the martial art of Taekwondo, as this enables them to develop an ability to control their emotions. In addition, Muslim male students are trained to become Imams so that they can facilitate the spiritual development of their soldiers. All cadets are encouraged to believe in God and practise good moral values.

Such extensive and deeply embedded intellectual and emotional standardisation provides an organisational capability for bold, intelligent and agile enterprises. Those who have experienced the same form of socialisation will have similar values, so they can be trusted to behave in predictable, helpful and responsible ways. This provides a foundation for systemic agility.

Key to the success of military units has been their extraordinary emphasis on the capabilities of decision-makers. Although the word intrapreneur is not used in a military context it is clear that military officers are expected to demonstrate internally orientated entrepreneurship. The breadth of competencies developed in individuals provides a sound behavioural foundation for a person to act as an agility champion. In a well-run military organisation decision-makers are capable, resilient, proactive and collaborative in predictable ways. This provides a capacity to do difficult, new and arduous things, despite difficulties that would overwhelm many of us.

Military psychologists have demonstrated the importance of specific personality attributes, especially a human quality that they call 'hardiness', which is closely connected to the quality of grit, discussed earlier. Those who are high in hardiness will be strongly committed to themselves and to others. They feel they can control or influence situations and desire to do this. Others see them as being confident. Tasks that are difficult or demanding will be energetically addressed. Hardy people are conscientious, persistent and will maintain an intelligent calmness in changing conditions. They accept that setbacks and problems are a normal part of life, but the impact can be minimised. We can describe them as agilepreneurs.

Hardiness and grit have been shown to be strong predictors of leader performance in circumstances that require agility (Von Culin, Tsukayama, & Duckworth, 2014). These are personality characteristics that enable a leader to be resilient and function effectively in arduous or uncertain circumstances. The psychological quality of hardiness develops early in life and can be strengthened or weakened by training, experiences and other circumstances. It is deeply embedded in personality so organisations seeking to be agile need to find ways to recruit people with these qualities for roles in the agile intensive parts of their organisation.

The METL

There have been many attempts over the past 70 years to develop measurement systems that can provide an assessment of the agility of a person, process or system. Despite setbacks, as some dimensions can not be measured accurately, the ability to assess objectively the agile capability of an organisation has proved to be a primary tool for managing and facilitating improvement.

As many military units are required to be agile it is essential that they use an assessment regime that is wider than a formal measurement process, as it is too easy to prioritise only aspects of a system that are easy to measure. An effective agility-specific assessment regime was developed for military use and is known as METL, or a Mission Essential Task List (Flynn, 1996).

The METL approach appears to be simple. Each unit must list a small number of tasks (3 to 5) that have been defined as being mission essential. They envision what would be happening if each mission essential task is performed in a way that can be considered as exemplary. They practice performing these mission essential tasks until the unit is satisfied it can meet the required high standard. Trials, supervised by external assessors, will be arranged to see whether the unit actually can achieve the exemplary standard.

But simple it is not. First, it is far from easy to determine which tasks are mission essential as the main criterion is 'what does the wider system need from this unit?' Secondly, the word 'exemplary' must be defined in the context of international exemplars, which requires a substantial benchmarking task. For example, the German Bundeswehr have a Cyber and Information Space Command that will need to be compared with the best military and civilian centres that perform a similar role. Thirdly, mission essential tasks need to be defined with sufficient specificity to enable them to be managed. Lastly, tests need to be good enough to rank the unit authoritatively and determine precisely where improvement is needed.

Despite such complications, the use of METL has proved to be valuable for military and those civilian organisations that have used it. It focuses management attention on the required functions or contributions from their area of responsibility. Equally important is that it renders agility to be a manageable, rather than an aspirational, construct.

In Conclusion

The military have much to teach us about requisite agility (indeed they were the first to use the term). Many organisations will neither have the need for the depth of agility capability possessed by armed forces nor will they have the resources to devote to this task. But there are opportunities for frugal adaptation. Military agility is a source of insight into ways of improving agility-orientated organisational development. Fortunately, many of the relevant studies are freely available from NATO and other sources. They nourish our imagination.

Study Eight: Devolved Agility

In 1995 an article was published with a somewhat undramatic title. It was called 'Projectification' of the Firm: The Renault Case (Midler, 1995). Its author, Christophe Midler, described how the French car company Renault had changed its organisational design fundamentally between the 1960s and 1990s. Early on, Renault had a classic hierarchical structure but, by 1990, its major divisions were organised around projects. Midler described this change process as 'Projectification', a term now widely used by organisational researchers.

Rarely can an academic researcher take a 30-year view, so Midler's study was particularly revealing. In the 1960s, an efficient functionally organised enterprise could thrive but, as market pressures grew, and competitive intensity increased, this form of organisation was incapable of being sufficiently dynamic. If it was to survive, Renault required rapid innovation, targeted product/market strategies and new forms of competitive differentiation that customers valued. Renault had no option but to become, at least in part, an agile enterprise and, in their case, that meant projectification.

Projectification is an organisational design principle where people are responsible for delivering currently unavailable outputs rather than delivering standardised outputs. An example assists us to understand this point. In his 2019 article, also about Renault, Midler wrote about the development of a new model of a car called the Kwid (Midler, 2019). This model was targeted towards the entry-level segment of the Indian market. It is manufactured in Renault's factory in Chennai, South India, and, as I write this section, sales of the Kwid place it second in its market segment.

A specification of required characteristics was prepared before a strategic decision was taken to develop the Kwid. The car would need to be competitively attractive when compared with Renault's best guess of what its rivals, like Suzuki, Hyundai and Tata, would offer in four years' time. Developing it would be a huge challenge. The Kwid had to cost about half as much as had previously been achieved, sell for €3500 and be fitted with a newly designed engine and gearbox. The quantity of innovation required meant that an agile organisation would be needed to deliver a product with multiple new features.

Once the go-decision had been made, a temporary project organisation was created to deliver the Kwid. The project manager was supported by a core team of about 30 highly experienced managers. This team had sufficient credibility, and the specialised knowledge, to challenge existing policies and practices. This was essential as the team knew that Renault's standard processes for managing new product development would not deliver the quantity of frugal innovation initiatives that had been specified. In effect, the Kwid project team developed an alternative corporate culture with its own core processes, reporting arrangements, structures and routines. Within the Kwid project organisation, there were multiple sub-projects, most with considerable interdependencies. Each was organised using similar design principles to the overall project.

Some of the organising principles used in the Kwid project were adopted widely as Renault's factories became increasingly automated, with routine work being undertaken by robots. People worked in temporary teams to complete non-routine tasks. A wave of project methodologies diffused widely across Renault in adaptive but influential ways. This enabled the quantity of agile initiatives to be increased. By the third decade of the 21st century Renault had adopted multiple innovation-orientated project management methods, like Design Thinking, Innovation Labs and Design to Cost Processes.

Midler's research provided new insight into a dimension of organisational agility that had previously been under-explored. He found that gaining advantage from agility required configurations of temporary organisations that were focused, well resourced, had fit-for-purpose cultures and routines, integrated development activities and facilitated flows of complementary innovation. His insight provided new avenues for agility-orientated organisational development and, although I cannot prove this assertion, I believe that projectification has been the single most productive approach to exploiting agility for advantage yet discovered.

Scrum

In February 2001, 17 friends, all software development specialists, met in a ski resort in Utah. Apart from enjoying the magnificent ski runs they spent time discussing what was wrong with software project management methods. It was an important topic. Developing computer software was a young but hugely important industry. Those who managed programmes and projects often used classic project management techniques. After all, it was argued, specialists could be given well-defined tasks and they only needed to complete their assignments as directed. There was a structured approach available for managing projects in this way, known as the Waterfall Method. This provided tools and disciplines to exercise project-wide control and to ensure that sub-tasks were tightly defined and logically related to main tasks. Planning was separated from doing, as it was considered to be unreasonable to expect a junior person to have the discretion to vary specifications. The Waterfall Method was widely used by rapidly growing software companies in the last decades of the 20th century but, there were four big problems. Many software projects were slow to deliver, failed to supply what customers wanted, exceeded their budgeted costs and wasted time and resources.

The friends shared their managerial experiences in the ski lodge. They knew that many software projects were developed in an environment where the situation or context can change quickly, changing customer needs require frequent schedule adjustments, unexpected threats occur and technical problems can disrupt progress. Tasks are intellectually demanding, specialised, complex, tailor-made for clients, contain uncertainties, are influenced by industry-wide methodological developments and can be progressed by relatively small teams. The friends asked the question: is the Waterfall Method fit-for purpose of managing such projects? Their answer was 'no'. It might be perfect for building a cruise ship but not for software development projects. A quite different managerial approach was needed, one that was sufficiently agile for the task.

Between ski runs the friends' discussions had wide-ranging implications. They produced the Agile Manifesto (Fowler & Highsmith, 2001). This brilliant document presented a markedly different approach to project management. Its principles encapsulated much of what had been learnt from psychological studies of work group performance and used collective intelligence, rather than a rigid schedule, for project control. Moreover, it expressed key principles simply and powerfully. The Manifesto provided an organisational template for undertaking planning and doing in parallel, thereby building agility into the fabric of a cellular form of organisation. It advocated using structured but human-centred organising principles. Importantly, the principles were elaborated into roles, disciplines, processes, structures and resource-requirements that became a managerial practice, known as Scrum (Schwaber, Hundhausen, & Starr, 2015).

The word Scrum refers to a set-piece in the sport of rugby where a team's players work to win ground, despite the best endeavours of the opposing team to stop them. In a rugby Scrum the players must work as a team to push the opposing team so they cannot gain possession of the ball. This provided a useful analogy for an approach to project work that abandons the notion that the best way to get complex things done is to freeze a plan for an entire project schedule in advance. Rather,

Scrum provides a disciplined and iterative framework in which granular teams have considerable autonomy, planning is adaptive, progress made in short cycles, the interests of customers are strongly represented, there is full transparency about progress (or the lack of it) and team members' ideas are used for frequent cycles of improvement. Control is exercised by explicit norms, transparent processes, defined accountabilities, dynamic processes (sprints), structured planning, an expectation of momentum, physical proximity and rituals for celebration. There have been many cases where Scrum has proved to be an outstandingly effective format for managing projects that require high levels of agility.

A Scrum team is unlike that found in many organisations as authority is shared, rather than being invested in a leader. Substantial responsibility is delegated to a team with between 5 and 10 members. The aim is to make rapid progress by constructively using the intelligence and expertise of all team members. Scrum's principles were based on a deep understanding of the distinctive mindsets, structures, processes and behaviours that provide proactive, fast, responsive and effective creative action. Insights had been drawn from humanistic psychology, problem-solving techniques, studies of effective and ineffective self-managed groups, and user-centred innovation. Importantly, Scrum had structure, discipline and a deep commitment to performance.

The transformation wrought by the availability of Scrum was that it provided managers with confidence that they could devolve responsibility for certain categories of tasks to largely autonomous teams. This development has revolutionised the use of self-managed teams that, previously, had a patchy record of success. Although Scrum was developed to improve software development it is now used much more widely. A structure of Scrum teams provides the organisational model for fast-developing companies like Spotify and Netflix. Perhaps surprisingly, it is also used in banking with ING. This Netherlands owned bank fundamentally re-engineered its headquarters' organisation to adopt the Scrum framework with several hundred teams (Birkinshaw, 2018).

Scrum is capable of being scaled with coordinating mechanisms providing organisation-wide coherence. These mechanisms include: Tribes, a group of perhaps 10 Scrums or Squads that contribute to common goals; Chapters, that bring together people with similar specialisms to share knowledge and Guilds, which are groups of people who share tools, materials and methods. The fact that Scrum is scalable is a major advantage from a senior managerial perspective. Some large tasks can be broken down into discrete projects and undertaken by a Scrum-based organisational form that had sufficient fractal-like integrity to provide coherence and alignment, which reduces the risk of duplicating work unnecessarily or missing essential requirements.

As Scrum has became widely practiced there were reports that the promised benefits were hard to achieve (Conboy & Carroll, 2019). It became clear that the adoption of Scrum was far from simple. Those involved need to be willing and able;

skillsets that seem easy to achieve when described theoretically are difficult to demonstrate behaviourally in stressful and demanding situations and the required granularity or extreme delegation can result in dysfunctional disintegration.

When organisations get Scrum right, productivity can improve by a factor of three (Rigby, Sutherland, & Takeuchi, 2016). Employee engagement improves markedly. Upgrades or new products can be released within weeks or months. Speed of innovation increases, as does customer satisfaction. If Scrum frameworks can greatly enhance productivity, whilst improving employee satisfaction dramatically, then it becomes the managerial equivalent of a magician's wand. So, should all managers dismantle their bureaucratic organisations, empower self-managed teams, redefine the role of managers so that they become facilitators and coaches and let the wisdom of the crowd guide their future? The answer is sometimes 'yes' and sometimes 'no'. We knew that it wouldn't be easy, didn't we!

Scrum's organising principles have similarities to those used in the Lean Startup, which is another valuable framework for managing agility, targeted at kicking-off a new enterprise. Lean Startup abandons the notion that new ventures benefit from preparing long-term plans and multi-year profitability forecasts. Rather, it promotes the principle that it is necessary to get started somehow, experience the realities of trading, frequently review to improve and be intelligently agile.

In Conclusion

Taken together, Scrum and Lean Startup have transformed the manageability of forms of agility as they provide inherently agile project management. Neither Scrum nor the Lean Startup are easy managerial stratagems to adopt as they are dependent on recruiting, motivating and aligning able people who are venturesome, reliable, prudent, disciplined and cooperative. Such people can be hard to find, and hard to keep! In Step Six we will explore this point further.

Study Nine: The Rise of the Machines

In recent years a force so extensive that it has been called the 4th Industrial Revolution has fundamentally reshaped the construct of agility (Schumacher, Nemeth, & Sihn, 2019). It is driven by the potential of digital and other science-based technologies that are merging the physical, digital and biological worlds. Machines and systems with built-in intelligence are now available at relatively low cost. In many industries, from farming to tourism, this capability has fundamentally revised the shape, dynamism, criticality and size of opportunity spaces that are available for agile initiatives. In addition, the 4th Industrial Revolution has created new categories of threats that need to be understood, mitigated and, where possible, transformed into advantages. In future decades the digital technologies that underpin machine and system intelligence will continue to evolve, meaning that 'do-different' agile capabilities will become a strategic imperative for many enterprises.

Many technologies facilitate agility, for example, democratised data empowers devolved decision-making; augmented intelligence increases the probability that individuals will take prudent and timely decisions; embedded analytics provides immediate feedback on efficiency and effectiveness; platform technologies integrate systems and 'data literacy for all' allows benefits from technologies to be widely used.

The scale of the likely impact can be understood by reviewing earlier industrial revolutions. It was the discovery that steam could power engines that initiated the first Industrial Revolution, shown when Thomas Newcomen installed the first working engine in a mine in 1712. Later, it was found that steam engines could power centralised factories enabling efficient production systems to be used. Society changed from being largely rural to urban with factories dominating wealth creation (Cardwell, 2017).

The second Industrial Revolution was based on electric power. The first efficient electrical generators became available in the 1870s. Larger factories created greater wealth that was partly used for research and development, providing advances such as the telegraph and telephone, chemical synthesis, the Bessemer steel making process and fertiliser production. Society changed as products and services became increasingly available and the consumer gained greater power.

A third industrial revolution occured in the second half of the 20th century that owed much of its transformative power to the fast-increasing capabilities of electronics, especially transistors, microprocessors and computers. For industry, this revolution drove waves of automation including using programmable machines and robots. Integration of information technology and computers became commonplace. Society changed as connectivity and information became increasingly available and much of the world became a global village.

Industry 4.0 is energised by interconnectivity and smart systems. It drives systemic transformation by using digital integration and intelligent sub-systems. Machines become entities that can redefine their functionality and take decisions autonomously, within parameters. The virtual and tangible worlds can interconnect seamlessly. Industry 4.0 is characterised by the integration of such assets as cyber–physical systems, advanced robotics, rapid innovation, machine intelligence, additive manufacturing, virtual and augmented reality, cloud computing, big data analytics and data science.

Industry 4.0 offers a promise of transformation agility. Online shoppers already have next-day delivery of items and may be wearing a heart monitor that uses cloud-based algorithms to detect abnormalities that will be available to healthcare providers in seconds. For military defence, radar systems have machine intelligence to discriminate between missile types, calculate launch and impact points, and perform scheduling tasks in just a few seconds. Police forces use algorithms to focus on areas were crime is more likely to occur. Traders in stocks and shares use algorithmic trading programs to send computer-generated orders in fractions of a second. The Internet of Things provides production managers with reports on the status of work processes at a level of detail never before available, allowing potential problems to be solved before they occur. National electrical distribution systems protect themselves automatically in the event of lightning strikes. Robots conduct initial job interviews to reduce the workload of HR professionals.

In each of these examples some forms of agility are dramatically enhanced by interconnectivity and smart systems. The application of digital technologies does not only enable organisations to increase their 'do better' agile capability, it also creates 'do different' zones of opportunity. We look to scenario planners, technology forecasters, those undertaking thought experiments and even science-fiction writers for inspiration. Enterprises that can be reshaped by digital technologies must look beyond conventional sources of input to shape their strategies.

Networks have grown vastly in importance as machine intelligence evolved in standardised ways, which enables interoperability. Increasingly agile capability requires focused effort to acquire and develop networks that serve five functions: namely (i) finding/creating opportunities, (ii) selecting promising prospects, (iii) gaining commitment to specific initiatives, (iv) effective deployment and (v) exploiting fully the advantages gained.

When machines and technologies are components of an organisation's portfolio of resources then zones of opportunities can be extended, or their boundaries redrawn. Some opportunities will change their status from being 'available to someone else', to now being 'available to us'. The possession of machines and technologies can cushion an organisation from threats and equip it to be ready to thrive for a different future.

Imagine that you are the director of a university in a city in Africa. You have had a strong academic faculty with an international reputation for African Art History that attracts about 60 students each year. Currently, courses are being delivered conventionally, with lectures, seminars, guided reading etc. Then a benefactor provides you with the required hard technologies (machines and systems) and soft technologies (expertise and skills) that are required for virtual classrooms, online courses, video production and so on. Now, you can become an online educational provider, reaching people anywhere in the world who are interested in African Art History. If exploited, the machines and technologies will have broadened and redefined your agile scope, opened new revenues streams and provided at least some protection from other universities, who could have become strong rivals. You will have more real options: your university's agile capability has been strengthened.

It is not axiomatic that acquiring machines and technologies will increase organisational agility, as they need to be prudently selected, adopted and used. That this was a far-from-easy process became clear in the middle of the 20th century as the UK was recovering from the ravages of the Second World War (Trist & Bamforth, 1951). At that time, it was essential to do everything possible to improve the economy and this required huge quantities of coal to supply energy requirements. About 700,000 men worked in Britain's coal mines. The coal was dug using pickaxes and shovels by small teams or gangs who used the same methods as did their fathers and grandfathers. Their working conditions seemed like those in a nightmare as miners had little light, were covered with coal dust, sometimes had to kneel to work and they were fearful of rockfalls, explosions or accidents with machinery.

New ways were becoming available to increase productivity. A major innovation was longwall mining, which used an enormous machine to cut coal mechanically. The UK's National Coal Board installed several longwall machines in suitable mines and expected substantial productivity gains. But they were disappointed. Miners were unhappy with the changes. Many wanted to leave the industry and absenteeism averaged 20%. Something was very wrong.

The Tavistock Institute in London were pioneers in investigating factors that influenced workplace productivity. They were asked by the National Coal Board to examine why the longwall method was failing to achieve its promise. Ken Banfield, an industrial psychologist who had been a miner himself, visited several of the newly mechanised mines. He came away perplexed. It seemed that, from a miner's point of view, the longwall method was better in every way. It was safer and less physically demanding. Bonuses were easier to achieve, and jobs had greater status as they required technical skills.

After a detailed study the Tavistock researchers found that in traditional coalmines everyone knew that the old short-wall method was extremely dangerous and that the work was hard. Men depended on each other completely. Gangs of miners often worked together for years and developed closer bonds than in many families. They would not hesitate to help a fellow gang member whenever it was needed. The men felt that they were valued members of a community.

After the longwall machines were installed many things changed. Operators were isolated from others. Their main task became to look after machines rather than work as a team. Previously there had been deep mutual interdependence. Now, increasingly, there were superficial relationships and it was 'each man for himself'.

In Conclusion

The Tavistock team realised the factors that helped or hindered an organisation from adopting new machines or technologies were shaped by interlocking human and technological factors. Their conceptual model, known as the Socio-Technical

Systems Framework, was developed to increase understanding of how technology shapes behaviour, and how behaviour shapes technology. We have learnt that joint optimisation is essential, meaning that social and technical systems must be designed so that they are positive for productivity and employees. This is particularly important in agile-intensive organisations as they require high levels of buy-in, commitment and willingness to 'go the extra mile' from key people. It is no surprise that the latest generation of giant global corporations have re-engineered people management so that able people clamour to work there. Requisitely agile organisations must dynamically integrate human and non-human worlds.

The Step One Workshop – Orienting: *What is known about achieving requisite agility?*

Preparation
A room with a large whiteboard or wall where Post-it type notes can be mounted or an equivalent virtual space will be required.

Time
About 2 hours and 15 minutes (larger teams take longer).

Workshop Structure

1. The ADT leader introduces the first EAfA Workshop by saying that its purpose is to enable ADT members to develop a shared understanding of the construct of agility that will underpin the work of completing the EAfA Process. It is important to emphasise that this will be an educational, not a decision-making, session. All the work of the ADT should be focused exclusively on the defined Unit of Analysis (5 minutes).
2. The ADT leader invites members of the team to agree on what would be great outcomes of this session. These can be written on a whiteboard or a flip chart so that they remain in view during the workshop (10 minutes).
3. Separately, each member of the ADT should post their notes of their three selected insights from the pre-work on the whiteboard and explain why she or he selected each one (3 minutes for each person).
4. Once everyone has presented their notes, they should be reorganised into logical clusters by the group, with one team member acting as the facilitator. After the clustering task has been completed everyone should vote for the three clusters that they consider will be the most relevant to the work of their ADT. The selected key clusters should be discussed in order of their perceived significance to explore how

the insights might be helpful. After each cluster has been discussed the leader should summarise what has been learnt from the exercise (60 minutes).

5. Team members agree what follow-up action should be taken to improve the conceptual understanding of organisational agility by ADT members (time as required).

6. ADT members privately answer two questions: 'What is one thing that worked well in this session?' and 'What is one area where we could improve next time?' After one or two minutes the answers to these questions should be shared and between three and five suggestions for improvement noted (10 minutes).

7. After the workshop photographs of the clusters of Post-it type notes should be taken and circulated, so that these can be reviewed as the remaining steps of the EAFA process are undertaken, especially for Step Seven.

7 Step Two – Predicting: *How might we need to change in the future?*

The focus of this step is *predicting*. It provides a method to enable the members of an ADT to explore the impact of possible future scenarios. This will deepen understanding of what needs to be done to increase the probability that a Unit of Analysis will be ready to grasp new or different opportunities and, particularly, to avoid threats in a different future.

Guidance for the ADT Leader

In Step Two the members of the ADT will begin to develop an informed view of how their Unit of Analysis may need to change in the foreseeable future. Notice that the task is to 'begin to develop an informed view'. As teams progress through the later steps of the EAfA Process they will continue to reflect on possible futures. Accordingly, the ADT leader should advise the team that their output from the Step Two Workshop will be provisional and one member of the team should take responsibility for upgrading the team's foresight analysis after each subsequent workshop.

If the ADT works at the strategic level then team members will explore how the future may be different from the present in those industries where their enterprise currently competes, or is considering competing. Not-for-profit organisations can undertake a similar task, with the goal of gaining and sustaining enduring comparative advantage.

An ADT that works at the local level will begin to develop an informed view of how their Unit of Analysis may need to change in one or more of the 6P areas described below. For the Step Two workshop it may make sense to expand the ADT by including additional participants who have different mindsets, experience and skills. This can help the team to be more ambitious but everyone attending the Step Two workshop will need to complete the pre-work, as directed.

During the workshop, the ADT leader should emphasise that the task requires analytical thinking but will be, inevitably, speculative. The leader should encourage team members to stretch their thinking into the future. The task will be challenging as radical and extensive changes are occurring in scientific, technological, political, environmental, competitive, demographic, legal and economic domains. Although the topic is complex, ADT members will find that many individuals, institutes, think-tanks and even novelists have spent years striving to develop reliable foresight and they can mine existing data to explore possible futures.

When completing Step Two the ADT will not undertake a fundamental analysis. Rather, team members will collect informed and relevant foresight investigations

https://doi.org/10.1515/9783110637267-008

conducted by others, synthesise (combine ideas from different sources) and assess the relevance to their Unit of Analysis.

Before the Step Two Workshop the ADT leader (and ACA, if available) should read the description of how to prepare a Change Drivers Map, explained in the pre-workshop reading and they may wish to view my video available at https://vimeo.com/ondemand/industryscenarios

The leader, or a team member delegated to lead this task, should practise developing a trial Change Drivers Map on a topic of their choice in advance of the workshop. It is *essential* that at least one person in the team has had hands-on experience of the Change Drivers Mapping method before the workshop, so that she or he can guide team members through the process. The trial map will need to be shown to the members of the ADT during the workshop and the person who completed it should be ready to describe how to undertake the task.

Before the workshop a large sheet of paper should be obtained for the Change Mapping Exercise; a long sheet of white wallpaper is best. A set of Sharpie fine marker pens or the equivalent will also be required.

The Pre-Workshop Tasks for Step Two

Purpose
To identify what needs to be done for the Unit of Analysis to become better prepared to exploit opportunities for advantage in the future.

Goals
i.   To provide those concerned with developing requisite organisational agility with foresight insights that enables them to define likely change drivers.
ii. To prioritise change drivers in terms of importance and urgency.
iii. To begin to define what requisite agility your Unit of Analysis will need to acquire now (the one-year view), in the foreseeable future (the three-year view) and in the middle-distant future (the seven-year view). This will be a preliminary assessment to be developed further in subsequent steps.

Process
Read the pre-work to prepare for the Step Two Workshop. ADT members should work alone, or in pairs, so that there will be a diversity of inputs for the workshop.

Core Task
Develop scenarios of the effect of change drivers on your Unit of Analysis and consider the consequences for acquiring requisite organisational agility.

Sub-Tasks
1. To use a foresight technique to define likely change drivers.
2. To prioritise change drivers in terms of importance and urgency.
3. To conceptualise of the effect of change drivers on your Unit of Analysis in one, three and seven years.
4. To begin to clarify an agility development agenda.

Time Required
About 2.5 hours for the pre-work and 3 hours and 40 minutes for the workshop (including breaks).

The Pre-Work for Step Two

To prepare for Step Two the members have two tasks. The first is to read the section entitled 'How to Have a Great Foresight Workshop'. As you read this you should highlight points that could help the ADT to have a successful foresight workshop. This task will take about 30 minutes.

Your second task is to spend two hours searching for informed foresight studies that are relevant to your Unit of Analysis. Try accessing professional associations, think-tank reports, academic investigations and TED talk videos to gain insights. Make notes of (i) *all* the change drivers that may reshape the work of your Unit of Analysis, using the 6Ps Model; (ii) when each could have an effect and (iii) the likely impact. Take your notes to the Step Two Workshop (about 2 hours).

How to have a Great Foresight Workshop

During the Foresight Workshop, the members of the ADT will work together to improve their understanding of how their Unit of Analysis may need to change in the foreseeable future. This requires developing a deeper understanding of existing change drivers, identifying possible new change drivers and predicting how these may evolve. This increases the probability that, in their own area of responsibility, managers, and key individual contributors, can develop the capabilities needed to thrive in the future.

The Step Two workshop is time-limited and will not go into great depth. It will provide an experience of using a structured process for developing foresight that can be developed further, in subsequent sessions, if necessary.

Why Foresight is Important

About 490 BCE, the great Chinese General, Sun Tzu (Tzu, 1981), wrote: "what enables the wise sovereign and the good general to strike and conquer, and to achieve things beyond the reach of ordinary men, is foreknowledge".

A key characteristic of a requisitely agile organisation is that it acquires the capabilities to thrive in a different future. This means that managers need to work on developing what Sun Tzu described as foreknowledge, that, today, we describe as foresight. Knowing what forces may impact the organisation in the future increases the probability that agility-orientated organisational development will take place.

Predicting Likely Futures

Predicting requires speculation, guesswork, collective intelligence and judgement. It will be assisted by data, analyses and projections but dimensions of prediction can never be entirely evidence-based. There will be unknowns, imponderables and uncertainties. Inevitably, assumptions will prove, at least in part, to be wrong. The task of forecasting is so 'wicked' (ill-defined and complex) that one senior management team undertaking this EAfA step purchased a large crystal ball and placed it in their workshop room. They felt that they needed the help of a magician!

When predicting, managers should try to use the skills of wise gamblers who win more often than they lose. And when wise gamblers lose, they suffer less than others. Successful gamblers study horses intensively. They know their pedigree, their success record, which jockeys they like, what sort of ground they prefer, whether they are happy in bad weather and so on. They do not allow uncertainties to prevent them from making a commitment but will not depend on luck alone.

Predicting can be a demanding task as many managers have been schooled in the importance of analytical decision-making. For this step, managers should adopt the mind-set of designers as they strive to predict the future, recognising that their decisions will also shape their own future.

Using the 6Ps Model for Foresight Development

In Chapter 3 the 6Ps Model was introduced. EAfA uses this model to deepen foresight analyses. It works in this way. Rather than ask the broad question: 'What do we need to do to be future ready?'

The EAfA approach is to ask six questions: How might we need to change . . .

. . . the outputs that we deliver (product agility)?

. . . ways that we get things done (process agility)?

. . . communication with stakeholders (positional agility)?

... our organisation's driving force (paradigm agility)?
... ways we obtain the resources (provisioning agility)?
... the use platforms for advantage (platform agility)?

Using these six questions provides greater depth in the analysis phase, as explained below.

The Three Phases for Deepening Foresight

For our purposes, we will see deepening foresight as a three-phase process: analysing, designing and testing.

In the *analysis phase*, specific to the work of your Unit of Analysis, you will gather information from the authoritative predictions of others about trends, change drivers and patterns of competition, that may affect one or more of the 6P areas (product, process, position, paradigm, provisioning and platform) in your Unit of Analysis (an example is described below). Your task will be to make sense of the information that you gather.

In the *design phase* you will construct descriptions of several future viable organisational models that could be relevant for your Unit of Analysis. Your goal will be to have a choice of several future-ready organisational models, as this facilitates creativity.

In the *testing phase* you will test your future-ready organisational models to assess their viability and determine what would be involved in transforming them from being a proposal into a reality.

Understanding the Three Phases Framework: An Example

It is helpful to consider an example to understand how the three-phase framework for deepening foresight can be used. Imagine that the president of the EFG University had decided to increase the probability that her university will be fit for the future. This is what happened:

In the *analysis phase* the members of the university's TMT gathered data. They collected analyses of change from authoritative sources and identified change drivers such as (i) changing governmental views of the future role of higher education, (ii) progress in the online delivery of courses, (iii) the likely impact of technology on young people's career prospects, (iv) how artificial intelligence may replace human teachers, (v) the growing interest in developing emotional intelligence rather than promoting traditional academic skills and (vi) the variety of ways that leading universities are preparing for a different future.

They concluded, using the 6Ps framework, that (i) the university's products would need to change so that more use would be made of online delivery; (ii) processes would increasingly use machine intelligence; (iii) the university could reposition itself as a character building institution; (iv) the role (paradigm) of a university would need to change as society evolved; (v) sources of funding (provisioning) would have to be expanded and (vi) platform thinking could provide previously unavailable opportunities.

These data were organised using the Change Drivers Mapping method. This required (i) defining the Unit of Analysis; (ii) listing the forces that have shaped the present; (iii) defining the type of each change driver (e.g., technological, political or environmental); (iv) assessing the likely degree of impact of each change driver and (v) identifying what new change drivers might reshape the landscape of opportunities in the future. During the Foresight Workshop, it became clear that there will be major changes in what students will expect to learn, the range of alternatives that will be available and how universities may be organised in a digitally enabled world.

In the *design phase* of their workshop TMT members were asked to ignore the realities of their university at the moment, reflect on the findings of their foresight analysis and answer the question: 'if you had 50 million dollars available for investment, what kind of university would you create that will be viable in twenty-years' time?' Participants used Design Thinking (Kolko, 2015) as a framework for creating concepts of possible futures, as this provides ways to explore what could be, rather than what is. It was agreed that three alternative university models could be viable in the long term. These were for the university to become (i) a Whole-Person Personal Growth Centre, (ii) a Low-Cost Online Provider of Specialised Knowledge and (iii) a World-Class Centre of Focused Research Excellence.

In the *testing phase* of the workshop team members reviewed the three possible future university models with multiple stakeholders to assess what would be involved in transforming each of them from being a conceptual proposal into a reality. The effect of this phase analysis was to provide deeper insight into the consequences of choosing each model as a strategic commitment.

A Great Foresight Workshop is . . .

Exciting and stimulating. Creativity thrives when diversity is present and divergent thinking is encouraged, so that multiple perspectives can be heard and discussed. Ramakrishna (Shah, 1993) made this point beautifully in his famous story of a group of six blind men encountering an elephant. Each approached the elephant. The one who grasped the leg said, 'The elephant is like a pillar', the man who held an ear said, 'No, the elephant is like a fan'. Another touched the tail and said, 'You are both wrong, an elephant is like a rope'. Every perspective makes a distinctive contribution but only when a consensus is developed can there be a platform for break-through thinking.

The Step Two Workshop – Predicting: *How might we need to change in the future?*

Preparation
A room with a wall on which a long (approximately 3 m) sheet of paper is fixed. A flip chart pad with marker pens is required.

Time
3 hours and 40 minutes (including breaks).

Workshop Structure

1. The ADT leader invites members of the team to agree on what would be great outcomes of this session. These can be written on a whiteboard or a flip chart so that they remain in view during the workshop (10 minutes).
2. At the end of the Step One Workshop participants were asked to list 'things that worked well and areas for improvement'. These points should be reviewed in order to assist the team to work more effectively during the current session (5 minutes).
3. In order for ADT members to tune into their task the Leader should inform them that (i) this workshop will provide an initial orientation to the Change Drivers Mapping method. It may be necessary to undertake further sessions to complete the foresight assignment; (ii) the workshop process will be helped if all participants adopt a proactive outward-looking approach, one that welcomes challenge and (iii) the workshop has three phases: analysis, design and testing (5 minutes).
4. The Leader should introduce the Analysis Phase of the workshop by explaining that a well-constructed Change Drivers Map improves the probability that the ADT can make prudent bets about which future change drivers will be impactful. Constructing a Change Drivers Map enables ADT members to see the scope and scale of the forces that may have an impact on the selected Unit of Analysis, and it shows how forces relate together. It will be helpful if the person who prepared a trial map before the workshop shows that map and explains how to complete the task. Questions should be encouraged (10 minutes).
5. The *Analysis Phase* requires that four tasks are completed by the whole ADT, specifically (i) take the large sheet of paper and draw a timeline across the bottom, going back for three years and forward for seven years; (ii) identify and name each separate change driver, show it as an arrow and indicate when it started and when it could cease to be a significant force for change; (iii) the width of the arrow indicates the extent of the impact and (iv) look into the future to predict additional possible change drivers. Add these to your map (1 hour).

6. For the *Design Phase* participants are divided into pairs. Each pair is given one sheet of flip chart paper and, working separately, pairs have 20 minutes to review the Change Drivers Map that was just created. Each pair's task is to devise one hypothetical organisational model that could be a winner in seven-years' time (as had been done by the team at EFG University, described in the pre-work). Their hypothetical model should be given a name and up to five key characteristics described. On the sheet of flip chart paper an imaginative drawing of their hypothetical model should be made, with key features explained. After 20 minutes the completed flip charts should be collected and displayed. Pairs are invited to briefly explain their logic. Three possible future winning organisational models should be selected for further development by agreement or voting (45 minutes).

7. For the *Testing Phase* participants are divided into three sub-groups. Each is assigned the task of taking one of the three selected possible future winning organisational models identified in the Design Phase. Each sub-group works on a different model. Sub-groups, working separately, have 20 minutes to undertake a thought experiment, which requires them to assess the practical implications of adopting their assigned hypothetical organisational model. Each sub-group should suggest (i) what would need to be done more or better, (ii) what would need to be done less or stopped, (iii) what new things would need to be done and (iv) what will remain the same. After 20 minutes each sub-group is asked to give a five-minute summary of their conclusions (40 minutes).

8. Conclude this step by selecting just one of the possible organisational models (the one that may be most viable) and begin to define what requisite agility that you would need to acquire now (the one-year view); what requisite agility would be needed in the foreseeable future (the three-year view) and what requisite agility would be needed in the middle-distant future (the seven-year view) (20 minutes).

9. ADT members privately answer two questions: 'What is one thing that worked well in this session?' and 'What is one area where we could improve next time?' After one or two minutes the answers to the questions should be shared and between three and five suggestions for improvement noted (10 minutes). After the workshop photographs of the completed Change Drivers Map and flip charts should be circulated so that these can be reviewed as the remaining steps of the EAFA process are undertaken.

8 Step Three – Diagnosing: *Do we have the capabilities to be agile?*

The focus of this step is *diagnosing*. It provides a method for assessing whether a Unit of Analysis has the required capabilities to deliver requisite agility. If needed, this diagnosis can be undertaken again after Step Six.

Guidance for the ADT Leader

There are similarities between core athletic capability and core agile capability, as each provides the readiness required to undertake defined categories of action successfully. In this step the members of an ADT will assess whether their selected Unit of Analysis possesses required agile capabilities.

The EAfA Agile Capabilities Reference Model describes 20 components of organisational agility that, if present, drive core agility or, if weak, become agility blockages. An agility driver is an attribute that increases the probability that required agility deliverables will be gained. An agility blockage is the presence of an attribute that hinders or prevents required agility deliverables from being gained. It will be the balance between drivers and blockages that determines the 'now' situation.

The Reference Model can be used to examine agile capability two levels. First, at the enterprise (systemic) level to diagnose the readiness of an entire organisation to be capable of (i) achieving strategic and systemic agility and (ii) promoting requisite local agility. Secondly, the Reference Model is used at the local or organisational sub-unit level for divisions, departments, LoBs, major projects etc. The guidance contained in this step assumes that ADT's focus will be on local units of analysis.

Some background may be of interest. The EAfA Agile Capabilities Reference Model was constructed using grounded theory techniques following several research studies undertaken by the author between 1998 and 2020. Initially 106 organisations that they had gained significant benefits from being prudently opportunistic were studied. The model presented in this step has not previously been published and incorporates findings from recent longitudinal research investigations. However, the research sample size (152 organisations in total) is too small for the Reference Model to be definitive, so it should be viewed as a set of orienting concepts rather than as a proven framework.

About two weeks before the Step Three Workshop the ADT members should be briefed on their pre-workshop tasks. Immediately before the workshop the ADT leader should ensure that the EAfA Agile Capabilities Reference Model Diagram (below) is copied on to a whiteboard in the workshop room. Pens suitable for writing on whiteboards will need to be available.

https://doi.org/10.1515/9783110637267-009

The Pre-Workshop Tasks for Step Three

Purpose
To assess whether the Unit of Analysis has necessary organisational capabilities and identify areas where improvement is needed to acquire requisite agility.

Goals
i.   To enable the members of the ADT to develop a consensus on the current agility drivers (factors helping agility) and blockages (factors hindering agility) in the Unit of Analysis.
ii. To define the nature of gaps between the Now Situation and the Desired Situation.
iii. To prepare a preliminary statement of what needs to change, that will be elaborated during later steps of the EAfA Process.

Process
Work alone or in pairs, in completing the pre-work as the workshop will be more effective if each team member has an opportunity to make a distinctive contribution.

Core Task
To rate whether the Unit of Analysis is strong or weak in each of the 20 components of the EAfA Agile Capabilities Reference Model.

Sub-Tasks
1. Review the explanations provided for each of the 20 components of the Reference Model.
2. Assess each separately to decide whether you consider it to be an agility driver or an agility blockage in relation to the Unit of Analysis being investigated.
3. Each component should be rated on a 6-point scale. If it is a very strong driver of requisite agility then a score of 6 points should be given, if it is an extremely significant blockage then a score of 0 points should be given. Points between 1 and 5 should be allocated to represent your personal assessment.
4. Make a note of your own scores for the each of the 20 components of the Reference Model and take this to the Step Three workshop.

Time Required
About 3 hours for the pre-work and 2 hours and 30 minutes for the workshop.

The Pre-Work for Step Three

Requisitely agile organisations need to be capable of being situational responsive, prudently opportunistic, capable of minimising threats and prepared to thrive in a different future. In order for these deliverables to be mainstreamed an organisation needs specialised core capabilities. In this step you will assess whether your Unit of Analysis has the required organisational capabilities.

In all, 20 organisational capabilities need to be evaluated. These are shown in the wheel diagram below. The model has five domains (identified by Roman numerals), each of which has four components (identified by English alphabet letters). The first domain (I) focuses on strategic-level and TMT issues, the second (II) on organisational routines and processes, the third (III) on the wider ecosystem, the fourth (IV) on resources and capabilities and the last (V) on dynamic capabilities and sources of momentum.

The wheel shape demonstrates that the components are interdependent and the hub of the wheel symbolises a constant process of grasping opportunities and avoiding threats. A wheel will be weakened if a spoke is absent, broken or fragile. It is the same with organisational agility, if any components are under-developed then they become blockages and the organisation's systemic agile capability is weakened.

In the following pages you will find a brief explanation of each of the 20 components shown on the wheel (see Figure 1). It will be your task to rate each one using the scoring system described above.

Component Ia: Top Team Commitment

The EAfA Process defines a top team as the group of people who determine the strategy for an enterprise. For example, in a hospital the TMT will be the group of people who lead and manage all aspects of the hospital from diagnostics and clinical support to procurement and maintenance.

Top Team Commitment is rated as 'high' when all the members of the TMT promote requisite agility proactively, wherever this will be productive. The TMT has prepared, and is actively deploying, an Agility Ambition that shapes strategies, vision, mission and values within the Unit of Analysis.

The TMT will be committed to gaining advantage from becoming requisitely agile. Team members understand, in depth, the different forms of value that can be provided by agility, its challenges, risks and associated organisational development requirements. They orient strategies, leadership, direction, policies, alignment and goals to drive the adoption of agility as a systemic capability in relevant parts of their organisation and into its ecosystem.

TMT members view agility as being an outcome of creating, resourcing, orienting and mobilising many interacting and interdependent resources that include human resources, autonomous systems, processes, ecosystem capabilities, organisational structures, stakeholders and cultural memes. Each of these resources is aligned to contribute to the organisation's capabilities to deliver requisite agility. This requires that TMT members adopt policies and practices that provide their organisation with

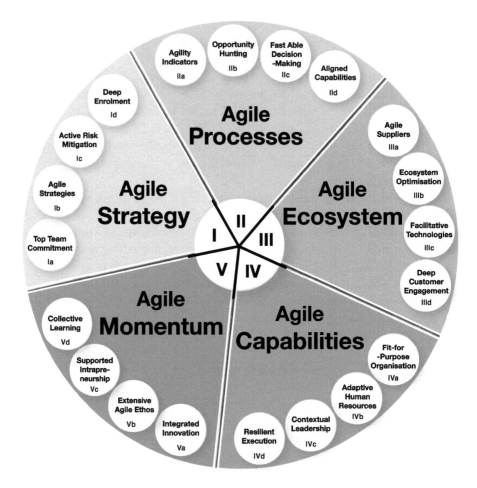

Figure 1: The EAfA Agile Capabilities Reference Model.

the necessary configurations of dynamic capabilities to deliver their organisation's Agility Ambition and they proactively address all agility blockages.

The TMT has adopted agile processes itself, so that strategies are formulated and enacted rapidly, often in days rather than weeks or months. The team is an efficient and effective working group. Everyone gives his or her full commitment and implements team decisions. The members know that top teams are vulnerable to generic weaknesses, particularly groupthink, which is an unwillingness to listen to divergent views and an unhealthy tendency to give excessive respect to the most senior members. Potential team weaknesses are avoided, as team members are aware of their potentially negative effects.

All TMT members act as role models. Members are optimistic but realistic. They respond effectively to situational changes: they create, find and exploit opportunities; they take steps to avoid or mitigate threats and they strive to prepare the organisation to be able to thrive in the future. Members keep up to date with developments about the agile modality of organising from new research and they study case studies related to the management of agile enterprises.

Key questions:
- Do members of the top team have an informed understanding of the role of agility in a high-performing organisation?
- Do members of the top team always act in ways that demonstrate agility is a core value for this organisation?
- Do members of the top team ensure that the organisation acts quickly to remove all blockages to agility?

Your Rating

If the description of this component is entirely accurate in relation to your Unit of Analysis, then Top Team Commitment will be a strong driver of requisite organisational agility and a score of 6 should be given. If a lack of Top Team Commitment is a significant blockage then a score of 0 should be given. Scores between 1 and 5 should be allocated to reflect your assessment of the degree to which this component is helping or hindering the Unit of Analysis to be requisitely agile.

Component Ib: Agile Strategies

Agile Strategies are rated as 'high' when the real (not espoused) strategy model that is used in the enterprise acts to promote situational adaptiveness, prudent opportunism, threat mitigation and future readying. In a requisitely agile organisation, strategies will (i) focus on high-level ambition, not long-term goals; (ii) emphasise the development of strategically significant capabilities; (iii) facilitate real-time emergent, not episodic, strategy formulation; (iv) clarify the required deliverables from requisite organisational agility; (v) delegate aspects of strategy formation to capable sub-units and (vi) specify the agile contribution that sub-units need to make to the wider organisation and to other stakeholders.

Agile Strategies are challenge-orientated, meaning that much time is invested in specifying what needs to be done to transform ambitions into actuality. For this reason, there is no clear separation between strategy-making and operations management. There is a strong focus on cycle times and capabilities, so that things get done, fast and effectively.

Strategies are deliberately aligned to realise the organisation's Agility Ambition as this defines the desired direction of travel. Strategies ensure that the Agility Ambition (i) integrates the organisation, (ii) determines the logic for its organisational structure,

(iii) clarifies the range of capabilities needed, (iv) defines productive human-machine relationships and (v) supports the organisation's Basic Business Concept or Driving Force (its chosen formula for adding superior value to internal or external customers/users within a sustainable cost structure).

Agile Strategies are integrated by the requirements of a single selected Basic Business Concept. It was the insightful work of Tregeo and Zimmerman (Tregoe & Zimmerman, 1980) that enabled us to understand that organisations need just one dominant integrating concept. This is because no organisation can do everything and needs to be fit for a specific purpose. For example, an emergency room in a hospital cannot develop new vaccines, and the research scientists in a pharmaceutical laboratory cannot run an efficient emergency room, even though both are staffed by medical doctors. Their organisations have different Basic Business Concepts. The emergency room needs to be agile in its capacity to configure its resources for the most urgent health needs of its patients at the time. The pharmaceutical laboratory needs to be agile in its capacity to configure its resources to exploit cutting-edge knowledge in scientifically responsible ways.

The EAfA Model identifies seven possible Basic Business Concepts. Our model builds on Treacy and Wiersema's pioneering construct of value disciplines (Treacy & Wiersema, 1993). Strategies will be primarily orientated to agility and required for excellence in one of these Basic Business Concepts: (i) *Customer Intimacy*: possessing organisational systems that respond to deep insights into customers' real needs and wants; (ii) *Frontier Innovation*: making and exploiting new-to-the-world breakthroughs; (iii) *Operational Effectiveness*: providing reliable products or services conveniently, and at lower prices than rivals; (iv) *Mandate Fulfilment*: meeting a set of predetermined aims, for example, in a police force or charity; (v) *Multiple Opportunism*: finding and capturing value from opportunities as they occur; (vi) *Product Leadership*: providing innovative products and/or services that are superior to those of rivals and (vii) *Technology Exploitation:* using technological innovations to create hitherto unavailable and desirable products and services.

Key questions:
- Is everyone aware of where and how we need to be agile in the future?
- Do our strategies change quickly to take full advantage of opportunities?
- Are there sufficient resources to help us overcome the challenges involved in getting things done quickly but effectively?

Your Rating

If the description of this component is entirely accurate in relation to your Unit of Analysis, then Agile Strategies will be a strong driver of requisite organisational agility and a score of 6 should be given. If a lack of Agile Strategies is a significant blockage then a score of 0 should be given. Scores between 1 and 5 should be allocated to reflect your assessment of the degree to which this component is helping or hindering the Unit of Analysis to be requisitely agile.

Component Ic: Active Risk Mitigation

Risks can be defined as the possibility of being disadvantaged as a result of actions or inactions. Active Risk Mitigation is rated as 'high' when risks are identified early; then are promptly and systematically reviewed to see whether they can be mitigated, eliminated or transformed into opportunities. Agile organisations cannot be risk averse but they must be risk prudent.

In an agile organisation, every decision-maker is a trained risk manager and automated systems have been designed to support risk identification and mitigation. Although it may seem otherwise, deep and wide proactive risk management is a required dynamic capability for systemically agile enterprises.

Stratagems for risk mitigation are used widely in a requisitely agile enterprise. For example, (i) by undertaking multiple development routes for initiatives while the cost is low, so that choices are greater and knowledge is deeper; (ii) insisting that investment proposals have assumptions clearly stated, opportunities identified, evidence presented, risks assessed and implications clarified and (iii) developing a tradition of intensive reflective learning to ensure that mistakes are analysed and causes of successes are understood. Learning is a shared practice and insights flow into the development of routines that reduce the risk that mistakes will be repeated and increases the probability that formulas for success will be understood, reinforced and enacted.

Decision-making processes are rigorous, as agile initiatives can add uncertainty, incur high costs, expend resources uselessly, undermine efficiency and expose the organisation to unknown, perhaps unknowable, risks. It is understood that bold decisions can absorb resources but not further an enterprise's Agility Ambition, thereby blurring focus and becoming a strategic risk. For these reasons care is taken to make prudent decisions that are aligned to the organisation's Agility Ambition and its chosen Basic Business Concept. This is often done quickly, as indecision is a source of increased risk.

Managers in agile enterprises know that they can not foresee the future, but they have routines in place to increase the probability that their strategies have a higher than average probability of success. They see the future not as a blank page, but rather as a series of out of focus images, some of which are clearer than others. Agile organisational competencies provide the strength to overcome setbacks and not be unduly disadvantaged by failed initiatives.

Key questions:
- Do those proposing new initiatives define associated risks?
- Is everyone trained in risk management?
- Is there an effective process for identifying when risks increase unexpectedly?

Your Rating

If the description of this component is entirely accurate in relation to your Unit of Analysis, then Active Risk Mitigation will be a strong driver of requisite organisational agility and a score of 6 should be given. If a lack of Active Risk Mitigation is a significant blockage then a score of 0 should be given. Scores between 1 and 5 should be allocated to reflect your assessment of the degree to which this component is helping or hindering the Unit of Analysis to be requisitely agile.

Component Id: Deep Enrolment

Deep Enrolment is rated as 'high' when people act proactively, frequently and competently to support the realisation of their organisation's Agility Ambition. Put simply, people will do whatever it takes to make a positive contribution to delivering requisite agility.

It is not easy to work in an agile enterprise. Each of the four deliverables that an organisation is entitled to expect from agility (situational adaptiveness, prudent opportunism, threat mitigation and future readying) can be demanding for individuals. *Situational adaptiveness* requires that people, perhaps helped by big data analyses, undertake complex and time-consuming searches for often weak or partly hidden signals that must be assessed to understand their significance, before formulating smart responses. *Prudent opportunism* is rarely straightforward, as there are always more opportunities than can be grasped. Once an opportunity has become a proposal then much work will need to be done to explore its merits and demerits. Then comes the often-difficult task of winning approval from those whose support is needed. Robust *threat mitigation* presents similar difficulties, as risks can be increased by taking agile initiatives and the consequences of failure may be high. Enabling an enterprise to be *future ready* is, perhaps, the most demanding task of all, as it requires finding a future strategic position that will be beneficial to all stakeholders and overcoming the inevitable challenges that will need to be faced.

If an organisation is to achieve these deliverables, then colleagues cannot avoid working in a stress inducing and demanding environment. Managers expect a lot from the people who work in, or for, an agile enterprise and not everyone will thrive in an organisation that is often in flux. People only feel deeply enrolled if they consider that their leaders and managers are fit to govern. This means that everyone serving the interests of the organisation needs to be treated with respect, feel valued, helped to overcome problems and rewarded in ways that are important to them.

In larger agile organisations the role of the human resource management department is central. People who are technically capable, and possess high emotional intelligence, must be recruited, motivated and helped to cope with complexity, uncertainty and an ongoing struggle to maintain a work-life balance. Agile organisations are choosy about who they employ and they win wars for talent. They seek people with psychological characteristics that include a can-do attitude, self-confidence, a commitment to learning, strong cognitive abilities and constructive teamworking skills. Agile organisations need people who make things happen in the real world. Deep Enrolment provides an energising force that drives organisational agility and supports colleagues though inevitable setbacks.

Key Questions:
- Do our organisation's values attract people who are great at getting things done?
- Are colleagues at every level willing to act as agents of change?
- Does almost everyone say: 'this is a great place to work'?

Your Rating

If the description of this component is entirely accurate in relation to your Unit of Analysis, then Deep Enrolment will be a strong driver of requisite organisational agility and a score of 6 should be given. If a lack of Deep Enrolment is a significant blockage then a score of 0 should be given. Scores between 1 and 5 should be allocated to reflect your assessment of the degree to which this component is helping or hindering the Unit of Analysis to be requisitely agile.

Component IIa: Agility Indicators

Agility Indicators are rated as 'high' when they (i) reliably demonstrate whether an organisation is superior to its rivals in each of the four dimensions of agility (situational adaptiveness, prudent opportunism, active threat mitigation and future readying) and (ii) enable an assessment to be made as to whether the enterprise's Agility Ambitions (systemic and local) are being delivered.

It is important that agile indicators assess whether an organisation is achieving requisite agility, not total agility. Often, the best source of insight into the quantity and type of agility required to achieve wanted agility deliverables is customers and potential customers. For example, a bespoke bedroom furniture company may have defined agility as: responding in 24 hours to enquiries, completing surveys in 3 days, producing finished designs in 2 days, customising fixtures with five times as many options as rival companies and meeting customers' preference for fitting dates at least 90% of the time. Achieving these performance levels will increase costs, so the key question is 'will sufficient numbers of customers pay more for this agile service?' If the answer is 'no' then striving to acquire this quantity of agility will be dysfunctional.

The constructs of Success Criteria and Success Indicators are used to devise assessment tools. Success Criteria are identified by answering the question: 'what precisely will we define as success?' And, Success Indicators by answering the question: 'how can we assess whether we are making good progress?' Notice that not all success indicators are measurable. Why? If only those dimensions that can be accurately measured are being managed, then there is a temptation to ignore other important factors.

Six Agility Scorecards can be prepared, one for each of the four dimensions of agility and two related to the Agility Ambition. Scorecards are most useful when they assess agility performance against rivals, potential rivals and best-in-class enterprises. The suggestions below of criteria that may be used for each scorecard are illustrative, not comprehensive.

Agility Scorecard One targets Situational Adaptiveness, which is a function of five key capabilities, namely (i) early identification of game-changing factors; (ii) rapid evaluation of potential impact of external events; (iii) identification of previously unrecognised opportunities; (iv) producing coherent situation analyses and (v) effective communication to those who can use the intelligence gained.

Agility Scorecard Two targets Prudent Opportunism, which is a function of five key capabilities, namely (i) defining promising opportunity spaces; (ii) specifying or creating specific opportunities; (iii) assessing potential value creation and cost implications; (iv) fully considering risk factors and (v) committing to exploiting selective opportunities.

Agility Scorecard Three targets Threat Mitigation, which is a function of six key capabilities, namely (i) the ability of managers to assess risk; (ii) early identification of possible threats; (iii) rapid evaluation of potential impact; (iv) exploration of a range of threat mitigation options; (v) adopting a comprehensive threat mitigation policy and (vi) effective execution.

Agility Scorecard Four targets Being Future Ready, which is a function of four key capabilities, namely (i) developing future scenarios of market and industry development; (ii) analysing relevant change drivers; (iii) identification of vulnerabilities and (iv) business model redesign.

Agility Scorecard Five targets enterprise-level Agility Ambition, which is a function of three capabilities, namely (i) clarity of the organisation's systemic Agility Ambition; (ii) extent to which the enterprise-level Agility Ambition shapes objectives, standards and success criteria across the organisation and (iii) extent to which feedback is available on progress in achieving the enterprise-level Agility Ambition.

Agility Scorecard Six targets local-level Agility Ambition, which is a function of four capabilities, namely (i) clarity of the local Agility Ambition; (ii) extent to which the local Agility Ambition defines objectives, standards and success criteria; (iii) extent to progress on achieving the local-level Agility Ambition is transparent and available in real-time and (iv) degree to which there is alignment between local and enterprise-level Agility Ambitions.

Agility Scorecards facilitate benchmarking. For example, manufacturing firms may benchmark their performance in terms of comparative flexibility, responsiveness, market position, technological innovation, application of smart technology or human resource capability against best-in-class enterprises, which are not necessarily rivals. Benchmarking has limitations as a dimension of the mission of an agile organisation may be to progress beyond accepted best practice. Despite its limitations, benchmarking provides a source of ideas and exemplars.

Key Questions:
- Does our organisation have agility-orientated Agility Scorecards that compares us with best-in-class exemplars and rivals?
- Do our Agility Scorecards tell us exactly where improvement is needed?
- Are there separate Agility Scorecards for those parts of the organisation that need to be intensively agile?

Your Rating

If the description of this component is entirely accurate in relation to your Unit of Analysis, then Agility Indicators will be a strong driver of requisite organisational agility and a score of 6 should be given. If a lack of Agility Indicators is a significant blockage then a score of 0 should be given. Scores between 1 and 5 should be allocated to reflect your assessment of the degree to which this component is helping or hindering the Unit of Analysis to be requisitely agile.

Component IIb: Opportunity Hunting

Opportunity Hunting is rated as 'high' when flows of potential opportunities drive effective development in one or more of the 6P target areas outlined below. The word 'hunting' demonstrates that much effort and skill is used to find and evaluate opportunities.

An opportunity is 'a potential wellspring of advantage'. They are transformed into advantages by a process that has five interlinked sets of activities, each requiring a different modality of organising, namely (i) searching; (ii) exploring; (iii) committing; (iv) realising and (iv) exploiting (see Chapter 3 for an explanation of this model).

The 6Ps Model targets Opportunity Hunting on (P1) improving or transforming outputs, or what is being produced (products); (P2) how activities are organised (processes); (P3) how relationships with the external environment are managed (position); (P4) the way that the organisation sees itself, specifically its choice of Basic Business Concept and Agility Ambition (paradigm); (P5) how resources are obtained (provisioning) and (P6) how that which is offered integrates with other products and services (platform). It is necessary to hunt for promising opportunity spaces in each of the 6P areas separately, as this provides a method for finding good hunting grounds.

Opportunity Hunting has three modalities: wide, deep and evaluative. *Wide Opportunity Hunting* benefits from the input of divergent thinkers and looks beyond obvious targets, detects weak signals, investigates multiple possibilities and strives to find fruitful future opportunity spaces. Hunters involved in wide-scanning engage in many face-to-face investigations, read widely, use virtual resources and the like. They build networks to explore many possible lines of enquiry.

Deep Opportunity Hunting is selective and intensive. Promising opportunities will be systematically investigated by a dedicated individual or team. Intelligence reports and thought pieces will be prepared to capture insights and to facilitate sensemaking. The aim is to understand selective opportunities in depth, with the intention of finding those that may be promising.

Evaluative Opportunity Hunting focuses on increasing the probability that opportunities will be prudently selected for exploitation. It examines how others, rivals for example, are grasping similar opportunities to learn about the advantages and disadvantages of exploitation and determine whether significant benefits can be obtained by being an early mover. Developing an evidence-based business case subsequently provides a mechanism for increasing the probability that prudent commitments can be made to exploit promising opportunities for advantage.

Key Questions:
- Do many people take time deliberately to hunt for opportunities outside of the organisation?
- Do managers receive a flow of intelligence reports about what is happening in the wider world that could affect us?
- Are teams often set up to explore potentially promising opportunities?

Your Rating

If the description of this component is entirely accurate in relation to your Unit of Analysis, then Opportunity Hunting will be a strong driver of requisite organisational agility and a score of 6 should be given. If a lack of Opportunity Hunting is a significant blockage then a score of 0 should be given. Scores between 1 and 5 should be allocated to reflect your assessment of the degree to which this component is helping or hindering the Unit of Analysis to be requisitely agile.

Component IIc: Fast, Able Decision-Making

Fast, Able Decision-Making is rated as 'high' when (i) decision-cycle times are quick and (ii) decisions receive the degree of attention that they require to permit prudent commitments to be made.

Decisions that commit an organisation to a particular path can be difficult or impossible to reverse. The aim is to ensure that all decisions are 'able', meaning that they (i) facilitate the realisation of the corporate and local Agility Ambitions; (ii) utilise evidence systematically; (iii) are tested for validity; (iv) incorporate wise intuition; (v) are taken rapidly and (vi) are deployed effectively.

Able decision-making is especially challenging in agile organisations for six main reasons, namely (i) the consequences of decisions can be unknowable (uncertainty); (ii) decision-makers may not be in the best position to assess the relevant factors (lack of proximity); (iii) windows of opportunity are often time-limited (urgency); (iv) decision choices are difficult to evaluate (complexity); (v) dysfunctional commitments can be made that result in the organisation taking a sub-optimal path (significance) and (vi) a hard-to-acquire coalition of support may be needed to enact decisions (need for buy-in). Able decisions in in an environment that is characterised by one or more of these six characteristics (uncertainty, lack of proximity, urgency, complexity, significance and need for buy-in) requires competent managerial processes.

Agile organisations take more decisions than non-agile organisations. Some of these will be speculative and there can be multiple decision-making processes. This means an agile organisation must be configured as a smart decision-taking entity. The capability will not be gained easily. It is a key task for the TMT to construct an organisation that is capable of Fast, Able Decision-Making. This requires specialist knowledge in the design of smart decision-taking entities in the digital age, where socio-technical systems are often central and intelligent machines may become active agents in decision-making.

Speed is a key characteristic of an agile organisation and the velocity of decision-making can provide competitive or comparative advantage, but only if able decisions are made. Sometimes it is more important to be right than fast. Formal processes for taking decisions, such as using the war-room concept, can be invaluable. An integrated organisation, where aligned and reliable systems allow information to flow rapidly throughout an organisation, assists decision-taking to be informed, rapid and effective.

Devolving decision-making authority is required in many, but not all, types of agile organisations. This requires that people act as intelligent agents rather than as performers of predetermined roles. Key risks in devolving decision-making authority include incompetence, neglect and non-alignment. It is necessary to develop individual and collective competence in decision-making by selecting able people, developing skills, setting standards and giving feedback. Alignment is facilitated by extensive, real-time briefing on context, priorities and the availability of evidence-based information.

Key questions:

- Have the strengths and weaknesses of our decision-making processes been analysed systematically?
- Has everyone who is expected to make decisions been fully prepared to do this effectively?
- Would it be true to say that this organisation has history of taking fast, able decisions?

Your Rating

If the description of this component is entirely accurate in relation to your Unit of Analysis, then Fast, Able Decision-Making will be a strong driver of requisite organisational agility and a score of 6 should be given. If a lack of Fast, Able Decision-Making is a significant blockage then a score of 0 should be given. Scores between 1 and 5 should be allocated to reflect your assessment of the degree to which this component is helping or hindering the Unit of Analysis to be requisitely agile.

Component IId: Aligned Capabilities

Aligned Capabilities are rated as 'high' when all the components of an organisation, including its sub-units and ecosystem, work together to facilitate the achievement of the corporate Agility Ambition. Resources will be reconfigured on an as-needed basis to provide ongoing real-time, fit-for-purpose effectiveness, thereby supporting the organisation's principal Basic Business Concept.

Alignment is provided by (i) the intensive and extensive communication of corporate vision, mission and values; (ii) clarity about the enterprise's Agility Ambition; (iii) descriptions of key challenges; (iv) direct contact across hierarchical divisions; (v) the standardisation of mindsets and skills, so that similar values are shared and (vi) protocols for proactive integration, consultation and communication.

Aligning forces need to be strong in agile organisations, so that when people use the word 'we' they mean the enterprise as a whole, not their work group. This high-level degree of cohesion can be difficult to achieve. In a non-agile organisation alignment will be maintained without undue effort, as roles are tightly specified and this provides clarity about the contributions of individuals to the organisation. In agile organisations roles are often fluid, meaning that shared aims, not routines, provide alignment.

Infrastructure is key. Smart enterprise-wide management and control systems facilitate ongoing dynamic alignment. Available mechanisms include (i) standardised IT infrastructures; (ii) commitment by sub-units to the organisation as a whole; (iii) power being held by people who have cooperative mindsets; (iv) win-

win psychological contracts, so that people feel respected and (v) positive recognition for proactive cooperation between subunits.

Alignment does not require comprehensive uniformity. Parts of the organisation will operate as differentiated fractals to deliver their specialised outputs to the wider organisation, as if they are sections of an orchestra contributing to a single symphony. Much operational alignment will be the result of on-going mutual adjustment between work groups, as they clarify roles, agree deliverables, establish communication processes and the like.

Lack of alignment is an ever-present danger in agile organisations. For example, ad hoc organisations, such as quasi-autonomous teams, perhaps partly staffed with temporary colleagues may work in short cycles with flexible membership. These atomised groupings can diversify radically from the parent organisation, resulting in confusion and disorganisation. When power moves to the edge of an organisation then decisions can be taken that are right for the sub-unit but disadvantageous for the organisation. Such dysfunctional outcomes need to be avoided if the organisation is to be requisitely agile.

Key questions:
- Are different parts of the organisation highly cooperative in getting things done?
- Are temporary resources (people and systems) quickly orientated so that they become high performing quickly?
- Do top managers take fast action if parts of the organisation are not working well together?

Your Rating

If the description of this component is entirely accurate in relation to your Unit of Analysis, then Aligned Capabilities will be a strong driver of requisite organisational agility and a score of 6 should be given. If a lack of Aligned Capabilities is a significant blockage then a score of 0 should be given. Scores between 1 and 5 should be allocated to reflect your assessment of the degree to which this component is helping or hindering the Unit of Analysis to be requisitely agile.

Component IIIa: Agile Suppliers

Agile Suppliers are rated as 'high' when they facilitate their client's Agility Ambition and meet its requirements for exceptional frequency, responsiveness, quality, cost, transparency and cooperativeness. Suppliers' inputs are often mission-critical, as a slow, unintegrated or unreliable supply chains markedly degrade an organisation's agile capability.

An agile organisation needs suppliers that can, and will, proactively help it in each of the four dimensions of agility (situational adaptiveness, prudent opportunism, threat mitigation and future readying). Suppliers can alert clients to situational changes and propose ways that these can be used for advantage; they will frequently highlight opportunities and may provide the means to grasp them; they do the same with threats and provide input about trends, so that an organisation becomes effectively forewarned on what it needs to do differently in the future.

From a suppliers' point of view, the complexity of dealing with agile organisations is a two-edged sword. Clients' changing demands will stretch suppliers in many ways. This can have benefits as it helps suppliers to improve and orders can be lucrative. But agile organisations change strategies and tactics frequently, so their needs are dynamic, which adds cost, complexity and uncertainty. Suppliers react by being choosy. They will not take all potential clients but select those whose values and operating processes fit with their own. The relationship between suppliers and clients must be a win-win, if it is to facilitate requisite agility.

Relationships between suppliers and agile clients are often personal, as everyone involved must build trust by being competent, solution-orientated, honest, direct, and honourably. Comprehensive legal contracts cannot substitute for the quality of human relationships. Eliminating interpersonal barriers, sharing goals, building partnerships and an interchange of people facilitates a high level of integration and sharing of accrued benefits.

Suppliers are an integral element in deploying Agile Strategies. They are key assets in an organisation's ecosystem and often need to be proactive agents in a functioning and dynamic network. This is enabled by interactive and interoperable IT systems, joint problem-solving capability and extensive cooperation between suppliers. Of importance is transparency, early recognition of potential problems and all parties contributing proactively to maintaining high levels of systemic agility for the client organisation.

Changes in any of the 6P areas may require different suppliers. Hence, finding new suppliers, completing due diligence checks and building win-win-relationships is a cornerstone of agile supply strategies.

Key Questions:
- Does our organisation have a history of working effectively with suppliers?
- Do we find suppliers that are reliable, cooperative and exceptionally creative?
- Do many of our suppliers actively help us to become better?

Your Rating

If the description of this component is entirely accurate in relation to your Unit of Analysis, then Agile Suppliers will be a strong driver of requisite organisational agility and a score of 6 should be given. If a lack of Agile Suppliers is a significant blockage then a score of 0 should be given. Scores between 1 and 5 should be allocated to reflect your assessment of the degree to which this component is helping or hindering the Unit of Analysis to be requisitely agile.

Component IIIb: Ecosystem Optimisation

Ecosystem Optimisation is rated as 'high' when an organisation's agile capability is strengthened through contacts with external entities, such as sources of funding, trade associations, government agencies, investors, research institutes, distribution chains, learning facilities, innovation hubs, resource providers etc. (Supply chains and customers are part of an agile ecosystem but are dealt with separately, as they have significantly different roles.)

That ecosystems can facilitate agility has been known for many centuries. Enterprising merchants in the early middle-ages sought to be connected to the city of Venice, as it had developed a wide range of resources to support profitable international trade. Agile-friendly ecosystems are complex, sometimes industry specific and multi-faceted. There is a large informal dimension, as they are created, in part, by the social interaction of proactive and talented people that share similar aspirations. Today's most energising agile-friendly ecosystems include Silicon Valley, Dubai, Shenzhen and Bengaluru.

Ecosystem advantages are strengthened by facilitative government policies, stimulated by engaged universities, resourced by exceptional talent, energised by an entrepreneurial local culture and enabled by capital availability. The close presence of competent rivals drives progress but is unforgiving, as enterprises will only thrive if they are prudently but boldly agile.

Much depends on geography. If you want to build a Formula One racing car the best place to site your factory will be in South East England, as 3,500 motorsport companies are based in Motorsport Valley, the home of about 80% of the world's high-performance automotive engineers. The presence of a critical mass of focused endeavour enables a cluster to form that benefits many players.

In agile enterprises managers at all levels need to exploit the benefits of ecosystems but often they contribute actively as well. This is necessary as vibrant ecosystems only emerge if nourished by mutually beneficial interactions. They are communities that thrive if there is reciprocal and respectful mutual benefit.

Some organisations must function in ecosystems that are less than agile-friendly. But they are not helpless, as in a connected world, it is possible for managers to construct virtual ecosystems. For example, in remote Namibia, away from any industry, I discovered that managers in a uranium mine had found ways to become a world-class user of kaizen (continuous improvement). The mine's managers had used the internet to work with Japanese centres of excellence, interact with kaizen enthusiasts across the world and gain help from universities to publish articles. They had created a facilitative virtual ecosystem.

Such ecosystems can provide capable partners for large or complex initiatives. In such partnering arrangements, if they work well, competition is replaced by what has been called 'coopetition', which is a combination of cooperation and competition, that enables agility to be enhanced by access to an extended resource base (Brandenburger & Nalebuff, 1997). Using this model of relationships enterprises share competencies and build temporary network-based capability. Coopetition can be an effective way to develop technologies and products, procure critical resources, investigate new markets and complement organisational competencies.

Key questions:
- Would it be correct to say that this organisation is particularly efficient in finding good partners?
- Does our organisation get the very best from its connections with the outside world?
- Do the sub-units in our organisation frequently reach outside the organisation to get inspiration and support?

Your Rating

If the description of this component is entirely accurate in relation to your Unit of Analysis, then Ecosystem Optimisation will be a strong driver of requisite organisational agility and a score of 6 should be given. If a lack of Ecosystem Optimisation is a significant blockage then a score of 0 should be given. Scores between 1 and 5 should be allocated to reflect your assessment of the degree to which this component is helping or hindering the Unit of Analysis to be requisitely agile.

Component IIIc: Facilitative Technologies

Facilitative Technologies are rated as 'high' when an organisation's agile capability is enhanced by acquiring, integrating and using technologies. The relationship between technology and agility is close, complex and dynamic.

Both hard and soft technologies play a major role in facilitating systemic and local agility. Hard technologies are largely science-based (e.g., deep learning algorithms, 3D printing or blockchain security). Soft technologies are practice-based (such as problem-solving methods or online learning). In some industries, the adoption of hard and soft agile enhancing technologies is the fastest way to achieve required agile deliverables, some of which may be disruptive and may provide completely new landscapes of opportunity.

Technologies need to be chosen to support the corporate Agility Ambition and serve the four dimensions of agility described earlier. The acquisition of appropriate suites of technologies requires well-informed top management direction, competent internal resources, integration of specialist external capabilities, extensive multi-level visioning, disciplined project management and frequent proofs of concept.

The process of technology acquisition can be integrated by defining technology portfolios. This enables technologies to be aligned, as often they will be interconnected and interactive. Examining the technology strategies of peers and best-in-class rivals provides a valuable input for developing agility-enhancing technology portfolios but this analysis, by itself, will be excessively present-orientated. Foresight into likely technological developments will be needed along with justifiable caution as to the realism of promises made by vendors.

Technological landscapes can change quickly and facilitate multiple innovations. For this reason, agile enterprises actively routinely study how technologies are likely to evolve, often using an insightful method known as a Delphi Study. This iterative process collects and synthesises opinions from experts who may be academic research faculty members at leading universities or speakers at relevant global seminars or conferences. Typically, a Delphi Study requires repeated questioning of experts, with phases of controlled feedback to inform each expert about the views of others, thereby stimulating new thinking. Typical questions asked might be: 'What would you consider as the Three Top Trends in relevant technologies over next 10 years?' 'What will be the top five most significant consequences?'

Some technologies can be dysfunctional for agility. For example, in 2020 it was still possible that a doctor in a UK hospital would need to log in separately to 20 databases to find information about a patient's medical history. Existing and prospective technologies need to be evaluated to assess whether they are (i) providing industry leading situational awareness, (ii) enabling enterprise-wide and local prundent opportunism, (iii) identifying and mitigating threats and (iv) are upgradable and future-orientated.

Key Questions:
- Would it be true to say that the organisations' systems greatly help us to be agile?
- Do our technological systems help us to know what we need to do to thrive in the future?
- Do our technological systems give us clear advantages over our rivals?

Your Rating

If the description of this component is entirely accurate in relation to your Unit of Analysis, then Facilitative Technologies will be a strong driver of requisite organisational agility and a score of 6 should be given. If a lack of Facilitative Technologies is a significant blockage then a score of 0 should be given. Scores between 1 and 5 should be allocated to reflect your assessment of the degree to which this component is helping or hindering the Unit of Analysis to be requisitely agile.

Component IIId: Deep Customer Engagement

Deep Customer Engagement is rated as 'high' when there are multi-level, fast, close and mutually beneficial relationships with internal or external customers, or potential customers. This requires that (i) internal and external actual and potential customers become targets for gaining high-level situational awareness, (ii) evidence-based insights are transformed into promising opportunities, (iii) potentially damaging threats are identified and (iv) all those with agency in an organisation share a common conceptualisation of how customers' needs may change in the future.

Deep customer engagement needs to provide evidence-based answers to five questions. How agile are we perceived to be? How do we compare with rival organisations? Would customers like us to be agile in different ways? How much would our increased or different agility be valued by our customers (if at all)? How do customers envisage that their need for us to be agile may change in the foreseeable future? It is possible that agility is a low priority for customers with other criteria, for example cost, being more important. This depth of insight is needed for the EAfA Process to facilitate devising an ambition for achieving requisite agility, not maximum agility.

Methodologies for achieving Deep Customer Engagement are widely practiced. Requisitely agile organisations use these methodologies assiduously, principally as market research tools. This facilitates the development of intimacy with customers, provides data that enables the reimagining of customers' journeys and facilitates finding opportunities to add value from the moment of awareness to achieving long-term loyalty. The Information Technology revolution has extended the range of tools available and reduced the costs of deep customer engagement. The internet provides easy access to customers who can act as informed users, co-developers, testers and evaluators. Many customers can become proactive agents in the process of designing, developing, using and improving products and services. On a larger scale, marketing departments use digital tools and big-data analytics to gain a greater depth of understanding.

A fruitful target group for targeting deep customer engagement are lead users, that are individuals or groups at the cutting-edge of an activity (von Hippel, 1986). For example, mountain rescue guides know more about rescue equipment than the equipment makers, as they have experience of using them in the worst weather conditions. Leading-edge users can often articulate a new concept for an improved product and may develop or test prototypes. This knowledge provides invaluable input for designers and may reduce new product development cycle times.

Achieving deep customer engagement greatly facilitates the task of defining Agility Indicators (see Component IIa) as an enterprise will have gained clarity about what increased agility is likely to be worth. Deep customer engagement provides a litmus test of whether value is being, or could be, added from agile initiatives. This is relevant at the enterprise (systemic) level and for sub-units who have internal or external customers.

Key Questions:
- Does our organisation become deeply engaged with customers?
- Do we collect evidence on why agility is important to our customers?
- Does our organisation co-develop products or services with customers?

Your Rating

If the description of this component is entirely accurate in relation to your Unit of Analysis then Deep Customer Engagement will be a strong driver of requisite organisational agility and a score of 6 should be given. If a lack of Deep Customer Engagement is a significant blockage then a score of 0 should be given. Scores between 1 and 5 should be allocated to reflect your assessment of the degree to which this component is helping or hindering the Unit of Analysis to be requisitely agile.

Component IVa: Fit-for-Purpose Organisation

Fit-for-Purpose Organisation is rated as 'high' when an organisation's style, structure, systems, capabilities and culture facilitate the acquisition, renewal and retention of requisite agility, thereby providing the deliverables specified in the organisation's Agility Ambition. The form of organisation strengthens its ability in each of the four high-level dimensions of agility (situational adaptiveness, prudent opportunism, active threat mitigation and future readying).

A fit-for-purpose agile organisation has selected and effectively deployed the types of agility that fit its current requirements. These change over time, sometimes rapidly. In 2020, for example, many organisations found that the impact of coronavirus was so destructive to their current business model that they were forced to look for new or different opportunity landscapes. Eight types of agility can be identified. Each requires a different managerial modality and is functional only in certain conditions. Fit-for-Purpose Organisations select the most appropriate types of agility and provide all of the capabilities that are needed for the selected types of agility to be deployed efficiently and effectively. This key construct will be briefly introduced below and described in depth in Step Six.

Top-Down Agility enables selected objectives to be achieved despite difficulties. It is especially relevant where new initiatives, that require extensive coordination, are needed to deliver priorities are contentious and need the deployment of scarce or expensive resources.

Routines-Based Agility enables a fast, capable and flexible response to be provided for predictable situations, such as a large building on fire or a health emergency. A pre-organised plan, that specifies roles and defines processes, provides contingent requisite agility.

Project-Based Agility enables major new tasks to be completed efficiently and effectively if they are variants of tasks previously completed, such building a cement plant, making a film or launching a marketing campaign.

Socio-Technical Agility enables technical and human resources to be combined to deliver an effective response that could not be achieved without the productive synthesis of these two domains of action.

Skunk Works Agility enables innovation to be targeted to achieve challenging new tasks that have never been previously completed, such developing a new vehicle for space exploration or dealing with unsolved environmental challenges.

Intrapreneurial Agility enables the latent entrepreneurial talents of multiple individuals to be liberated and channelled into driving initiatives that would not otherwise be undertaken.

Granular Agility enables qualified individuals or teams to take responsibility for directing activities locally, thereby delivering customised solutions.

Networked Agility enables the talents and resources of multiple organisations to be combined, thereby providing a capacity to undertake tasks that none of the individual organisations could accomplish alone.

Key Questions:
- Can our organisation reorganise quickly to take advantage of new opportunities?
- Does our organisation use the types of agility that are most efficient and effective?
- Are we more effectively agile than rival organisations?

Your Rating

If the description of this component is entirely accurate in relation to your Unit of Analysis, then Fit-for-Purpose Organisation will be a strong driver of requisite organisational agility and a score of 6 should be given. If a lack of Fit-for-Purpose Organisation is a significant blockage then a score of 0 should be given. Scores between 1 and 5 should be allocated to reflect your assessment of the degree to which this component is helping or hindering the Unit of Analysis to be requisitely agile.

Component IVb: Adaptive Human Resources

Adaptive Human Resources are rated as 'high' when the people that work in, or with, an organisation are able and willing to work effectively in an agility-orientated environment and they strive to do everything possible to enable both corporate and local Agile Ambitions to be achieved.

There is a long list of generic personal qualities needed to enable people to function successfully in agile organisations. In addition to relevant and deep technical competence, personal skills are critical. These include intellectual curiosity, proactivity, team-orientation, co-working with machines, resilience and a willingness to undertake roles as needed by the situation. People working in agility intensive roles need personal grit, emotional maturity, theories of action and a capacity to work with smart systems. These personal qualities will be supplemented with role-specific capabilities that vary according to which type of agility is being used, as will be explained in greater detail in Step Six.

The importance and complexity of recruiting, training, retaining and motivating people with the required generic attributes, and role-specify competencies, means that all but the smallest agile enterprises need creative and forward-looking human resource management policies and practices. This requires that the human resource management department is a genuine strategic partner and has the influencing power to ensure that all managers take responsibility for win-win people management. The importance of this has been shown by world-class agile organisations like Google or Spotify, which are lead developers of methods for people management that treat everyone differently, rather than as a member of a category.

Studies of the differences between top and average performing individuals suggest that, in some occupations, the best can be about 10 times more productive than those who are average (Evers, Anderson, & Voskuijl, 2017). As agile organisations are heavily dependent on high performing individuals there is a clear message: if you want to be agile, you need great people. Such talent is in high demand, so agile organisations must be great places in which to work. Acquiring high-end talent is a mission-critical requirement for those parts of an organisation that need to be intensively agile.

Those organisations may have legacy Human Resource Management departments that remain dominated by twentieth century good-practice as they continue to adopt policies that promote conformance, risk avoidance, rigid job descriptions, legal compliance and the implementation of formalised procedures. Such legacy practices become systemic agility blockages.

Until relatively recently the dominant driver of agility was people. Now smart systems are adding previously unavailable agile capabilities. Where this occurs, the emergence of socio-technical enabled agility changes the portfolio of skills needed. Organisations need to learn to be agile in new ways.

Key Questions:
- Do talented people want to work here?
- Does the human resource management department work in ways that facilitate organisational agility?
- Do most visitors comment that there is a sense of positive energy in our organisation?

Your Rating

If the description of this component is entirely accurate in relation to your Unit of Analysis, then Adaptive Human Resources will be a strong driver of requisite organisational agility and a score of 6 should be given. If a lack of Adaptive Human Resources is a significant blockage then a score of 0 should be given. Scores between 1 and 5 should be allocated to reflect your assessment of the degree to which this component is helping or hindering the Unit of Analysis to be requisitely agile.

Component IVc: Contextual Leadership

Contextual Leadership is rated as 'high' when leaders and managers flex their style according to the needs of the moment. Effective leadership in agile organisations requires a diversity of styles that EAfA describes as Contextual Leadership. The key styles are explained below in sequence but will be adopted flexibly. The styles described relate directly to the innovation management modalities, described earlier.

The *Searching Leadership Style* is used when situations, needs, opportunities, hazards or resources are insufficiently understood. Proactive searching enables intelligence and insights to be gathered so that possible opportunities and threats can be identified. What do you have when searching is complete? Perhaps hundreds of undifferentiated ideas and possibilities. This style requires the development of a temporary organisational culture that promotes open-minded, inquisitive and outward-looking enquiry.

The *Exploring Leadership Style* is used when there are many ideas for initiatives but their strengths and weaknesses are unknown. Some may be nuggets of gold whilst others will be impractical, irrelevant or unlikely to create value. Solid, disciplined detective work will be needed. The leader will emphasise the need to understand, in depth, the potential benefits of ideas or opportunities, their downsides, risks and the implications of possible adoption, as this knowledge will improve the quality of evidence for decision-making. This style requires the development of a temporary culture that promotes disciplined investigation of the merits and demerits of opportunities or ideas.

The *Committing Leadership Style* is used when decisions are made as to which ideas and proposals should be adopted as commitments. The key question is 'should we do this?' Answering this question requires moving beyond assessing whether a proposed initiative is a 'good idea'. It requires deciding whether it 'is a good idea *for us?*'. After a commitment decision is made, then the necessary resources and funding must be provided. Only so much can be done at once. If an initiative is adopted as a managerial priority, then those whose support will be needed must 'sign-up' to become proactive facilitators and enablers. This style requires the development of a temporary culture that promotes considered decisions and the aligned mobilisation of managerial effort and organisational resources.

The *Realising Leadership Style* is used to transform a commitment into something useful. Often a team or project organisation will be required. Team members need to work within the disciplines of task management. The membership of the team may change over time but its main requirement remains the same: to make a service, product or other artefact that creates greater value than the costs incurred. A realising culture promotes focused, coordinated and agile teamwork and emphasises performance. This style requires the development of a culture that builds an adaptive but temporary project organisation to get things done efficiently and effectively.

The *Exploiting Leadership Style* is used to gain the maximum advantage from initiatives. It may be that possible users are unaware of advantages that they are missing. Or, there might be opportunities for upgrades in the service or product. Also, there will an emphasis on learning how to improve in the future. This style requires the development of a temporary culture that focuses attention on exploiting advantages fully.

Key Questions:
- Do leaders and managers flex their styles to suit the stage of development of initiatives?
- Are initiatives managed so that they progress quickly and effectively?
- Do leaders and managers give people the help that they need to get new things done?

Your Rating

If the description of this component is entirely accurate in relation to your Unit of Analysis, then Contextual Leadership will be a strong driver of requisite organisational agility and a score of 6 should be given. If a lack of Contextual Leadership is a significant blockage then a score of 0 should be given. Scores between 1 and 5 should be allocated to reflect your assessment of the degree to which this component is helping or hindering the Unit of Analysis to be requisitely agile.

Component IVd: Resilient Execution

Resilient Execution is rated as 'high' when things get done effectively and efficiently, despite problems or setbacks. Inadequate or failed execution is a serious problem for agile enterprises as it undermines the satisfaction of customers, creates unnecessary work, saps collective confidence, questions the efficacy of a can-do ethic and diverts management attention into 'fire-fighting'. For agile organisations reliable and fast execution is a required mission-critical capability.

The word 'resilient' is important. In this context it means delivering on promises despite uncertainties, complexity, systems failures and other predictable or unpredictable contingencies. Achieving Resilient Execution is especially demanding for agile enterprises for three main reasons: (i) over the last decade there have been considerable improvements in every aspect of execution, from product and service quality to maintaining close contact with customers, suppliers etc. This sets a high standard for all enterprises that is difficult to attain; (ii) agile enterprises are dynamic, meaning that their offers change frequently and this adds complexity, thereby increasing the risk of unexpected vulnerabilities and (iii) urgent cooperative, adaptive and orchestrated action across organisational sub-units requires a hard-to-achieve level of internal coordination.

TMTs in requisitely agile enterprises will have clarified what 'good' execution means in practice and blockages in execution receive immediate management attention. TMTs will have a theory of action as to how to acquire the relevant characteristics from High Reliability Organisations, such as Air Traffic Control Systems or Nuclear Power Plants. Many agile organisations draw from quality management and lean process improvement as overarching disciplines. These constructs and methodologies need to be deeply embedded in practice.

Lean thinking provides valuable templates for developing execution capabilities, as it focuses on the elimination of non-value-adding activities and installing high-reliability processes that have a built-in capacity for continuous improvement and self-healing (see Step One for an explanation of Lean Thinking). Lean process are necessary but not sufficient as robustness needs to be designed into organisational resources including facilities, equipment, systems, sub-contracted services, controls, management routines, information processes and technological support. Rapid Resilient Execution leverages bundles of aligned capabilities to transform intentions into actions effectively, efficiently, rapidly and economically.

Smart systems and human problem-solving skills facilitate Resilient Execution. Smart systems provide real-time performance management, progress analytics and may enable easy benchmarking comparisons and displays of systemic effectiveness. This enables managers to monitor the efficiency of execution across their organisation. Human problem-solving skills, including systematic problem-identification and structured problem-solving are essential for all colleagues, including outside contractors. When there is deep collective competence in problem-solving then symptoms of problems will be identified quickly and sufficient resources allocated to find effective solutions. If this does not occur then inertia becomes a way of life. An organisation that is slow in identifying and solving problems finds its creative energies become absorbed in rectification and minor improvement, not in finding and seizing opportunities.

Key Questions:
- Is fast, reliable execution (getting things done efficiently, effectively and on-time) a strength of this organisation?
- Does everyone in the organisation have the ability to solve problems systematically?
- Are problems in execution quickly solved?

Your Rating

If the description of this component is entirely accurate in relation to your Unit of Analysis, then Resilient Execution will be a strong driver of requisite organisational agility and a score of 6 should be given. If a lack of Resilient Execution is a signifi-cant blockage then a score of 0 should be given. Scores between 1 and 5 should be allocated to reflect your assessment of the degree to which this component is help-ing or hindering the Unit of Analysis to be requisitely agile.

Component Va: Integrated Innovation

Integrated Innovation is rated as 'high' when an organisation uses appropriate modes of innovation in the service of delivering its Agility Ambition.

The EAfA Process views innovation as specialised work packages that transform selected opportunities into value. Our perspective is unconventional. A commonly used definition of innovation is 'the successful exploitation of ideas that are new to the Unit of Adoption'. This helpfully differentiates innovation from invention. However, agile organisations frequently outsource, buy or lease novel solutions rather than do the work of creating them, in order to avoid any potential disadvantages of acting as the original innovators. EAfA defines *successful* innovation as 'doing the work of transforming opportunities into value, where the advantage gained is greater than the financial and non-financial costs incurred'.

Agile organisations must be initiative-intensive, but they do not need to take the full burden of innovating on themselves. Often, ideas and opportunities can be appropriated or adapted from outside, as is done by fast followers. However, agile organisations will innovate where they can gain at least one of three possible bene-fits, which are (i) enabling the innovator to be a first-mover, as this, on average, has proven advantages; (ii) increasing the probability that the outcome from innovation can become a valuable asset that is owned by the innovator and can be protected and (iii) by doing the necessary work the organisation acquires valuable and battle-tested knowledge. These benefits can be game-changing, meaning that innovation needs to be integrated into the core capability profile of many agile organisations.

Eight modes of innovation are widely found in agile organisations. These are (i) *Creative Team Process* (furthers innovation by creative team interaction); (ii) *Reviewing to Improve* (develops insights from systematic analysis of past events); (iii) *Proactive Imitation* (looks for comparable experiences or products from elsewhere that can be imitated or adapted); (iv) *Creative Re-Examination* (finds conceptually different ways to analyse situations find solutions); (v) *Experimentation* (tests ideas in practice to collect evaluation data); (vi) *Resourced Initiatives* (undertakes directed and resourced innovation projects); (vii) *Design Thinking* (focusing on what could be, rather than what is) and (viii) *User Co-Creation* (where ideas are co-developed with users, often internal or external customers). Each mode of innovation has a different function. Selecting appropriate modes effectively is a key requirement.

Innovation may be needed in five zones. *Strategic Innovation* enables strategic commitments to become actualities. *Functional Innovation* enables specialist groups to upgrade their contribution to the organisation. *Workplace and User Innovation* brings about changes in what is done or how it is done, driven by the insight of the people who are directly involved. *Specialist-Driven Innovation* uses experts to advise on which innovations should be adopted. *Network Innovation* constructs an ecosystem to gain benefit from new ideas between interdependent agents. Agile organisations may need innovate in all these zones.

Key Questions:
- Is our organisation's approach to innovation increasing our ability to be agile?
- Are we innovating sufficiently to be ready for a different future?
- Are we faster at innovating than our rivals?

Your Rating

If the description of this component is entirely accurate in relation to your Unit of Analysis, then Integrated Innovation will be a strong driver of requisite organisational agility and a score of 6 should be given. If a lack of Integrated Innovation is a significant blockage then a score of 0 should be given. Scores between 1 and 5 should be allocated to reflect your assessment of the degree to which this component is helping or hindering the Unit of Analysis to be requisitely agile.

Component Vb: Extensive Agile Ethos

Ethos is the distinctive spirit of a culture, community or organisation. Extensive Agile Ethos is rated as 'high' when everyone feels that they want to contribute positively to fulfilling their organisation's Agility Ambition. Agile organisations are characterised by promoting an adventurous but prudent ethos.

As mentioned earlier (see Chapter 2) agile organisations are aligned by a shared ambition, rather than by shared routines. The EAfA Process emphasises that it is a leadership task to shape the development of what sociologists have called a 'collective consciousness' or the 'hive mind' (Yolles, 2005). This develops when people share aspirations and feel that they are part of a whole. They prize belonging, identify their fortunes with their organisation and feel emotionally connected. Values and beliefs become unified and the organisation evolves as a social entity. As collective consciousness grows in influence so the organisation will develop an identity (how it is perceived from the outside); a personality (a shared stance to work), a culture (agreement about 'this is how we get things done') and an ethos (its distinctive spirit).

The notion that agile organisations possess a distinctive organisational personality, identity, culture and ethos is consistent with the EAfA view that they can be considered to be organisms with a form of life force, rather than as machines or systems. Agile organisations seem to be intelligent and alive, not soulless bureaucracies. The language needed to describe such an organisation, and the metaphors that we use to make sense of its intelligent wholeness, is organic, dynamic and fluid.

The ethos of requisitely agile organisations is cooperative, as they only thrive when the values-in-action are integrity, reliability and predictable quality of performance, otherwise they can fall into chaos. Agility requires inner-directed discipline.

Agile organisations have a distinctive and often idiosyncratic ethos that, unlike the notion of an organisational brand, has been created from actions by multiple stakeholders. When an agile-friendly ethos is extensively embedded, then the organisation will possess a capacity to liberate and align human energy in ways that often feel extraordinary.

Leaders actively shape their organisation's ethos by what they say and, more importantly, what they do, and by what they do not do. However, leadership is not sufficient as everyone who has influence, that is possesses agency, serves to create their organisation's personality moment-by-moment by their actions and inactions. In a requisitely agile organisation, the connection between individuals and the organisation is deep. Much is required from colleagues who must engage in multiple novel and uncertain activities, take responsibility for decision-making, work flexibly in various work groups, maintain just-in-time learning, experience stressful situations and cope with variable, probably unpredictable, workloads. The extent of this commitment requires that people will dedicate much of themselves to their organisation. This will only be undertaken when individuals feel deeply connected to their organisation by being part of the hive mind.

   Key Questions:
- Does everyone feel that they are privileged to work here?
- Does the ethos of the organisation promote agility?
- Is there extensive cooperation between sub-groups?

Your Rating

If the description of this component is entirely accurate in relation to your Unit of Analysis, then Extensive Agile Ethos will be a strong driver of requisite organisational agility and a score of 6 should be given. If a lack of Extensive Agile Ethos is a significant blockage then a score of 0 should be given. Scores between 1 and 5 should be allocated to reflect your assessment of the degree to which this component is helping or hindering the Unit of Analysis to be requisitely agile.

Component Vc: Supported Intrapreneurship

Supported Intrapreneurship is rated as 'high' when many people in an organisation find, develop and exploit many opportunities and senior managers support bottom-up initiatives. Intrapreneurship provides a mechanism for facilitating multiple acts of prudent opportunism.

   The term intrapreneur may be unfamiliar. You can think of it as internally directed entrepreneurship. An intrapreneur possesses entrepreneurial talent and uses it to benefit their organisation, not primarily themselves. EAfA recognises that there is a sub-type of intrapreneur that we call an agilepreneur. Someone playing this role has the skills to embed an entrepreneurial ethos in their areas of influence, by acting as a change agent.

   Traditionally entrepreneurs focused on products and markets. Agile organisations TMTs enlarge this entrepreneurial scope in two main ways. First, they deliberately design their organisations to support, develop and exploit intrapreneurial talent, if this type of agility is needed. This is achieved by legitimising agilepreneurship as a change dynamic, providing resources to empower intrapreneurial proactivity and visibly adopting selected proposals, thereby encouraging agilepreneurship.

   Secondly, intrapreneurial ability will be targeted on *all* the 6P target areas (see Chapter 3 for an explanation of the 6Ps Model). These are (P1) Products (outputs), (P2) Processes (activities), (P3) Positions (external communication), (P4) Paradigms (business models), (P5) Provisioning (resources) and (P6) Platforms (ways of exploiting network effects). For example, one intrapreneur can focus her or his energies on finding better ways to organise work (P2) whereas another finds new ways to communicate with potential customers (P3).

Intrapreneurship is strengthened by allocating time and resource for experiments, prototyping, testing and learning from comparable organisations' cutting-edge initiatives. It thrives in a climate that does not punish failure unless it was the result of neglect. The benefits of intrapreneurship must be honoured within the organisation, so that it becomes a culturally valued activity.

Although intrapreneurship provides a valuable mechanism for facilitating multiple acts of prudent opportunism it can be a high-risk organisational policy. Not everyone is capable of making prudent judgement decisions about where to invest time and resources, so intrapreneurial initiatives can result in dysfunctional fragmentation. Additionally, effort can be invested disproportionately in developing novel proposals rather than contributing to current priorities. Despite such risks, promoting intrapreneurship remains an essential option for organisations seeking to acquire requisite agility.

Key Questions:
- Does our organisation deliberately support those with entrepreneurial passion?
- Are there policies and practices in place to help intrapreneurs to be effective?
- Do intrapreneurs target their proposals on taking the organisation forward?

Your Rating

If the description of this component is entirely accurate in relation to your Unit of Analysis, then Pervasive Intrapreneurship will be a strong driver of requisite organisational agility and a score of 6 should be given. If a lack of Pervasive Intrapreneurship is a significant blockage then a score of 0 should be given. Scores between 1 and 5 should be allocated to reflect your assessment of the degree to which this component is helping or hindering the Unit of Analysis to be requisitely agile.

Component Vd: Collective Learning

Collective Learning is rated as 'high' when an organisation learns at a pace that gives it comparative or competitive advantage. This enriches, aligns and strengthens the contribution of individuals to the organisation. It is distinct from individual learning, as it is the organisation that acquires intelligence (Lau, Lee, & Chung, 2019). Collective learning reshapes how people think, feel and act. Increasingly, autonomous systems add to organisational learning capacity as a modern agile enterprise requires socio-technical learning capability.

We came to understand that collective learning is mission-critical in an unexpected way. Some years ago, a group of social scientists spent months on an American aircraft carrier studying how the crew could manage complex, technical and dangerous tasks reliably and adjust quickly to unexpected situations, in other words to be agile. They found that everyone understood her or his impact on the total system and this enabled them to make intelligent real-time decisions in the interest of the whole. When things went wrong those involved developed solutions autonomously, thereby practicing what was described as 'heedful interrelating' (Weick & Roberts, 1993). It was concluded that such aligned collective learning enhances sociological coherence, a necessity in agile organisations.

In Chapter 2 it was suggested that: "Agile organisations are best viewed as organisms, not machines. They are capable of being venturesome, intelligent and self-healing." This implies that it is possible for an organisation to learn. An example shows that this is possible. The day that the new Terminal Five was opened at London's Heathrow Airport there were a host of problems. In all, 34 flights had to be cancelled. A few years later another new terminal was opened at Heathrow without any of the earlier problems. Flights were moved to the new terminal in stages, systems were tested multiple times before the opening day and back-up resources were in reserve in case of problems. The managers had learnt from their previous experience. They did not make the same mistakes twice. There had been detailed analyses of failures that identified, in detail, the factors that caused them. The lessons learnt were widely shared. Time was taken to build a consensus amongst managers, as to the best way to commission new terminals. Heathrow had learnt as an entity.

The pace of collective learning needs to be fast in an agile organisation, as does unlearning (moving on from 'old' ways of thinking and acting). Agility requires that people and systems can change frequently, so much needs to be done without a raft of experience being available for guidance. Rapid collective learning can be facilitated by digital and face-to-face training, but the most significant enabling force will be role modelling by leaders and senior managers. It makes a huge difference if leaders and senior managers are seen to be open to new constructs, listen to divergent views, review critically current operations, study the alchemy of success assiduously and receive personal feedback positively. Such behaviours help to develop a learning-oriented ethos in the enterprise.

In agile organisations those whose actions can shape the future of the enterprise need to be exposed, in depth, to the pulse of the world in which they operate. If individuals are not in touch with developing themes within their area of responsibility, then their thinking cannot expand in ways that promote requisite agility. Interestingly, agile organisations are more intellectual than others, as there needs to be a substantial quantity of time spent on the development of evidence-based constructs about how things could develop. Within explorations of future spaces for opportunity lies the possibility for initiatives that are not rooted in current situation.

Key Questions:
- Do those in leadership positions actively promote collective learning?
- Do those in leadership and management positions behave in ways that show that they are personally open to learning?
- Are there frequent opportunities to get together and learn from recent successes and identify areas for improvement?

Your Rating

If the description of this component is entirely accurate in relation to your Unit of Analysis, then Collective Learning will be a strong driver of requisite organisational agility and a score of 6 should be given. If a lack of Collective Learning is a significant blockage then a score of 0 should be given. Scores between 1 and 5 should be allocated to reflect your assessment of the degree to which this component is helping or hindering the Unit of Analysis to be requisitely agile.

The Step Three Workshop – Diagnosing: *Do we have the capabilities to be agile?*

Preparation
A room that has a large image of the EAfA Wheel Reference Model on a whiteboard or similar.

Time
2 hours and 30 minutes.

Workshop Structure

1. The ADT leader invites members of the team to agree on what would be great outcomes of this session. These can be written on a whiteboard or a flip chart so that they remain in view during the workshop (10 minutes).
2. At the end of the Step Two workshop participants were asked to list 'things that worked well and areas for improvement'. These points should be reviewed in order to assist the team to work more effectively during the current session (5 minutes).
3. The ADT leader shows the Agile Wheel Diagram and he or she asks members if it they have questions about the model (5 minutes).

4. In the workshop session, individuals should share their pre-work scores component-by-component before each component is discussed. By consensus, each of the 20 components should be rated by the team using a 6-point scale with the lowest scores indicating that it is a blockage or hindering factor and high scores indicating that it is an agility driver (60 minutes).
5. By consensus or voting, the top three blockages and top three agility drivers are identified and listed separately. Then the ADT spend 20 minutes discussing the significance of the blockages and 20 minutes discussing how the agility drivers could be strengthened (60 minutes).
6. ADT members privately answer two questions: 'What is one thing that worked well in this session?' and 'What is one area where we could improve next time?' After one or two minutes the answers to the questions should be shared and between three and five suggestions for improvement recorded (10 minutes).
7. At the end of the workshop, the top three drivers and blockages should be listed, and notes saved as they will be needed in Step 6.

Going Deeper

Some organisations may wish to gather systematic data using an organisational survey. A condensed version of the EAfA Systemic Agility Reference Model Survey can be downloaded freely from https://www.richmondconsultantsltd.com, which includes guidance for administration.

9 Step Four – Envisioning: *What will we be like when we are requisitely agile?*

The focus of this step is *envisioning*. In this step the ADT will develop a draft Agility Ambition, that will continue to be refined as later steps are completed.

Guidance for the ADT Leader

Many organisations have a mission statement, a definition of their strategic intent, a list of core values or a vision of the future. Such constructs align an organisation towards achieving shared goals and, clarify its formula for gaining competitive or comparative advantage. Fewer organisations have clarity about what they seek to achieve from being requisitely agile. This means that there will be divergent views about the functions of agility in the organisation, a lack of clarity about which types of agility are needed and few, if any, ways to assess how success can be assessed.

In this step the members of an ADT participate in an Agility Ambition Workshop. The Unit of Analysis can be the organisation (the systemic level) or sub-units (the local level). It is preferable if the TMT define the corporate Agility Ambition first, as this will enable sub-units to frame their local Agility Ambitions within the context of the wider organisation's requirements. However, the task is worthwhile if undertaken by sub-units working alone.

ADT leaders should note that the EAfA perspective on organisational agility is contingent, not absolutist. This is because not all organisations need to be agile; not all parts of an organisation need to be equally agile and not all organisations need to adopt the same type of agility. Hence, in the briefing for the workshop the ADT leader should emphasise that the task of the ADT is viewing agility as an organisational capability that may, or may not, be relevant to them and realise that it has great potential but also incurs costs and risks.

The workshop task is to 'to prepare a draft realistic and progressive Agility Ambition statement'. ADT leaders should note the word 'draft'. As the ADT works through the remaining steps of the EAfA Process the Agility Ambition statement will continue to be refined. It may also need to be discussed with senior managers and other stakeholders.

It will be important to refer, if available, to relevant guidance notes that have been prepared by your senior management, as sub-units need to be aligned with their wider organisation's corporate Agility Ambition.

https://doi.org/10.1515/9783110637267-010

The Pre-Workshop Tasks for Step Four

Purpose
To prepare a draft realistic and progressive Agility Ambition Statement for our Unit of Analysis.

Goals
i. To enable ADT members to understand the functions of an Agility Ambition.
ii. To produce a draft Agility Ambition that can be developed further in subsequent steps of the EAfA Process and used as the basis for wider consultation.

Process
Work alone, or in pairs, in completing the pre-work as the workshop will be more effective if each team member has an opportunity to make a distinctive contribution.

Core Task
To prepare a draft Agility Ambition statement.

Sub-Tasks
1. Read the Guidelines for Defining an Agility Ambition.
2. As you read the Guidelines you should make your own list of 'things that we should do to prepare a realistic, constructive and aspirational Agility Ambition Statement' and 'things that we should avoid doing'. After you have read the Guidelines in full, select what you consider to be the three most important 'things to do' and the most important three 'things not to do'. Take these points to the workshop.

Time Required
About 2 hours for the pre-work and 3 hours and 15 minutes for the workshop.

The Pre-Work for Step Four

In this step the ADT will develop a draft Agility Ambition statement, that can be used for discussion with stakeholders. Your Agility Ambition statement will be a description of what your Unit of Analysis will be like when it becomes requisitely agile, meaning that it has not too much agility, nor too little, of the right type and is delivering the wanted agility deliverables. An Agility Ambition should not promote agility because it is being seen as a 'good thing'. Agility needs to be viewed as an optional strategic capability rather than a foolproof formula for success. The Agility Ambition for your Unit of Analysis could be to become less agile!

Sub-units often have Agility Ambitions that are different from others. There can be situations where the Agility Ambition of an enterprise is bold and aspirational, but some of its sub-units will need to focus on developing other capabilities, such as conformance to standard operating procedures. For example, a film production company can have a stretching Agility Ambition but the primary task of its equipment maintenance department is to achieve high levels of reliability, which is more important than being agile. Your aim will be to find ways to exploit agility for advantage in your own area of responsibility.

We can learn about the functions of an Agility Ambition by studying the following example. It is a remarkable story of the development of a pioneering social enterprise (Horne, 1995). It was in 1965 when a huge riot laid waste to many buildings in Watts, a poor community in Los Angeles. By the end the third day, the unrest covered 50 square miles. Watts looked like a war zone and violent destruction continued for another three days. Eventually, peace was restored but high unemployment, poor schools, inferior living conditions, police aggression and generalised alienation remained. One man made a difference in the months and years that followed. He was Ted Watkins, a black man born in the 1920s who, at the age of 13, on his own, had moved to Watts to find a job. He worked in automobile factories and became an official of the United Auto Workers Union.

After the Watts riots Watkins formed a group called the Watts Labor Community Action Committee (WLCAC). It began with responsible people willing to give time and energy to a social project. There were few resources and the needs were enormous. A decade later, the WLCAC had 1,400 employees, almost all were previously unemployed residents of Watts; they had planted 28,000 trees; won contracts for 49 work programmes and were one of the largest social enterprises of its kind in the world ("Watts Labor Action Committee," n.d.).

How was this achieved? Watkins had an ambition. He wanted to contribute to the transformation of Watts. He believed that young people's potential was corrupted by unemployment and that working would improve their lives for the better. His ambition was to bring work to Watts. That would require that young people learnt how to work efficiently and effectively.

Watkins did not know how to achieve this ambition and he formed the WLCAC as a learning organisation, led by a Governing Board that was committed to find promising opportunities for those who most needed help. Watkins himself, with the members of the Governing Board, became the wellspring for hundreds of initiatives.

Values were key and, once agreed, they were imposed consistently, thereby providing an organisational glue. For example, Watkins said: "we do not try to find recreational activities: we find a way for youth to become productive so that they could end up with a job" and "we demand production". Such values shaped decision-making (these comments are extracts from my video interview with Ted Watkins that you can find at https://vimeo.com/234332754) Put simply, the ambition was 'to find ways to bring enough work into Watts and get work done well by our people'. This intent could not be achieved without an Agility Ambition.

One story provides an insight into how Watkins's Agility Ambition shaped policy development. In 1966, about a year after the riot had been quelled, Watkins was driving through the district when he saw about twenty young people standing on a street corner. He stopped his car and went to talk to them. The young people told him that they were waiting for a WLCAC volunteer to take them to a music venue, but she had not arrived. He waited with them for about half an hour before taking the younger ones to their homes. The next morning Watkins learnt that the volunteer had planned to meet the young people on that street corner, but her husband had arranged a surprise dinner, and she had no way of contacting them to postpone the evening's entertainment. A few days later Watkins chaired a meeting of the Governing Board and he told them that 'we cannot run this organisation with volunteers. We need paid staff to deliver our services'. His recommendation was accepted.

The story of the absent volunteer demonstrates that Watkins identified a problem and, faithful to his ambition, he cared sufficiently to take decisive action. Many of us might have seen this as a trivial incident. Watkins saw it as an unacceptable consequence of a systemic problem that was a threat to his ambition. He analysed the causes, found a solution and convinced Board Members to act. A new policy was devised and comprehensively implemented. As a result, the organisation grew stronger. Watkins's actions demonstrated that agility needs to be focussed inwards as well as outwards, which we can describe as paradigm agility.

A supremely agile organisation, like the WLCAC, could not have emerged without a resourceful, bold and capable leader who had developed an inspiring and comprehensive ambition. Watkins was willing to devote himself to this effort. Values and orientating principles were developed, embedded and demanded. The WLCAC became an organisation capable of creating opportunities and delivering on its promises. It became requisitely agile. And remains, so, with new objectives but the same core Agility Ambition.

Why have an Agility Ambition?

The Agility Ambition of the WLCAC was about the essence of organising, not the specifics of what needed to be achieved. At the highest level it was an ambition to do everything possible to support socially constructive action in a specified community. How this would be interpreted would depend on the opportunities currently available. It is correct to describe this Agility Ambition as a 'call for action'.

An Agility Ambition is a future-orientated sensemaking tool that orientates people to a chosen direction of travel. Its managerial purpose becomes clearer if an example is considered. Imagine that Jane Smith joins the LMN organisation as a manager and she is given an explanation of the enterprise's Agility Ambition. Afterwards she should be able to say: "I understand what is meant by agility here, the things that we need to do to make it happen, why it is important to us and how I can help". Notice that the Agility Ambition was communicated to Jane in sufficient depth for her to visualise how it might be applied in practice. Agility Ambitions are nothing unless they guide multiple endeavours. If wisely constructed, and extensively adopted, an Agility Ambition provides inclusive and focused cultural cohesion.

The Functions of an Agility Ambition

A well-constructed Agility Ambition, embedded in the ethos of the organisation, provides a range of benefits to the wider organisation that, using a sociological perspective, we will describe as 'functions'. These are the contributions that a part makes to the whole.

An Agility Ambition can function to empower individuals and it provides a tool for enrolling others. This point becomes clearer if we return to the history of the WLCAC. If Ted Watkins did not have an ambition, then nothing would have happened. His ambition was not a defined goal but a description of the desired life force of an organisation that would continue to flex as a construct and facilitate multiple forms of opportunism. Hence it was an *agile* ambition, one that inspired him and, later, others. Watkins worked at developing his ambition to ensure that it was (i) based on clear values, (ii) integrated, (iii) comprehensive, (iv) evidence-based and (v) could continue to evolve over time.

An Agility Ambition should function to inspire, align and mobilise groups. The Governing Board of the WLCAC had attracted a group of experienced, influential and proactive members (we can describe them as agilepreneurs) who provided wider perspectives, resources, guidance and momentum. They helped Watkins to look for insights about how to scale-up, eventually using the Roman Catholic Church as an organisational model. The WLCAC created, or found, opportunities, and detected threats, for both internally and externally focused initiatives. Their Agility Ambition enabled the WLCAC's strategies to evolve over time.

We learnt from remarkable people like Watkins that forming an Agility Ambition is a leadership and strategic act. It gains power when it provides orienting concepts for people to know 'this is what we are working to achieve'. Agility Ambitions are demonstrated by actions, especially during critical incidents. When effective, they integrate, align, inspire and mobilise initiatives. Agility Ambitions provide an architecture of meaning to organisations that require prudent opportunism as a core capability.

An Agility Ambition should illustrate what deliverables will flow from the possession of agility to owners, employees, other stakeholders, customers and those who may be socially or environmentally impacted. It helps individuals to realise that their working lives cannot be entirely pre-planned, as forms of uncertainty will be a constant companion but facing this reality has benefits as it facilitates personal growth.

When do we need an Agility Ambition?

Agile Ambitions are needed where one or more of three conditions apply, which are that (i) agility is a core element of an organisation's identity; (ii) the work undertaken requires inputs from enhanced situational responsiveness and/or more rapid and consequential prudent opportunism and/or robust threat avoidance and/or deliberately preparing to be future-ready or (iii) it is possible that external or internal change drivers will require an agile response in the foreseeable future.

An Agility Ambition as a Career Choice

A useful way to understand the essence of an Agility Ambition is to compare it with a career choice made by a person. An individual must identify, and take action to satisfy, his or her inner creative forces that, once identified, act as career drivers. These emerge from an individual's personality, abilities, values and self-image and are revealed rather than selected. People learn what excites and fulfils them. They reach a point where they feel that 'this is who I want to be and what I want to contribute to the world'. Career drivers are an unseen hand that guides personal decision-making. An Agility Ambition serves a similar purpose, as it liberates and channels energy and resources into multiple aligned and attuned endeavours.

An Agility Ambition can be to avoid Agility!

All organisations have Agility Ambitions, whether they know it or not. But they do not have to be enthusiastic about agility as a broad concept. Organisations can have ambitions to avoid agility. I recall visiting the directors of a mass-transit railway where the managers of operations and maintenance departments actively fought against deviations from required standards, as there had been examples where this had led to inefficiencies and accidents. Their managerial ambition was to achieve 100% skilful, timely and responsible conformance to tried-and-tested routines. Agility played a minor role (they had a kaizen process) except when major changes were introduced, such as major upgrades to signalling systems, that needed phases of increased but top-down agility.

An ambition to avoid agility or demote it to become a low-priority capability, can be exactly what is needed. The Ponte Vecchio Bridge was built in Florence in 1345 and, close by, there are traditional jewellery workshops that keep alive the unique Florentine tradition of jewellery-making that began in the 12th century. The competitive advantage of these traditional jewellers is that they eschew fashion, thereby enabling customers to enjoy newly made medieval masterpieces. For these jewellery workshops agility, at best, will be a minor asset, perhaps helping them to find better ways to recruit talented apprentices or to use social media for marketing.

How does an Agility Ambition differ from other Strategic Tools?

An Agility Ambition is different than a mission statement, strategic intent or a play-book, although these constructs have value and overlap in constructive ways. An Agility Ambition is aspirational, emotional, open and has attraction power. It is akin to the motive force that gets a middle-aged parent, who has promised her son to run a marathon next year, to get out of bed at 4am to go for a run on a wet and cold winter morning. There are rational arguments to support this ambition, but the driving force lies deeper. It comes from a desire to make a difference.

An Agility Ambition is an essential building block in transforming an intention to become an agile organisation into a reality. When effective, an Agility Ambition articulates, in depth, the function of agility within a specific organisation in ways that everyone can understand, embrace and use to guide their priorities. An effective organisational Agility Ambition will be a managed consensus that is constructed and reconstructed in real time as people with agency decide what is important, or not important and what will be done, or won't be done.

Agility Ambitions and Organisational Values

These is a close relationship between an Agility Ambition and organisational values. It is our values that tell us what is important. They shape the personalities of individuals and organisations. Shared values are fundamental elements of a corporate genetic code that defines an organisation's identity, ethos and personality. Core values become effective when they determine behaviour whether someone else is watching or not. When a core value is enacted widely and frequently then it becomes an aligning force.

The way that core values are practiced will adapt to changing requirements. Imagine an up-market retail store that prides itself on being highly customer-orientated. A few years ago, this core value was interpreted to mean that its sales staff were required to be extremely helpful on a customer-by-customer basis during face-to-face interactions. Today, many customers are virtual, and it is the store's online systems and automated processes that have taken over much of this requirement. The store's core value ('being highly customer-orientated') remains the same but the way that it is enacted has changed with the times.

Agile Agility Ambitions

An Agility Ambition is a living sensemaking intent that will be revised and re-shaped over time. Waves of radical agility can occur. Consider, for example, a medical school. Their Agility Ambition is to do whatever it takes to prepare their medical students to be great doctors. In their anatomy department for almost 200 years students had learnt from books like Gray's Anatomy that was first published in 1858. In the early 2020s interest grew in using a very different learning approach. Now medical students use augmented reality headsets to study the intricacies of the human body. Other developments in learning technologies are reshaping how anatomy is understood. Neuroscience is enabling more effective learning processes to be designed. Connectivity between medical schools, perhaps on different continents, permits virtual classrooms to be effective. The medical school's Agility Ambition remains the lodestone or guiding principle but the way that it is enacted changes as opportunities for improvement become available.

Deploying Agility Ambitions

Before a systemic-level Agility Ambition is formally rolled out (deployed) it needs to be codified. The tool for achieving codification is to develop a policy statement, that can be disseminated systematically. The policy deployment communication strategy may include roadshow presentations, town hall meetings, video newsletters, infographics or succinct publications. The aim of formal deployment of an Agility Ambition is to win hearts and minds, thereby feeding a movement that enables it to be understood and prized by everyone involved. Informal deployment is perhaps more influential. Two key stratagems for achieving wide understanding, and buy in to an Agility Ambition, are storytelling and role modelling.

Stories shape how people think and feel. They provide a means by which people make sense of shared possibilities and enable them to construct mental images of 'who we are' and 'what we can become'. Stories are richer than rational explanations, as they deal with emotional factors like hopes, anxieties and desires. They feed the development of a collective aspiration that helps to give an Agility Ambition the power to be ambitious. Ways need to be found for all opinion leaders, at every level, to become actively enrolled in the 'big story' of who we are, what we want to become and which challenges need to be overcome. Stories provide vehicles for capturing characteristics of culture and passing them to others. They explain how the world works and provide answers to existential questions like 'what is important?' 'How should I behave?' 'Who do I trust?' 'What is the value of what we do?' 'How should we react to change? And 'how outward looking should we be?'

Role modelling requires that people with power or influence within an organisation act in ways that are consistent with the ambition statement. This has been described as 'walking their talk'. Only when opinion leaders actively support the Agility Ambition in times of decision will the message become real.

The Agility Playbook

Once an Agility Ambition has become an organisational property it may need to be elaborated so that people know what it means in practice. One tool for achieving this an Agility Playbook. This describes how responses to signals or events should be handled in ways that are consistent with the Agility Ambition.

Playbooks are helpful when complex things need to be done, as roles can be defined explicitly. Without a playbook, it is difficult to avoid being under-organised, wasting time and losing agile momentum. In a requisitely agile organisation playbooks are illustrative rather than texts specifying standard operating procedures. They provide clarity as to who owns what and how issues should be addressed in ways that are consistent with the Agility Ambition.

The Step Four Workshop – Envisioning: *What will we be like when we are requisitely agile?*

Preparation
A room with space for members of the ADT to divide into four sub-groups. Four flip charts and sets of fine marker pens need to be available.

Time
3 hours and 15 minutes, including break.

Workshop Structure

1. The ADT leader invites members of the team to agree on what would be great outcomes of this session. These can be written on a whiteboard or a flip chart so that they remain in view during the workshop (10 minutes).

2. At the end of the Step Three workshop participants were asked to list 'things that worked well and areas for improvement'. These points should be reviewed in order to assist the team to work more effectively during the current session (5 minutes).

3. An ADT member is asked to read aloud ONE item from his or her list of the most important three 'things to do' when preparing an Agility Ambition and spend 30 seconds explaining the reason for the choice. As ADT members suggest items these should be noted on a whiteboard or flip chart. The Leader then asks another ADT member to read ONE item from his or her most important three 'things to do' list that is different from the first and will be given 30 seconds to explain the reason for the choice. This process is repeated with the third and subsequent ADT members. When all items have been described and listed the Leader should summarise the notes made on the whiteboard or flip chart (15 minutes).

4. Repeat the exercise using the same format but identifying important 'things not to do' (15 minutes).

5. Divide the group into four sub-groups. Each sub-group should use a framework suggested to the author by Dr Roger Harrison, which is to draw four columns on their flip chart (Harrison, 1995). The heading for the first column is 'More or Better', for the second column is 'Less or Stop', for the third column is 'New Things to Start' and for the last column is 'Things to Continue' (5 minutes).

6. Using these four column categories Sub-Group One will answer the question: 'In our Unit of Analysis what do to become requisitely Situationally Adaptive in 3-years' time, Sub-Group Two will do the same with Prudently Opportunism, Sub-Group Three with Proactively Mitigating Threats and Sub-Group Four with Becoming Future Ready. Each Sub-Group should spend approximately seven minutes focusing on each column (e.g., a Sub-Group will spend seven minutes listing answers to the question: 'In our Unit of Analysis what things will we need to be doing More or Better in order to be requisitely Situationally Adaptive in three years' time?') This will be repeated for the second column and so on (30 minutes).

7. Sub-Groups share their completed flip charts with the other members of the ADT with minutes for presentation and five minutes for discussion for each Sub-Group (40 minutes).

8. Pairs of ADT members are formed (there can be one trio). Each pair will answer the same question: 'Based on everything that we have done in the ADT what should be the Agility Ambition for our Unit of Analysis in about 30 words?' Write your answer on one sheet of flip chart paper (15 minutes).

9. The completed flip charts should be fixed on a wall and members of the ADT discuss each to ensure that they understand the suggestions made. These flip charts should be retained, as they will be needed in the Step Five workshop (20 minutes).

10. The ADT leader agrees to take all the proposed Agility Ambition flip charts and produce a composite draft for circulation to members of the ADT within one week. This draft Agility Ambition will become an input into the Step Five Workshop process.

11. ADT members privately answer two questions: 'What is one thing that worked well in this session?' and 'What is one area where we could improve next time?' After one or two minutes the answers to the questions should be shared and between three and five suggestions for improvement recorded, as they will be needed for the next step (10 minutes).

10 Step Five – Scoping: *Where, when and how, do we need to be agile?*

The focus of this step is *scoping*. In this step the ADT will identify what requisite agility will be needed urgently (the one-year view), in the foreseeable future (the three-year view) and in the middle-distant future (the seven-year view).

Guidance for the ADT Leader

This step builds on the output of Step Four and the flip charts that were produced should be available during this workshop session. It is necessary to review which Unit of Analysis will be used for the task, as this may be different than for previous workshop sessions. The Unit of Analysis can be the entire organisation, including its ecosystem, a LoB, an activity stream or other form of sub-unit. If a different Unit of Analysis is selected for this step than has been used previously, then the membership of the ADT is likely to need to change.

The ADT leader or an ACA should ensure that a flip chart pad will be available for the workshop, along with highlighters in the following colours: deep red, red, pink, light blue, blue and, optionally, brown and yellow.

The Pre-Workshop Tasks for Step Five

Purpose
To identify what requisite agility will be needed urgently (the one-year view), in the foreseeable future (the three-year view) and in the middle-distant future (the seven-year view).

Goal
To enable ADT members to understand where increased, decreased or different agility is needed in their Unit of Analysis.

Process
Work alone, or in pairs, in completing the pre-work.

Core Task
All members of the ADT should study the Guidelines for Preparing Agility Heat Maps (below) and make notes of points that they feel should to be discussed by the ADT.

https://doi.org/10.1515/9783110637267-011

Time Required
About 1 hour for the pre-work and 3 hours for the workshop.

The Pre-Work for Step Five: Guidelines for Preparing Agility Heat Maps

This task will enable you to assess the degree of need for agile-orientated organisational development in your Unit of Analysis. This is required as not all parts of an organisation need to be equally agile and it is important to identify where agility can be exploited for advantage. You should use the output from the previous workshop (Step Four, Envisioning) to provide input for this assignment.

It helps to have a mental picture of what will emerge from this workshop. Imagine a poster that shows your Unit of Analysis, situated within its ecosystem. Some organisational areas are coloured deep red, others red, pink, light blue or blue. Each colour represents the ADT's assessment of the area's requirement for agility development.

Now imagine that there are three posters using the same colour scheme. The first shows what requisite agility is needed now (a one-year view), the second takes a three-year forward-looking view and the last, a seven-year view. These posters will be the tangible deliverables from this workshop.

The heat-map format will be used as this will clearly illustrate the agility requirements of different parts of the organisation. Your heat maps should be ready to be shown to a TMT to explain what agility-orientated organisational development initiatives are needed.

In order to prepare for the workshop, it is necessary for you to (i) read the guidelines; (ii) reflect on the Astoria Theatre case study and (iii) list questions or discussion points about the heat-map method to be reviewed at the start of the workshop. In addition to studying these guidelines, it will be useful for those unfamiliar with the method to undertake an internet search to understand current best practice in constructing heat maps.

Defining Areas of a Heat Map

There is no standard way to define the areas that are relevant for a heat-map, so it will be best if you experiment with different formats, beginning by using your organisational structure chart or organigram as a template.

Agility Readiness Criteria

A five-point scale is usually sufficient to indicate the need for more or better agile capability. The criteria listed below have proved, but situations vary, and it will make sense for you to develop a scale that is meaningful for your own Unit of Analysis.

Deep red – There is an urgent and mission-critical need for this area to be stronger in situational adaptiveness, and/or prudent opportunism, and/or threat mitigation and/or future readying.

Red – High priority for this area to be stronger in situational adaptiveness, and/or prudent opportunism, and/or threat mitigation and/or future readying.

Pink – Significant priority for this area to be stronger in situational adaptiveness, and/or prudent opportunism, and/or threat mitigation and/or future readying.

Light blue – Low priority for this area to be stronger in situational adaptiveness, and/or prudent opportunism, and/or threat mitigation and/or future readying.

Blue – This area is adequately agile.

Some users have added two other colours. *Brown* for areas of the organisation that are currently excessively agile and *yellow* for areas of the organisation that may need new capabilities in the future.

Although it is not recommended for an initial workshop, as the additional task will be time consuming, it is possible to go to another level of detail and assess the four dimensions of agility separately. If this is to be attempted then separate heat map maps will show which parts of your organisation need to be (i) more intensively situationally adaptive, (ii) faster and more frequently prudently opportunistic, (iii) more resilient to predictable threats or (iv) ready for a different future. Four additional heat maps will be prepared for each of the one-, three- and seven-year views, making twelve in total.

Making Assessments

How do we know if an area is requisitely agile? The output from steps two, three and four provides an essential input. In this step will explore the four generic agility attributes. Later, you can extend your analysis to include your Agility Ambition. Where data are lacking, an agility-orientated benchmarking exercise can be undertaken. Often, it will not be sufficient to look locally, as comparisons with the best-in-class are necessary. It has been said that, 'you don't become a world class tennis player by comparing yourself only with those in your local club'!

Heat Mapping in Action: The Astoria Theatre Case Example

In order to understand how heat maps can be used for this task it is helpful to consider an example. The mini-case study below is a real story, but details have been changed, so that the organisation cannot be identified.

There is a theatre called the Astoria in Sydney, Australia. Almost every week it puts on a different show. There are special events for children, visitors take tours around the century-old building and outside organisations can hire the theatre for private events. Some of the theatre's organisational sub-units are highly routinised as, for example, each day the building must be cleaned, tickets sold, suppliers paid, safety systems checked and windows cleaned. Extremely limited agility is required for these routinised sub-units but there may be episodes when the agility level needs to be increased. For example, when theatre tickets became available on smart phones there was a phase of greatly heightened agility required in the ticketing department.

Some of the Astoria Theatre's organisational sub-units must be frequently flexible, adaptive and inventive. For example, a new theatrical production will present known and unforeseen challenges, perhaps requiring unique special effects or dramatically different lighting arrangements. Such out-of-the-box challenges cannot be managed using standard operating procedures. In each case, a temporary project organisation will be formed so that teams work creatively, often with outside specialists, to find solutions. Yet other sub-units must be almost permanently agile. These include the units that book visiting theatre companies, those that promote the theatre to new audiences, or those that devise processes to use novel digital technologies.

Imagine that the Astoria's one-year view agility heat map has one sub-unit coloured deep red, which is the development department. This team is responsible for developing fundraising strategies, writing grant applications, seeking sponsorship and finding for commercial partnerships. Why was the development department assessed to have an urgent and mission-critical need to be stronger in situationally adaptiveness, prudent opportunism, threat mitigation and/or future readying? It is because the Astoria's revenues do not cover expenses and the fabric of the theatre needs major refurbishment, so additional sources of funds are needed urgently. As the development department's success in fundraising has declined in recent years, and other city theatres have been more successful, it was obvious that opportunities were missed. The theatre's directors, acting as an ADT, concluded that they have an entitlement to expect upper-quartile fundraising effectiveness as an agility deliverable from the development department, but this is not being achieved. So, the deep red colour on the heat map is appropriate.

The Astoria's three-year view heat map has a different sub-unit coloured deep red, which is the technical department. This team manages technical aspects of shows and events including sound, lighting and digital effects. There are many technological innovations in theatre management, but the Astoria's technical department lacks the capacity to find and incorporate them. Over the next one or two years the strategy, role and capabilities of the technical department will need to be greatly strengthened to attract the world's most progressive theatre companies.

The Astoria's seven-year view heat map is based on a prediction by the theatre's directors that new forms of competition could render traditional theatres obsolete unless they offer exciting new experiences. It has been predicted that future theatre goers will wish to experience a play, rather than just watch it, meaning that members of an audience become immersed and can interact in real-time with a play. This will be a totally new model of a theatrical experience that will be dependent on revolutionary developments in digital technologies. All the areas of the organisation that would need to be involved in this transformation of the theatre's product were coloured deep red on the seven-year heat map. The ADT considered that the Astoria would need to reinvent itself when the new technologies become available if it is to survive. The implications would be organisation-wide or systemic.

It is important not to assume that it is the fault of those involved if an area is deemed to need agility enhancing interventions. Often a lack of resources or management scorecards that measure things other than agility are causes of inadequate deliverables. Even a frontier agile organisation will not need every sub-system to be equally agile. Participatively developing and sharing agility heat maps widely, and discussing their implications, is a requisite agility enhancing practice.

Ecosystems and Heat Maps

Heat maps become more powerful when they expand outside of the boundaries of the organisation to include its ecosystem. Organisations are not islands, they have many and varied interactions with outside nodes, including customers, suppliers, rivals, advisers, resource-providers, government authorities and the like. These interactions form an ecosystem that, to some extent, can be managed. A sub-unit will have an ecosystem that includes other internal sub-units and external interdependencies.

Agile organisations need a supportive ecosystem. To date, there has not been sufficient academic research for us to understand definitively what are the characteristics of a fully supportive ecosystem, but we know that at least five dimensions are important. These are to ensure flows of (i) inspiration, (ii) insight into the wants and needs of (external or internal) customers and potential customers, (iii) predictions of likely changes in opportunity spaces, (iv) early recognition of threats and (v) assessments of the strength and positioning of potential rivals and collaborators.

The Step Five Workshop – Scoping: *Where, when and how do we need to be agile?*

Preparation
A room with space for members of the ADT to stand close to a whiteboard or flip chart. The flip charts from the previous step should be displayed as should other relevant material from previous steps. Highlighters need to be available in the following colours: deep red, red, pink, light blue, blue and, optionally, brown and yellow. Both thick and thin (sharpie type) board markers will be needed.

Time
3 hours, including break.

Workshop Structure

1. The ADT leader invites members of the team to agree on what would be great outcomes of this session. These can be written on a whiteboard or a flip chart so that they remain in view during the workshop (10 minutes).
2. At the end of the Step Four workshop participants were asked to list 'things that worked well and areas for improvement'. These points should be reviewed in order to assist the team to work more effectively during the current session (5 minutes).
3. The ADT leader asks whether anyone has questions or points for discussion about the heat-map method. Issues should be listed on a whiteboard or flip chart and resolved before progressing further (10 minutes).
4. The Unit of Analysis for the heat-map task should be confirmed (5 minutes).
5. An infographic outline of the Unit of Analysis is to be prepared on a whiteboard or flip chart. Key areas to be identified and each discussed to decide which colour best represents the distance between current agility level and requisite agility in the short-term (the one year view) using the colour coding scale: *deep red* (an urgent and mission-critical need), *red* (high priority), *pink* (significant priority), *light blue* (low priority) and *blue* (no action needed) (50 minutes).
6. The same task is undertaken to develop a three-year view, preparing a second infographic (30 minutes).
7. The same task is undertaken to develop a seven-year view, preparing a third infographic (30 minutes).
8. The ADT review the draft heat maps and plan how to consult with others to refine them over the next few weeks. The aim is not to be 100% accurate but to have a sufficiently well-defined overview to define the requirement for organisational development initiatives (15 minutes).

9. ADT members privately answer two questions: 'What is one thing that worked well in this session?' and 'What is one area where we could improve next time?' After one or two minutes the answers to the questions should be shared and between three and five suggestions for improvement noted (10 minutes).

11 Step Six – Customising: *What types of agility do we need?*

The focus of this step is *customising*. In this step the ADT will identify the optimal types of agility needed to provide requisite agility.

Guidance for the ADT Leader

Exploiting agility for advantage requires using appropriate types of agility. It is a core principle of EAfA that there are multiple types of agility, each with different functions. Put simply, one type of agility will be functional in some circumstances but dysfunctional in others. The EAfA Agility Typology Model, used in this step, was developed by the author for this book to facilitate designing agility-orientated organisational development programmes.

The typology is used for developing both systemic and localised agility, depending on the Unit of Analysis selected. Selecting the best type to meet required agility deliverables requires judgement as, at the time of writing, there are no authoritative research findings that show definitively which types of agility are most productive in specific circumstances.

During an initial briefing session, the ADT leader should emphasise that is essential that the pre-work task, which is substantial, is completed diligently, in order to ensure that every member of the ADT has a sufficiently deep understanding of the EAfA Typology to contribute competently to the workshop.

The EAfA Agility Typology Model can be used in several ways but managers working through the EAfA Process often choose to augment the heat maps that they had prepared in Step Five. It is this method that will be described in this step but ADT leaders should feel free to experiment with other formats for using the typology.

The EAfA Agility Typology Model is an original conceptual framework, so please reference the source when you use it. Secondly, if you are willing to share your analysis anonymously please send a copy to the author at agility@richmondconsult.com so that future editions of this book can be improved.

The Pre-Workshop Tasks for Step Six

Purpose
To assist managers to select optimal types of agility for their organisation's needs.

https://doi.org/10.1515/9783110637267-012

Goals
i.   To enable ADT members to understand, in depth, the eight types of agility.
ii. To use the EAfA Model to assess whether optimal types of agility are used currently.
iii. To decide what needs to be done to exploit different types of agility for advantage.

Process
Work alone, or in pairs, in completing the pre-work as the workshop will be more effective if each team member has an opportunity to make a distinctive contribution.

Core Task
To be prepared to make a well-informed contribution to the Agile Typology Workshop.

Sub-Tasks
1.   Read the pre-work, to understand the significance of agility types.
2.   Study each of the types carefully before (i) preparing a summary (about 50 words) of the key distinguishing features of each type, (ii) listing three situations where it should be used and (iii) three situations where it should not be used.

Time Required
The pre-work for this task is particularly demanding and at least 3 hours should be allocated to complete it. The workshop will take 2 hours and 45 minutes.

The Pre-Work for Step Six: Why Types of Agility are Important

In Chapter 1 the story was told of the competitive struggles between Nokia and Apple in the first decade of the 21st century, which led to Nokia losing its dominance of the mobile telephony market. Jorma Ollila, their CEO at the time, had steered Nokia to become the dominant player in the mobile phone market but he had become concerned that Nokia's innovative energy was waning. Guided by visionary business consultants, Nokia embraced agility as its core organisational philosophy in the late 1990s and the company adopted a fluid, decentralised and emergent version of the Agile Paradigm using Intrapreneurial and Granular types of agility (more about these types of agility later). The result was loss of focus and greatly reduced effectiveness.

Apple was an exemplar of a different type of agile organisation, as it used a Top-Down type of agility, largely shaped by its CEO, Steve Jobs. Apple had an integrated organisational model that enabled it to be prudently opportunistic on a grand scale. Steve Jobs demanded perfection in every task and was famously ill-tempered with those who were less than fully competent. In interviews that I conducted with Apple executives at the time one compared Jobs to General George S. Patton, known as 'Old Blood and Guts', because of his hard-driving personality and his philosophy of leading by taking fast and aggressive offensive action. Another Apple manager told me that: "Steve is a megalomaniac! There is only one thing that makes this acceptable and is that he is often right about what needs to be done. We love him for that".

Both Nokia and Apple had adopted agility as their managerial policy but had chosen different types. We learn from this example that key management tasks are to decide why agility is required (i.e. its required functions and what agility deliverables are expected), select the most appropriate agility type or types available, understand their required modalities, construct a fit-for-purpose organisation, remove agility blockages and energise sub-systems to be requisitely agile.

Definitions: Types and Modalities

We will use the word 'type' to mean a form of organisational design with common characteristics and a 'modality' as the way that something is done. These constructs overlap but have a different emphasis. Type is primarily concerned with definition and modality with how action happens.

The EAfA Agility Typology Model is heuristic, rather than one developed from grounded theory. The agility types specified are those that the author found helpful in his research and have proved useful for managers and students undertaking agility-orientated organisational development.

Types of Agility

There are eight agility types in the EAfA Model. An agility type has distinctive functions that, if appropriately selected and well-executed, provides required agility deliverables. Every agility type has distinctive strengths and weaknesses and each requires a different organising modality and a distinctive form of organisation. Organisational development requirements are contingent on the type of agility adopted.

A note of caution. Typologies are useful managerial tools, but they have a dark side. They are useful, as a typology clarifies key features of a complex and multifaceted phenomenon. But they can be dangerous, as typologies are inherently rigid and may not be entirely appropriate for local situations. On balance, advantages outweigh the disadvantages, but it helps to see a typology as a set of orientating concepts rather than an immutable taxonomy.

Multiple Types of Agility

The question is often asked: 'can an organisational unit have more than one agility type?' The answer is 'yes but be careful'. Organisations are organised for specific purposes, which requires specialisation. No organisation, or sub-unit, can do everything equally well. Hence, it is important to ensure that each type of agility is managed differently and resourced appropriately. Every agility type requires a different facilitating modality that will need to be delivered by a specialised fit-for-purpose organisation. If two, or more, agility types are adopted then organisational complexity increases and coherence can be undermined or lost.

There are two principle choices available if more than one type of agility is required. The first is to form differentiated sub-organisations with the specialised set of capabilities required for just one agility type. The second choice is to train those involved to be able to reconfigure their mindsets and ways of working so that they can deliver different agility types when needed. This is demanding but sometimes required, for example in military units.

The Eight Types of Agility

Type One: Top-Down Agility

Top Down Agility

Top-Down Agility is delivered by centralised decision-making and the effective deployment of corporate policies and practices. It is leadership intensive, authoritarian and situationally adaptive. This approach to delivering agility is distinctly unfashionable in the West but remains widely used in some geographies, especially where authoritarian decision-making is legitimate.

Put simply, the modality of Top-Down Agility is that 'the boss decides'. There is one single node for decision-making so, if a responsible top manager, or team, is available, competent and effective then fast and decisive decisions can be taken and resources made available, facilitating agility.

Top-Down Agility appears to be uncomplicated. Key decisions will be taken by one, or a few, top managers who deal personally with key issues. These top managers determine decision rules, for example specifying how arguments are to be put when approval is sought for an initiative, specifying what evidence is needed and determining the optimum velocity for decision-making. Some, probably most, decisions will be made quickly, often after short meetings, but complex or strategically significant issues will be investigated in great depth.

Capable top managers, who share a vision of what their organisation is striving to achieve, can greatly enhance agility as they take a wide view, can be decisive, are able to be bold and will make resources available to implement decisions. Anyone who doubts that top-down agility is a viable modality for achieving agility can reflect on an initiative taken in China in 2003 to address the outbreak of Severe Acute Respiratory Syndrome (SARS) that caused more than 8,000 cases (Zhaohong, 2003). When the severity of the infection became clear, an executive order was given by the Chinese government to increase the availability of isolation hospitals beds. The entirely new Xiaotangshan Hospital was built in Beijing to accommodate patients showing symptoms. It was reportedly constructed in seven days, with X-ray and CT rooms, an intensive-care unit and a clinical laboratory. About 4,000 people built this 1,000-bed hospital, working day and night. The instruction from the top was: 'get it done fast, no matter what it costs!' This was not a one-off initiative. In the city of Wuhan in 2020 a 1,000 bed hospital was built in just 10 days to treat patients suffering from the newly discovered coronavirus. It is difficult to imagine a rapid response of this magnitude could have been achieved by anything other than Top-Down Agility.

Top-Down Agility can only be effective when those further down an organisation take responsibility for intelligently contributing to the priorities of the moment. Hence, a TMT needs to be close to people at every organisational level to avoid decisions being taken in an 'ivory tower'. Also, top managers must have gained the trust of those lower down the organisation so that upwards communication is authentic, even on difficult issues.

Despite its efficacy, Top-Down Agility has multiple vulnerabilities. Top managers can be overloaded, inadequately briefed, misguided, domineering, suffer from groupthink or be insufficiently influential for their decisions to be enacted. They can stifle agility as well as enable it.

The core operating principle of this mode of agility is hierarchical, organic and uses bureaucracy as an instrument for mobilising controlled action. Top-Down Agility, when effective, embeds an almost real-time capability for situational responsiveness, prudent opportunism and threat mitigation, as has been demonstrated in many military conflicts.

An Example of Top-Down Agility

In 1929 Edwin Land filed a patent for an optical filter that blocked certain polarised light waves that later became the first product of the Polaroid Corporation and was used for sunglasses, photographic filters and other applications (Thadamalla, Dadhwal, & Sonpal, 2009).

Land was highly ambitious and he was a persuasive advocate of the technologies that he developed. In 1937, at the age of 28, Land became president and director of research of the Polaroid Corporation. His passion for innovation, and willingness to be boldly opportunistic, was demonstrated by the well-known story of how he invented the instant camera.

In 1943 Land was on vacation in Santa Fe with his three-year old daughter, Jennifer, and he took a photograph of her. She wanted to see the photograph and asked her father why it was not possible to see the picture immediately. Land reflected on Jennifer's question and, in an hour, he had worked out how to construct an instant camera and the chemistry required for a self-developing film.

After much laboratory work patents were filed and, in 1948, Polaroid's Model 95 began to be sold, which provided users with a dry photograph in a minute. Over the next 30 years numerous improvements were made and Polaroid cameras were sold worldwide. In 1977 revenues were $1 billion and the company was highly profitable.

A new and advanced product called Polavision was launched in 1977. This was an instant movie film that Land believed would compete with the video camcorders that were becoming available at that time. Polavision failed as it was expensive, visually inferior and could not be edited in the normal way. The system was discontinued in 1979, costing Polaroid at least $70 million and using many years of work by talented researchers. It was said that no systematic market research had ever been undertaken. Edwin Land resigned soon after.

I visited Polaroid two years after Edwin Land had resigned from being president, chairman of the board and the director of research. I found an enterprise that felt devoid of momentum. I recall being told that: "without Land we lost our soul". One manager told me that Land had been so dominant that he once said in a meeting: "I won't have a deputy, but I will have lots of great people to get the things done that I want to get done".

Polaroid went through two bankruptcies between 2001 and 2009 and, at the time of writing, it licenses its name to manufacturers who make products that Polaroid believes will be attractive to consumers. Currently, Polaroid is a profitable but niche marketing business and a shadow of its former self.

Learning from the Example

The rise and fall of Polaroid demonstrated the unique strengths of Top-Down Agility and its limitations. Land excelled in finding and exploiting opportunities. His genius created an entirely new market segment and he successfully transformed scientific research into wanted consumer products.

Land's insight that instant photography was technically possible after an apparently whimsical request from his three-year old daughter was a great achievement. Even more extraordinary was his willingness to devote countless hours to developing prototypes that needed extensive scientific and technological innovation without any proof that they could be exploited for advantage. Other remarkable achievements followed. A unique product was developed, patented, marketed, defended against the might of Kodak who sought to capture the instant film market for themselves. It became a globally fashionable item, delivered a robust profit margin (using the razor blade revenue model) and was followed by generations of improved products.

It was not a story of success-after-success. Land's commitment to instant movie film and his Polavision system illustrates the hazards of Top-Down Agility. Polavision was a product that had little or nothing to offer and was ridiculously expensive. Normal film could be processed overnight with much higher quality. No serious film maker ever adopted Polavision on a long-term basis. Polavision, was entirely 'Land's baby' but its multiple disadvantages meant that it was always destined to be a dead duck. Land had made a foolish bet, but his dominance meant that Polaroid became committed to a pathway of self-harm.

Uses of Top-Down Agility

This modality of agility is beneficial where the leader is an extraordinarily able individual, or there is a very capable small leadership group with the talent and enthusiasm to be pioneers. It is needed when crisis, or complex and uncertain, situations occur. If a ship hits an iceberg, a film production needs direction, or a do-different innovation is failing then Top-Down Agility can be the only way to provide necessary coordination and control.

As mentioned earlier, this modality is unfashionable. But this does not mean that that it should be abandoned. There are times when Top-Down Agility will be the optimal managerial approach and it will be greatly valued by followers. A key challenge is to avoid placing power in the hands of those who will abuse it or use it foolishly.

Type Two: Routines-Based Agility

If...........

Then do........

Routines-Based Agility

Routines-Based Agility delivers adaptive but prescribed flexibility. It enables an organisation to respond to predefined categories of complex needs. Many organisations use this modality for facilitating agility. A factory will have routines to meet unexpected large orders, a police department's routines will enable it to cope with rare but serious cases of civil unrest and television stations use routines for news gathering when disasters strike.

Routines-Based Agility is optimal when predictable situations occur that are so complex that it would be impossible to organise sufficiently quickly unless there are pre-prepared plans and available mission-essential capabilities. The core operating principle of this modality of agility is to possess the capability for the efficient deployment of best-in-class, and often technologically supported, routines that have been fine-tuned for possible scenarios. The required organisational form is hierarchical, structured with predefined policies and/or processes to deal with unexpected variations.

Developing competence in this modality of agility begins with scenarios that describe categories of possible requirements. For example, a Fire Department may realise that there is a remote possibility that a train transporting dangerous chemicals is derailed locally, so they will develop a scenario to specify how they will respond. It is probable that simulations will be needed to understand likely challenges in depth. Often, past experience, including that of other organisations, will provide guidelines that enable contingency plans to be devised. Rehearsals will be needed so that people and systems learn to act effectively. Specialist resources may be required that are kept for a just-in-case scenario. A playbook will describe the required patterns of interdependent actions to be taken by people and non-human actors in response to predefined signals or conditions. As unexpected factors can cause scenario playbooks to be inadequate it will be necessary for real-time managerial mechanisms for effective adaptation to be built into the structure of routines.

Each time a scenario is enacted, either as a simulation or as real case, there will be opportunities for organisational learning. Routines for effective review-to-improve sessions provide key inputs for developing the capabilities required for Routines-Based Agility. Organisations that excel in this modality will actively seek insights from similar situations elsewhere. For example, the experience of a fire department fighting a chemical fire in Vietnam can be used by firefighters in New York to improve their routines for similar eventualities.

Routines can adapted, within limits, according to the logic of the situation. Such role flexibility needs to be rehearsed as variations can undermine systemic integrity. Routines reduce job complexity, increase proactivity and facilitate interdependence, as people know what to expect of others. In the last decade Routines-Based Agility has been greatly enhanced by capable smart systems that, for example, run virtual scenarios, provide real-time information and automate certain routines.

An Example of Routines-Based Agility

A hospital's emergency department has the task of responding quickly and effectively to serious or urgent health problems. Mostly, they cope with a similar injuries and illnesses day-after-day. But there can be major exceptions. A plane crash may cause mass injuries or there could be an unexpected outbreak of a rare tropical disease. Emergency departments must be capable of responding to such incidents efficiently, with little time to prepare.

Sets of routines kick-in from the moment a new patient enters an emergency department. Structured triage determines treatment pathways using routines that specify ways to process pre-defined categories of patients. Frequently, such routines will not be locally determined but have been derived from the findings of randomised controlled trials, as these are the gold-standard guidelines for driving innovation in medical contexts.

Routines can incorporate values, such as respect for patients' dignity and they will specify where and how clinical judgements are to be made. Hence, routines can humanise what could be a mechanistic process. In a hospital, control and coordination is exercised through a strict but compassionate managerial hierarchy. Those in positions of leadership act as proactive agents of improvement in the routines system of the emergency department, by learning from conferences on their specialisms, reading technical journals and being audited by peers and external expert bodies.

Emergency departments operate efficiently and effectively if those involved are able and willing to adopt, adapt and conform to multiple and complex sets of routines. These will be embedded in socio-technical systems, as communication and control systems, equipment and resources can enable routines to be deployed more efficiently and effectively. The role of non-human agents in delivering Routines-Based Agility is growing, some being driven by cyber-physical systems that ensure computers interact directly with the physical world and deploy routines autonomously.

The adoption of different sets of routines will be triggered by pre-determined signals. If, for example, the emergency room receives a warning that a group of people suffering from hypothermia are about to arrive they will immediately adopt routines suited to this form of medical emergency. Hierarchical management enables those with decision rights to reconfigure the organisation flexibly to respond to current priorities. Sets of routines often require interdependent action by several people that will have been incorporated in formal specifications. Focused and structured communication, for example displays of patient wait-times, enables the fine-tuning of operations, so that the routines system has a degree of intelligent adaptability.

In a hospital sets of routines can always be improved, which benefits from collaborative review-to-improve learning experiences, often involving patients and other stakeholders. Such learning loops improve the service to patients, exploit insights from those who know most about the reality of this form of work and provide input for continuous improvement, also known as kaizen. An example clarifies this point. The Flinders Medical Centre in South Australia had tried many of the normally used techniques for reducing congestion in their emergency room, but these were largely ineffective. Members of the management group studied Lean Thinking techniques and used its conceptual tools to construct a schematic representation of how their emergency room actually functioned (King, Ben-Tovim, & Bassham, 2006). When this was available it became straightforward to highlight areas where different routines were needed. Once proven, these improvements were codified as improved routines for managing workflows, resulting in a highly significant reduction in the number of did-not-wait patients.

From time to time emergency departments may need to cope with non-routine medical emergencies. I recall being at a London Hospital, working on a non-connected research assignment, shortly after a terrorist bomb had exploded nearby. Normal procedures were instantly abandoned and, within a few minutes, medical staff from the hospital were in the street attending to victims. In this case, no predetermined set of routines was available, but the health workers had been trained in good medical practice and it was these embedded disciplines, combined with mutual adjustment, that enabled life-saving treatment to be given.

New situations prompt managers to expand their list of possible scenarios and develop situation-specific policies, routines and rehearsal requirements. Some years ago, in an English city, a Novichok chemical warfare weapon was used and several people were injured. They were taken to hospital, where doctors had no routines available for dealing with this kind of emergency. A temporary and partly virtual Skunk Works (see later for a description of this type of agility) was needed to develop treatment methods and, later, these were codified into routines that were made available widely, should there be another attack of this kind.

Learning from the Example

What can we learn about Routines-Based Agility from this example? It is that agility can provided by an efficient bureaucracy that has competent leadership and an empowered chain of command. This modality requires that people and systems behave in predictable ways and their autonomy will be confined. This is not to say that creativity and individual initiative are eliminated. Rather the opposite, as these qualities become embedded in sets of routines to enable effective situational responsiveness (Volberda, Foss, & Lyles, 2010).

The roles of leaders and managers are central when this modality of agility is used. Routinely, they must identify examples of relevant best-in-class performance and embed the lessons learnt into improved sets of routines. When executive decisions are needed, often within seconds, it must be clear who has the decision rights required to make judgement calls. Obedience from others involved will be necessary to enable timely and coordinated action; unless there is evidence that a decision is poor when routines for challenging decisions should kick-in.

Training and practice are important as Routines-Based Agility needs to become second nature. Techniques like gamification and virtual reality can add realism to simulation exercises. Subsequent analysis of video recordings taken of processes in action provides input for improvement and gives confidence to those involved. Multi-unit simulations offer opportunities to practice interoperability. Such planning can never provide sufficiently detailed routines to deal with every eventuality, but it provides an essential framework for competent Routines-Based Agility.

Periodically, continuous improvement will not be sufficient to provide best-in-class Routines-Based Agility. Returning to the emergency room example, imagine that they are about, for the first time, to use drones for the transport of automatic defibrillators to people who have suffered a heart attack with the drone providing instructions on using the equipment to help the victim. As routines for using this new technology do not exist in the unit of adoption, what happens? Typically, a contract will be agreed with a specialist provider to buy the drones, install the necessary ancillary equipment, train members of the emergency room team and provide ongoing maintenance. The use of outside resources enables competent routinisation to be completed quickly. Why do not the emergency room team do this themselves? For them, it would distract from core tasks, require a long learning curve and require Project-Based agility, which requires different competences, as we will see later.

Sometimes organisations that are meant to deliver Routines-Based Agility fail, because of inadequacies of management, unintegrated sub-units, cumbersome bureaucracy, lack of discipline, low levels of motivation etc. When this happens, an externally driven organisational development programme may be required as dysfunctional routines are hard to change. The aim must be to construct an intelligent, motivated and efficient bureaucracy able to deliver this modality of agility.

Uses of Routines-Based Agility

Many organisations use the Routines-Based Agility modality. For example, in Las Vegas, a company called Acrylic Tank Manufacturing designs and installs exotic fish tanks for wealthy individuals and companies. Rarely will two fish tanks be the same. One customer may want a tank to be built into part of a motor truck, another desires that exotic fish are swimming around the products of her company ("Acrylic Tank Manufacturing," 2020). Tanks range from 200 to 200,000 litres in size. Those who work in Acrylic Tank Manufacturing have elaborate routines for identifying customers' needs, developing design concepts, providing healthy environments for exotic fish, sourcing materials, fabricating reliable installations etc. These routines embed imagination and creativity into design processes. Their agility is confined to fish tank design and installation but, within this opportunity space, the company has requisite systemic agility, essential to compete successfully in a high-end interior fashion design business.

Other examples of the use of Routines-Based Agility include film units, pit-stop teams for racing cars, fine-dining restaurants, factory maintenance technicians and workers in an Apple store. Within larger organisations there will be sub-units that use this modality. For example, in a University there will be a department that deals with assessing whether research proposals meet ethical and data security regulations and they will have routines for this purpose. In a software supplier there will be routines for escalating customers' problems to senior management when these are not being solved quickly. In a travelling circus there will be routines for dismantling the Big Tent before moving to another location. Routines-Based Agility provides an invaluable modality for managing flexible and rapid responsiveness to predictable scenarios.

Type Three: Project-Based Agility

Project-Based Agility

Project-Based Agility enables an organisation to respond effectively to large, complex or demanding opportunities, or confront major threats, for which it has relevant previous experience. This organisational modality provides the resources, disciplines and momentum required to get largely known, but important and often difficult, things done. Project-based agility lacks deep innovation capability and it important to note that opportunities that require radical or disruptive 'do different' innovation are likely to be best managed using the Skunk Works modality, as described later.

Projects vary according to whether they are routine or pioneering and are often answers to the question: 'how can we take advantage of this big opportunity?' A civil engineering company will establish a project to build a new water treatment plant in Mongolia. A charity will form a project team to launch a major new funding initiative. An internet platform provider will task a project team to report on the implications of a new generation of cellular network technologies.

Routine projects achieve their goals largely, but not entirely, by using existing assets and tried-and-tested processes. These have been acquired as project delivery teams completed similar assignments previously. This will enable, for example, a company experienced in building cement plants across the world to build a new plant with a relatively small degree of customisation as most of the required tasks will be variants of known practices and processes. The cement plant builder will have departments with a deep knowledge of specialised systems, vulnerabilities and key success factors, many of which will be industry specific. Centralised corporate resources provide services to project delivery teams within an organisational ethos that promotes high levels of inter-team cooperation. Routine project agility is facilitated by the capability to effectively leverage, and build on, accumulated know-how.

Pioneering projects transform new or hard-to-achieve opportunities into hard or soft artefacts that have fundamental differences from previously competed tasks. Here deep professional competence, supported by resources, including machine intelligence, provides high-level problem-solving capability, often facilitated by Design Thinking. Requisite agility is provided by specialist experts working together intensively, undertaking experiments, and being supported by structured processes that allow for complexity to be managed with a degree of efficiency. Such projects need a supportive ecosystem with flows of responsive, timely, apt and expert services from corporate sources, partners or sub-contractors. Many of the factors that can hinder the performance of a pioneering project lie not within the project organisation itself but on its dependence on others. Strengthening pioneering project capability requires that the project-in-its-ecosystem be the unit of improvement. In pioneering projects, the mode of management needs to hands-on, assertive, collaborative, demanding and proactive.

Pioneering projects require do-different agility but not new-to-the-world innovation. They will have multiple uncertainties, as goals are often unclear and can change over the life of the project. Tasks present challenges that have never previously been overcome by those involved. Expected and unexpected difficulties abound, errors will be made, cost and time requirements can be impossible to predict accurately and organisational complexity can be profound. Why, you may be wondering, should any sane management team undertake this kind of initiative? The answer is that rewards can be high, as it is pioneering projects that create the future, so an organisation that can deliver them will acquire valuable future-orientated agile capabilities.

Resources are key for both routine and pioneering projects. Great people, with apt experience and creative commitment, are core but technical systems and physical resources provide multiple forms of support. Virtual or physical co-location is vital for frequent strategy reviews and next-steps planning. Suites of project management tools improve decision-making, especially software to facilitate scenario exploration or advanced simulation.

The key building block of project-based agility is a temporary organisation that is established for a specific purpose. Of great importance will be access to the accumulated craft wisdom of a few battle-hardened senior project managers, as project success will be highly dependent on the personal qualities of a small number of key actors. The senior project management team must be technically capable, strategically aligned, unfailingly cooperative, managerially sophisticated and remarkably persuasive: a quality of team-working that is hard to achieve in practice.

An Example of Project-Based Agility

In order to explore project-based agility, a disguised case will be examined in greater detail. As a core part of its mission, the Hope and Light Church (H&LC) provides help for people in those parts of the world that are desperately deprived. Historically, many of those attending H&L churches in affluent countries gave donations to support humanitarian initiatives in places like the slums of Brazil or poor villages in the arid north of Nigeria. H&LC builds clinics and schools to support to those in the greatest need of help, such as street children, abused women and impoverished elderly people. A TMT leads H&L and they became concerned that donations from their churches in affluent countries were falling markedly. The financial shortfall was so great that existing initiatives were curtailed and few new ones were starting. In recent years, other charities had found new ways to encourage donors, but H&LC had not adapted to the new ecology of charitable giving. The members of H&LC's TMT knew that their methods for raising funds had changed little in the past 30 years. They discussed the problem in a top team meeting and decided that H&LC needed to 'innovate in provisioning' (i.e. how they raise funds). A project team was formed to explore what could be done.

H&LC's project team was given a name: Giving 4 Good. A 'heavyweight' project manager was appointed, who had the power, and a budget, to do whatever was necessary to make progress. He was committed to the H&L Church and had previously led similar investigations for government and industry. Six others joined the team. Each agreed to give five weeks full-time to the assignment and travel where necessary, at their own expense. Two were H&LC priests, who had years of experience in providing help to people in remote or troubled places. Two were ordinary or lay members of the H&L Church. The other members were specialists in charitable giving, one was a consultant in strategic management and the other an organisational development change agent, with experience in working with religious organisations.

All seven members of the project team met for a kick-off three-day workshop. Hypotheses were developed as to why H&LC funding was declining and what were the characteristics of similar organisations that were succeeding in fund raising. Evidence was to be collected to validate or disprove these hypotheses. A month-long programme of fact-finding activities was arranged, including focus groups with churchgoers, interviews with those engaged in humanitarian initiatives, studies of other charities, experiments to test the reaction of churchgoers to various marketing strategies and crowdsourcing suggestions. As evidence was collected during the four weeks of fieldwork it was shared by daily SKYPE calls between all team members. Current humanitarian initiatives were visited, some virtually. Other charities provided comparative data. Insights from team members were organised using standardised data extraction forms. One member of the team compiled inputs using a qualitative analysis software programme and produced a 'this is what we have learnt in the last week' report each Saturday. After five weeks, another three-day workshop was held to explore options and prepare recommendations that, on the final day, were shared with H&LC's TMT and discussed extensively. It was agreed that a new approach be taken to promote charitable giving, including ensuring that donors would, in future, have a direct connection with those who had benefited from their gifts. Some months later, the flow of funds was sufficient.

Learning from the Example

What can we learn about Project-Based Agility from this example? For the H&L Church, this was a pioneering project as it was, for them, a 'do different' process. An opportunity had been identified (to improve fund raising methods) but it was neither fully understood by those with the power to manage the situation nor was there sufficient momentum to drive change. Wisely, an empowered temporary organisation, a project team, had been formed with the task of helping the TMT to take informed decisions about a key, but poorly understood, issue. In this case the problem was known but the solution was unknown.

The members of the project team had a comprehensive range of skills and they were willing to dedicate themselves to an intensive and disciplined work programme. Sufficient time (the first kick-off workshop) was invested by team members in becoming a high-performing team. They developed a schedule of tasks and designing a temporary organising structure to ensure that findings from their data collection could become a team asset. Systematic methods were used to conduct market research studies. All team members were kept aware, almost in real time, of the progress being made by everyone else. Team members were valued for their differences and made distinctive, often creative, inputs. Adjustments in workflow were made as data were organised and the project pathway evolved in ways that had not been predicted. The team's proposed actions were achievable, affordable and fitted with the church's values and goals. There was a comprehensive hand-over to the client at the end of the assignment.

What happened later? The Giving 4 Good project provided evidence-based proposals for new fund-raising strategies that resulted in an improved flow of revenues. There was another outcome considered to be important by H&LC's top team. The success of this project team, and the methods that they had used, had been shown to be effective and were absorbed into the Church's organisation. H&LC began to use similar temporary project organisations to help it to adjust to a changing world, thereby increasing its capacity for maintaining requisite agility.

Uses of Project-Based Agility

A strength of Project-Based Agility is that stretch goals can be set early and, importantly, adequate resources assigned to the task with defined outputs expected, indeed demanded. This provides focus, clarity and momentum. Additional outside resources can be incorporated into project structures providing a capability that would not otherwise be available.

Over time, Project-Based Agility has become more efficient, driven by greater managerial insight into the challenges of effective project management (e.g., the Scrum approach) and the use of novel technologies for team coordination and remote working, including facilities like cloud computing and easy access storage data retrieval, automated or smart search, rapid prototyping and advanced simulation. Put simply, excellent project capability should be a moving target. That which represents best practice today may become out-dated, and a rigidity, in years to come.

Project-Based Agility has many applications. It is important for the strategic level of an organisation, as projects can examine issues for which senior managers lack the necessary bandwidth to see all the opportunities, let alone to seize them selectively. If a government needs a new airport, a bank requires a new software program or a television studio undertakes a technological an upgrade then requisite agility will be provided using the project-based modality.

Many businesses in entertainment, construction, aerospace, engineering providers, film studios, consultancies, legal firms, marketing and advertising companies undertake routine and pioneering projects. However, as our example shows, not-for-profit organisations can also benefit. The word 'projectification' was coined to capture the essence of this key managerial method for achieving big-picture agility (Maylor & Turkulainen, 2019).

Type Four: Socio-Technical Agility

Socio-Technical Agility

The outputs of many agile organisations are a function of interactions between human endeavour and technical systems. The technical dimension is increasingly capable and able to increase situational awareness, provide opportunities, change the nature of threats and redefine how future-proof organisations can be designed. Effectively interlinking social and technical domains makes a mission-critical contribution to organisational agility in many, but not all, 21st century enterprises.

The scope of socio-technical enabled agility is enormous, as the following examples illustrate. Artificial Intelligence programmes, using machine learning, natural language processing and text analytics, are testing hypotheses in pharmaceutical research laboratories at a rate that was previously impossible. Teachers are using machine learning to ensure that students can only progress after they have mastered earlier content. Police plan the deployment of resources to those parts of a city that learning algorithms predict are likely to experience crime on that day.

These examples demonstrate that socio-technical agility not only aids human work but it does work that cannot be done by humans, no matter how capable they are. For example, many spacecrafts now have autonomous systems that automatically detect and avoid debris. Such technologies expand and change the dimensions of opportunity landscapes.

The socio-technical framework (Crick & Chew, 2017) views an organisation as having two domains, one human and the other technical. For all practical purposes, the domains are inextricably interrelated. An organisation's capability for agility depends on a symbiotic relationship between these domains. When change occurs, for example if a new technical system is introduced, then human factors cannot be ignored.

Socio-technical systems present three distinctive managerial challenges. These relate to (i) selection, (ii) integration and (iii) human reaction.

Selection is a significant managerial challenge, as finding (or inventing) suitable technical systems, or acquiring advanced tools, requires understanding, in depth, their potential costs, benefits and limitations. New or improved technical systems frequently become available in fast-changing and science-based sectors. Not all enterprises have sufficient readiness to absorb new technologies nor are all managers able to determine the relative advantages and disadvantages of different technological trajectories.

Frequently, new technologies will need to be integrated into existing systems. This often generates difficulties that will be specific to a particular organisation, as ready-made solutions may not be readily available. For example, when a bank upgrades its systems for processing transfers of funds it may need to incorporate these into legacy systems that were installed decades earlier. Integration is not an event but a process of mutual adaptation. People encounter technologies and technologies encounter people: both are changed.

That technical systems can increase systemic and local organisational agility is not new. For example, in the 20th century a jukebox would be the centre piece of many bars and cafés. Jukeboxes selected a song requested by a customer after a coin was inserted. An early model was unveiled in 1889 at Palais Royal Saloon in San

Francisco and, for the next 80 years, it underwent waves of technical development. Jukeboxes provided café owners with a new landscape of opportunities. Young people would gather in those coffee bars with the most modern jukeboxes. Enterprising café owners realised that a jukebox was more than accessory, as it offered an opportunity for a different paradigm or business model to be adopted. With the arrival of the jukebox, even small cafés could become entertainment hubs with the advantages that they played up-to-the-minute popular music, attracting more customers and received additional revenue from the machine itself. The jukebox did more than fulfil a market need as it created new market segments and, later, through the connectivity of the Internet the jukebox inspired the development of universal music sharing services through platforms like Spotify and Apple Music.

High-level convergence of data processing systems, combined with the increasing capabilities of digital assets and technologies, has enabled a vast expansion of opportunities for do-better and do-different agility. For example, factories, and other production facilities, have seen paradigm-shifting changes resulting from the integration of technologies such as enterprise resource planning, machine-to-machine communication, the Internet of Things, machine learning, artificial intelligence, coordinated and smart robotics and predictive analytics. Such digital infrastructures provide unprecedented levels of control over areas such as resource utilisation, energy use and waste management. Automated systems identify areas of production processes that are failing to deliver expected performance levels. Electronically enabled surveillance enables production control systems to be fine-tuned, sometimes autonomously, so that late changes can be assimilated, new products or services will be introduced quickly, design-to-delivery cycles are dramatically shortened, and risks associated with using human operators are reduced.

The function of technical devices in enabling agility is demonstrated powerfully by the range of aids available for blind people. Scanners can read product barcodes in shops and speak to blind customers; GPS can be built into walking sticks to locate buildings or hazards and voice-controlled assistants will warn when a wanted bus is approaching. The ingenuity of such aids is truly remarkable. They greatly extend blind people's opportunity spaces but, possibly more important, some aids mitigate threats. For example, an audio label maker enables a blind person to save a sound file on items in the kitchen, like foods, medicine and cleaning products, that will be heard when touched with a special pen. Such labellers reduce the risk that the wrong medicine will be taken, or that a cleaning product will be incorrectly used.

An example of Socio-Technical Agility

Amazon is headquartered in Seattle, Washington and operates globally (J. Smith, 2018). At the time of writing, it has a market capitalisation of more than $1 trillion and more than 550,000 employees. Studying Amazon provides valuable insights into the organisational characteristics of a modern company that adopted socio-technical agility as one of its core operating principles (a second core operating principle for Amazon is Type 6, Intrapreneurial agility, that is used for managing product, service and process innovation and is discussed below).

Amazon thinks big. The company began by retailing books on-line and now sells almost everything, as well as offering cloud services, music, films, healthcare and professional services. Every month about 200 million people visit their website. In the United States, Amazon's share of the ecommerce market is close to 50%. Including sellers on Amazon Marketplace about 350 million products are available and 5 billion items are delivered to customers each year.

Amazon.com was launched in 1995 and developed a mission to be Earth's most customer-centric company, where customers can find almost anything they might want to buy online and endeavours to offer its customers the lowest possible prices. This apparently simple set of aims acts as the energising and aligning force that shapes managerial decisions across a vast and complex business.

Achieving superior customer centricity in this form of large enterprise cannot be achieved without socio-technical agility. In the early days of internet shopping customers waited for hours for deliveries to arrive. Amazon listened and devised systems that tracked every order and automatically sent a flow of e-mails to customers telling them about progress, asked where to deliver a package should they be out and, later, provided automated pick-up points in convenient locations. This was powered by a complex and coordinated system, including integrated connectivity with suppliers, sensors for tracking packages, dedicated IT systems, hand-held devices for delivery drivers and easy interfaces for customers.

Only automated systems can manage a business such as Amazon. Many factors must be highly integrated, including global variations, numbers of customers, range of products offered, diversity of supplies, complexity of operations, customisation and an emphasis on speed and reliability. Amazon's agility would have been unachievable without 21st century technical systems.

Once an improvement is made in Amazon's processes it will be rapidly diffused to Amazon's facilities worldwide, as standards for delivering customer service and customer centricity are upgraded systemically and frequently. This increases the agility of the total system as any node can become an originator of improvement in their global smart system. Artificial Intelligence algorithms diagnose causes of failures, decide on maintenance requirements and order parts and tools needed without human intervention thereby reducing downtime and limiting the cost of maintenance.

Amazon is not only a user of autonomous systems, it develops them. This was greatly helped by the purchase of the specialist robot manufacturing company Kiva. Amazon's managers realised that opportunities which arise from socio-technical innovation can provide new competitive advantages, so the company could not afford to be a fast-follower in key areas. Selectively, it needs to be an innovation leader, which requires owning state-of-the-art assets and gaining world-class expertise in socio-technical innovation, adoption and diffusion.

Learning from the Example

The case of Amazon provides important insights into the implications of adopting the concept of socio-technical systems. They require the integration, alignment and application of multiple technologies, some of which are evolving quickly. This will be managed by a part of the organisation that Henry Mintzberg described as 'the technostructure', as it provides an organisational capability for new or improved technologies to be found, developed, integrated and embedded (Lunenburg, 2012). An effective technostructure makes socio-technical agility possible.

Interestingly, some companies outsource aspects of their technostructure. Despite being attractive, there are generic risks in outsourcing technostructure capabilities, as the buyer receives largely commoditised solutions. For Amazon this restriction would curtail their mission to be a leader in socio-technical agility. Hence, Amazon acquired many capabilities themselves, but will buy-in technology and services from outside suppliers where this will accelerate progress.

Uses of Socio-Technical Agility

Socio-Technical Agility is multi-functional. It can increase situational adaptiveness, provide comparative or competitive advantage and helps to future-ready an organisation. Increasingly, as prices fall, technically enabled agility become more affordable, is low risk and may be easily implemented.

It is difficult to think of an organisation that cannot benefit in some way from socio-technical agility but the organisations that benefit the most are those that use complex processes to create value. However, dependence on technically enhanced agility is not without risk. Catastrophes can occur. In 1859 an intense solar storm severely damaged the telegraph communication systems available at that time and a similar event today would destroy satellites and digital systems. Agile organisations do not only use socio-technical systems: they take steps to protect themselves if these systems fail, as minimising risk needs to be a key deliverable from possessing requisite agility.

Type Five: Skunk Works Agility

Skunkworks Agility

In 1934, Al Capp, an American cartoonist, first published a comic strip that would run for 43 years, have 60 million readers and be syndicated in 28 countries. The main character was Li'l Abner Yokum, a mountain hillbilly, who lived in the small town of Dogpatch somewhere in America's remote mountain regions. Another inhabitant was Big Barnsmell, who ran the Skonk Works, a dilapidated factory that cooked dead skunks (that smelly animal) along with old shoes, to make oil for a purpose that was never disclosed. Barnsmell was a loner and he was never invited to social gatherings. 'He has an air about him' those in Dogpatch frequently observed.

During World War II, the US Government became aware that the German Luftwaffe had acquired a jet fighter that was faster than any Allied plane. The Lockheed Corporation was commissioned to develop a jet fighter that would be superior to that possessed by the Luftwaffe (Larsson, 2019). A group of engineers was secretly brought together in a circus tent in Burbank that had been erected next to a plastics factory that polluted the air with foul-smelling chemicals, rather like Big Barnsmell's Skonk Works in Dogpatch. The Lockheed team began answering the phone by saying 'Skonk Works here' but later the term used was changed to 'Skunk Works' and their modality for accelerated technological innovation became centre stage.

Skunk Works Agility provides a capability for an organisation to undertake novel, complex, and often disruptive, innovation initiatives. This distinguishes Skunk Works Agility from Project-Based Agility, its close cousin, that is characterised by a lower requirement for complexity, integration or radical innovation. Skunk Works can be viewed as R&D Departments on Steroids! They must be at the cutting edge of (usually science-based) knowledge, or be extending it. Those who work in Skunk Works will be experts in translating advanced knowledge into systems, artefacts etc. Skunk Works are organisations-within-organisations that can reliably produce radical innovations.

Skunk Works Agility enables previously unobtainable categories of opportunities to be grasped or hard-to-achieve hypothesised opportunities to be transformed into products or services. For example, it may be that developments in bioengineering create an opportunity to improve current aids for paralysed people using a new form of embedded sensors, but many practical, technical and scientific difficulties have yet to be solved. Allocating this task to a specialised Skunk Works may well be the best way to make progress.

That agility can be achieved by constructing bespoke and specialised organisations-within-organisations is neither a new idea, nor is it confined to commercial companies. In 1774 the Roman Catholic Church established an astronomy study group that remains active to this day. The Vatican Observatory Research Group studies topics like black holes and singularities (it has a telescope in Arizona) and is exploring a newly developed perspective called Quantum Theology, demonstrating that not all activities of skunk works relate to science-based innovation.

The Skunk Works organisational model has become sufficiently well-articulated to become a reliable organisational option. Famously, Steve Jobs used this organisational form to develop the first Apple Mac. The Ford Motor Company's Skunk Works developed ways to radically improve vehicle interiors. Netflix has established many Skunk Works, combining them with Scrum principles (more about this later). There are examples of Skunk Works being created informally, in organisational corridors of indifference, that have resulted in innovative changes, like the development of the first artificial hip joints in the Columbia Hospital in South Carolina or the design for a new generation of microcomputers in Data General Corporation by a group of new college graduates that was described so powerfully in the book *The Soul of a New Machine* (Kidder, 1981).

Skunk Works are a powerful management tool but are far from easy to manage. Invariably, they are highly dependent on the capabilities of key individuals. They require the dedication of the brighter and the best, who must be skilled interpersonally as well as technically. Skunk Works can only survive if they are protected from their parent organisation and they need strong top management sponsorship, which can be difficult to achieve. These are complex organisations as decision-making must be technically proficient, speculative, frequent and fast. Errors will be made; learning must be shared and Design Thinking mastered. But there are situations where Skunk Works are indispensable drivers of 'do different' agility. They enable large companies to emulate the agility of innovation-intensive small enterprises. Especially in fast-moving technology companies, Skunk Works have become an institutionalised managerial device.

An Example of Skunk Works Agility

Exploring in greater depth the organisation of the Lockheed Skunk Works is revealing. The first thing to note is that it was elitist from the very beginning. A brilliant young engineer, Clarence 'Kelly' Johnson, was selected to design an organisational format that could deliver disruptive innovation. Widely recognised as an engineering genius, Kelly had designed his first aircraft as a 13-year-old schoolboy.

Kelly studied aeronautical engineering at the University of Michigan, and he joined Lockheed as a tool designer after graduation. Early in his career, Kelly confronted the chief engineer with his analysis that one of the company's aircraft would be fundamentally unstable if an engine failed. This potential fault had not been recognised by experienced design engineers, but Kelly's calculations proved to be correct and he solved the airplane's stability problems. At the age of 23 he joined Lockheed's prestigious aeronautical engineering team.

In 1943, Kelly was asked to design the first US jet fighter. He realised that Lockheed's standard administrative and engineering management systems would inhibit or prevent progress. Something quite different would be required. The famous circus tent was hired, and the newly formed Skunk Works developed its own rules. Even senior Lockheed executives were not allowed to enter unless they had been invited. Kelly constructed an organisation that, to use Henry Mintzberg's term, was a genuine adhocracy, in that it was inherently flexible and was regulated by shared principles and the real-time judgements of hand-picked, on-the-spot engineers. In adhocracies the organisation will be frequently reconfigured ad hoc, or according to the logic of the situation. Standardised routines or broad-brush corporate policies had no place in the Lockheed Skunk Works.

In Lockheed's Skunk Works the engineers and technicians worked together in ways that were reminiscent of primitive hunting bands. They knew each other as individuals, so that interactions were brief, constructive and cooperative. Each person kept the others in mind and would take steps to avoid problems for colleagues. Collective mindsets evolved that stimulated creative solutions that were radically different from any previously used. Later, a theory of action was codified that became known as Design Thinking but when we examine descriptions of everyday life in Lockheed's Skunk Works it is clear that many of the principles were practiced in the 1940s.

Kelly was assertive, opinionated, bold and intolerant of inadequacy. Engineers' accounts of the experience of working in the Skunk Works describe him as being direct, controlling, principled, demanding, authoritarian but brilliant. His leadership style was domineering but inclusive. The centrality of Kelly's role provided a single point of decision-making that ensured alignment between teams, which was essential as many decisions had implications for other parts of an aircraft's systems. The process for providing systemic coordination was Kelly's hands-on intervention in every consequential detail.

Kelly's principles show that a Skunk Works is a managed enterprise that maintains high engineering standards and has rules related to customer relationships, financial accountability, required processes and decision-making protocols. Skunk Works have an open and permissive environment, but this is counterbalanced by demanding leadership expectations, a managed culture and a pervasive demanding ethos. A Skunk Works' culture is stronger, deeper and it expects more from participants than do many forms of organisational culture. Working in a Skunk Works is akin to becoming a member of a world-class sports-team that can compete with the world's best.

One reason why the Lockheed's Skunk Works was successful was that the talented engineers were deeply embedded in the task of designing aircraft and they had developed what some have described as a sixth sense or an artistic intuition into what would be an effective aeronautical design. This capacity for subject-specific mastery is hard to replicate but may explain why flows of outstanding initiatives emerged from Lockheed's Skunk Works.

Importantly, Kelly published his operating principles. They provided a conceptual scaffolding for Skunk Works that is still used today. His fourteen principles include that a manager must be fully empowered to control completely a programme, should only be accountable to a very senior corporate executive and teams should be kept small but everyone has to be on-top-of-their-game.

The Lockheed Skunk Works was designed to be revolutionary, not evolutionary. Interestingly, this required not only escaping from rigidities of routine organisations but also avoiding the limitations of evolutionary R&D departments. In order to create an organisation that would be capable of reliably making technological leaps a distinctive set of organisational attributes was required These were explicit, needed to be coherent and included the following elements:

- Isolated: physically separate from the main organisation, including R&D.
- Customer-centric: adopting an on-going customer-intimacy strategy.
- Focused: having one goal at a time for a team.
- Technically led: the boss is deeply technically knowledgeable.
- Multi-disciplined: all needed specialisations need to be available.
- Total dedication: everyone's energies 100% for the current project.
- Countercultural: the goal is to 'do different'.
- Elitist: Only the best people can work for us.

Apple did precisely this when it developed the first Mac computer. The Mac development team commandeered a separate building, flew a pirate's skull and crossbones flag from the roof, abandoned the rules and regulations of the core organisation, brought their sleeping bags to the office and created the first truly customer-friendly computer, demonstrating the efficacy of the Skunk Works model of organising that had been pioneered in World War II.

Learning from the Example

The Lockheed Skunk Works addressed frontier technological challenges. It showed that there could be great benefits in constructing an organisational unit that was elitist, demanding, disciplined and expected that all members did whatever was needed to be done for each of them to be on top of their game. In some cultures, this organisational principle might be considered as insufficiently concerned with work-life balance or outdated. But the success of the Skunk Works, and comparable experience with top sports teams, suggests that there are some tasks that can only be achieved by exceptional talent and exceptional dedication.

The Skunk Works organisational model has other applications. Radical government policies can be developed in Skunk Works, as can bold marketing strategies or new models of educational programmes. Mini-Skunk Works can be used for addressing wicked (complex with no apparent solution) problems or opportunities.

Type Six: Intrapreneurial Agility

Intrapreneurial Agility

Intrapreneurial Agility facilitates the adoption and exploitation of multiple initiatives that have not been originated by an organisation's TMT. It can be delivered by human and/or non-human agents. The key building block of this mode of operating is intrapreneurship (internally directed entrepreneurship) that empowers and enables individuals, teams or autonomous systems to find, progress and exploit opportunities for the benefit of the organisation (Desouza, 2012).

Agility from intrapreneurship requires four conditions: (i) people with entrepreneurial talent are hired or developed, motivated and supported; (ii) senior managers promote entrepreneurship and adopt a proportion of proposed initiatives; (iii) entrepreneurs' efforts are aligned with the wider needs of the organisation and (iv) resources are made available for initiatives that are sufficient for a successful outcome.

The rationale for promoting intrapreneurship as a modality for achieving requisite agility is that, except in small or non-agile enterprises, top-down agenda-setting and decision-making cannot supply the required quantity of timely developmental initiatives needed for an organisation to achieve its Agility Ambition. Organisations that adopt intrapreneurial agility can harness the creative energy, wisdom and specialist knowledge of many people, that is an often-neglected resource. In effect, the organisation becomes a federation of internal entrepreneurs.

Managing an intrapreneurial organisation is not easy for five main reasons: (i) people with entrepreneurial talent can find it unrewarding to operate within a corporate environment, (ii) ideas or proposals may be strategically unaligned or impractical, (iii) resource allocation procedures do not support the development of initiatives from outside of the conventional organisational structure, (iv) commitment to current tasks reduces the time available for talented people to generate viable out-of-the-box proposals and (v) specialised skills are lacking.

Despite such potential difficulties, harnessing intrapreneurial talent has been shown to be a remarkably productive form of organisational agility, that can be targeted externally or internally. For example, internally, at the shop-floor level intrapreneurs can use frameworks like kaizen, or continuous improvement, to harness shop-floor level entrepreneurial energy to bring about multiple micro-improvements. Externally targeted intrapreneurship can be focused on areas like improving ecosystem processes or creating new products, platforms or services. Those in the middle of organisations, managers or specialists, often have constructive ideas in one or many of the 6P areas described earlier.

The skills required are distinctive as intrapreneurship is neither a science nor an art, it is a craft. It helps to acquire specialised areas of knowledge, undertake skills training, gain experience in nurturing opportunities, participate in focused networking and use structured processes. But those who excel as intrapreneurs will add something extra. They have passion and a willingness to learn from master practitioners, which shapes how they live their lives. They discover how to acquire exceptional agency. This is rarely an easy developmental journey. Intrapreneurs will have setbacks and difficult choices must be made. An intrapreneur must be assertive, proactive, persuasive and opportunistic. She or he builds credibility over time by taking intrapreneurial initiatives and succeeding often. This involves finding new ideas and different ways of doing things, sometimes breaking rules, challenging habits and cutting through a morass of dysfunctional bureaucracy. It requires becoming an agilepreneur.

Institutionalising intrapreneurship as a modality for increasing agile capability is a strategic decision, as members of the TMT must redefine their role and become responsible for proactively enhancing the initiative-taking capability of their organisation. Senior people can kill an idea with a lack of enthusiasm, by putting a proposal low on a priority list or, sometimes, merely a weary look is sufficient to undermine confidence. In this, the roles of champions and initiative sponsors are vital. Of course, not all proposals can be timely, beneficial or practical. When an idea must be rejected a skilful sponsor will recognise the contribution of the disappointed individual for her or his initiative.

Intrapreneurship has attractions for individuals with entrepreneurial talent. Not all will want to establish their own businesses. Larger organisations can be attractive places for venturesome people, as they have access to resources such as talented colleagues, marketing capability, technologies, finance, networks etc.

Successful intrapreneurs need to benefit personally from investing their life-energy for the benefit of the organisation, with rewards including financial bene-fits, status, recognition and freedom to explore.

An Example of Intrapreneurial Agility

The 3M (Minnesota Mining and Manufacturing) corporation was founded in 1902. Today it is a successful diversified technology innovator, owning more than 100,000 patents. The company was awarded the US government's highest award for innova-tion. Over a 20-year period 3M's return on assets averaged 29%, which is remarkably high. 3M was highly ranked in Fortune magazine's survey of America's Most Admired Corporations and has been listed as one of the World's Most Ethical Companies (Coyne, 1996).

In the early days, such success seemed unachievable. Things began to change in 1907, when, at the age of 20, William McKnight began to work for the company as an assistant bookkeeper. In his role in the Finance Department, McKnight discov-ered that the company was close to bankruptcy. He suggested insightful and practi-cal ideas for new products and for cutting costs. McKnight's rise to the top was meteoric and he became President in 1929. For the next 43 years McKnight was a top 3M executive and he is credited with defining the set of strong core values that has become deeply embedded in the company's culture.

In 1948 McKnight wrote: "As our business grows, it becomes increasingly neces-sary to delegate responsibility and to encourage men and women to exercise their initiative. This requires considerable tolerance. Those men and women, to whom we delegate authority and responsibility, if they are good people, are going to want to do their jobs in their own way. Mistakes will be made. But if a person is essentially right, the mistakes he or she makes are not as serious in the long run as the mistakes that management will make if it undertakes to tell those in authority exactly how they must do their jobs. Management that is destructively critical when mistakes are made kills initiative. And it's essential that we have many people with initiative if we are to continue to grow." He later added: "If you put fences around people you get sheep. Give the people the room they need" (Hayton & Kelley, 2006, p. 97).

As a researcher, I have interviewed several 3M people. They think differently from other companies as their executives do not operate from a succinct set of man-agement principles. Rather 3M managers have a comprehensive managerial philoso-phy, communicated through stories, that they explain in depth. This deep consensus about ends and means has constructed a deeply human-centric enterprise, but not one that is egalitarian. 3M is a strict meritocracy.

During my interviews with 3M managers the following comments were made: "we keep one eye looking down to determine our next steps and the other eye looks far away to the horizon". "3M is an evolving organism that is fed because we consciously and systematically develop the skills needed to change as the world changes". "We avoid feeling that we can relax as things are going well right now". "Life without innovation would be unthinkable".

From such comments we learn that 3M's culture is a balance of opposites. It is liberating and confining, confident and anxious, present-orientated and future-focused, permissive and demanding. It is in this duality that strength lies. The ethos of the company attracts talented people, especially engineers who tell researchers like me that "you don't work for 3M, you become part of 3M".

The company gives its employees an option to work on projects of their own choosing, without management approval, for 15% of their time. Individual inventors can request seed capital for initiatives from their own business unit managers to support their proposals and, if a request is denied, they can seek funding from other business units. Proposals for new ventures from inventors will be vigorously examined by senior managers for viability but, if accepted, the company's buy-in to provide support for an initiative will be rock solid.

Boldness, proactivity and resilience are prized. Successful agilepreneurs are recognised and their career progress will be accelerated. Those with technical prowess and entrepreneurial energy acquire a special status. Scientists do not have to become managers to make career progress as there is a dual career ladder. Professional groups come together to explore scientific opportunities with the highest honour being becoming a member of the 3M Technical Hall of Fame.

There is a strong emphasis on questioning customers to understand, in depth, what would delight them. 3M recognises that the process of seizing opportunities is rarely tidy. The company's distinctive approach becomes culturally embedded by short innovation stories, including stories of failure, each establishing a principle of agilepreneurship.

The famous Post-it Notes™ story captures 3M's focus on the exploitation of new ideas (Coster, 2017). 3M had developed a weak adhesive for which a commercial use could not be found. A researcher, named Art Fry, explored the potential of this reusable, pressure-sensitive adhesive that could be applied to a piece of paper and removed without damaging the surface underneath. Fry used samples to mark the hymns chosen to be sung at church on the next Sunday and he was pleased that his bookmarks no longer became misplaced.

Fry believed that this could become a new line of business and he had trial packs of Post-it Notes™ produced. There was little interest from senior managers. Fry decided to supply packs to the secretaries of top managers, and he asked them to evaluate them. Quickly they became popular and Fry supplied more and more, until one day he stopped meeting requests saying that the trial had ended. Several secretaries were disappointed and they complained to their bosses. This brought Post-it Notes™ to the attention of top management which led to a Business Case being developed, presented and accepted. After Post-it Notes™ became an initial success, 3M optimised their product line by searching for ways to extend the initial concept. Product variants have included different colours, various sizes and shapes, flip chart versions, extra-strong glue and waterproof notes.

Learning from the Example

The 3M case shows that is possible and profitable to adopt intrapreneurship as a core operating principle. But it is not easy! For decades 3M executives have presented their company's success formula in conferences and numerous articles or books have been written about them. Yet the company remains highly distinctive. Relatively few other enterprises have succeeded in institutionalising intrapreneurial agility as successfully.

The essence of 3M's differentiation lies in the core values of those who have positions of power and influence, both managerial and technical. They pride themselves on running a technology-based business, with the word 'business' being important. It is impossible promote intrapreneurship without those in the power elite of an organisation relishing the risks, competitiveness, demands, uncertainties and dramas of business life.

Uses of Intrapreneurial Agility

Modern corporations, especially those that thrive by capturing opportunities created by the Information Age, have little option but to evaluate whether to adopt this type of agility. This is because many opportunities require customised technical innovation or localised intrapreneurship/entrepreneurship that cannot be managed from the top. This applies in many industries. For example, banks, insurance companies and government departments have found that they benefit when intrapreneurship becomes deeply embedded in parts of their organisations. Its importance grows as routine work becomes increasingly automated for, as yet, intrapreneurship is largely a human endeavour focused on both internal and external customers. Intrapreneurial agility can be intricately linked to granular agility, as we will see in the next section, but some forms of intrapreneurial agility are large-scale, strategically significant or costly, so cannot be progressed locally. For this reason, it is necessary to differentiate these two modalities.

Type Seven: Granular Agility

Granular Agility

Something is granular when it is composed of discrete entities that are not deeply interconnected with others. This word defines an organisational form in which work groups are largely self-managing and can be relatively weakly connected to others. Granularity delivers agile deliverables that are hard to achieve using other modalities.

Granular organisations are found frequently. If you walk around a business school you may pass a room where a class of students are listening to a lecture, in the next room small groups can be discussing a case-study, further down the corridor there is a noisy debate about the benefits of diversity in top teams and in the last room individual students are receiving one-to-one career counselling. Each room is a discrete entity that is not deeply interconnected with others. The organisational form is granular.

A granular organisation is intensely customised, organised for specific purposes, can be self-managing, has acquired deep task-specific capabilities, uses facilitative technologies and its human members have become a close, high performing team. Consider a complex police investigation that requires DNA analysis, knowledge of the Russian Mafia, covert electronic surveillance and an ability to trace funds in tax havens. Each of these activities is highly specialised and the police investigation will need individuals or teams that are expert in their assigned tasks, have access to required resources and are largely self-managing. Clearly, the output of teams will be pieces of a jigsaw puzzle that must be integrated but the core work is localised and granular.

Granular agility is based on a different view of motivation than other modalities. It is based on an assumption that many people do not have a deep sense of ownership for their work and feel that they are just another resource for an organisation. However, if they are given ownership of local strategy and tactics then their sense of ownership deepens, untapped talents emerge and they will take multiple responsible actions. The roots of granular agility lie in the Human Potential Movement that emerged in the middle of the last century (Gardner, 2020). Opinion leaders, like the psychologist Carl Rogers and A. S. Neil, head teacher of the student-led school

Summerhill, had shown the positive effects that a regime that encouraged self-responsibility provided, including increases in autonomy, empowerment and community consciousness. These attributes enable people to be responsible for reacting constructively to circumstances and taking positive action. Hence, individuals increase their ability to become more capable agility agents.

Granular agility has been so productive for modern organisations that it has become the best-known approach to developing organisational agility, largely by using variants of the Scrum Methodology (Verheyen, 2019). This powerful set of integrated and structured managerial practices has enabled teams to become requisitely agile as they address locally defined or highly specialised tasks. Impact studies have shown that huge leaps in productivity can result from the adoption of Scrum (see Step One for a detailed explanation).

An Example of Granular Agility

In the late 1960s General Foods (currently part of the Kraft Heinz Company) owned the Gaines Plant in Kankakee, Ohio, which made dog food. There were endless problems, especially between workers and management. Absenteeism was high, productivity was low and there were frequent cases of sabotage—once when paint was deliberately mixed with dog food. One day, a new employee started to work diligently on a production line, but his co-workers realised that they would need to work harder just to keep up. The new worker was punished for his diligence by being tied with duct tape to a downpipe in a remote part of the factory, where he was left until his cries for help were eventually heard.

In 1961 the Kankakee factory began to make a new kind of dog food. It was the Gaines-Burger, a hamburger for dogs that was marketed with the catchy slogan 'the canned dog food without the can'. Gaines-Burgers became a runaway success and, as production increased, it was realised that a new production facility would be needed. Two visionary managers reflected on the plant's management problems and decided to spend months studying the world's most productive manufacturing plants to discover how they were managed and organised.

The lessons learnt were adopted in a new dog food plant built in the small city of Topeka in Kansas. Although not intended, the Topeka Plant became a bold experiment in industrial organisation, using techniques such as self-managed teams, multi-skilling, structured multi-level self-directed performance reviews and supervisors acting as facilitators. Although the term was not then used, the social structure of the plant was designed to exploit granular agility. At one point the Topeka Plant was one of the most discussed industrial experiments in the world (Walton, 1977).

I visited this plant twice and found it to be outstandingly agile. Work teams had real responsibility and they took it seriously. I recall a meeting with two plant operators being cut short as they had to join a panel of employees recruiting a new worker without any member of management being involved. This was revolutionary. That workers could have the power to recruit others and, later, decide if they were fit for promotion was contrary to advice in widely used management textbooks. But it worked. The level of commitment of all associates was inspiring.

Those employed in the Topeka Plant had been carefully selected. Once there, responsibility was given and accepted. Everyone I met looked for opportunities for improvement and they thought about ways to solve them. Hazards were identified early and imaginative steps taken to avoid them. Things were done quickly, often without a requirement to gain the permission of managers or supervisors. Being there was exciting. It felt that 'this is the way that a factory should be'. There was an energised, proactive and committed culture that facilitated multiple acts of micro-agility. The Topeka Plant had a very distinctive organisational personality.

The core manufacturing process of the plant had been designed by professional engineers and could not easily be changed. But there were many opportunities for improvement. At the time that I visited there was a heartfelt commitment from every employee to make the plant the best that it could become. Individuals were proactively agile within their own areas of responsibility and they helped each other, even between departments and work groups.

Employees were treated as stakeholders, for example all were involved in financial planning. I was told that: "everyone in the plant participates in the process of putting together a budget for the next fiscal year: we (the senior managers) go to the people and say here is what we have, now we have to put together a plan of what should we be shooting for in production and yield and spoilage for the next fiscal year".

Although visitors left with an overwhelming sense of optimism there were top corporate executives in General Foods who were unconvinced. I was told that Topeka Plant was scathingly known as the 'Funny Farm' in Corporate Headquarters. Three years after the plant opened a team of forensic accountants was sent to examine claims that the Topeka Plant was more effective than other comparable plants. They found that, in the areas of cost the plant could control, the Topeka Plant, depending on the process, was between 20% and 40% better than comparable plants anywhere in the country. These findings convinced top managers on General Foods and they went on to implement organisational in-sights from its Topeka Plant in its factories around the world, especially in other parts of the United States and the UK.

Learning from the Example
The Kankakee and Topeka plants made almost identical products but everything about the factories felt different. The organisational personality of the Kankakee Plant was such that workers saw management as an occupying force. Topeka had a different organisational personality. Those who worked there felt a deep responsibility for the betterment of the plant. They organised themselves, sought opportunities attentively

and made improvements. If there was trash in a corridor it would be removed by the next person who passed, if an unexpected noise was heard from a machine then a maintenance technician would be alerted immediately. Those who worked in Topeka read magazines on factory management in their breaks and discussed what they read over coffee with their co-workers.

The success of the Topeka Plant demonstrates that granular agility is wider than the disciplined Scrum methodology. The principles of extending ownership and facilitating inner-directed responsible agency can be seen in such diverse work groups as those undertaking complex surgery, recording classical operas or undertaking a large archaeological dig.

Uses of Granular Agility
This form of agility offers deliverables or benefits that are difficult to gain from other modalities. These begin with harnessing the commitment and talent of individuals. In industrialised societies many people feel alienated from their work, which is understandable as they may be treated as replaceable components of organisational machines. Granular agility negates alienation as the agency of everyone is prized. It is fulfilling for the person and, if constructively exercised, for the organisation as well.

Type Eight: Networked Agility

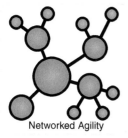

Networked Agility

If you visited the television department of the British Broadcasting Corporation (BBC) in London fifty years ago you would have found that producers and directors would be BBC employees but a freelance scriptwriter might be employed, independent camera people (known as stringers) would capture film footage in distant places, self-employed actors were hired, stock footage came from commercial film libraries and technical services purchased from independent film laboratories. This network of capabilities provided the BBC with huge systemic agility, as they were able to configure internal and external task-specific resources on a programme-by-programme basis.

The BBC had found that networked agility was far from easy to achieve. At worst, those asked to provide inputs could be unreliable, inconsistent, incompetent or produce outputs that were contrary to the project concept. These risks were diminished when external contributors were known, had a reputation for being reliable, were closely managed and/or a strong legally binding contract was in place. Managing such dynamic and complex networks was a daunting task for the senior people in the BBC and it took years of trial-and-error learning for them to develop effective processes for managing such ad hoc structures.

Later, in the BBC, the role of networked agility became even greater. First, they commissioned outside companies to create entire TV programmes. This extended the corporation's systemic agility. It allowed the BBC to expand its landscape of opportunities by acquiring do-different capabilities that were outside of its current portfolio of competencies. Non-BBC producers or directors brought innovative constructs, different values, new perspectives and advanced technical capabilities into the production department. Secondly, co-productions could be undertaken with other broadcasting organisations around the world, which provided more and different resources and enabled production standards to approach those of feature filmmakers.

The BBC's agility, vital for a world-class broadcaster, was dependent on its capacity to be the hub of a network and an effective integrator of resources and systems. But integration alone would have been insufficient, as the BBC needed to be a concept-developer. As in an orchestra, a brilliant composer and a skilled conductor need be the heart of each venture. Creative leadership provided the BBC with the capability to be a pioneer.

The BBC's network-based agility has enabled the corporation to maintain its status as a world-class broadcaster over generations. It provides a powerful demonstration of the deliverables that can be gained from networked agility. However, the construct is broader. This is because networking is a core mechanism by which Open Innovation and Organisational Learning can be achieved.

Open Innovation and Agility

The term Open Innovation describes a distinctive modality for developing new (for an enterprise) products, processes, marketing positions, organisational models or paradigms, sources of resources (provisioning) or platforms. Open Innovation requires abandoning a belief that it is always best to manage innovation only by using corporate resources (Marcolin, Vezzetti, & Montagna, 2017). Rather, a policy is adopted that innovation is best managed, at least in part, by finding and using outside inputs. This avoids the need to replicate development activities already undertaken by others and adds to corporate resources in cost-effective ways. Open Innovation is based on a recognition that, in a networked world, few organisations can justify owning all of the assets that are required to sustain flows of cost-effective initiatives that create opportunities or provide ways by which they can be exploited (hence contribute to systemic agile capability).

Although forms of Open Innovation have been practiced for thousands of years, it has grown in importance, as it is now increasingly cost-effective to implement. Until relatively recently it would have been impossible for people working on progressing a novel initiative to gain fast access to globally available advice, guidance, experience and resources. Now, facilitated by the internet, with advanced search facilities and other forms of digital communication, such information flows easily. The reduction of barriers to the sharing of knowledge, combined with access to numerous, easy-to-reach, low-cost and highly specialised information sources, and resource providers, has been a major factor in changing the modalities that can be used to manage innovation initiatives. Multiple forms of input can be sought, including advice, critique, connections, offers of help, co-development of proposals, insight into stakeholders' viewpoints, cautionary guidance, specialist resources and market intelligence. Open Innovation facilitates assumptions to be tested, new constructs to be explored, experiments to be undertaken and it challenges groupthink.

Avoiding destructive groupthink is necessary if prudent opportunism is to be practiced. Put simply, being opportunistic is easy, being prudently optimistic is difficult. Groupthink is an enemy of prudence. This insight became widely known when a political scientist, Irving Janis, investigated why TMTs made major policy decisions that went disastrously wrong. He found that team members had become victims of groupthink, which is a form of cohesive, collective thinking that develops in a close group where members come to think in the same way and they reinforce each other's views (Janis, 1972). Those who think differently will be rejected. Increasingly, such close groups come to believe their own prescriptions are correct. Janis's work had a revolutionary effect on those studying organisational effectiveness. It was realised that, in certain circumstances, a top team could become a destructive force that would lead their organisation into acting unwisely or unethically.

Organisational Learning and Networked Agility

During the height of the coronavirus epidemic in 2020 many thousands of people around the world were in hospital suffering the worst effects of this respiratory disease. They needed oxygen to be artificially pumped into their lungs if they were to survive but there was a global shortage of the required specialised equipment. A breakthrough came when a team of engineers from University College London worked with medical clinicians and the Mercedes Formula One Motor Racing Team to build a device that delivers oxygen to the lungs without needing a ventilator. It had taken about a week to design a new version of the device that could be manu-factured quickly in large quantities. Existing knowledge assets were combined in new ways in a dynamic learning adhocracy and the complete dedication of a tempo-rary team accelerated learning and enabled a new design to be prepared, prototypes built and tested in days. Rarely has networked agility been so valuable.

Effective collective learning is an essential capability in an agile enterprise. It requires being connected with the wider world using a myriad of modalities. Also, networks of learning ecosystems need to be developed at the individual, team, sub-unit and organisational levels. As was discussed earlier (see Chapter 2), agile organisations are best conceptualised as organisms rather than as machines. This viewpoint enables organisational or collective learning to become a managerial priority.

Agile organisations take a focused approach to promoting organisational learn-ing, specifically addressing four questions: how can we learn to be more intelligently situationally aware? How can we learn to find, select and exploit opportunities bet-ter? How can we learn to define significant threats and find ways to diminish them? How can we learn to prepare ourselves to thrive in a different future? Invariably an-swering these questions requires looking inwards and outwards.

Inwards-looking agility-orientated learning identifies the factors that are help-ing or hindering the organisation from being strong in the four dimensions of or-ganisational agility (the questions listed above). This frequently requires internal learning networks to be established that can be described as Communities of Practice (Borzillo, Schmitt, & Antino, 2012). For example, an international charity might have a Community of Practice reviewing the agility of its fundraising activi-ties and another looking at the agility of its safeguarding practices for children and vulnerable adults.

Outward-looking agility-orientated learning identifies how similar and best-in-class organisations are addressing the same four questions. Here, external networks facilitate learning and may include international standard-setting organisations, universities, professional bodies, lead organisations etc. For example, an interna-tional charity may have a team assessing best-in-class techniques for assessing the impact of its programmes, which requires an understanding of current best practice in monitoring and evaluation drawing from guidance from the United Nations, World Bank, Leading Universities and other charitable initiatives.

An Example of Networked Agility

In 2014 an outbreak of Ebola occurred in Sierra Leone; a country that was ill-prepared to address this terrible health epidemic. Initially, the virus spread with frightening speed. After the funeral of one victim about 300 mourners contracted the disease. Ebola spread relentlessly to Guinea and Liberia with 11,310 deaths reported. Totally inadequate resources were in place to handle such an outbreak. There were no vaccines, no treatments, inadequate diagnostics, no public health plans and poor medical facilities (Preston, 2019).

Two years later, there were safe treatment centres, effective public health programmes, trials of new vaccines, improved medical care and early warning systems in case of another outbreak. This was an example of a multi-dimensional agile networking on a gigantic scale.

How was Ebola defeated in this outbreak? The answer is through the development of effective and networked partnerships. The US Centre for Disease Control (CDC) and the World Health Organisation established operations centres, military organisations sent medical teams and equipment, the Red Cross and Red Crescent Society supplied newly developed isolation tents, UNICEF gave sleeping mats and cooking equipment and the World Bank paid for the airlift of 20 ambulances. University teams provided specialised medical research facilities and pharmaceutical firms undertook crash programmes to develop vaccines and therapeutic drugs.

This complex web of networks within networks required control and coordination. Here the CDC played a key role. There were Health Alert Network notifications and a dedicated Ebola website for information, guidance, case counts, maps and resources. Information was sent to state and local partners, including hospitals, healthcare systems, health partners and emergency management partners. Hundreds of guidance documents were prepared and online learning packages, that included video lectures and downloadable presentations, were frequently updated with the latest information and developments.

Mechanisms were put in place to recruit and enrol partners. For example, the Wellcome Foundation has enormous experience of gathering world-class experts to address current medical challenges and, in August 2014, they created an Ebola Research Fund and invited applications from researchers. The UK's Medical Research Council and Department for International Development became joint sponsors. Very soon after there were trials of promising vaccines undertaken by the Guinean authorities, World Health Organization, Médecins Sans Frontières and the Norwegian Institute of Public Health. A new organisation, the Coalition for Epidemic Preparedness Innovations, was formed to promote scientific research. Such inter-organisational cooperation provided almost unprecedented agility: a process for creating a vaccine normally takes years. In this case one was ready for testing in eight months.

Learning from the Example

It is impossible to know how many people and organisations contributed to network-based organisation fighting the Ebola epidemic, but some estimates suggest more than 50,000. Sub-networks developed for different purposes, involved in areas such as fundraising, basic research, financing, public-health, training and nursing.

International organisations showed extraordinary proactive leadership, reminiscent of that which is required for a military intervention. A consensus was built around the vital importance of this disease outbreak and the urgency of the need. Political support was obtained. Temporary organisations were formed and coordinated using the war-room approach. There was an overarching commitment to two hard-to-achieve ambitions, which were to beat this Ebola crisis and be better prepared for future outbreaks.

The high degree of consensus achieved provided an emotional and intellectual superstructure. Multiple organisations and individuals contributed strategically and operationally, sometimes leading, sometimes following. The building of political will was key. Such comprehensive and coordinated agility required a network of networks that possessed profound strategic alignment.

Uses of Network Agility

Physical or virtual networks can be formally constructed to act as agility enablers. This requires an explicit agreement about mission, shared values, management, objectives and organisation structure. It will be necessary to agree what resources will be provided and who will take decisions. In addition, processes for assuring confidentiality and data security will need to be put in place. It will be important to have a means of assessing performance and a policy for retaining knowledge, including databases and repositories for tacit knowledge.

Both formal and informal networks play a key role in strengthening organisational agility. They enhance capacity to gain situational awareness; recognise, evaluate and grasp opportunities; identify threats and acquire ideas as to what will be required to thrive in the future.

Gaining situational awareness is facilitated by learning networks, especially those that are inter-organisational. They (i) enable experience to be shared, (ii) focus attention on situation analysis, (iii) explore pathways for progress and (iv) produce evidence that improves the quality of decision-making.

Prudent opportunism can be facilitated by resource-providing networks. Often these enable resources to be located. For example, a film production company will access specialised skills from personal contacts and a specialist training company may source resources for its new app from internet searches.

Threats can be identified by using the 'the wisdom of the crowd' as this is more likely to detect subtle or weak signals than can be achieved in a single organisation. Many threats are latent, as they depend on a flow of events that may not occur in the ways hypothesised. Threats are multiple and varied. Networks, including those that possess big-data analysis capabilities, are more likely to identify them and track their development.

Future readying has proved to be the most difficult aspect of organisational agility to manage. Two methods have proved at least partly successful. One is to look for change drivers and try to predict their trajectory. This can answer four questions: Is there a dominant design in our industry? Is the dominant design likely to change? What might happen if the dominant design changes? Can we lead the development of the next dominant design? Secondly, it is necessary to track organisations that are positioning themselves for long-term survival to assess their capability development priorities. This kind of analysis cannot provide a proven success format, rather it offers a provocative input to focus attention on long-term organisational development priorities.

The Step Six Workshop – Customising: *What types of agility do we need?*

Preparation
A room with space for members of the ADT to stand close to a whiteboard or flip chart. The flip charts from the previous step should be displayed as should other relevant material from previous steps.

Time
3 hours including break.

Workshop Structure

1. The ADT leader invites members of the team to agree on what would be great outcomes of this session. These can be written on a whiteboard or a flip chart so that they remain in view during the workshop (10 minutes).
2. At the end of the Step Five workshop participants were asked to list 'things that worked well and areas for improvement'. These points should be reviewed in order to assist the team to work more effectively during the current session (5 minutes).
3. Dedicate one hour to deepening your understanding of the eight types of agility. Allocate seven minutes for each of the eight types. For the first type one person reads their summary of the key distinguishing features and lists situations where it should be used and where it should not be used. Others add comments and suggestions. The leader or ACA summarises the discussion before moving on. Then discussion moves to the next type with a different member of the ADT giving their summary and suggestions for where the type should be used and where it should not be used. Repeat until all eight styles have been discussed (60 minutes).

4. Your task will be to produce Augmented Heat-Map graphics of your organisation, within its ecosystem, that shows which types of agility are, or will be, needed. For each area of your heat map select one of the eight types of agility, as described in the pre-work, that you consider could be most beneficial. You can use the code numbers given below for clarity. Begin with the one-year view, followed by the three-year view, If you have time also complete the seven-year view (60 minutes).

Agility Types Codes

T1 – Top-Down Agility: enables an organisation to respond to a unified command structure.

T2 – Routines-Based Agility: enables an organisation to respond flexibly to a largely predictable variety of complex needs.

T3 – Project-Based Agility: enables an organisation to be reconfigured so that it can achieve big tasks within its existing range of competences.

T4 – Socio-Technical Agility: enables an organisation to gain agility through the integration of human and non-human assets.

T5 – Skunk Works Agility: enables an organisation to deliver innovation-intensive agility.

T6 – Intrapreneurial Agility: enables an organisation to exploit the entrepreneurial talent of key individuals.

T7 – Granular Agility: enables an organisation to exploit the entrepreneurial talent of its human resources.

T8 – Networked Agility: enables an organisation find and coordinate internal and external resources to meet short-term needs.

---

5. When the Augmented Heat Map is complete the members of the ADT assess whether the current organisation is fit for purpose (25 minutes).
6. ADT members privately answer two questions: 'What is one thing that worked well in this session?' and 'What is one area where we could improve next time?' After one or two minutes the answers to the questions should be shared and between three and five suggestions for improvement recorded (10 minutes).

12 Step Seven – Delivering: *How can we make progress?*

The focus of this step is *delivering*. In this step the ADT will reflect on its learning journey and identify where organisational development initiatives will be needed.

Guidance for the ADT Leader

In this step ADT members will have an opportunity to look back at their journey through the EAfA Process, draw out key points and prepare a specification for an organisational development plan. ADT leaders should ensure that all the flip charts or images of whiteboards completed in earlier steps can be displayed in the workshop room, as these will remind participants of the work that they have done previously.

Optionally, senior managers and (if available) specialists in organisational development can be invited to act as observers. If observers are to be present, then they should be asked not to participate in the main workshop activities but may contribute at the end of the workshop. This will extend the time required for the workshop by at least 15 minutes.

The Pre-Workshop Tasks for Step Seven

For this step of the EAfA Process a technique known as Force Field Analysis will be used to identify what needs to change. Before you attend the Step Seven workshop you should read the notes on Force Field Analysis, practice using the method on a change issue that you are considering at the moment and you may find it helpful to view a few of the many videos about Force Field Analysis that are available on the web. You should come to the workshop ready to use Force Field Analysis without further explanation.

Force-Field Analysis

The EAfA process has helped you to diagnose the 'now' situation and 'wanted' situation in relation to requisite agility in your Unit of Analysis. Almost always there will be a gap between what is wanted and what is present. Progress will be made by undertaking action to close this gap, once its nature is clearly understood (Swanson & Creed, 2014).

An effective way to understand what is necessary to close the gap is to use Kurt Lewin's Force Field Analysis. This tool is widely known but has often been misunderstood. Only when Force Field Analysis is used rigorously can it provide the degree of

https://doi.org/10.1515/9783110637267-013

insight into the nature of the gap that is needed to enable an effective organisational development intervention to be designed.

Force Field Analysis is uniquely insightful. The word 'field' is important, but it is far from obvious what it means in this context. Lewin used the word to describe a zone or entity within which different forces interact, somewhat like a fish tank. Within a fish tank there will be water, a heater, thermostat, fish, plants an oxygenator etc. All these components interact to become an aquarium that is more than the sum of its parts, as the interaction between components produces something new. Lewin used the word 'field' to describe the nexus of forces that interact together to create a different entity.

Lewin was interested in how different kinds of forces coalesce to determine the amount and trajectory of personal and organisational change. An example helps to explain the principle. Lewin might be interested in how someone addicted to drugs could achieve detoxification. He finds that there will be forces helping, or driving, a person to move towards successful detoxification (like medical advice, family support, a structured detox programme and one-to-one therapy) and other forces hindering, or preventing, the addicted person from becoming drug-free (like painful withdrawal symptoms, having to leave the social community of other addicts and the pleasures of drug-induced highs). Lewin determined that the balance between helping and hindering forces largely explained whether change could occur. Put simply, he argued that if the helping forces were weak, and the hindering forces were strong, then the present situation would be likely to be frozen, with change unlikely to occur.

The field holding a situation in place at a moment in time is a balance of helping and hindering forces. This balance can be changed by using one or more of the three options that are available. These are (i) strengthening existing helping forces, (ii) adding new helping forces and (iii) weakening or eliminating hindering forces.

Lewin realised that successful change usually requires acting on several of the most influential forces at the same time. For example, if an addicted person is provided with medicine to ameliorate the effects of withdrawing from use of a drug but he or she remains in a social group with other addicts, and no other hindering force is weakened, then the probability that detox will be successful is greatly reduced. Lewin concluded that those who want to manage change should consider the field, not only individual forces, as the unit of analysis.

If change is to be planned, then a goal must be set. Imagine a large restaurant where the general hygiene standards are dangerously low. The restaurant manager set a goal to achieve 5-star hygiene standards (the highest available). A list was prepared of forces that hindered the achievement of high hygiene standards and the few that helped. The definition of forces was evidence-based where possible, and inputs included the findings of external inspections, observations of restaurant employees, scientific tests of types of contamination, interviews with staff members etc. Judgements were made where objective data could not be obtained. It became clear that the forces that hindered progress towards the goal included ignorance of good hygiene practices, lack of cleaning materials and no reliable process for checking cleanliness. As a separate exercise, the restaurant manager undertook research to find what criteria were used in the best restaurants to rate food hygiene standards in order to achieve a 5-star standard. She investigated how the best restaurants had reached the goal. With these insights a Force Field Analysis Diagram was prepared. Existing forces, both helping and hindering, were added to a graphic, each was given a name and an assessment made as to the power of the force.

The Force Field Analysis Diagram was prepared with a vertical line in the middle that represents the 'now' situation and is an outcome of a balance between helping and hindering forces. In the diagram below the helping and hindering forces are illustrated by arrows of different length and thickness to indicate their importance (length) and strength (width). Note that a force can be human or another factor (e.g., the availability of funds for investment or the lack of a management information system could be forces).

In order to manage change, a clear statement of intention was set. The wanted situation was worded as precisely as possible ('to achieve 5-star hygiene standards as assessed by an external inspector within three months'), that was later broken down into monthly milestones with clear statements of what will be happening 'more or better', 'less or stop', 'new things to start' and 'things to continue' on a particular date over the time scale of the change programme.

Figure 2: The Force Field Analysis Framework.

A Force Field Analysis Diagram becomes a master change plan. Each force that needs to become stronger, weaker or newly added becomes an item for analysis and planning. The key questions include: 'How can we build on strengths?' 'What needs to be done to unblock the blockages?' What new things can we do? What will be the most effective way to facilitate change? How can we track progress?

The Step Seven Workshop – *Delivering: How can we make progress?*

Preparation
A room with space for members of the ADT to stand close to a flip chart. A flip chart pad will be needed. The completed flip charts from all the previous steps should be displayed around the walls. Three flip charts will be needed with fine (sharpie type) marker pens available.

Time
2 hours and 15 minutes, including break.

Workshop Structure

1. The ADT leader invites members of the team to agree on what would be great outcomes of this session. These can be written on a whiteboard or a flip chart so that they remain in view during the workshop (10 minutes).
2. At the end of the Step Six workshop participants were asked to list 'things that worked well and areas for improvement'. These points should be reviewed in order to assist the team to work more effectively during the current session (5 minutes).
3. The ADT should be divided into three sub-groups. Each is asked to prepare a Force Field Analysis Diagram with the Wanted Situation being 'Achievement of our Agility Ambition' on a sheet of flip chart paper (30 minutes).
4. Each sub-group presents their analysis and explains each of the forces identified (10 minutes for each sub-group, 30 minutes in total).
5. The ADT, who may be joined by senior managers, now working as a single group, develop a single Force Field Analysis Diagram that will be a composite of the earlier versions (45 minutes).
6. The ADT discuss how to make best use of their analysis and roles are allocated (10 minutes).
7. Each member of the ADT has one minute to write a note of one thing that he or she appreciated about being involved in the EAfA Process. These comments to be shared before the workshop is closed (10 minutes).

Bibliography for Part II

Acrylic Tank Manufacturing. (2020). Retrieved March 30, 2020, from https://www.acrylicaqua
riums.com

Alberts, D. S., Bernier, F., Farrell, P. S. E., Pearce, P., Bélanger, M., Lizotte, M., . . . Phister,
P. W. (2014). SAS-085 Final Report on C2 Agility.

Alberts, D. S., & Hayes, R. E. (2003). Power to the Edge: Command, Control in the Information Age.
CCRR Publication Series.

Bernstein, P. L. (2010). Wedding of the Waters: The Erie Canal and the Making of a Great Nation
(ASIN: B004). W. W. Norton & Company.

Birkinshaw, J. (2018). What to expect from Agile? MIT Sloan Management Review, 59 (2),39–42.
Retrieved from www.forbes.com,

Blank, S. (2013). Why the Lean Start-Up Changes Everything. Harvard Business Review.

Borzillo, S., Schmitt, A., & Antino, M. (2012). Communities of practice: Keeping the company agile.
Journal of Business Strategy, 33(6),22–30.

Brandenburger, A. M., & Nalebuff, B. J. (1997). Co-Opetition (2nd ed.). Profile Books.

Bratton, W. J., & Knobler, P. (1998). The Turnaround: How America's Top Cop Reversed the Crime
Epidemic. Random House.

Cardwell, D. (2017). The Development of Science and Technology in Nineteenth-Century Britain.
Taylor & Francis.

Cheung-Judge, M.-Y., & Holbeche, L. S. (2015). Organization Development: A Practitioner's Guide
for OD and HR (2nd ed.). London: Kogan Page.

Conboy, K., & Carroll, N. (2019). Implementing large-scale agile frameworks: challenges
and recommendations. IEEE Software, 36(2),44–50.

Coster, J. (2017). Lessons from 3M Corporation: managing innovation over time and overcoming the
innovator's dilemma. Retrieved from www.kth.se

Coyne, W. E. (1996). Building a Tradition of Innovation. In The UK Innovation Lecture. London: DTI.

Crawley, R. W., & Kloman, E. H. (1972). NASA Seminar on Organization and Management.

Crick, C., & Chew, E. K. (2017). Business processes in the agile organisation: a socio-technical
perspective. Software and Systems Modelling, 16(3),631–648.

Desouza, K. C. (2012). Intrapreneurship: Managing Ideas Within Your Organization (Kindle).
Rotman-UTP Publishing.

Duckworth, A. (2016). Grit: The Power of Passion and Perseverance. London: Penguin.

Eisenhardt, K. M., & Martin, J. A. (2000). Dynamic Capabilities: What Are They? Strategic
Management Journal, 21(10/11), 1105–1121.

Evers, A., Anderson, N., & Voskuijl, O. (Eds.). (2017). The Blackwell Handbook of Personnel
Selection. Blackwell Publishing Ltd.

Flynn, M. J. (1996). Battle Focused Training for Peacekeeping Operations: A METL Adjustment
for Infantry Battalions.

Fowler, M., & Highsmith, J. (2001). The Agile Manifesto. Software Development, 9(8),28–37.

Francis, D., & Woodcock, M. (1999). Developing Agile Organizations: Theory and Interventions.
Aldershot, Hampshire, UK: Gower Publishing.

Gabriel, R. (2011). Hannibal: The Military Biography of Rome's Greatest Enemy. Potomac Books.

Gardner, H. (2020). Of Human Potential: A 40-Year Saga. Journal for the Education of the Gifted,
43(1),12–18.

Gerstner Jr., L. V. (2002). Who Says Elephants Can't Dance?: Inside IBM's Historic Turnaround.
London: HarperCollins.

Ghoshal, S., & Butler, C. (1992). The Kao Corporation: A Case Study. European Management
Journal, 10(2),179–192.

https://doi.org/10.1515/9783110637267-014

Harrison, R. (1995). The Collected Papers of Roger Harrison. San Francisco: Jossey-Bass.

Hayton, J. C., & Kelley, D. J. (2006). A competency-based framework for promoting corporate entrepreneurship. Human Resource Management, 45(3),407–427.

Horne, G. (1995). Fire This Time: Watts Uprising and the 1960s (Carter G. Woodson Institute Series in Black Studies). University of Virginia Press.

Janis, I. L. (1972). Victims of groupthink: A psychological study of foreign policy decisions and fiascos. Boston: Houghton Mifflin Company.

Johnson, S. (2001). Emergence: The Connected Lives of Ants, Brains, Cities and Software. New York: Scribner.

Kao: R&D Philosophy. (2020). Retrieved March 20, 2020, from https://www.kao.com/global/en/re search-development/basic-concepts/philosophy/

Kidder, T. (1981). The Soul of a New Machine. Boston: Little and Brown.

King, D. L., Ben-Tovim, D. I., & Bassham, J. (2006). Redesigning emergency department patient flows: Application of Lean Thinking to health care. EMA – Emergency Medicine Australasia, 18(4),391–397.

Kolko, J. (2015). Design Thinking Comes of Age: The approach, once used primarily in product design, is now infusing corporate culture. Harvard Business Review, (September), 66–71.

Larsson, A. (2019). The seven dimensions of Skunk Works: a new approach and what makes it unique. Journal of Research in Marketing and Entrepreneurship, 21(1),37–54.

Lau, K. W., Lee, P. Y., & Chung, Y. Y. (2019). A collective organizational learning model for organizational development. Leadership and Organization Development Journal, 40(1),107–123.

Lunenburg, F. C. (2012). Organizational Structure: Mintzberg's Framework. International Journal for Scholarly, Academic, Intellectual Diversity, 14(1),1–8.

Marcolin, F., Vezzetti, E., & Montagna, F. (2017). How to practise Open Innovation today: what, where, how and why. Creative Industries Journal, 10(3),258–291.

Maylor, H., & Turkulainen, V. (2019). The concept of organisational projectification: past, present and beyond? International Journal of Managing Projects in Business.

Meredith, S. E., & Francis, D. L. (2000). Journey towards agility: the agile wheel explored. The TQM Magazine, 12(2),137–143.

Midler, C. (1995). "Projectification" of the firm: the Renault case. Scandinavian Journal of Management, 11(4),363–375.

Midler, C. (2019). Crossing the Valley of Death: Managing the When, What, and How of Innovative Development Projects. Project Management Journal, 50(4),447–459.

Mintzberg, H., Quinn, J. B., & Ghoshal, S. (1998). The Strategy Process (REVISED Eu). Hemel Hempstead, UK.: Prentice Hall Europe.

Nagel, R. N., & Dove, R. (1991). 21st Century Manufacturing Enterprise Strategy: An Industry-Led View. Iacocca Institute. Bethlehem.

Naylor, J. Ben, Naim, M., & Berry, D. (1999). Leagility: integrating the lean and agile manufacturing in the total supply chain. International Journal of Production Economics, 62, 107–118.

O'Reilly III, C. A., & Tushman, M. L. (2004). The Ambidextrous Organization. Harvard Business Review, 82(4),74–82.

Potts, R., Vella, K., Dale, A., & Sipe, N. (2016). Exploring the usefulness of structural–functional approaches to analyse governance of planning systems. Planning Theory, 15(2),162–189.

Preston, R. (2019). Crisis in the Red Zone: The Story of the Deadliest Ebola Outbreak in History, and of the Outbreaks to Come (1st ed.). Penguin Random House.

Rigby, D. K., Sutherland, J., & Takeuchi, H. (2016). Embracing agile: How to Master the Process that's Transforming Management. Harvard Business Review, 94(5),40–50.

Roethlisberger, F. J., & Dickson, W. J. (1939). Management and the Worker. Cambridge, Mass: Harvard University Press.

Schmidt, E., Rosenberg, J., & Eagle, A. (2015). How Google Works. London: John Murray.

Schumacher, A., Nemeth, T., & Sihn, W. (2019). Roadmapping towards industrial digitalization based on an Industry 4.0 maturity model for manufacturing enterprises. Procedia CIRP, 79, 409–414.

Schwaber, K., Hundhausen, R., & Starr, D. (2015). Agile Project Management with Scrum (2nd ed.). Microsoft Press.

Shah, I. (1993). Tales of the Dervishes. Octagon Press.

Smith, J. (2018). How Jeff Bezos Built an E-Commerce Empire: The Unwritten Story of Amazon.com. Kindle Edition.

Smith, M. (1998). Station X: The Codebreakers of Bletchley Park. Channel 4 Book.

Swanson, D. J., & Creed, A. S. (2014). Sharpening the Focus of Force Field Analysis. Journal of Change Management, 14(1),28–47.

Taylor, F. W. (1911). The Principles of Scientific Management. New York: Harper.

Teece, D. J., & Pisano, G. (1994). The Dynamic Capabilities of Firms: an Introduction. Industrial and Corporate Change, 3(3),537–556.

Ten things we know to be true. (n.d.). Retrieved March 25, 2020, from https://www.google.com/about/philosophy.html

Thadamalla, J., Dadhwal, V., & Sonpal, A. (2009). The Downfall of Polaroid: Corporate Lessons (A). IBS Research Center.

Tidd, J., & Bessant, J. (2014). Strategic Innovation Management. New York: John Wiley & Sons Inc.

Treacy, M., & Wiersema, F. (1993). Customer Intimacy and Other Value Disciplines. Harvard Business Review, 71(1),84–93.

Tregoe, B. B., & Zimmerman, J. W. (1980). Top Management Strategy: What It Is and How to Make It Work. London: John Martin Publishing.

Trist, E. L., & Bamforth, K. W. (1951). Some Social and Psychological Consequences of the Longwall Method of Coal-Getting: An Examination of the Psychological Situation and Defences of a Work Group in Relation to the Social Structure and Technological Content of the Work System. Human Relations.

Tzu, S. (1981). The Art of War. In J. Clavell (Ed.). London: Hodder and Stoughton.

Verheyen, G. (2019). Scrum: A Smart Travel Companion (2nd ed.). Van Haren.

Vogelsang, J., Townsend, M., Minahan, M., Jamieson, D., Vogel, J., Viets, A., . . . Valek., L. (2012). Handbook for Strategic HR: Best Practices in Organization Development from the OD Network. AMACOM, a division of American Management Association.

Volberda, H. W., Foss, N. J., & Lyles, M. A. (2010). Absorbing the Concept of Absorptive Capacity: How to Realize Its Potential in the Organization Field. Organization Science, 21(4),931–951.

Von Culin, K. R., Tsukayama, E., & Duckworth, A. L. (2014). Unpacking grit: Motivational correlates of perseverance and passion for long-term goals. Journal of Positive Psychology, 9(4),306–312.

von Hippel, E. (1986). Lead Users: A Source of Novel Product Concepts. Management Science, 32(7),791–805.

Walton, R. E. (1977). Work Innovations at Topeka: After Six Years. The Journal of Applied Behavioral Science, 13(3),422–433.

Watts Labor Action Committee. (n.d.). Retrieved March 30, 2020, from http://www.wlcac.org

Weick, K. E., & Roberts, K. H. (1993). Collective Mind in Organizations: Heedful on Interrelating Flight Decks. Administrative Science Quarterly, 38(3),357–381.

Womack, J. P., & Jones, D. T. (1996). Lean Thinking. New York: Simon and Schuster.

Yolles, M. (2005). Organisational intelligence. Journal of Workplace Learning, 17(1–2), 99–114.

Zhao-hong, L. I. (2003). The Thinking of Xiaotangshan Hospital Construction in Emergency Situation. Hospital Administration Journal of Pla, 4, 10.

Part III: **Resources**

13 Theory, References and Follow-Up Reading

Readers may have noticed that there are only selective academic references in the main body of this book. Hopefully, this enabled the text to be read more easily but it means that there will be insufficient depth of explanation for some readers. Part III attempts to fill this gap. Here you will find additional support for the arguments made in the book. The topics are arranged alphabetically. The notes and comments in this part of the book are not intended to be authoritative literature reviews, rather they provide a historical background and selected scholarly perspectives. References are provided for further reading but these should be viewed as indicative, not comprehensive.

Further information on recent organisational developments for requisite agility and diagnostic surveys can be found online at https://www.richmondconsultantsltd.com and the author can be contacted by e-mail at enquiries@richmondconsult.com with the term 'EAfA' in the subject line. You can help the author to be agile by sharing your experience of using the EAfA Process to improve subsequent editions of this book.

Topic One: 3M and William McKnight

William L. McKnight (1887–1978) spent his entire career in the 3M corporation and is credited with enabling 3M to be consistently and requisitely agile over many decades. Conceição et al. (2002, p. 32) explained that "3M's culture is based on McKnight's management principles laid out in 1948". More than a great manager McKnight was also a business philosopher, who created a corporate culture that encourages employee initiative, entrepreneurship and innovation. 3M's commitment to proactive opportunism, using an organic analogy, was summarised by Coyne (2001, p. 21) as to "achieve long-term growth in such an environment, technology companies need to be capable of constant adaptation. Like evolving organisms, they must be adept at transforming their behaviour and their properties based on changes in the world around them". Coster (2017, p. 38) emphasised the importance of the role of shared values stating that the 3M "culture can be seen as strong because employees continuously state the same values and as the values are reinforced through different reward and recognition programs. Yet, the company culture includes values of entrepreneurship, innovation, creativity, collaboration and openness, therefore, one might argue that the core values of 3M's organizational culture is allowing flexibility and adaptability. Moreover, as 3M has facilitated capabilities to learn and unlearn, it indicates that their organizational culture can change".

https://doi.org/10.1515/9783110637267-015

Further Reading

Conceição, P., Hamill, D., & Pinheiro, P. (2002). Innovative science and technology commercialization strategies at 3M: A case study. Journal of Engineering and Technology Management – JET-M, 19, 25–38.
Coster, J. (2017). Lessons from 3M Corporation: managing innovation over time and overcoming the innovator's dilemma. Retrieved from www.kth.se
Coyne, W. E. (2001). How 3M Innovates for Long-Term Growth. Research Technology Management, 44(2), 21–25.

Topic Two: Absorptive Capacity

It is far from obvious what the term 'absorptive capacity' means to anyone outside of a rather narrow academic circle. It is a term used to describe synthesis of four interconnected attributes namely (i) the capability of people in an organisation to look outside of their own organisation and find ideas, opportunities, connections and other possible useful or advantageous inputs; (ii) consider (absorb) each new possibility so that they understand its strengths and weaknesses; (iii) select the most likely to be beneficial to their own organisation and (iv) effectively implement the advantageous initiatives by having effective execution capability. Absorptive capacity is directly related to all agile enterprises as it assists an organisation to become highly situationally responsive.

Absorptive Capacity was explained by Easterby-Smith et al. (2008, p. 483) as "the ability to locate new ideas and to incorporate them into an organization's processes, and this is widely seen as a major contributor to organizational performance". Absorptive capacity can result in the beneficial exploitation of forms of knowledge and other potential resources, including ideas, technologies, requirements, standards, alternatives, factors affecting choices, implementation issues and resource availability. As this modality of finding beneficial initiatives does not require internally driven innovation it is often fast and low cost. In a seminal paper, Cohen and Levinthal (1990, p. 135) stated that Absorptive Capacity is relevant at "both the individual and organizational levels" and that it is accumulative as "prior knowledge permits the assimilation and exploitation of new knowledge". Efficient and effective absorption can be analysed in three categories:

Acquisition requires recognising the potential value of ideas from many sources (these can be in 'what is produced' (product), 'how things are done' (process), 'how communication takes place' (position), in 'ways of thinking' (paradigm), 'availability of resources' (provisioning) and/or 'environments to facilitate participation' (platform)). Relevant activities include learning about trends, possibilities and the experiences of leading institutions, assembling different sources of knowledge, focusing and categorising them, analysing where new ideas could fit in.

Assimilation entails exploring, a phase in which ideas and opportunities are organised, debated and analysed in order to understand them in depth. Ideas need to be tested; both to demonstrate that they are practical and to ensure (as far as possible) that adoption can add value faster than cost. The essence of this phase is coming to understand the full potential of promising ideas as well as their downsides. Experimentation and filtering help to narrow the field so that exploration effort can be placed where it is most likely to deliver an attractive return on investment.

In transformation, a commitment decision will be needed to adopt the new or improved offerings such as products, brands, services, communication, experiences, or efficiently to innovate processes. Mechanisms for managing adoption are needed in addition to the resources required to enable them to be implemented. Exploitation, involves the full implementation of new knowledge through integration into business areas such as processes, coordinating functions, aligning core values, training staff etc. and by delivering a coherent customer experience.

Further Reading

Cohen, W. M., & Levinthal, D. A. (1990). Absorptive capacity: a new perspective on learning and innovation. Administrative Sciences Quarterly, 35, 128–152.

Easterby-Smith, M., Graca, M., Antonacopoulou, E., & Ferdinand, J. (2008). Absorptive Capacity: A Process Perspective. Management Learning, 39(5),483–501.

Topic Three: Actor Network Theory

Actor Network Theory (ANT) is a sociological theoretical perspective, developed by Bruno Latour (2005), that provides a structured way of conceptualising how varied sources of agency interact to form a gestalt or whole. ANT is relevant to understanding organisational agility as multiple factors, including resources, structures, cultural characteristics, managerial dedication and communication capabilities, can serve to either help or hinder requisite agility. ANT examines the interaction of human and non-human actors. It considers reality as resulting from an interplay of actors (technically known as 'actants') within networks. Rydin (2013, p. 24) wrote that "with its emphasis on the lack of any boundary between society and technology or between the social and the natural worlds, (ANT) . . . can offer an analytic edge over existing planning theories that only engage with the material and natural world through the values and communicative action of social actors".

ANT provides a set of constructs that place non-human factors, such as artefacts, cultural memes, significant events and technological developments, in direct relation with social factors like attitudes, skills, values and patterns of interaction. It has been used in many empirical studies, so it provides a validated framework for analysis (Dedeke, 2017; Jørgensen, 2017; Palmer, 2016; Pollack, Costello, & Sankaran, 2013).

ANT provides a framework for academic scholars seeking to understand the messy nature of agile organisational life as Aka (2019, p. 526) found when exploring "the triggering of innovations by shocks, the proliferation of ideas, the frequent back-and-forth activities, the changes in the innovating unit, the key role of the manager, the shifting in the criteria over time, and the different and contradictory stakeholders' interests. These modifiers reside in what is known as the 'black box' of the innovation process".

Further Reading

Aka, K. G. (2019). Actor-network theory to understand, track and succeed in a sustainable innovation development process. Journal of Cleaner Production, 225, 524–540.

Dedeke, A. N. (2017). Creating sustainable tourism ventures in protected areas: An actor-network theory analysis. Tourism Management, 61, 161–172.

Jørgensen, M. T. (2017). Reframing tourism distribution – Activity Theory and Actor-Network Theory. Tourism Management, 62, 312–321.

Latour, B. (2005). Reassembling the Social: An Introduction to Actor-Network-Theory. Politica y Sociedad (Vol. 43). Oxford UK: Oxford University Press.

Palmer, M. (2016). Sustaining indigenous geographies through world heritage: a study of Uluṟu-Kata Tjuṯa National Park. Sustainability Science, 11, 13–24.

Pollack, J., Costello, K., & Sankaran, S. (2013). Applying Actor–Network Theory as a sensemaking framework for complex organisational change programs. International Journal of Project Management, 31(8),1118–1128.

Rydin, Y. (2013). Using Actor-Network Theory to understand planning practice: Exploring relationships between actants in regulating low-carbon commercial development. Planning Theory, 12(1),23–45.

Topic Four: Agency

The notion of 'agency' examines the role of individuals and groups in facilitating change (Giddens, 1986). This draws from sociological models, known as structuration theories, that explore the relationship between actors and social structures (Sarason, Dean, & Dillard, 2006) within the context of social change. A core notion is that, in some situations, actors can acquire agency meaning that they gain power or influence, at least to some extent, in the organisations within which they work. This view is supported by Abdelnour et al. (2017, p. 1781) who observe that "today, agency-centric trajectories consider individual actors, wittingly or unwittingly, to have an almost heroic capacity to manipulate institutions." Burkitt (2016, p. 323) notes that a widely used definition of "an agent is 'a person or thing that takes an active role or produces a specified effect', 'the doer of an action'". Harsch and Festing (2019, p. 49) point out that agile agents rarely gain power unless they are seen to make a positive contribution as "high achievers with potential, who act as multipliers and motivate not only themselves, but also other employees to improve the organization and build on its success. They are innovative, mobile, customer-oriented, resilient, and adaptable, have a high ability to learn and a high willingness to perform, and they call into question conventional practices".

Case studies enable us to explore the construct of agency in the context of organisational agility (e.g., Schlatmann & Jacobs, 2017) and show that individual agents are rarely the sole 'doers of action'. Rather they enter a context in which agency is ongoing and so the influence of a single person is always relational, in that it depends on 'doing the right things at the right time, to be influential and move things forward'. As Edwards (2005, p. 175) stated: relational agency requires a "capacity to recognize others as resources, to elicit their interpretations and to negotiate aligned action".

Further Reading

Abdelnour, S., Hasselbladh, H., & Kallinikos, J. (2017). Agency and Institutions in Organization Studies. Organization Studies, 38(12),1775–1792.

Burkitt, I. (2016). Relational agency: Relational sociology, agency and interaction. European Journal of Social Theory, 19(3),322–339.

Edwards, A. (2005). Relational agency: Learning to be a resourceful practitioner. International Journal of Educational Research, 43(3),168–182.

Giddens, A. (1986). The Constitution of Society: Outline of the Theory of Structuration. Polity Press. Cambridge, UK.

Harsch, K., & Festing, M. (2019). Dynamic talent management capabilities and organizational agility – A qualitative exploration. Human Resource Management, 59(43),43–61.

Sarason, Y., Dean, T., & Dillard, J. F. (2006). Entrepreneurship as the nexus of individual and opportunity: A structuration view. Journal of Business Venturing, 21, 286–305.

Schlatmann, B., & Jacobs, P. (2017). ING's agile transformation. McKinsey Quarterly, 1, 42–51.

Topic Five: Agility as a Strategic Issue

King (1982, p. 45) stated that a "definition of 'strategic issue . . . is a 'condition or pressure' on the organization that involves: (a) possible outcomes that are important to, or of possible high impact on, the organization's overall performance . . . and (c) strategy consequences, in that the various possible outcomes implied by the issue would prescribe that different strategies should be implemented". Laamanen et al. (2018, p. 626) found that "strategic issues tend to be learning episodes not only for the individuals involved but also for the organization as a whole".

A report by PA Consulting clarified that agility met King and Laamanen's criteria (2019, p. 9) and stated that "global business is facing unprecedented disruption. An increase in technology-based innovation and changing customer expectations is uprooting the old, established corporate order. This acceleration propels economies forward and creates new, market-beating growth opportunities for those who are willing to seize them. Nearly three-quarters of the leaders we spoke with believe that companies' ability to respond rapidly to change will make the difference between success and failure." PA's assessment of the strategic significance of agility emphasises the breadth of the construct and its central significance in shaping organisational personalities in the 21st century. They view agility as a current leadership zeitgeist, a perspective that has deep historical roots as Mayo & Nohria (2005, p. 60) explained when they wrote: "The central lesson we can take from business history is that context matters. The ability to understand the Zeitgeist and pursue the unique opportunities it presents for each company is what separates the truly great from the merely competent".

A survey conducted by McKinsey & Company went into detail about the scope of strategic initiatives connected with agility and found that (2017, p. 3) "when asked where their companies apply agile ways of working, respondents most often identify activities that are closest to the customer: innovation, customer experience, sales and servicing, and product management. This is not too surprising, since customer centricity is cited most often—followed by productivity and employee engagement—as the objective of agile transformations. Companies are also focusing on internal end-to-end processes. At least four in ten respondents say their companies are applying agile ways of working in processes related to operations, strategy, and technology, while roughly one-third say they are doing so in supply-chain management and talent management". This survey demonstrated that companies are applying agility selectively in different areas of their business, illustrating that agility is a generalised capability that must be customised for specific processes and implementation areas.

Military planners led the original thinking processes that resulted in the definition of the Agile Paradigm and they continue to make a major contribution. A 200-page NATO report obscurely titled 'SAS-085 Final Report on C2 Agility' (Alberts et al., 2014) presents the results of research, including experimental findings, into the challenges of coordinating resources to counter known and unknown threats. The authors state that: "The logical response to high degrees of uncertainty and complexity is to improve Agility. Agility, like any other 'good', is not an end unto itself and thus simply seeking maximum Agility is not the answer" (p. 48). Those shaping the future of the armed services see the potential of socio-technical advances providing previously unobtainable levels of agility. Ryan and Mittal (2019, p. 125) wrote "Currently, autonomous systems are supporting human analysts in virtually all of the subfunctions (of military operations), since they allow the analysts to more readily collect and process data. Unmanned aerial vehicles have been used for intelligence gathering for decades. Additionally, autonomous software codes are used for cyberspace monitoring to gather intelligence. There are also systems under development, such as the U.S. Special Operations Command's hyper-enabled operator, that will use a higher level of autonomy to automate the full intelligence process from collection to analysis". These observations provide evidence that agility is a plastic concept in that it is capable of being advanced and redefined as technological paradigms change. This can be seen within a broader context of Technological Paradigms as Cimoli and Dosi (1995) suggest in their evolutionary microeconomic theory of innovation and production.

That agility is not confined to commercial enterprises was clearly shown by a study of UNICEF by Amatullo (2015, p. 36) who writes "the agility again of the structure is seen as a positive that is also responsive of the larger changes the organization has to contend with in terms of the nature of the complexity of world problems and circumstances, which in turn influence the institutional logics of UNICEF".

When the construct of agility was launched in the early 1990s it was heralded as the answer to a moribund and dysfunctional industrial structure. We have matured. Now agility can be seen as a set of business excellence models that can be applied flexibly and integrated creatively. In short, we have learnt to apply the Agile Paradigm in an agile way! An important paper by Teece et al. (2016, p. 31) makes this point asserting that: "Organizational agility is a much-touted attribute and usually considered virtuous. However, there are associated costs, and the existing literature does not explain when agility is desirable, the nature of its foundations, and how, if at all, it relates to strategy". Agility can be expensive, unnecessary and incurs significant new risks. From a strategic viewpoint, if Teece et al. are correct, then a decision to adopt the Agile Paradigm is just one strategic option among many.

Darwinian forces are powerful they are not ubiquitous. Not all situations are equally win-lose (Lundin et al., 2015). Nevertheless, no organisation can afford to ignore agility and, looking ahead, to a world dominated by an increasingly capable set of technological platforms we see that agility is an increasingly important organisational imperative (Doz & Mikko Kosonen, 2008).

Further Reading

Alberts, D. S., Bernier, F., Farrell, P. S. E., Pearce, P., Bélanger, M., Lizotte, M., . . . Phister, P. W. (2014). SAS-085 Final Report on C2 Agility.

Amatullo, M. V. (2015). Innovation by Design at UNICEF: An Ethnographic Case Study. Case Western Reserve.

Cimoli, M., & Dosi, G. (1995). Technological paradigms, patterns of learning and development: an introductory roadmap. Evolutionary Economics, 5(3),243–268.

Doz, Y. L., & Mikko Kosonen, S. (2008). The Dynamics of Strategic Agility. California Management Review, 50(3),95–118.

King, W. R. (1982). Using strategic issue analysis. Long Range Planning, 15(4),45–49.

Laamanen, T., Maula, M., Kajanto, M., & Kunnas, P. (2018). The role of cognitive load in effective strategic issue management. Long Range Planning, 51(4),625–639.

Lundin, R. A., Arvidsson, N., Brady, T., Ekstedit, E., Midler, C., & Sydow, J. (2015). Managing and Working in Project Society: Institutional Challenges of Temporary Organizations. Cambridge, U.K.: Cambridge University Press.

Mayo, A. J., & Nohria, N. (2005). Zeitgeist leadership. Harvard Business Review, 83(10).

McKinsey & Company. (2017). How to create an agile organization. McKinsey & Company.
paconsulting.com. (2019). The Evolution of the Agile Organisation: Old dogs. Ingenious new
tricks. Retrieved from http://www2.paconsulting.com

Ryan, T., & Mittal, V. (2019). Potential for Army Integration of Autonomous Systems by Warfighting
Function. Military Review, (Sep-Oct), 122–133.

Teece, D. J., Peteraf, M., & Leih, S. (2016). Dynamic Capabilities and Organizational Agility: Risk,
Uncertainty, and Strategy in the Innovation Economy. California Management Review, 58(4),
13–35.

Topic Six: ACAs

The National Training Laboratories (NTL) was founded in 1947 and has been a highly
influential hub of advanced thinking about Organisation Development. It is based in
Washington, the United States and during the late 1940s, the term 'Change Agent'
was coined during discussions (Ottaway, 1983). Many of those helping 'client systems' found the term enabled them to clarify their role (Lippitt, Watson, & Westley,
1958). About the same time, in the UK, the Tavistock Institute of Human Relations
(TIHR) became actively involved in developing theories on how to facilitate organisation development as its mission was 'the promotion of the effectiveness of individuals
and organisations' (Neumann, 2005, p. 120). Both the NTL and the TIHR were deeply
influenced by the work of Kurt Lewin (Trist & Murray, 1993), especially Lewin's view
of the importance of action research that he (1947, p. 150) defined as "comparative
research on the conditions and effects of various forms of social action. Research,
that produces nothing but books will not suffice".

Change Agents conduct interventions intended to improve organisations (Church,
2017), that can be, for example, to facilitate an organisation to become requisitely agile
and remain so. We will refer to this role as an Agility Change Agent or ACA. An ACA is
an outsider to the client system that is the object of an intervention. He or she may
work in another part of the same organisation (an internal ACA), be contracted to provide specific services (an external ACA) or be imposed on the client system, perhaps by
members of senior management or a regulatory body (a supervisory ACA).

The overarching goal of an ACA's interventions is to facilitate the acquisition of
VRIN organisational assets (valuable, rare, inimitable and non-substitutable) (Nason
& Wiklund, 2018) both systemically and locally (Eisenhardt & Martin, 2000). The crucial requirement for an ACA is finding ways of being functional (i.e., to make a constructive contribution) for each new client. Being an ACA is a far from easy task. It
can be difficult to assess the competence level of an existing portfolio of agile capabilities; the readiness of key actors will be hard to determine as the possibilities for
radical or incremental improvement. A model developed by Talcott Parsons (1954)

provides a format for determining the generic functions that, if contributed in ways that lead to effective action, increase the probability that an ACA can add value (Sciulli & Gerstein, 1985). Parsons's framework indicates that ACAs need to facilitate, accelerate or strengthen a client system's capability to (i) be better resourced; (ii) allocate resources for long-term advantage, short-term efficiency and equity; (iii) achieve the willing engagement of everyone involved and (iv) maintain alignment and attunement (Harrison, 1995).

In all, about 30 scholars have sought to define the range of styles available to change agents and an excellent early article by Ottaway (1983) provided an explanation of the historical development of the role. Caldwell (2003) made a major contribution by expanding the definition of change agents to include managers, teams and others who can acquire agency. The mission of ACAs is not static as requisite organisational agility is a plastic construct. Today, the business ecosystem is characterised by waves of technical change that are shifting the logics required for organisational survival.

One of the earliest documented accounts of the work of ACAs is a detailed description of an intervention into the process of loading railroad trucks in the early years of the last century. A group of 'efficiency engineers', led by Frederick Winslow Taylor, analysed work processes in the Bethlehem Steel Company (Taylor, 1911) and facilitated a raft of improvements that would have been difficult, or impossible, for the incumbent managers to achieve on their own, thereby facilitating organisational agility. Taylor and his team spent months observing the micro-dimensions of efficiency and inefficiency using laboratory-style techniques of scientific enquiry and conducting controlled experiments. It was concluded that (2004, p. 5): "It is no single element, but rather this whole combination, that constitutes scientific management, which may be summarized as: Science, not rule of thumb; harmony, not discord; cooperation, not individualism; maximum output, in place of restricted output; the development of each man to his greatest efficiency and prosperity". The ACAs were (i) outside of the unit of intervention, (ii) had a range of different competencies from those in management positions, (iii) worked to a comprehensive theory of change that was described later in the hugely influential book *The Principles of Scientific Management* and (iv) worked collaborative with incumbent managers to change the constructs being used to organise work and managerial practices (Wrege & Perroni, 1974).

The Bethlehem Steel case study demonstrated that ACAs could create conditions that improved an organisation's efficiency and effectiveness. But this is not an intervention that will be successful in all cases. A review of the effectiveness of productivity-based interventions concluded that: "there may be isolated cases where a consultant achieves positive results in the face of an apathetic, uncooperative management or an obstructionist, hostile labour force, but these are the exception not the rule". It is reasonable to assume that two main factors increase the probability of a beneficial intervention by an ACA: one, being the openness and receptivity of people in the unit and the other being quality of fit between the skill, knowledge and methodologies used by the ACA and the specific needs of the client system.

ACAs need a high level of personal skills including (i) building collaborative relationships with clients while encouraging collaboration throughout the client system; (ii) striving for authenticity and encouraging this quality in their clients; (iii) being committed to developing self-awareness, interpersonal skills and lifelong learning; (iv) focusing efforts on helping everyone in the client organisation to increase their empowerment to levels that make the workplace and/or community agile, satisfying and productive; (v) drawing from multiple disciplines to inform an understanding of human systems, especially the applied behavioural sciences; (vi) approaching organisations and sub-units as open systems and acting with the knowledge that change in one area of a system results in changes in other areas; (vii) frequently re-examining, reflecting and integrating experience into practice and (viii) being focused on helping to bring about positive change and achieving desired outcomes.

Further Reading

Caldwell, R. (2003). Models of change agency: a four-fold classification. British Journal of Management, 14(2),131–142.

Church, A. H. (2017). The art and Science of Evaluating Organisation Development Interventions. OD Practitioner, 49(2),26–35.

Eisenhardt, K. M., & Martin, J. A. (2000). Dynamic Capabilities: What Are They? Strategic Management Journal, 21(10/11), 1105–1121.

Harrison, R. (1995). The Collected Papers of Roger Harrison. San Francisco: Jossey-Bass.

Lewin, K. (1947). Frontiers in Group Dynamics: Channels of Group Life; Social Planning and Action Research. Human Relations, 1(2),143–153.

Lippitt, R., Watson, J., & Westley, B. (1958). The Dynamics of Planned Change – A Comparative Study of Principles and Techniques. (W. B. Spalding, Ed.). Harcourt, Brace & World.

Nason, R. S., & Wiklund, J. (2018). An Assessment of Resource-Based Theorizing on Firm Growth and Suggestions for the Future. Journal of Management, 44(1),32–60.

Neumann, J. E. (2005). Kurt Lewin at the Tavistock Institute. Educational Action Research, 13(1), 119–136.

Ottaway, R. N. (1983). The Change Agent: A Taxonomy in Relation to the Change Process. Human Relations, 36(4),361–392.

Parsons, T. (1954). Essays in Sociological Theory. Glencoe: Free Press.

Sciulli, D., & Gerstein, D. (1985). Social Theory and Talcott Parsons in the 1980s. Annual Review of Sociology, 11, 369–387.

Taylor, F. W. (1911). The Principles of Scientific Management. New York: Harper.

Taylor, F. W. (2004). Excerpts: The Principles of Scientific Management 1910. Primary source collection: The Gilded and the Gritty: America, 1870–1912, p 5. National Humanities Center. Research Triangle Park, North Carolina.

Trist, E. L., & Murray, H. (1993). The Social Engagement of Social Science: The Foundation and Development of the Tavistock Institute to 1989.

Wrege, C. D., & Perroni, A. G. (1974). Taylor's Pig-Tale: A Historical Analysis of Frederick W. Taylor's Pig-Iron Experiments. Academy of Management Journal, 17(1),6–27.

Topic Seven: Agility Playbooks

An Agility Playbook is a tool that enriches an Agility Ambition so that everyone who can either help it to be achieved, or hinder its achievement, can gain a deeper understanding of what needs to be done. Gray et al. (2010, p. 5) describe the process as "to imagine a world; a future world that is different from our own . . . we need our goals to be fuzzy . . . a framework for exploration, experimentation, and trial and error".

The US military has developed a structured approach that can be used to develop a playbook. This was described by Mostashari et al. (2012, p. 2) as "a Concept of Operations (CONOPS) (that) is a document describing the characteristics and intended usage of a proposed or existing system from the viewpoint of its users. Its purpose is to communicate the quantitative and qualitative system characteristics to all stakeholders and serve as a basis for stakeholder discussions about the system. Moreover, the CONOPS can help reach a 'meeting of the minds' before the requirements process begins. Generated effectively, it may convey a clearer statement of intent than the requirements themselves".

As described elsewhere, 3M is an exemplar of an enduring agile enterprise. Their playbook is fragmented but extremely powerful. It is articulated through stories, as Shaw et al. (1998, p. 42) explained: "Stories are a habit of mind at 3M, and it's through them – through the way they make us see ourselves and our business operations in complex, multidimensional forms – that we're able to discover opportunities for strategic change. Stories give us ways to form ideas about winning".

The concept of a playbook was developed by sports coaches to enable teams to know how to respond to contingencies (Krueger, 2016). Playbooks vary in their specificity, sometimes defining roles and responsibilities precisely, whereas others describe wanted values and provide orienting concepts. Sociologists define playbooks as instruments of socialisation (Ardts, Jansen, & van der Velde, 2016), meaning that they serve to create social cohesion and act as a template for defining what is right social action.

Playbooks have another purpose. They convey what is important and they provide guidance about priorities. Weick (2005, p. 410) argued that sensemaking and sense-giving are key elements of the leadership process, explaining that "Plausible stories animate and gain their validity from subsequent activity . . . Students of sensemaking understand that the order in organisational life comes just as much from the subtle, the small, the relational, the oral, the particular, and the momentary as it does from the conspicuous, the large, the substantive, the written, the general, and the sustained".

Whatever form it takes, an Agility Ambition will be impotent unless ways are found to enable it to shape the behaviour of people and smart machines. This is a deep process, as the example of traditionally qualified London taxi drivers demonstrates. For research purposes brain scans were made of taxi drivers who had spent at about three years learning the detail of the streets of London (Maguire et al., 2000) before they could try to pass the required demanding examination. It was found that the back of the hippocampus in the brain that is the area that holds detailed memories was enlarged compared with a control sample. Socialisation can physically change a human being: it is a profound force!

Further Reading

Ardts, J., Jansen, P., & van der Velde, M. (2016). The breaking in of new employees: Effectiveness of socialisation tactics and personnel instruments. The Journal of Management Development, 20 (2),7–10.

Gray, D., Brown, S., & Macanufo. James. (2010). Gamestorming: A Playbook for Innovators, Rulebreakers and Changemakers. Sebastopol, CA: O'Reilly Media Inc.

Krueger, G. (2016). Legacy, 15 Lessons in Leadership: What the All Blacks Can Teach Us About the Business of Life.

Maguire, E. A., Gadian, D. G., Johnsrude, I. S., Good, C. D., Ashburner, J., Frackowiak, R. S. J., & Frith, C. D. (2000). Navigation-related structural change in the hippocampi of taxi drivers. Proceedings of the National Academy of Sciences of the United States of America, 97(8), 4398–4403.

Mostashari, A., McComb, S. A., Kennedy, D. M., Cloutier, R., & Korfiatis, P. (2012). Developing a Stakeholder-Assisted Agile CONOPS Development Process. Systems Engineering, 14(3), 305–326.

Shaw, G., Brown, R., & Bromiley, P. (1998). Strategic stories: how 3M is rewriting business planning. Harvard Business Review, 76(3).

Weick, K. E., Sutcliffe, K. M., & Obstfeld, D. (2005). Organizing and the Process of Sensemaking. Organization Science, 16(4),409–421.

Topic Eight: CENTRIM and the Freeman Centre

The Centre for Research in Innovation Management (CENTRIM) and Science and Policy Research (SPRU) were co-located in the Freeman Centre on the University of Sussex's Campus in the UK when the Agile Management Research Programme was undertaken. CENTRIM's focus was on the management of innovation whereas SPRU specialised in undertaking research into innovation policy (Outhwaite, 2017). The Freeman Centre, named after Professor Chris Freeman (Martin & Bell, 2011) was one of the largest academic bodies in the world studying science, technology, innovation management and organisational agility.

CENTRIM undertook social-science research to deepen understanding of the management of innovation, for both economic and social benefit. A key purpose of knowledge gained, apart from its inherent academic value, was to provide insight into ways to gain and sustain economic benefit, which, for commercial organisations, meant the acquisition and maintenance of competitive advantage. In addition,

CENTRIM's mission recognised that innovation is necessary in all domains of human life, including the maintenance of a healthy, fulfilled, coherent and positive society. Accordingly, CENTRIM researchers took the view that innovation can contribute to the development of institutions with social purposes and non-profit making enterprises (Bessant, Tsekouras, & Rush, 2009).

CENTRIM investigated the management of innovation by acquiring, developing and disseminating knowledge that met academic criteria for validity and was new in the sense that it provided additional information, insights or new syntheses of existing research-based knowledge for practitioners (Bessant, Caffyn, & Gallagher, 2001). CENTRIM's used a construct of knowledge acquisition that was termed 'closing the loop', as it was based on a dynamic dialogue between theory and action and a form of Engaged Scholarship (Van de Ven, 2007). The commitment to this form of enquiry required that CENTRIM researchers engage in 'the real world' to learn from practice, to assess the impact and consequences of theories, frameworks and analyses on practice, and test theoretical contributions for their efficacy. Over the lifetime of the Freeman Centre, there were more than 250 significant collaborations either with other academic institutions or industry.

CENTRIM was selected to be one of the first research groups in Europe to investigate organisational agility from a social-science perspective. From 1997–1999 six researchers, under the direction of Professor John Bessant, used action research methods (Coghlan, 2011) to study how case-study companies progressed on their individual journeys to adopt and use the Agile Paradigm (Bessant, Knowles, Briffa, & Francis, 2002). The term 'agility' was defined by the research team as an "organisation's capacity to gain competitive or comparative advantage by intelligently, rapidly and proactively seizing opportunities and reacting to threats" (Bessant, Francis, Meredith, Kaplinsky, & Brown, 2001, p. 487).

In addition to deepening understanding of the managerial challenges faced by managers as they sought to adopt the Agile Paradigm, CENTRIM's investigation contributed to innovation studies, as it provided insight into the requirements for absorptive capacity related to innovation in paradigm (Francis & Bessant, 2005).

Further Reading

Bessant, J., Caffyn, S., & Gallagher, M. (2001). An evolutionary model of continuous improvement behaviour. Technovation, 21(2),67–77.

Bessant, J., Francis, D. L., Meredith, S. E., Kaplinsky, R., & Brown, S. (2001). Developing manufacturing agility in SMEs. International Journal of Technology Management, 22 (1/2/3), 28–54.

Bessant, J., Knowles, D., Briffa, G., & Francis, D. L. (2002). Developing the Agile Enterprise. International Journal of Technology Management, 24(5/6), 484–497.

Bessant, J. Tsekouras, G. & Rush H. (2009) 'Getting the tail to wag: developing innovations capability in smes', Paper presented at CI Net 2009, Brisbane, Australia.

Coghlan, D. (2011). Action Research: Exploring Perspectives on a Philosophy of Practical

Knowing. The Academy of Management Annals, 5(1),53–87.

Francis, D. L., & Bessant, J. (2005). Targeting innovation and implications for capability development. Technovation, 25(3),171–183.

Martin, B. R., & Bell, M. (2011). In memory of Chris Freeman: Founding Editor of Research Policy 1971–2003. Research Policy, 40(7),895–896.

Outhwaite, W. (2017). Science of science at Sussex University. Zagadnienia Naukoznawstwa, 53:2(212), 149–156.

Van de Ven, A. H. (2007). Engaged scholarship: a guide for organizational and social research. Engaged Scholarship: A Guide for Organizational and Social Research. Oxford University Press. Oxford UK.

Topic Nine: Darwin and Evolution

Charles Darwin (1859, p. 2) wrote that: "as more individuals are produced than can possibly survive, there must in every case be a struggle for existence, either one individual with another of the same species, or with the individuals of distinct species, or with the physical applied with manifold conditions of life . . . Although some species may be now increasing in numbers, all cannot do so, for the world would not hold them". It is this analysis that underpins agility theory as organisations, like the organisms that Darwin studied, tend to proliferate to an unsupportable extent. Hence, those who are strongest survive and thrive and the weakest will perish. Individuals, groups and organisations can recognise this reality and try deliberately to be strong in the circumstances that they experience by becoming agile.

That evolutionary forces shape organisations was articulated by Moore (2005, p. xiv) who argued that an imperative is to create: "competitive advantage in an increasingly commoditizing world. To lead that effort you must continually reappraise what role your company is playing in the market ecosystem, how the landscape of competition is changing, where your competitive advantage has come from in the past and where it is likely to come from in the future, what kinds of differentiation will be most rewarded and what kinds of innovation will be most required".

Ruse (2009, p. 18) argues that: "Organisms compete against each other in lines, and improvement occurs; the prey gets faster, and hence the predator gets faster, and so forth". The implication is that freezing agility is never possible, rather it is necessary to recognise that survival grows more difficult over time and rigidity inhibits constructive adaptation. This stance is similar to that taken by those who support the practice and processual views of strategy as Paroutis & Pettigrew (2007, pp. 100–101) explain: "strategy as practice approach favours managerial agency, situated action, and strategy stability together with strategic change rather than focusing on a set of change events from a firm level of analysis, as most process studies tend to do".

Further Reading

Darwin, C. (1859). The origin of the species by means of natural selection (extracts). https://doi.
    org/10.5962/bhl.title.24329
Moore, G. A. (2005). *Dealing with Darwin: How Great Companies Innovate at Every Phase of their
    Evolution*. London: Penguin.
Paroutis, S., & Pettigrew, A. (2007). Strategizing in the multi-business firm: Strategy teams at mul-
    tiple levels and over time. *Human Relations*, *60*(1), 99–135.
Ruse, M. (2009). Charles Darwin on human evolution. *Journal of Economic Behavior and
    Organization*, *71*(1), 10–19.

Topic Ten: Defining Agility: Selected Key Concepts

Setilli (2014, p. 192) explains that the "word agile is derived from the Latin agilis, meaning to drive, act". The importance of 'driving and acting' is deeply rooted in human history. Sun Tzu's classic text, *The Art of War*, written around 320 B.C., was the first comprehensive study of the art and science of effective action. In it, Tzu wrote: "avail yourself of any helpful circumstances over and beyond the ordinary rules. According as circumstances are favourable, one should modify one's plans" (quoted in McCreadie et al. 2009, p.39).

Sun Tzu's explanation has several important components (Hou, Sheang, & Hidajat, 1991). By 'gaining advantage' Tzu recognises that there will be winners and losers but wise, timely action will change situational dynamics, thereby increasing the probability that the most agile players will win. By 'by possessing and mobilis-ing the required capabilities' Tzu emphasises the importance of being able to exe-cute decisions, which requires that resources can be made available and they can be deployed effectively and quickly. By 'respond proactively' Tzu recognises that it is necessary to understand, in depth, the logic of the current situation but not to be imprisoned by it, as effective action can exploit latent opportunities and reduce threats. By 'despite opposition and difficulty' Tzu recognised that it is rarely possi-ble to be perfectly prepared, but obstacles must become targets for action, not rea-sons for failure.

Aghina et al. (2017, p. 5) provide insight into the organisational requirements, observing that "truly agile organizations . . . are both stable and dynamic at the same time. They design stable backbone elements that evolve slowly and support dynamic capabilities that can adapt quickly to new challenges and opportunities". The authors identified three core organisational areas where balancing the inherent tension between stability and flexibility is important, which are organisational structure, governance and processes.

There has been a maturing of the concept of agility that is now seen to be an appropriate strategy based on need, for example, Naylor, Naim and Berry (1999, p. 117) write that "manufacturers should not be looking at operations in isolation from the rest of the supply chain. Whether to develop an agile capability or a lean manufacturing structure will be dependent upon where in the supply chain the members are located. This total supply chain perspective is essential, and companies should be striving for leagility that is carefully combining both lean and agile paradigms". Hence, agility can be seen as being a contingent stratagem, not one that is required universally and is not the only tool in the toolbox.

Today we can define agility as a construct located in the realisation that much of the world is, and will always be, ruled by Darwinian forces, meaning that harsh competition is the normal condition. But it is not inevitable that we will be passive victims of our situation. Wise, capable and timely action increases the chances that some will survive and thrive. But this is not easy, as 'only the paranoid survive' (Grove, 1998). There can be no fixed formula that can be guaranteed to deliver success. Rather the best tactic for survival will be wholeheartedly embracing responsiveness and acquiring the skills of a hunter. At the organisational level this requires the acquisition of capabilities, including human capital, that can be readily reconfigured to seize short- and long-term opportunities and, a high degree of intelligence, willingness and boldness amongst decision-makers to take advantage of the circumstances of the moment whilst avoiding the pitfalls that often beset the hasty (Blodgett, Conrad, & Kobren, 2008).

There is a consensus that the need for agile competences is growing as the forces that drive competition are becoming stronger, more formidable and increasingly disruptive (Routroy, Potdar, & Shankar, 2015). This has been explained by Geoffrey Moore (2005, pp. xiiv–xiv): "free market economies operate by the same rules as organic systems in nature: (so that) competition for scarce resources of customer purchases creates hunger that stimulates innovation; customer preferences for one innovation over another create a form of natural selection that leads to survival-of-the-fittest outcomes; each new generation restarts the competition from a higher standard of competence than the prior generation (and) thus over time successful companies must evolve their competence or become marginalised".

Further Reading

Aghina, W., Ahlbäck, K., De Smet, A., Fahrbach, C., Handscomb, C., Lackey, G., . . . Woxholth, J. (2017). The 5 Trademarks of Agile Organizations Written collaboratively by the McKinsey Agile Tribe. McKinsey & Company. https://www.mckinsey.com/business-functions/organiza tion/our-insights/the-five-trademarks-of-agile-organizations

Blodgett, C., Conrad, C. and Kobren, B., 2008. *Developing an integrated, agile, and high-performing future workforce: The DoD logistics human capital strategy*. Office of the Deputy Under Secretary of Defense for Logistics and Materiel Readiness Washington United States.

Grove, A. S. (1998). Only the Paranoid Survive: How to Exploit the Crisis Points that Challenge Every Company and Career. New York: Doubleday.

Hou, W. C., Sheang, L. K., & Hidajat, B. W. (1991). Sun Tzu: War & Management. Singapore: Addison-Wesley.

McCreadie, K., Shipside, S., & Phillips, T. (2009). Strategy Power Plays: Winning Business Ideas From the World's Greatest Strategic Minds. Oxford, U.K.: Infinite Ideas.

Moore, G. A. (2005). Dealing with Darwin: How Great Companies Innovate at Every Phase of their Evolution. London: Penguin.

Naylor, J. Ben, Naim, M., & Berry, D. (1999). Leagility: integrating the lean and agile manufacturing in the total supply chain. International Journal of Production Economics, 62, 107–118.

Routroy, S., Potdar, P. K., & Shankar, A. (2015). Measurement of manufacturing agility: a case study. Measuring Business Excellence, 19(2),1–22.

Setili, A. (2014). The agility advantage: How to identify and act on opportunities in a fast-changing world. Chicago: John Wiley & Sons Inc.

Topic Eleven: Dynamic Capabilities

In the 1970s two academically orientated consultants, Tregoe and Zimmerman (1980, p. 11) wrote a book entitled *Top Management Strategy* that explained that the authors had "explored strategy formation with more than 200 major organisations around the world . . . (and developed) the concept of Driving Force, the key to strategic thinking". They found that there were only nine possible core business models, each of which required a different set of aligned capabilities. A key insight was that "one and only one should be the Driving Force for the total organisation" (p. 43).

Tregoe and Zimmerman stated that organisational capabilities (resources) need to be developed in an aligned way so that a company becomes a good example of one of the nine types. To use a simple analogy to explain the principle, it would be rational for the Cape Town Opera to develop capabilities in staging operas (its offered product) but not in the transportation of performers or the manufacturing of stage lighting, as these are different forms of business and have other driving forces. In fact, an attempt to develop capabilities in multiple driving forces will become a distraction and disintegrate the organisation (Slywotzky, Morrison, Moser, Mundt, & Quella, 1999).

Although Tregoe and Zimmerman's Nine Driving Forces framework was a significant approach to develop a strategic-level organisational development methodology based on contingency theory, the strategic significance of resource ownership had been identified much earlier. For example, a case study by Penrose (1960, p. 22) asserted that "the growth of the firm is fundamentally constrained by the knowledge and experience of its existing personnel . . . But new bases are not acquired 'ready-made', so to speak, through extensive and rapid absorption of new people in new fields that are not easily integrated with some existing and internally developed unit in the firm".

The strategic significance of resources became clearer when Wernerfelt (1984, pp. 173–174) wrote "(w)hat a firm wants is to create a situation where its own resource position directly or indirectly makes it more difficult for others to catch up. To analyse a resource for a general potential for high returns, one has to look at the ways in which a firm with a strong position can influence the acquisition costs or the user revenues of a firm with a weaker position". A seminal paper by Barney (1991, pp. 105–106) stated that "not all firm resources hold the potential of sustained competitive advantages. To have this potential, a firm's resource must have four attributes: (a) it must be valuable, in the sense that it exploits opportunities and/or naturalizes threats in a firm's environment, (b) it must be rare among a firm's current and potential competition, (c) it must be imperfectly imitable, and (d) there cannot be strategically equivalent substitutes for this resource that are valuable but neither rare or imperfectly imitable". This viewpoint and has gathered academic momentum ever since, becoming known as the resource-based view (RBV).

The RBV was derived from economic analyses largely conducted in the 1990s that had shown that competitively successful companies possessed superior portfolios of industry-specific capabilities, accordingly, the true sources of competitive or comparative advantage lie in the possession of bundles of capabilities that, when appropriately selected, well-coordinated and operating effectively, enable winning strategies to be delivered (Nason & Wiklund, 2018).

It became clear that the RBV was unable to explain why some companies excelled in being agile. Fortunately, during the 1990s, Teece, Pisano and Shuen sought to understand the characteristic of largely high-tech companies that had succeeded in achieving profitable growth and they concluded that (1997, p. 515) the "(w)inners in the global marketplace have been firms that can demonstrate timely responsiveness and rapid and flexible product innovation, coupled with the management capability to effectively coordinate and redeploy market internal and external competences". The competences to deliver 'timely responsiveness and rapid and flexible product innovation' were different from 'ordinary' resources as they were forces for creative adaptation that Teece et al. defined as 'dynamic capabilities', explaining (1997, p. 515) that "term 'dynamic' refers to the capacity to renew competences so as to achieve congruence with the changing business environment; certain innovative responses are required when time-to-market and timing are critical, the rate of nature of future competition and markets difficult to determine. The term 'capabilities' emphasizes the key role of strategic management in appropriately adapting, integrating, and reconfiguring internal and external organizational skills, resources, and functional competences to match the requirements of a changing environment".

Teece (2007, pp. 1319–1320) explained that the construct of dynamic capabilities "includes difficult-to-replicate enterprise capabilities required to adapt to changing customer and technological opportunities. They also embrace the enterprise's capacity to shape the ecosystem it occupies, develop new products and processes, and design and implement viable business models". The argument is that dynamic capabilities enable organisations to destroy that which has become dysfunctional and to evolve, learn and reconfigure themselves to meet current and future challenges. Augier and

Teece (2009, p. 412) state that dynamic capabilities provide: "the ability to sense and then seize new opportunities and to reconfigure and protect knowledge assets, competencies and complementary assets with the aim of achieving a sustained competitive advantage". Eisenhardt and Martin (2000, p. 21) observe that dynamic capabilities are "very frequently used to build new resource configurations in the pursuit of temporary advantage".

In a later article Teece, Peteraf and Leih elaborated their construct, writing that (2016, p. 18) a "firm's dynamic capabilities govern how it integrates, builds, and reconfigures internal and external competences to address changing business environments . . . while strategy and capabilities can be analytically separated, as a practical matter they need to be developed and implemented together. While routines and processes are vital components of dynamic capabilities, in our framework strong capabilities are never based entirely on routines or rules. One reason is that routines tend to be relatively slow to change. Good managers think creatively, act entrepreneurially, and, if necessary, override routines. Put simply, managers matter in our framework".

There are close parallels between Teece's description of the leadership and managerial challenges faced by managers and that used in EAfA. Key differences include that the dynamic capabilities framework was developed from economics-based research and EAfA emerged from decades of engaged scholarship, as change agents attempted to help leaders and managers acquire the competences needed for timely responsiveness and rapid and flexible product innovation. This experience of agility-orientated organisational development interventions led to EAfA adopting a finer-grained perspective, arguing that agility needs to be adopted differentially in various parts of an organisation. EAfA also takes the view that agile capabilities are constructed continuously, following Bjerregaard and Jonasson (2014, p. 1507) who wrote "An institution is often considered to be a stable, taken-for-granted 'being' . . . we suggest an alternative ontology for understanding an institution as something unstable and always 'becoming'". Bjerregaard and Jonasson suggest that that organisations are best viewed as ongoing works-in-progress within which flows or figurations of activities, events, requirements, contextual factors, technological/other forms of knowledge, social memes and managerial actions construct and reconstruct organisations as social systems in real-time (Whittington, 2007). A similar theoretical viewpoint is already established in strategic studies, known as Strategy-as-Practice (Mirabeau, Maguire, & Hardy, 2018), but this has not been widely used for agility studies.

Despite such differences, it is important to note that EAfA is largely consistent with the dynamic capabilities framework and was, in part, developed from attempts to use it as a model for organisational development interventions. Those leading or facilitating the EAfA Process will gain from reviewing current literature on dynamic capabilities.

Further Reading

Augier, M., & Teece, D. J. (2009). Dynamic Capabilities and the Role of Managers in Business Strategy and Economic Performance. Organization Science, 29(2),410–421.

Barney, J. B. (1991). Firm Resources and Sustained Competitive Advantage. Journal of Management, 17(1),99–120.

Bjerregaard, T., & Jonasson, C. (2014). Managing Unstable Institutional Contradictions: The Work of Becoming. Organization Studies, 35(10),1507–1536.

Eisenhardt, K. M., & Martin, J. A. (2000). Dynamic Capabilities: What Are They? Strategic Management Journal, 21(10/11), 1105–1121.

Mirabeau, L., Maguire, S., & Hardy, C. (2018). Bridging practice and process research to study transient manifestations of strategy. Strategic Management Journal, 39(3),582–605.

Nason, R. S., & Wiklund, J. (2018). An Assessment of Resource-Based Theorizing on Firm Growth and Suggestions for the Future. Journal of Management, 44(1),32–60.

Penrose, E. T. (1960). The Growth of the Firm – A Case Study: The Hercules Powder Company. The Business History Review, 34(1),1–23.

Slywotzky, A. J., Morrison, D., Moser, T., Mundt, K. A., & Quella, J. A. (1999). Profit Patterns: 30 Ways to Anticipate and Profit from Strategic Forces Reshaping Your Business. Chichester, UK.: John Wiley & Sons Ltd.

Teece, D. J. (2007). Explicating Dynamic Capabilities: The Nature And Microfoundations Of (Sustainable) Enterprise Performance. Strategic Management Journal, 28(August), 1319–1350.

Teece, D. J., Peteraf, M., & Leih, S. (2016). Dynamic Capabilities and Organizational Agility: Risk, Uncertainty, and Strategy in the Innovation Economy. California Management Review, 58(4), 13–35.

Teece, D. J., Pisano, G., & Shuen, A. (1997). Dynamic capabilities and strategic management. Strategic Management Journal, 18(7), 509.

Tregoe, B. B., & Zimmerman, J. W. (1980). Top Management Strategy: What It Is and How to Make It Work. London: John Martin Publishing.

Wernerfelt, B. (1984). A Resource-based view of the Firm. Strategic Management Journal, 5, 171–180.

Whittington, R. (2007). Strategy practice and strategy process: Family differences and the sociological eye. Organization Studies, 28(10),1575–1586.

Topic Twelve: Flinders Medical Centre

The Flinders Medical Centre opened in 1976 and is a major public and teaching hospital located at Bedford Park, South Australia. It is a unit within the Southern Adelaide Local Health Network.

The centre provides an excellent example of a not-for-profit agile organisation that is active in each of the 6P areas described earlier in this book. Some examples make the point. It is a state-of-the-art facility for cancer care (product), has used advanced methods of managing the patient's experience (process), communicates extensively with patrons (position), conceptualises the organisation in terms of facilitating wellness (paradigm), is highly active in fund raising (provisioning) and provides research platforms for advancing medial knowledge (platform).

Relevant publications are 'Redesigning emergency department patient flows: Application of Lean Thinking to health care' (King, Ben-Tovim, & Bassham, 2006) and 'Comparison of three simulation-based training methods for management of medical emergencies' (Owen, Mugford, Follows, & Plummer, 2006).

Further Reading

King, D. L., Ben-Tovim, D. I., & Bassham, J. (2006). Redesigning emergency department patient flows: Application of Lean Thinking to health care. EMA – Emergency Medicine Australasia, 18 (4),391–397.

Owen, H., Mugford, B., Follows, V., & Plummer, J. L. (2006). Comparison of three simulation-based training methods for management of medical emergencies. Resuscitation, 71(2),204–211.

Topic Thirteen: Fractal Organisational Models

Lawrence and Lorsch (1969, p. 1) opened their book on developing organisations by writing that "practicing managers and students of administration are besieged with ideas and techniques for improving the effectiveness of their organisations . . . on the one hand they are told to encourage more autonomy and participation in decision-making . . . on the other hand they are advised to rely heavily on . . . programmatic decision techniques". They describe the forces that pull organisations in two opposite directions, one to integrate and the other to differentiate. Integration enables an organisation to operate facilitated by "the management hierarchy . . . (and) supplemental integrating devices, such as individual coordinators, cross-unit teams, and even whole departments . . . (to) achieve integration" (p. 13). Differentiation enables an organisation to adapt to its environment and tasks and the "needed differences are not minor variations in outlook but, at times, involve fundamental (different) ways of thinking and behaving" (p. 12). They concluded (1967, p. 47) that "differentiation and integration are essentially antagonistic, and that one can be obtained only at the expense of the other . . . But (certain) conditions . . . make it possible to achieve high differentiation and high integration simultaneously".

It was Hans-Jürgen Warnecke (1993) who provided a comprehensive methodology for facilitating requisite integration and differentiation with the construct that organisations can square this circle by becoming fractal enterprises. Warnecke used the mathematical construct of a fractal as a metaphor. He pointed out that all fractals are different from each other, but they share common design principles. This construct becomes easier to understand when an example is examined. In a world-class Hi-Fi Audio Products company everyone involved, including suppliers and distributors, must be devoted to delivering the highest quality sound experience for customers. This must be a core value, and an enacted and universally applied policy that underpins every decision, defines every process and specifies every practice. But, to be requisitely agile, some parts of the Hi-Fi company need a highly differentiated organisation. Those designing the next generation of speakers will be science-based, experimental and innovative whereas the quality control team will be structured, rigorous and intolerant of defects. Warnecke described the attributes that must be shared as being 'self-similar' and the differentiated parts as fractals with "the decisive characteristic of vitality" (p. 146).

The use of the construct of a fractal organisation provided a means by which organisational integrity can be preserved whilst specifying areas of opportunity for parts of the organisation to be entrepreneurial, to practice absorptive capacity and, in some cases, undertake original innovation initiatives. TMTs need to define what needs to be self-similar in every part of their enterprise (Paroutis & Pettigrew, 2007). This is facilitated by being definitive about their corporate Agility Ambition, as this provides a container within which units function in the interests of the whole, and by the specification and adoption of self-similar policies. This both constrains and liberates organisational sub-units. This requirement is so significant that achieving requisite agility requires that managers learn how to manage a fractal organisation.

Canavesio (2007, pp. 796–797) defines opportunities for fractal variation being facilitated by a manager being "an autonomous and intelligent actor or agent whose behavior is not strictly programmed, nor perfectly definable a priori and it is not predictable . . . The self-organization characteristic allows the fractal company to support the dynamic reconfiguration of network connections between projects and the creation of project instances in order to self-adapt internal and external changes. Thus, constantly new project instances and relationships between project managers are created and at the same time many of them disappear".

Further Reading

Canavesio, M. M., & Martinez, E. (2007). Enterprise modelling of a project-oriented fractal company for SMEs networking. Computers in Industry, 58, 794–813.

Lawrence, P. R., & Lorsch, J. W. (1967). Differentiation and Integration in Complex Organizations. Administrative Science Quarterly, 12(1), 1.

Lawrence, P. R., & Lorsch, J. W. (1969). Developing Organisations: Diagnosis and Action. (E. H. Schein, W. Bennis, & R. Beckhard, Eds.). Reading, Mass: Addison-Wesley.

Paroutis, S., & Pettigrew, A. (2007). Strategizing in the multi-business firm: Strategy teams at multiple levels and over time. Human Relations, 60(1),99–135.

Warnecke, H.-J. (1993). The Fractal Company: A Revolution in Corporate Culture. Berlin: Springer-Verlag.

Topic Fourteen: Harrods Department Store, London

The store is one of the world's largest and most famous department stores with more than 90,000 m2 of space (Dale, 1981). Harrods sells luxury and everyday items across seven floors, has 330 department and its motto is Omnia Omnibus Oblique or All Things for All People, Everywhere. Today, the store attracts 15 million customers each year. It was not always so. In the 1960s people still loved Harrods but other retailers were waking up. Sharp, aggressive and imaginative retailers were eating Harrods' business. The store was virtually unchanged since the 1940s. Many members of the staff were the essence of loyalty. They were traditional in attitudes, and their behaviour was equally conservative. The pressure for change was not coming from below! A new managing director called his senior team together, explained there was a deep problem. From then onwards Harrods has experienced waves of revolution and evolution redefining how its corporate personality is expressed (Harrod, 2017).

Further Reading

Dale, T. (1981). Harrods: the store and the legend. Pan. London.
Harrod, R. (2017). The Jewel of Knightsbridge: The Origins of the Harrods Empire. Stroud: The History Press.

Topic Fifteen: Innovation and Agility

Innovation is closely related to agility although the two are distinct. It is possible to be innovative without being highly agile, as is demonstrated by the rigid disciplines that govern R&D practices in pharmaceutical companies. Also, it is possible to be agile without being innovative by, for example, adopting an outsourcing business model that makes resources available on an as-needed basis.

Innovation is a grand force in organisations. If an organisation was a living creature then innovation would be the evolutionary response, providing the means to gain and sustain relative advantage and, consequently, survival. Although innovation is a fundamental driving force within organisations, it is not the only one. Innovation co-exists in an uneasy relationship with three other grand driving forces: the need for order, alignment and prudence.

Organisations need to be orderly so that they are understandable, efficient and predictable. For example, in a public swimming pool the quality of the water needs to be checked daily, swimmers must be observed constantly by a lifeguard and the pool must be opened at predictable hours so that swimmers know when they can take their morning exercise. The pool must be orderly.

Organisations need alignment. The parts cannot pull in too many different directions as they must be directed, just as a magnet causes iron filings to be oriented in the same direction. Alignment is essential as it is not possible to do everything well, so focus is needed. A hotel cannot be both a five-star retreat for the rich and famous and a backpacker's hostel. Choices are essential and alignment must follow. Alignment requires coherence in values, strategies and systems and in the competencies and attitudes of employees. At the deepest level, coherence shapes how people feel about their work identity: employees come to embody an organisation becoming its DNA.

Prudence is the last of the grand driving forces. It combines economy with appropriate concern for inappropriate risk. So, those running a fine hotel need to be protective, cautious and expect the worst; concern for the customer can be neglected through ignorance, complacency or indifference; costs can escalate; a fire can engulf the building; a rival hotel can offer superior facilities. It is necessary to prepare for the unexpected, the hazardous and the dangerous. In doing so, it is necessary to fight tendencies towards disintegration, neglect, and self-serving behaviour.

Innovation cannot be understood in isolation. It co-exists in a dynamic relationship with the other three grand driving forces, each pushing and pulling and, through dynamic conflict, providing the foundation for understanding, commitment and action. There is always an uneasy tension between competing imperatives as decisions are made. No single grand driving force has sufficient embedded wisdom to provide an organisation that is entirely fit for purpose. Although the drive for order, alignment and prudence may serve to limit, confine and constrain innovation, it is important to understand that they too are elemental and, like the juggler's balls in motion, the four grand forces are indivisible.

There will be periods when innovation is the dominant grand force, but at other times it needs to be curbed, evaluated and targeted. The push and pull between the four grand forces provides a fundamental rhythm—sometimes harmonious, sometimes discordant—that frames decisions, large and small. It is the task of those who make choices about what to do, and how to do things, to pay attention to each of the grand forces and to maintain them in dynamic tension.

Although there is no agreed definition of the term 'innovation' there is a consensus that the construct is broader than 'invention'. A definition provided in the OSLO Manual, prepared by the Organisation for Economic Co-operation and Development (OECD) (Gault, 2018, p. 618) states that "a common feature of an innovation is that it must have been implemented . . . In addition to being 'new or significantly improved' a product has to be 'introduced on the market' and a process or method has to be 'brought into actual use . . . The innovation takes place the moment the two conditions have been met". Galvez et al. (2018, p. 1) captured key features of innovation in their definition that "an innovation is the implementation of a new or significantly improved product (good or service), or process, a new marketing method, or a new organizational method in business practices, workplace organization or external relations". Innovation is therefore more, much more, than invention. We can conclude by defining innovation as a process of making that transforms ideas or opportunities, new to the unit of adoption, into tangible or intangible artefacts that add value.

The term 'adds value' requires further explanation. Until relatively recently, economic advantage was widely seen as the primary, perhaps the only, way that innovation can add value. As Kogabayev and Maziliauskas observed (2017, p. 63): "Schumpeter, who may be called the founder of the theory of innovation in the economy generally, regarded innovation as the economic impact of technological change". More recently, some have expanded typologies of where innovation could (and should) add value. Particularly influential has been John Elkington (2013) who developed 'people, planet and profits' formulation that is the basis of the Triple Bottom Line method of evaluating organisational performance.

Although examples of organisations capable of generating innovation are ancient (Brown et al., 2009), it is relatively recently that their management has been studied systematically. A sociological study, entitled *The Management of Innovation* (Burns & Stalker, 1961) is widely considered as a foundational contribution. Economists have been particularly influential for, as an engine of economic growth, innovation has been found to have no equal and Baumol (2002, p. 13) has convincingly argued that: "virtually all of the economic growth that has occurred since the 18th century is ultimately attributable to innovation". Another strand of research used the lenses of social psychology (e.g., Katz and Kahn (1978)) and ethnographic social anthropology (e.g., Kidder (1981)) to provide a fine-grain analysis of the behaviours that enabled innovation to occur effectively or ineffectively. The outcome of more than 50 years of cross-disciplinary research has been the development of a distinctive academic discipline (Krishnan, 2009) and a comprehensive theory of action that many managers have adopted (e.g., see the practice of Innovation Management; Miles, and Snow (2006)). The core constructs of Innovation Management draw from disciplines such as economic history, strategic management, engineering, organisational sociology, design studies, development studies, evolutionary biology and complexity science (Beaumont, Thuriaux-Alemán, Prasad, & Hatton, 2017; Cai, Liu, Huang, & Liang, 2019; Vidmar, 2019).

The study of Innovation Management is, quintessentially, transdisciplinary which Nicolescu (2014, p. 187) defines as a discipline that: "concerns that which is at once between the disciplines, across the different disciplines, and beyond all discipline. Its goal is the understanding of the present world, of which one of the imperatives is the unity of knowledge". The core constructs of Innovation Management combine a wide variety of pools of academic knowledge with an understanding that management is a form of craft rather than a profession (Mintzberg, 1987) that Sarason, Dean, and Dillard (2006, p. 287) explain requires acts: "of entrepreneurship (that occur) as the agent specifies, interprets, and acts upon the sources of opportunity".

Many organisations have recognised the need to improve their efficiency and effectiveness in managing innovation. These include commercial companies, government departments, hospitals, charities, NGOs and social work agencies (Amatullo, 2015; Berdegué, 2005; Tidd & Bessant, 2014; Tuominen & Toivonen, 2011). When not-for-profit organisations consider where value can be added from innovation, they are likely to be dissatisfied with current typologies. Five possible forms of added value can be considered as beneficial. These are:

1. For the innovators themselves, who are strengthened by the experience.
2. For the host organisation, as innovation can increase profitability, develop resilience and increase efficiency.
3. For those who receive the outputs.
4. For social and environmental ecosystems.
5. For cultural heritage of mankind.

Not all innovation initiatives will be successful. Some will add cost faster than value. Others will fail at some point in the transformation process. Those who are successful will add a distinctive contribution to one or more of the five possible beneficiaries listed above, in ways that are cost effective and help to deliver comparative or competitive advantage. Deciding which innovative proposals to adopt is a difficult managerial task as (i) in many organisations there are a myriad of ideas, some of which are unachievable, expensive, strategically inappropriate, risk-ladened or self-serving; (ii) organisations may possess systematic biases that screen out certain categories of ideas thereby limiting options before they have been considered fully; (iii) innovation requires a form of decision-making that, at times, resembles gambling since bets must be placed on prospects that can not, at that time, be understood fully; (iv) efforts to promote innovation are sometimes dysfunctional as they can be distracting, wasteful or unproductive; (v) within an organisation there may be a need for thousands of innovations to be undertaken at the same time, most of which will be narrow in scope and improvement orientated but a few may be transformational and require the destruction of existing assets, routines and mindsets; (vi) successful innovation requires that organisations possess a superior capability to execute—to get things new done effectively and efficiently and (vi) innovation must be integrated with the other things that an organisation needs to do, like ensure conformance, maintain quality, manage risk, be efficient etc.

Innovation does not take place in a vacuum and is shaped by disparate forces. These may be internal to the organisation, come from linkages (e.g., with suppliers or distributors), customers' expectations and requirements, the advantages gained by technological leaders, strategic choices, changes in overarching goals (e.g., an increasing recognition of the importance of sustainable development) rival firms etc. An organisation's innovation activities are influenced by, and may influence, political, economic, social, market-driven, ideological and/or technological phenomena.

Innovation can be described as a non-linear process having five principal phases: (i) someone sees an opportunity or has an idea (perhaps original, probably not), the idea is (ii) assessed, (iii) adopted, (iv) implemented and (v) benefits result. These stages offer a preliminary framework for understanding what is required to manage 'the successful exploitation of new ideas'. This non-linear process is not confined to new product development as organisations adopt new internal processes, position or reposition themselves in markets and invent or reinvent the business models that they use to define their identity—such initiatives are also innovations. Again, someone had an idea, it was assessed, adopted, applied and someone benefited.

Seeking to understand how organisations develop innovation capability presents distinct theoretical challenges as it is more complex than studying a single act of innovation. Nine factors help to explain why:

1. Not all innovation initiatives add more value than cost. Innovation can be either functional or dysfunctional – it is rarely neutral. Dysfunctional innovation undermines a firm if it adds cost faster than value, occupies resources on fruitless activities, undermines the existing core business by becoming a distraction or locks the firm into sustaining, rather than disruptive technologies (Christensen, 2015). Since innovation often, but not always, includes an element of risk it cannot offer a guaranteed formula for gaining or sustaining advantage.

2. Innovation can have the effect of increasing complexity, and uncertainty in an organisation and disturb existing policies, practices, mindsets and competencies

3. The known can be replaced with the unknown: that which is tried-and-tested replaced with promise or aspiration (Lord, DeBethizy, & Wager, 2005). Innovation can be a driver of change in which some are disadvantaged (Machiavelli & Bull, 1984).

4. In many organisations there are more ideas generated than can be implemented. Many must be killed-off, sometimes without a full understanding of their potential. The culling of ideas and proposals can demoralise their champions and there is a risk that promising ideas are not given the degree of commitment needed. Decisions about which innovations to adopt can be demanding and significant – a complex organisational process without certain benefit.

5. Assuring the needed quality and quantity of ideas is a demanding organisational task. It is possible that ideas available to one organisation are inferior to those developed by rival firms in terms of their capacity to exploit assets, create value to the firm and/or its customers. Not every firm has access to the 'best' ideas (McGourty, Tarshis, & Dominick, 1996). The quantity of supply of ideas is also variable.

6. Innovation capability cannot be conceptualised as a single linear process as it is better viewed as a multiplicity of non-linear processes, some interacting, that occur in a multiplicity of places within a company and within its wider value chain. This presents a management challenge, especially for the TMT, as the diffusion of multiple speculative innovation initiatives cannot be effectively

managed using conventional management-by-objectives (MbO) disciplines (Ashkenas, Ulrich, Jack, & Kerr, 1995).

7. Innovation initiatives often require co-operation across internal organisational boundaries, perhaps requiring the reorganisation of responsibilities – with the possibility that internal politics, interplay of personalities or lack of managed horizontal processes will retard effective implementation (Hastings, 2000). Lateral management processes are more complex than classic functional structures (Galbraith, Downey, & Kates, 2002).

8. Not all organisational forms encourage innovation (Mintzberg, Quinn, & Ghoshal, 1998). For example, an emphasis on conformance and reliability – important performance indicators for many firms – can diminish the motivation to be innovative and the skills to do so. An organisational form that facilitates innovation can be 'untidy', perhaps conflicting with other organisational values and policies.

9. A final factor renders innovation more complex than routine activities. This is the requirement for learning and unlearning (Argyris, 1976). Some innovations can be straightforward – the replacement of a slow computer printer for a faster one, for example. But other innovations can require the destruction of mindsets, routines, assets, authority structures and cultural imperatives (Hurst, 1995). New learning may be required, at the organisational, team and individual level. Unlearning and learning can be drivers of innovation as well as servants of it. The learning and unlearning process can be exploratory, anticipatory and speculative, thereby challenging organisational routines that provide stability, effectiveness and conformity. The significance of learning in innovation is difficult to underestimate, especially as much can depend on tacit knowledge. Moreover, codified learning can change from being an asset to be a 'rigidity' (Leonard-Barton, 1992).

These nine factors are illustrative rather than exhaustive. It may be that innovation should be regarded as more than just another management process as it is a kind of 'organisational alchemy'. The nature of the innovation process is, itself, subject to innovation (Cockburn, Henderson, & Stern, 2017). It has changed and, arguably, has become more efficient and diffused in the past century. There is a greater participation in the innovation process today than was historically the case. Many people contribute to workplace innovation (kaizen). It could be said that we live in an era of the democratisation of innovation and recent developments in internet technology have facilitated the development of open and user-led innovation (Chesbrough, 2003).

This exploration of the nature of innovation provides insight into a distinctive set of challenges that are faced by leaders and managers as they attempt to incorporate the principles and practice of effective innovation into their journey to become a requisitely agile organisation. Key questions are 'what should be the role of innovation in our organisation? What deliverables do we want from innovation?'

Further Reading

Amatullo, M. V. (2015). Innovation by Design at UNICEF: An Ethnographic Case Study. Case Western Reserve, Cleveland, Ohio.

Argyris, C. (1976). Single-Loop and Double-Loop Models in Research on Decision Making. Administrative Science Quarterly, 21(3),363–375.

Ashkenas, R., Ulrich, D., Jack, T., & Kerr, S. (1995). The Boundaryless Organization. San Francisco: Jossey-Bass Inc.

Baumol, W. J. (2002). The Free-Market Innovation Machine: Analyzing The Growth Miracle Of Capitalism. Woodstock, Oxon.: Princeton University Press.

Beaumont, M., Thuriaux-Alemán, B., Prasad, P., & Hatton, C. (2017). Using agile approaches for breakthrough product innovation. Strategy and Leadership, 45(6),19–25.

Berdegué, J. A. (2005). Pro-Poor Innovation Systems. Rome: IFAD.

Brown, K. S., Marean, C. W., Herries, A. I. R., Jacobs, Z., Tribolo, C., Braun, D., . . . Bernatchez, J. (2009). Fire as an engineering tool of early modern humans. Science, 325(5942),859–862.

Burns, T., & Stalker, G. M. (1961). The Management of Innovation. London: Tavistock Publications Ltd.

Cai, Z., Liu, H., Huang, Q., & Liang, L. (2019). Developing organizational agility in product innovation: the roles of IT capability, KM capability, and innovative climate. R and D Management, 49(4), 421–438.

Chesbrough, H. W. (2003). The Era of Open Innovation. MIT Sloan Management Review, 44(3),35–41.

Christensen, C. M. (2015). Disruptive Innovation Is a Strategy, Not Just the Technology. Business Today, 23(26),150–158.

Cockburn, I. M., Henderson, R., & Stern, S. (2017). The Impact of Artificial Intelligence on Innovation: An Exploratory Analysis. In NBER Conference on Research Issues in Artificial Intelligence. Toronto.

Elkington, J. (2004). Enter the Triple Bottom Line. In A. Henriques & J. Richardson (Eds.), The Triple Bottom Line: Does It All Add Up (pp. 1–19). Abingdon, UK: Earthscan.

Galbraith, J. R., Downey, D., & Kates, A. (2001). Processes and Lateral Capability. In Designing Dynamic Organizations: A Hands-on Guide for Leaders at All Levels (pp. 134–188). New York: AMACOM, a division of American Management Association.

Galvez, D., Enjolras, M., Camargo, M., Boly, V., & Claire, J. (2018). Firm Readiness Level for Innovation Projects: A New Decision-Making Tool for Innovation Managers. Administrative Sciences, 8(1), 1–17.

Gault, F. (2018). Defining and measuring innovation in all sectors of the economy. Research Policy, 47 (3),617–622.

Hastings, C. (2000). Strategic Management by Project Group: Lessons Learned. In Business-Driven Action Learning: Global Best Practices (pp. 169–178). Basingstoke, UK: McMillan Press Ltd.

Hurst, D. K. (1995). Crisis & Renewal: Meeting the Challenge of Organizational Change. (M. L. Tushman & A. H. Van de Ven, Eds.), The Management of Innovation and Change. Boston: Harvard Business School Press.

Katz, D., & Kahn, R. L. (1978). The social psychology of organizations. New York: Wiley.

Kidder, T. (1981). The Soul of a New Machine. Boston: Little and Brown.

Kogabayev, T., & Maziliauskas, A. (2017). The definition and classification of innovation. HOLISTICA – Journal of Business and Public Administration, 8(1),59–72.

Krishnan, A. (2009). What are academic disciplines? National Center for Research Methods, (January), 57.

Leonard-Barton, D. (1992). Core capabilities and core rigidities: A paradox in managing new product development. Strategic Management Journal, 13(S1), 111–125.

Lord, M., DeBethizy, D., & Wager, J. (2005). Innovation that Fits: Moving Beyond the Fads to Choose the RIGHT Innovation Strategy for Your Business. New Jersey, USA.: Pearson Education Limited.

Machiavelli, N., & Bull, G. (1984). The Prince. Harmondsworth: Penguin.

McGourty, J., Tarshis, L. A., & Dominick, P. (1996). Managing Innovation: Lessons from World Class Organizations. Int. J. Technology Management, Special Issue on the 5th International Forum on Technology Management, 11(3/4), 354–368.

Miles, R. E., Miles, G., & Snow, C. C. (2006). A Business Model for Continuous Innovation. Organizational Dynamics, 35(1),1–11.

Mintzberg, H. (1987). Crafting Strategy. Harvard Business Review, 65(4),66–75.

Mintzberg, H., Quinn, J. B., & Ghoshal, S. (1998). The Strategy Process (REVISED Eu). Hemel Hempstead, UK.: Prentice Hall Europe.

Nicolescu, B. (2014). Methodology of transdisciplinarity. World Futures, 70(3–4), 186–199.

Sarason, Y., Dean, T., & Dillard, J. F. (2006). Entrepreneurship as the nexus of individual and opportunity: A structuration view. Journal of Business Venturing, 21, 286–305.

Tidd, J., & Bessant, J. (2014). Strategic innovation management. New York: John Wiley & Sons Inc.

Tuominen, T., & Toivonen, M. (2011). Studying Innovation and Change Activities in Kibs Through the Lens of Innovative Behaviour. International Journal of Innovation Management, 15(2),393–422.

Vidmar, M. (2019). Agile Space Living Lab – The Emergence of a New High-Tech Innovation Paradigm. Space Policy, 49, 1–11.

Topic Sixteen: Learning Organisations

The construct of a learning organisation is based on a theoretical viewpoint that organisations are more than a collection of individuals: they have a distinctive identity, culture, sets of routines etc. (Durkheim, 1982). Moreover, organisations can learn and become, in effect, teachers using a process that has been called socialisation (Allen & Meyer, 1990). A key scholar who drew attention to the need for organisational learning to be deliberately developed was Senge (1992, p. 174) who wrote that "the discipline of managing mental models – surfacing, testing, and improving our internal pictures of how the world works – promises to be a major breakthrough for building learning organizations." Later, Thomas and Allen (2006, p. 125) explained that: "organisational learning is not a cumulative result of individual learning. Rather, organisations learn when discoveries, evaluations and insights by individuals are successfully embedded in the organisation's mental models or cognitive systems and memories". An effective learning organisation prioritises the acquisition of collective learning as an organisational asset and develops routines that enable different kinds of knowledge to be adopted as upgraded efficiently and effectively, along with processes for unlearning (by removing or diminishing dysfunctional mental constructs so that they no longer influence behaviour) (Senge, 1992).

We learnt that collective learning is important in an unexpected way (Weick & Roberts, 1993). Social scientists spent many months on an aircraft carrier striving to understand how the crew could undertake a host of a complex, technical and dangerous tasks reliably and adjust to unexpected situations. They found that everyone understood their impact on the system and took decisions in the interests of others in real time. When things went wrong those involved would develop their own solutions, practicing 'heedful' working.

Further Reading

Allen, N. J., & Meyer, J. P. (1990). Organizational Socialization Tactics: A Longitudinal Analysis of Links to Newcomers' Commitment and Role Orientation. Academy of Management Journal, 33(4),847–858.

Durkheim, E. (1982). The Rules of Sociological Method. (S. Lukes, Ed.). New York: The Free Press.

Senge, P. M. (1992). The Fifth Discipline: The Art & Practice of the Learning Organization. London: Random House.

Thomas, K., & Allen, S. (2006). The learning organisation: a meta-analysis of themes in literature. The Learning Organization, 13(2),123–139.

Weick, K. E., & Roberts, K. H. (1993). Collective Mind in Organizations: Heedful on Interrelating Flight Decks. Administrative Science Quarterly, 38(3),357–381.

Topic Seventeen: Organisation Development

The social technology of modern Organisation Development (OD) developed from social science research in the late 1940s. Its purpose was to bring about intentional organisational change based on a value system that was humanistic and inspirational. In brief, research into OD has shown that successful change requires (i) a consensus on shared values, (ii) clarity of goals, (iii) commitment of the guiding coalition, (iv) appropriate skills, (v) a realistic diagnosis of 'where we are' and (vi) a process for managing change.

In an influential book Argyris (1970) stated that OD needed (i) to focus on the conditions necessary to develop the competence of a social system and (ii) use a primary intervention cycle that Kolb and Frohman (1970) defined as having six steps: contract and entry, data collection and analysis, data feedback and negotiation of interventions, action and evaluation. Argyris emphasized that OD was (and is) more than a quasi-professional business-improvement practice as it is values-directed, being dedicated to promoting "humanistic values: respect for human dignity; integrity; freedom; justice and responsibility" (Garrow, Varney, & Lloyd, 2009, p. 6).

Not all agreed that values of OD were the only way by which change agents could help to 'develop the competence of a social system'. Although there has not been a comprehensive study of the underpinning values of different types of interventionists it is reasonable to argue that at least six alternatives but overlapping value-orientations emerged from the 1960s. These can be characterised as facilitating: Achieving Superior Economic Returns (gaining maximum return on investments), Market Leading (achieving a market position that wins lucrative orders), Innovation Intensive (maintaining timely flows of highly productive innovations), Strategic Positioning (becoming located in the most profitable parts of value chains), Efficiency and Effectiveness (being lean and agile) and Risk Minimization (protecting the organisation against hazards). These alternative approaches are largely derived from economic analyses and the diffusion of functionally-specific bodies of knowledge (like knowledge of digital factories or lean manufacturing) (Sturdy, 2011). They view the targets for organisational interventions as profitability and competitive/comparative advantage and human relations issues become relevant only so far as they are needed to support the primary goals.

In addition to a proliferation of targets and modalities for interventions, a different kind of challenge has emerged to the OD model of values-based change agency. It comes from process theories of organisations (Bjerregaard & Jonasson, 2014) and from constructs related to organisational agility (Doz & Mikko Kosonen, 2008). There is growing support for characterising organisations as always being in a state of 'becoming' – a status that becomes more acute as the rate of disruptive change, and therefore the need for agility, increases (Francis, Bessant, & Hobday, 2003), organisations become more network-based (Burke, 2014) and increasingly work is performed by robots and Artificial Intelligence systems (Church & Burke, 2017). For organisations in this condition, the primary OD intervention cycle is excessively dedicated to improving of the current client system and insufficiently focused on what the organisation can become (Uhl-Bien & Arena, 2018) neglecting the range of dynamic capabilities needed for productive continuous becoming (Salvato & Vassolo, 2018).

Further Reading

Argyris, C. (1970). Intervention Theory and Method. Reading, Mass: Addison Wesley.

Bjerregaard, T., & Jonasson, C. (2014). Managing Unstable Institutional Contradictions: The Work of Becoming. Organization Studies, 35(10),1507–1536.

Burke, W. W. (2014). Changing Loosely Coupled Systems. Journal of Applied Behavioral Science, 50(4), 423–444.

Church, A. H., & Burke, W. W. (2017). Four trends shaping the future of organizations and organization development. OD Practitioner, 49(3),14–22.

Doz, Y. L., & Mikko Kosonen, S. (2008). The Dynamics of Strategic Agility. California Management Review, 50(3),95–118.

Francis, D. L., Bessant, J., & Hobday, M. (2003). Managing radical organisational transformation. Management Decision, 41(1/2), 18–31.

Garrow, V., Varney, S., & Lloyd, C. (2009). Fish or Bird? Perspectives on Organisational Development (OD). Brighton: Institute for Employment Studies.

Kolb, D. A., & Frohman, A. L. (1970). An Organization Development Approach to Consulting. Sloan Management Review, 12(1),51–65.

Salvato, C., & Vassolo, R. (2018). The sources of dynamism in dynamic capabilities. Strategic Management Journal, 39(6),1728–1752.

Sturdy, A. (2011). Consultancy's consequences? A critical assessment of management consultancy's impact on management. British Journal of Management, 22(3),517–530.

Uhl-Bien, M., & Arena, M. (2018). Leadership for organizational adaptability: A theoretical synthesis and integrative framework. Leadership Quarterly, 29(1),89–104.

Topic Eighteen: Pinnacle Point

Pinnacle Point is located south of Mossel Bay on the coast of South Africa. It is the site of caves that have been inhabited for hundreds of thousands of years. Archaeological excavations have found that Middle Stone Age people lived there between 170,000 and 40,000 years ago. The inhabitants used stone tools and there is strong evidence that the techniques used for shaping stones evolved considerably over time. Particularly significant was the discovery that heat could make stones easier to work.

Brown et al. (2009, p. 861) observed that "Heat treatment provides the option of exploiting more-local but poorer raw materials and compensating by improving their quality. Heat treatment front-loads tool production costs by forcing the toolmaker to invest in fire production in order to improve the subsequent knapping process . . . The controlled use of fire was a breakthrough invention that allowed cooking, the production of warmth and light, and protection from predators . . . Heat treatment and its requirements signal an important technological advance, in that fire was now being carefully manipulated as an engineering tool". And in a later article Brown et al. (2012, p. 592) observed that "(e)arly modern humans in South Africa had the cognition to design and transmit at high fidelity these complex recipe technologies. This ability facilitated effective weapons grounded in microlithic technology, conferring increased killing distance and power over hand-cast spears. Microlith-tipped projectile weapons increased hunting success rate, reduced injury from hunting encounters gone wrong, extended the effective range of lethal interpersonal violence, and would have conferred substantive advantages on modern humans as they left Africa and encountered Neanderthals equipped with only hand-cast spears".

Further Reading

Brown, K. S., Marean, C. W., Herries, A. I. R., Jacobs, Z., Tribolo, C., Braun, D., . . . Bernatchez, J. (2009). Fire as an engineering tool of early modern humans. Science, 325(5942),859–862.

Brown, K. S., Marean, C. W., Jacobs, Z., Schoville, B. J., Oestmo, S., Fisher, E. C., . . . Matthews, T. (2012). An early and enduring advanced technology originating 71,000 years ago in South Africa. Nature, 491(7425),590–593.

Topic Nineteen: **Projectification**

Projects are a key organisational device for facilitating organisational agility. Accordingly, projectification is a central construct in agility-orientated organisational development. Although projects are structured, they are temporary organisations constructed to achieve specific ends. Mintzberg's studies of organisational structures (1983, pp. 253–254) identified the 'adhocracy' as a distinctive form of an organisational "configuration . . . required of a space agency, an avant-guard film company, a factory manufacturing complex prototypes, an integrated petro-chemical company . . . (as it requires a distinctive organisational) configuration . . . that is able to fuse experts drawn from different disciplines into smoothly functioning ad hoc project teams". Mintzberg described the characteristics of an adhocracy as (i) requiring an organic rather than a mechanistic structure; (ii) having a high degree of job specialisation; (iii) needing to manage the frequent redeployment of staff as activities change; (iv) installing crucial liaison mechanisms that facilitate coordination and (v) an inability to manage centrally, hence the need for selective decentralisation. Tellingly, Mintzberg observed that: "of all of the (organisational) configurations, Adhocracy shows the least reverence for the classic principles of management, especially unity of command . . . the Adhocracy must break through the boundaries of conventional specialisation and differentiation: the professionals must amalgamate their efforts (and) different specialists must join forces in multi-disciplinary teams" (p. 255–256). According to Mintzberg there are significant downsides associated with an Adhocracy that it, "is simply not an efficient structure . . . the root of its inefficiency is the Adhocracy's high cost of communication" (p. 277) but if an ad hoc organisation seeks to bureaucratise in order to become more efficient then it "risks falling into a schizophrenic state, continuing wavering between two kinds of structure, never clearly isolating either, to the detriment of both" (p. 279).

Davis and Brady (2000) drew from constructs used in the resource-based theory of the firm (Eisenhardt & Martin, 2000) and introduced the notion of 'project capabilities', which are "important activities (e.g. bidding, project design, implementation and de-commissioning involved in supplying CoPS)" (p. 932) and include a requirement for "strong capabilities in tendering or bidding activities i.e. pre-sales marketing, proposal preparation, conceptual design, risk assessment and contracts that have to be carried out prior to commencing a project" (p. 937). Davis and Brady suggested that the principle instrument for developing project capabilities would be the effective use of a learning cycle. In addition, they drew attention to difficulties of exploiting learning noting that: "the ability of a firm to adapt to changing business requirements depends in part on a capability called 'absorptive capacity'. Largely a function of a firm's prior knowledge and experience, absorptive capacity refers to the ability to recognise the value of new, external knowledge and information, assimilate it and apply it to meet new commercial objectives" (p. 935). Specific processes are mentioned as contributing to the acquisition and deployment of project capabilities, including project manuals, internal consulting groups, service level agreements and project reviews.

Gann and Salter (2000), considered project capabilities that provided a wealth of new insights. They investigated two areas that had not previously been explored fully, which were (i) the importance of: "delivery and feedback mechanisms linking one firm's technical capabilities with those of other enterprises, with whom the firm collaborates, in order to produce one-off projects" (p. 955). Gann and Salter emphasised the importance of behavioural and inter-personal competencies as: "success often depends upon the knowledge that people at every level of the organisation bring to bear in new, semi-autonomous and often temporary, cross-functional teams" (p. 967). Projects require that people are highly cooperative, proactive, outgoing, realistic, positive and behaviourally skilled: in short, they demonstrate emotional intelligence (Goleman, 1996). The work by Gann and Salter greatly expanded our understanding of the need for high quality of interpersonal relationships and advanced problem-solving skills, that provided a useful antidote to those whose solutions to the task of managing projects were control orientated, systems-based, bureaucratic or technocratic.

Hobday (2000) took a broader perspective. He demonstrated that undertaking projects required a supportive ecosystem that he called a project-based organisation (PBO). Hobday argued that the PBO form of organisation, rather than functional or matrix form, could provide for constructive symbiotic relationships between complex projects and a wider corporate structure that provides resources, exercises control, owns technical and other capabilities, develops processes, clarifies values, offers learning opportunities and supplies reputational assets. Tellingly Hobday observed that the relationship between a project and the wider organisation can be replete with difficulties, as many areas of tension can exist. Project managers need to satisfy internal masters as well as external customers. However, Hobday's research showed that: "the PBO form was more effective than the functional form in integrating different types of knowledge and skill, learning within the project boundary and coping with project risks and uncertainties" (p. 892). Later research (Thiry & Deguire, 2007) provided further understanding of the range of control and coordination mechanisms that PBO companies develop, especially the role of key role of project management offices.

Further insights came from Manning and Sydow's study of the key role played by enduring personal relationships in TV film production (2011), Ahola et al.'s study of the dynamics of trust building between suppliers and customers in the Russian gas industry (Ahola, Kujala, Laaksonen, & Aaltonen, 2013) and Lindkvist's insightful analysis of formal and informal learning mechanisms using evolutionary theory (2008). Söderlund (2008) observed that: "the duality of operational and dynamic capabilities in project operations highlights the need of a broad look at learning processes operating in project contexts . . . the nested character of learning highlights the need to foster various types of learning processes and knowing, that capability building involves codification, articulation and experience accumulation, and that these learning processes complement each other . . . Capability building in project settings involves many different actors, including project managers, project team members, project office managers and top managers" (p. 63). From this viewpoint an organisation's capacity to become an effective learning organisation would be the focus of its organisational development efforts. How, exactly, such learning was to be promoted was something of a black box as were ways in which the benefits could be appropriated.

Whyte et al. (2015) pointed out that the competences required to be an effective project-type company are not static, writing that: "today, mobile hardware, cloud computing and integrated software are becoming used for storage and retrieval, automated search, and prototyping and simulation functions. As such technologies are adopted in project-based industries, their use is breaking the mould of established approaches to project management, enabling more rapid and agile forms of organizing" (p. 1). This insight provides an important insight for scholars as, to put it simply, excellent project capability must be conceptualised as a moving target. That which represents best practice now may be outdated, and therefore a rigidity, in years to come (Kanter, 2006).

Echoing the work of Mintzberg on adhocracies that we mentioned above, a few scholars have asserted that 'we have got it all wrong'! It was argued that the conceptual apparatus adopted for the analysis and interpretation of projects is implicitly rooted in logical-positive viewpoints that are fundamentally inadequate. For example, a leading advocate of this view, Christophe Bredillet (2007) stated that it is necessary to develop "an understanding of project management as an 'entrepreneurial' activity (vis-à-vis 'operational' activity); and as a mirror used for action and reflection" (p. 7). Put simply, Bredillet's argument is this: we have come to believe that the best way to manage projects is to enforce multiple forms of intellectual standardization (using project manuals and the like). In fact, projects are, fundamentally, entrepreneurially driven complex adaptive systems that require intelligent and informed agents to 'do their best when they find themselves'. Hence, the pursuit of a form of organisation that seeks to impose codified forms of best practice denigrates the need for individuals and teams to be powerfully and proactively responsive (i.e., to possess the qualities of a good agilepreneur).

This argument for adopting a constructivist perspective (and diminishing the supremacy of the positivist perspective) to the problem of managing projects echoes the stance taken by Mintzberg (1987) when, discussing 'crafting' strategy, he wrote: "What, then, does it mean to craft strategy? Let us return to the words associated with craft: dedication, experience, involvement with the material, the personal touch, mastery of detail, a sense of harmony and integration. Managers who craft strategy . . . are involved, responsive to their materials, learning about their organizations and industries through personal touch" (p. 73). It did not require a significant conceptual leap to see that a distinctive feature of a project is that each can be considered as a strategically distinctive entity as, by definition, it is a one-off endeavour that is as large, in itself, as many medium-sized businesses. Hence, a high quality of governance can be seen as an essential core capability.

Now, it is understood that uniformity and conformance are only part of the solution and that intrapreneurship, agility, judgement and aligned proactivity are important as well. If the findings of relevant literatures are combined then it seems that project-based companies thrive on combinations of opposites: they need to be tightly planned yet agile, disciplined yet organic, integrated yet deeply specialised, technically proficient yet business orientated, and systems-driven yet intrapreneural. Perhaps this is why even well-resourced projects that are led by elite managers can fail to deliver their promises (Brady & Davies, 2010).

In a project-based company, much of the required work can not be atomised, knowledge intensity is high, design tasks are massive and multi-disciplinary, the experience effect (that yields efficiencies through repetition) is fragmentary, risks are endemic, sales processes are long and arduous and interdependencies are pervasive and rhizomic (Chia, 1999).

Further Reading

Ahola, T., Kujala, J., Laaksonen, T., & Aaltonen, K. (2013). Constructing the market position of a project-based firm. International Journal of Project Management, 31(3),355–365.

Brady, T., & Davies, A. (2010). From hero to hubris – Reconsidering the project management of Heathrow's Terminal 5. International Journal of Project Management, 28, 151–157.

Bredillet, C. N. (2007). Shikumidukuri vs. one best (no) way! Project and Programme Management for Enterprise Innovation (P2M): towards a new paradigm? In In International Research Network of Organizing by Projects-IRNOP 8. Brighton, UK.

Chia, R. (1999). A 'Rhizomic' Model of Organizational Change and Transformation: Perspective from a Metaphysics of Change. British Journal of Management, 10, 209–227.

Davies, A., & Brady, T. (2000). Organisational capabilities and learning in complex product systems: towards repeatable solutions. Research Policy, 29(7–8), 931–953.

Eisenhardt, K. M., & Martin, J. A. (2000). Dynamic Capabilities: What Are They? Strategic Management Journal, 21(10/11), 1105–1121.

Gann, D. M., & Salter, A. J. (2000). Innovation in project-based, service-enhanced firms: the construction of complex products and systems. Research Policy, 29(7–8), 955–972.

Goleman, D. (1996). Emotional Intelligence: Why it Can Matter More Than IQ. London: Bloomsbury Publishing Plc.

Hobday, M. (2000). The project-based organisation: an ideal form for managing complex products and systems? Research Policy, 29(7–8), 871–893.

Kanter, R. M. (2006). Innovation: The Classic Traps. HBR, (November), 73–83.

Lindkvist, L. (2008). Project organization: Exploring its adaptation properties. International Journal of Project Management, 26(1),13–20.

Manning, S., & Sydow, J. (2011). Projects, paths, and practices: sustaining and leveraging project-based relationships. Industrial and Corporate Change, 20(5),1369–1402.

Mintzberg, H. (1983). Structure in Fives: Designing Effective Organisations. Eaglewood Cliffs, N.J., USA: Prentice-Hall.

Mintzberg, H. (1987). Crafting Strategy. Harvard Business Review, 65(4),66–75.

Söderlund, J. (2008). Competence Dynamics and Learning Processes in Project-Based Firms: Shifting, Adapting and Leveraging. International Journal of Innovation Management, 12(01), 41–67.

Thiry, M., & Deguire, M. (2007). Recent developments in project-based organisations. International Journal of Project Management, 25(7),649–658.

Whyte, J., Stasis, A., & Lindkvist, C. (2015). Managing change in the delivery of complex projects: Configuration management, asset information and 'big data".' International Journal of Project Management, 34, 339–351. https://doi.org/10.1016/j.ijproman.2015.02.006

Topic Twenty: Requisite Agility

Two British sociologists, Burns and Stalker (1961a) were amongst the first social scientists to examine the texture of work in modern organisations. They found that there were vast differences between the work patterns of people who undertook predictable tasks compared with those who had to respond to situations as they occurred. They described the difference between these two modalities as operating in mechanistic or organic systems. Burns and Stalker (1961b, pp. 103–104) explained this distinction thus: "Mechanistic systems (namely 'bureaucracies') define his (the employee's) functions, together with the methods, responsibilities, and powers appropriate to them . . . In organic systems, the boundaries of feasible demands on the individual disappear. The greatest stress is placed on his regarding himself as fully implicated in the discharge of any task appearing over his horizon, as involved not merely in the exercise of a special competence but in commitment to the success of the concern's undertakings approximating somewhat to that of the doctor or scientist in the discharge of his professional functions". The analysis between mechanistic or organic systems has clear relevance to analyses of organisational agility, since most agility types are essentially organic. Whether a part or whole of an organisation operates in an organic modality is contingent upon environmental conditions. Since Burns and Stalker's pioneering studies much work has been undertaken in what has become known as contingency theories (Hanisch & Wald, 2012).

Lawrence and Lorsch (1967) made significant advances and found that the degree of environmental uncertainty, including the rate of innovation, pace of market changes and/or radical changes process technology were key determinates. Their analysis found that extensive cross-functional teamwork and co-ordination mechanisms were necessary to facilitate adaptation. Mintzberg (1983) found multiple contingency factors including organisational age, size, predictability of tasks, degree of innovation required and, later, leadership values. In a later work Mintzberg argued that turbulent and uncertain environments require strategies to be opportunistic, frequently revised and pursued with vigour despite contextual ambiguities—a working definition of agility. Mintzberg et al. (1998) used the term 'emergent strategy' to describe such managerial stances in contrast with formal, planned 'deliberate strategy'. In essence, an emergent strategy is one in which a firm's strategy makers accept that there are too many unknown or unknowable variables for prudent plans to be prepared well in advance and it is necessary for strategies to be developed in real time according to factors that prevail at that time. Emergent strategies depend on assessments and commitments made by the power elite of an organisation and are particularly responsive to serendipitous innovation opportunities. Indeed, it is reasonable to argue that a capacity to adopt an emergent strategy is a necessary element in innovation capability.

An article with the startling title "The Curse of Agility" by Lamberg et al. (2019, p. 16) studied the role of agility in Nokia and concluded: "When examining the period of 2006–2010, the dominant picture is that these (agile) ideas materialised in a near-hysterical corporate climate … Nokia was inconsistent in its reactions, launching numerous projects and strategies to counterattack its emerging rivals". This case demonstrated that agility is not a universally beneficial managerial strategy. Teece et al. (2016, pp. 13–14) take this point further when they write: "We suggest that when inflection points emerge, uncertainty is enhanced, and change is necessary for firms to remain competitive. However, because change is costly and achieving agility often involves sacrificing efficiency, one cannot assert that business firms should organize continuously for agility. Knowing when (and how much) agility is needed and being able to deliver it cost effectively is a crucial managerial capability".

Further Reading

Burns, T., & Stalker, G. M. (1961a). The Management of Innovation. London: Tavistock Publications Ltd.

Burns, T., & Stalker, G. M. (1961b). The mechanistic and organic systems of management (Abridged). In The Management of Innovation (pp. 103–108). London: Tavistock Publications.

Hanisch, B., & Wald, A. (2012). A Bibliometric View on the Use of Contingency Theory in Project Management Research. Project Management Journal, 43(3),4–23.

Lamberg, J. A., Lubinaitė, S., Ojala, J., & Tikkanen, H. (2019). The curse of agility: The Nokia Corporation and the loss of market dominance in mobile phones, 2003–2013. Business History, 1–47.

Lawrence, P., & Lorsch, J. W. (1967). Organization and Environment. Boston: Harvard Business School.

Mintzberg, H. (1983). Structure in Fives: Designing Effective Organisations. Eaglewood Cliffs, N.J., USA: Prentice-Hall.

Mintzberg, H., Quinn, J. B., & Ghoshal, S. (1998). The Strategy Process (REVISED Eu). Hemel Hempstead, UK.: Prentice Hall Europe.

Teece, D. J., Peteraf, M., & Leih, S. (2016). Dynamic Capabilities and Organizational Agility: Risk, Uncertainty, and Strategy in the Innovation Economy. California Management Review, 58(4), 13–35.

Topic Twenty-One: Targeting Agility on Sustainable Development

Agility is an organisational capability that can be used for many purposes Increasingly, momentum is growing for agility to be targeted on organisations adopting the mindset that they are citizens of the world and their actions should improve the human condition and be environmentally caring. In short, organisations need to make a positive contribution to humanity, the world and stakeholders.

The phrase triple bottom line (TBL) accounting was coined in the early 1990s (Elkington, 1994) to review the consequences of organisational activities in three categories: people, planet and profit. TBL requires redefining 'what a good organisation is and does' as it holds, as a core value, that organisations should meet the needs of all their stakeholders, not just the interests of owners and, therefore, balance sheets should present hard data on performance in relation to all of the three domains.

Auditing performance using TBL criteria may lead to defining new targets for innovation. All companies have financial performance indicators (driven by statutory requirements) but few have environmental or social performance goals. Once goals are set in the environmental or social domains, then there is increased motivation to find new ideas to achieve improvements.

In general, those interested in TBL approaches do not concern themselves with financial performance, since this is already a daily preoccupation of owners, shareholders and managers. Rather they focus on environmental sustainability (ensuring that a company is prudent in the use of 'natural capital' (e.g., raw materials, plants, and animals). Also, it limits or avoids any form of damage to the natural world) and practices social responsibility (adopting a humanistic approach to employees, conforming to an ethical code and taking actions to improve the quality of human life by assisting communities to be educated, developed, skilled, with strong justice and communication systems).

Ivory and Brooks (2018, pp. 349–350) point out that TBL "has its foundations in output-based accounting which purports to calculate the economic, social, and environmental bottom lines of an organisation . . . but . . . measuring outputs may provide useful information about past programmes, focusing on outputs, especially in dynamic and turbulent environments . . . limits an organisation's ability to appropriately allocate the assets, capabilities, and competencies, which form the foundation of their future actions and outcomes". It may be that construct of stakeholder capitalism, the theme of the 2020 Davos Conference, provides a better foundation for managerial decision-making.

Whilst there are strong arguments in favour widening the definition of organisational success criteria, there are counter arguments as well. Refocussing a company on multiple stakeholders can be seen as undermining the clarity of purpose of the firm since decision-making becomes complex, more voices need to be heard, differing criteria must be considered, risks may be increased, and the definition of 'success' becomes blurred.

As mentioned in the main body of this book, agile organisations are prudently optimistic and this phrase can be interpreted as being stakeholder orientated. Wiraeus and Creelman (2019) found that the Balanced Scorecard (Kaplan & Norton, 1992) can be reworked so that it becomes dynamic and (2016) suggest modifications to the widely used EFQM (Kim, Kumar, & Murphy, 2010) model to enable it to be useful to agile enterprises.

Sustainable development is an immense need and an immense challenge. It requires innovation in paradigm—the way that we think—as well as innovation in process, products and values. Sustainable development requires us to change how we define "good"—individuals and organisations will need to unlearn their 'old' ways of thinking and adopt new ones that are more complex, responsible and may contain inherent contradictions.

Further Reading

Dubey, M. (2016). Developing an Agile Business Excellence Model for Organizational Sustainability. Journal of Global Business & Organizational Excellence, 35(2),60–67.

Elkington, J. (1994). Cannibals with Forks: the Triple Bottom Line of 21st Century Business. Oxford, U.K.: Capstone Publishing Ltd.

Ivory, S. B., & Brooks, S. B. (2018). Managing Corporate Sustainability with a Paradoxical Lens: Lessons from Strategic Agility. Journal of Business Ethics, 148(2),347–361.

Kaplan, R. S., & Norton, D. P. (1992). The balanced scorecard – measures that drive performance. Harvard Business Review, January-Fe, 71–79.

Kim, D. Y., Kumar, V., & Murphy, S. a. (2010). European Foundation for Quality Management Business Excellence Model: An integrative review and research agenda. International Journal of Quality & Reliability Management, 27(6),684–701.

Wiraeus, D., & Creelman, J. (2019). Agile Strategy Management in the Digital Age: How Dynamic Balanced Scorecards Transform Decision Making, Speed and Effectiveness. Cham, Switzerland: Palgrave Macmillan.

Topic Twenty-Two: Top Management Teams

Requisite organisational agility requires strategic commitment, hands-on leadership and energised and coherent top management teamwork (Denning, 2018). Accordingly, TMTs provide an essential set of functions in an agile organisation as they promote, design, lead, provide resources for, support and renew programmes for agility-orientated organisational development. The complexity of the task is substantial, as TMTs need to facilitate productive flows of agile initiatives that (i) meet a wide variety of needs; (ii) employ a variety of modalities for facilitating agility that need to be bundled, aligned and mutually supportive into integrated configurations and (iii) are difficult, or impossible, to evaluate using a cost-benefit model. In addition, TMTs have a key role in setting their organisation's Agility Ambition and acting as champions, agenda-setters, key decision takers and efficiency drivers (this last role is important as agility can be costly, wasteful or misguided) (Daisley, Economides, Gillespie, & Quest, 2018).

Agility is not the only aspect of an organisation that TMTs need to consider. Equally important can be issues such as strategies for gaining competitive or comparative advantage, achieving financial goals, making sound investment decisions, defining technology strategies and being environmentally friendly (Doz & Kosonen, 2010). Accordingly, TMTs need to fit agility into their wider role, which requires answers to questions such as these:

i.   Where does our organisation need (and not need) requisite agility (this is the question that the EAfA Process addresses)?
ii. How should agility relate to our organisation's other priorities?
iii. What proportion of our resources should be dedicated to the different possible modalities for facilitating agility?
iv. What configuration or bundle of modalities for facilitating agility is appropriate for the next stage in our organisation's development?
v.   How should the costs of, and value-added from, agility be assessed?
vi. What should be our parenting model (as a TMT) to facilitate flows of functional (rather than dysfunctional) agility?

Arguably, the modern approach to the study of top teams began in the 1960s with Henry Mintzberg's research into the actual behaviour of managers (Mintzberg, 1973). Observing directly what managers did, rather than what they were believed to do, provided extraordinary insight into the wide variety of tasks that were performed. Many years later Mintzberg (2009) revisited his original study and he concluded that managing is a practice, learnt through experience. The top managers that Mintzberg observed led busy, fragmented lives and interacted with many individuals and groups, often having hundreds of interactions in a single day. Mintzberg's research demonstrated that the notion that a top team operates like a closed work group does not apply to those in the strategic apex. Rather a nexus of relationships, coalitions, agreements and processes is constructed and then reconstructed frequently. An effective TMT, in Mintzberg's view, is an open adaptive system.

Earlier a political scientist, Irving Janis (1972), made a major contribution to understanding the dynamics of TMTs when he investigated the reasons why some major policy decisions had gone disastrously wrong. He found that the major cause was that the ruling coalition, the TMT, became the victims of groupthink, which he defined (1971) as "a quick and easy way to refer to the mode of thinking that persons engage in when concurrence-seeking becomes so dominant in a cohesive ingroup that it tends to override realistic appraisal of alternative courses of action" (p. 84). Janis's work had a revolutionary effect on those who were studying organisational effectiveness at the time. It was realised that, in certain circumstances, a top team could become a destructive force that would lead their organisation into acting stupidly, unethically or be bent on self-destruction. This insight enabled scholars to see more clearly the dysfunctional potential of a TMT.

From the late 1970s there was a growing interest in the contribution of sociologists who explored the notion that managers were not mere playthings of the situation, as they were, or could become, proactive actors or agents that drove change. Giddens's theory of structuration (1986) provided a new way of interpreting the roles played by TMTs. Structuration theory posits that people are not entirely free to choose their own actions, but they may possess 'agency' as they can make a difference. Giddens asserted that it is people who construct social entities, but are, also, constrained by them. Structures, the patterns of social life, are created, maintained and changed by actions. However, not everyone has the same amount of agency. Within organisations, the need for control, alignment and coordination requires a hierarchical structure to form that has a strategic apex (Paroutis & Pettigrew, 2007). It is reasonable to hypothesise that the TMT functions as the brain of the firm and can do so as increased quantities of agency have been captured. Although Giddens's theory can be hard to grasp, it did demonstrate that sociologists could help to explain issues that were outside of economists' conceptual arena (Jones, Edwards, & Beckinsale, 2000).

Michael Porter's book *Competitive Strategy* (1980) caused a revolution in strategic studies that continues to be felt to this day. The book was a study of the principles that underlie winning strategies and it clarified the kinds of commitment decisions made by top managers. Porter asserted that not every competitive strategy can be pursued at the same time. Strategic choices are far from easy to make since they depend on deep knowledge of markets, competitors, technologies, cost-structures and sources of value creation. In effect, Porter was telling top teams that, 'you have special work to do. Only you can determine your company's competitive strategy and it is hard work'. With Porter's framework in hand TMTs had greater clarity about their collective task and, not long after, not-for-profit organisations began to analyse their strategy to seek to achieve comparative advantage. The work of the modern top team began to be fully defined.

During the 1980s, having been influenced by the work of Mintzberg, Janis, Porter and others, the study of top teamwork became increasingly differentiated from general studies of organisational groupings, as sociologists, management theorists, consultants and top managers realised that there was something special about TMTs. This was elaborated by an influential study of top management decision-making in 12 successful American corporations (Donaldson & Lorsch, 1983). The authors stated that, "daily in the executive suites . . . complex choices (are made) about corporate goals and the means to achieve them, choices that outline the strategic direction of the company" (p. 6). Donaldson and Lorsch concluded that there must be a 'deep consensus about ends and means at the top' (personal communication). The use of the term 'ends and means' was significant: it is not enough to decide what is required; it is necessary to find ways to achieve it. Execution—the ability to get things done—was identified as a core task of TMTs.

Almost at the same time as Donaldson and Lorsch published *Decision Making at the Top,* another highly significant book was published (Tregoe & Zimmerman, 1980) with the title, *Top Management Strategy.* The work was comprehensive and radical and it served to elaborate the agenda for the work of TMTs. Their book argued that all strategic business units (SBUs) must possess a single strategic driving force that should be selected from one of eight types that are available. As the different strategic driving forces are mutually exclusive, it was necessary to make a choice and shape the organisation to become a good example of type. This approach, quite different from, but complementary to, that of Porter (see above), served to further define the distinctive work of TMTs. Tregoe and Zimmerman's emphasis on the importance of alignment and cohesion helped TMTs to understand that establishing the principles of a coherent organisational design were mission critical. Although they did not use the term, in effect, Tregoe and Zimmerman were asserting 'that the TMT needs to become an organisation's chief architect'.

Arising from a parallel stream of work undertaken in the early 1980s, an article introducing the construct of Upper Echelons was published by Donald and Phyllis (1984), who argued that "organizational outcomes, both strategies and effectiveness, are viewed as reflective of the values and cognitive bases of powerful actors in the organization" (p. 193). Hambrick and Mason argued that: "each decision maker brings his or her own set of 'givens' . . . (that) reflect the decision maker's cognitive base . . . they also reflect his or her values: principles for ordering consequences or alternatives according to preferences" (p. 195). The authors suggested that: "the manager's field of attention, those areas to which attention is directed, is restricted" (p. 195). Arguably, in addition to describing these personalised characteristics, the main contribution of Upper Echelons Theory was to provide a framework for exploring how the composition of the TMT would affect its capacity to act effectively and affect organisational outcomes. Later, Hambrick (2007) provided an update on the original paper and was able to report that "many subsequent studies have verified that organizational outcomes depend, at least in part, on TMT composition" (p. 334). Also, Hambrick shares refinements that have been made to the theory including the observation that "several studies have shown that managerial discretion is a pivotal moderator of upper echelons predictions of organizational outcomes" (p. 335). In this observation, Hambrick makes a similar point to that made by Giddens (discussed above) that the construct of agency is essential for explaining the efficacy of TMTs.

A few years before Hambrick's publication of the article that introduced the Upper Echelons Theory, a UK scholar, Meredith Belbin (1961), published an insightful work entitled *Management Teams: Why They Succeed Or Fail.* Based on seven years of action research at the Administrative Staff College at Henley-on-Thames in England, Belbin found that an effective team needs its members to play nine key roles if it is to work effectively. We do not know if Hambrick was aware of Belbin's work (it is not cited in the bibliography of his paper) but the notion that individuals play different, complementary and essential roles extends the Upper Echelons Theory that it provides a rationale as to why a team is required. One of Belbin's key insights was that: "imperfect people can make a perfect team" (personal communication).

By the end of the 1980s, many of the building blocks for understanding TMTs were in place and structured processes for top team building began to be available. We can summarise key components of the TMT studies at this time as follows:

i.   TMTs make a critical contribution to organisational effectiveness
ii.   If TMTs are to exploit their potential, then they need to gain agency: the capacity to 'make a difference'.
iii. TMTs have distinctive properties: they have significant differences from other work groups.
iv.   TMTs can be dysfunctional, particularly if they suffer from groupthink.
v.   There is a body of knowledge and a set of tools required to determine an organisation's drive to adopt a strategy to gain competitive or comparative advantage, which needs to be understood and implemented by the TMT.
vi.   For a TMT to be successful, there must be a deep consensus about ends and means, so implementation capability is required in addition to policymaking.
vii. It is the role of the top team to align the organisation around a clear organising principle.
viii. The personal capabilities of members of TMTs make a significant difference to organisational outcomes.
ix.   Effective teams require a full range of roles to be played, not all of which can be played by one person.

Research findings are extending our understanding of how TMTs perform their tasks. For example, the ways in which TMTs relate to middle managers has been explored (Raes, Heijltjes, Glunk, & Roe, 2011). It is the middle managers in larger organisations who work with the members of TMTs to define and implement strategies, especially those related to development in areas such as research and development, operations, human resource management, marketing etc. Raes et al.'s article presents an interface model that examines how TMTs and middle managers interact together and the authors conclude that: "The proposed relationships in our model imply at least three main temporal forms by which the interface may develop over longer periods of time: a stable interface, a positive spiral, and a negative spiral . . . with decreasing levels of TMT participative leadership and middle management's active engagement, as well as decreases in cognitive flexibility and integrative bargaining" (p. 117). By presenting their interface model and the notion of negative or positive spirals Raes and her co-authors, take forward our understanding of the problem of strategy deployment. Their article extends our understanding of the scope of TMT research that needs to move towards seeing TMTs from an open systems perspective. In fact, as practitioner literature demonstrates (Lafley & Charan, 2008) TMTs do not work in isolation, rather they are nodes within a complex web of interactivity that extends far beyond the boundaries of organisations.

Further Reading

Belbin, M. (1961). Management Teams: Why they Succeed or Fail. London: Heinemann.
  Daisley, M., Economides, M., Gillespie, D., & Quest, L. (2018). Here's How To Bring Agility Into The Boardroom.
Denning, S. (2018). The role of the C-suite in agile transformation: The case of amazon. Strategy and Leadership, 46(6),14–21.
Donald, C., & Phyllis, A. (1984). Upper Echelons: The organization as a reflection of its top managers. Academy of Management Review, 9(2),193–206.
Donaldson, G., & Lorsch, J. W. (1983). Decision Making at the Top. New York: Basic Books.
Doz, Y. L., & Kosonen, M. (2010). Embedding Strategic Agility: A Leadership Agenda for Accelerating Business Model Renewal. Long Range Planning, 43(2–3), 370–382.
Giddens, A. (1986). The Constitution of Society: Outline of the Theory of Structuration. Polity Press. Cambridge, UK.
Hambrick, D. C. (2007). Upper Echelons Theory: An Update. Academy of Management Review, 32(2), 334–343.
Janis, I. L. (1971). Groupthink. Psychology Today, 5(6),43–46. Retrieved from http://agcommtheory.pbworks.com/f/GroupThink.pdf
Janis, I. L. (1972). Victims of groupthink: A psychological study of foreign policy decisions and fiascos. Boston: Houghton Mifflin Company.
Jones, O., Edwards, T., & Beckinsale, M. (2000). Technology Management in a Mature Firm: Structuration Theory and the Innovation Process. Technology Analysis & Strategic Management, 12(2),161–177.
Lafley, A. G., & Charan, R. (2008). The Game-Changer: How You Can Drive Revenue and Profit Growth with Innovation. New York: Random House.
Mintzberg, H. (1973). The Nature of Managerial Work. London: Harper & Row.
Mintzberg, H. (2009). Managing. San Francisco, Cal.: Berrett-Koehler Publishers.
Paroutis, S., & Pettigrew, A. (2007). Strategizing in the multi-business firm: Strategy teams at multiple levels and over time. Human Relations, 60(1),99–135.
Porter, M. E. (1980). Competitive Strategy: Techniques for Analyzing Industries and Competitors. New York: The Free Press.
Raes, A. M. L., Heijltjes, M. G., Glunk, U., & Roe, R. A. (2011). The Interface of the Top Management Team and Middle Managers: A Process Model. Academy of Management Review, 36(1),102–126.
Tregoe, B. B., & Zimmerman, J. W. (1980). Top Management Strategy: What It Is and How to Make It Work. London: John Martin Publishing.

Topic Twenty-Three: Vision, Mission and Values

We can consider Vision as an elaborated and codified description of what an organisation seeks to become, described by Lipton (1996, p. 85) as giving "people the feeling that their lives and work are intertwined and moving towards recognizable, legitimate goals". Mission as a definition of the contribution that organization intends to make to the wider world provides a raison d'être, that Ekpe et al. (2015, p. 135) explain provides "an enduring statement of purpose". Values, in this context, are a specification of the components of an institutional belief-system that will contribute to fulfilling the promises of the organisation's vision and mission, combined with meeting the expectations of key stakeholders, which is described by Bourne et al. (2017, p. 2) as having "a significant role in representing the intent of organisations to operate in particular ways and to encourage particular behaviours from organizational members".

The construct of 'values' is often difficult to address, as values are (to some extent) personal and they can be beneath the level of consciousness (Russ, 2018). But values are there, like the foundations of a building. We can see values are internal agents that tell us what is important or unimportant, good or bad. Values tell us what to fight for and what to neglect, what to cherish and what to despise.

When all of the elements of a vision, mission, values (VMV) provide competitive or comparative distinctiveness, are widely held and deeply understood, then they provide core elements of a shared identity that is enacted by instruments such as managerial hierarchies and systems, cultural imperatives, reward policies and, increasingly, the application of directed digital intelligence (Collins & Porras, 2002).

Although VMVs differ from organisation to organisation there is a degree of self-similarity as all organisations need to be capable of surviving in their current ecosystems (Warnecke, 1993). Organisational ecosystems are influenced by the prevailing social milieu that, in the second decade of the 21st century, has been described by sociologists as Late Modernity (Giddens, 1991) in which the influence of tradition has been greatly weakened and people construct and reconstruct themselves as self-development projects. This existential fluidity, combined with other generic change drivers such as the pace of digital transformation and increased levels of globalised competition, creates a need for organisations to strive to possess five attributes. They need to be (i) agile (foreseeing opportunities and threats, responding quickly and effectively and innovating efficiently); (ii) intelligent (using human and machine intelligence to increase productivity, efficacy, coordination and adaptation); (iii) productive (creating value faster than increasing costs); (iv) responsible (operating in ways that enhance the quality of society and are sustainable environmentally) and (v) promote healthy organization (i.e., compassionate, affirmative, open, fair and meritocratic).

Further Reading

Bourne, H., Jenkins, M., & Parry, E. (2019). Mapping espoused organizational values. Journal of Business Ethics, 159(1), 133–148.

Collins, J. C., & Porras, J. I. (2002). Built To Last: Successful Habits of Visionary Companies (Paper). New York: HarperBusiness Essentials.

Ekpe, E. O., Eneh, S. I., & Inyang, B. J. (2015). Leveraging Organizational Performance through Effective Mission Statement. International Business Research, 8(9),135–141.

Giddens, A. (1991). Modernity and Self Identity: Self and Society in the Late Modern Age. Cambridge, U.K.: Polity Press.

Lipton, M. (1996). Demystifying the development of an organizational vision. MIT Sloan Management Review, 37(4), 83.

Russ, H., 2018. Metaphysical mapping: A methodology to map the consciousness of organizations. Methodological Innovations, 11(2), p.2059799118788998.

Warnecke, H.-J. (1993). The Fractal Company: A Revolution in Corporate Culture. Berlin: Springer-Verlag.

Topic Twenty-Four: VUCA

The term VUCA was coined by the US Army War College in the late 1990s to describe the dynamic nature of our world and is short for 'volatility, uncertainty, complexity and ambiguity'. Horney et al. (2010, p. 33) define the key terms as follows: "Volatility (is) The nature, speed, volume, magnitude and dynamics of change; Uncertainty (is) The lack of predictability of issues and events; Complexity (is) The confounding of issues and the chaos that surround any organization; and Ambiguity (is) The haziness of reality and the mixed meanings of conditions".

An elaborate definition of each of the four elements of VUCA and reframing these as challenges was developed by Bennett and Lemoine (2014, p. 27) who suggest that volatility requires "slack and (devoting) resources to preparedness . . . investment should match the risk"; uncertainty requires Investing "in information . . . in conjunction with structural changes, such as adding information analysis networks, that can reduce ongoing uncertainty"; complexity requires "specialists, and . . . resources adequate to address the complexity" and ambiguity requires "Understanding cause and effect (that) requires generating hypotheses and testing them. Design your experiments so that lessons learned can be broadly applied".

Schoemaker et al. (2018, p. 19) state that "under VUCA (it is essential to develop) sensing capabilities in an integrated manner. For example, tools for external scanning and scenario planning . . . linked systematically to dashboards that monitor key trends and uncertainties, or other types of decision support systems". VUCA is a much-discussed topic and needs to be explored in relation to many aspects of sectors and organisational arrangements (Mack, Khare, Krämer, & Burgartz, 2015) including projects and programmes, risk management, customer relationships, pricing, sourcing, environmental impact and information systems.

Examining the military implications of functioning in a VUCA world Soykan (2015, p. 3) observed that: "NATO forces will require more agile (responsive, flexible, adaptive, innovative, resilient, versatile expeditionary capabilities to create the desired effects and maintain sufficient freedom of action to accomplish the mission at hand".

Reviewing micro-level implications, specifically the style versatility of those in leadership positions, Teece (2018, p. 27) states that they "must be like classical musicians who follow a tight script for the part of the strategy deemed robust, as well as jazz performers who can improvise around key themes as necessitated by unexpected change. Leaders must develop the individual capacity to better manage these inherent paradoxes and must create organizations adept at developing strong dynamic capabilities".

Further Reading

Bennett, N., & Lemoine, G. J. (2014). What VUCA really means for you. Harvard Business Review, 92(1–2), 27.

Horney, N., Pasmore, B., & O'Shea, T. (2010). Leadership agility: A business imperative for a VUCA world. Human Resource Planning, 33(4),33–38.

Mack, O., Khare, A., Krämer, A., & Burgartz, T. (Eds.). (2015). Managing in a VUCA World. Basel: Springer International Publishing Switzerland.

Schoemaker, P. J. H., Heaton, S., & Teece, D. J. (2018). Innovation, dynamic capabilities, and leadership. California Management Review, 61(1),15–42.

Soykan, B., & Alberts, D. S. (2015). Moving C2 Agility from a theory to a NATO Practice. In 20th ICCRTS "C2, Cyber, and Trust."

Teece, D. J. (2018). Dynamic capabilities as (workable) management systems theory. Journal of Management and Organization. HQ, NATO Supreme Allied Command Transformation. Norfolk, VA, USA.

Index

https://doi.org/10.1515/9783110637267-016